The Pathology of the U.S. Economy Revisited

The Pathology of the U.S. Economy Revisited

The Intractable Contradictions of Economic Policy

Michael Perelman

palgrave

THE PATHOLOGY OF THE U.S. ECONOMY REVISITED: THE INTRACTABLE CONTRADICTIONS OF ECONOMIC POLICY

First published 2002 by PALGRAVE™
175 Fifth Avenue, New York, N.Y.10010 and
Houndmills, Basingstoke, Hampshire RG21 6XS.
Companies and representatives throughout the world.

PALGRAVE is the new global publishing imprint of St. Martin's Press LLC Scholarly and Reference Division and Palgrave Publishers Ltd (formerly Macmillan Press Ltd).

ISBN 0–312–29472–7 hardback
ISBN 0–312–29317–8 paperback

Library of Congress Cataloging-in-Publication Data
Perelman, Michael.
The pathology of the U.S. economy revisited : the intractable contradictions of economic policy / by Michael Perelman.
p. cm.
Includes bibliographical references and index.
ISBN 00-312-29472-7—ISBN 0-312-29317-8 (pbk.)
1. United States—Economic policy—20th century. 2. United States—Economic conditions. 3. Industrial relations—United States. 4. Monetary policy—United States. 5. Finance—United States. 6. Wages—United States. I. Title: Pathology of the US economy revisited. II. Title.
HC103.P417 2001
330.973—dc21

2001044659

A catalogue record for this book is available from the British Library.

Design by Letra Libre, Inc.

First edition: January 2002
10 9 8 7 6 5 4 3 2 1

Printed in the United States of America.

Contents

INTRODUCTION

Setting the Stage

Writing a book about the recent state of the economy is always a risky business, perhaps akin to herding cats. By the time an author convinces himself that he has finally got a reasonable fix on the economy and commits his views to paper, the economy is liable to take on an entirely new complexion. Other times the economy will appear to be entering an unprecedented new phase, only to slink back unceremoniously into its previous incarnation. In short, the economy can be a cruel subject for those who are foolhardy enough to pretend that they can master it.

To make matters even more difficult, over and above the changes in the economy itself, the interpretation of the same economic event continues to evolve in light of recent economic thinking many decades afterward. For example, economists still hotly debate the ultimate causes of all previous depressions. Virtually nothing remains settled. I am reminded of the response attributed to China's long-time foreign minister during Mao's leadership, Chou En-Lai, upon being asked what he thought about the French Revolution of 1789. He responded that it was still too early to tell.

Even so, understanding the economy is of the utmost importance, since most people are at the mercy of economic forces. Perhaps the best an economist can do is to tell an interesting and coherent story in the hope that it can help people to understand the economy better today and to assist other people who will tell even better stories in the future.

This book mostly considers the economy from the perspective of the U.S. experience, only because I happen to know the U.S. economy better than any other. It emphasizes the Golden Age following World War II and the subsequent decline that began at the end of the 1960s and persisted into the early 1990s.

I should be clear about my use of the term "decline." The absolute size of the economy did not decline, but much of that growth came from more people working more hours rather than from improvements in productivity. The rate of profit, perhaps the key indicator within the mindset of a capitalist economy, did decline, at least until the 1980s. By the late 1990s by many measures, the economy seemed quite vigorous, so much so, that many commentators announced the beginning of a new economy.

I approach the so-called new economy more tentatively than I do when treating the earlier postwar period. Some observers have confidently pronounced that the emergence of modern technologies has created a new stage of development that makes virtually all previous economic logic obsolete. I hesitate to reach a decisive conclusion about such matters. My own impression is that the strengthening of intellectual property rights in recent years represents a far more revolutionary turn than the acceleration of technological progress. For the most part, I put off such questions until the final chapter.

Even within the limited terrain of the U.S. economy, knowledge is embarrassingly imperfect. For example, the rate of profit and the Gross Domestic Product are two of the most important commonly used indicators of economic health. Although neither measure offers a full picture of the economy, both are useful.

The Gross Domestic Product, corrected for inflation, reflects the overall level of economic activity. This measure rose fairly steadily in the early years of the twentieth century. The first experience of an actual decline was 1913–14, when the economy suffered a minor setback. Soon thereafter, with the outbreak of World War I, the economy grew rapidly. The first serious decline came in 1920. The economy fell sharply, only recovering the lost ground by 1927.

Then in 1929, another major calamity struck. The Great Depression, associated in the United States with the collapse of the stock market, began relatively mildly, and then picked up momentum as a whirlwind of economic devastation annihilated jobs, banks, businesses.

Despite the hoopla about the New Deal, the GDP never recovered its 1929 peak until 1941, when the upsurge in wartime demand finally got the economy going again. Except for a slight decline in 1946, the momentum of wartime prosperity continued during the early postwar years. The next couple of decades came to be known as the Golden Age, because the economy performed better than it ever had previously. Wages grew. Profits were high. Everything seemed almost perfect—at least for a large fraction of the population.

By the late 1960s, the bloom was wearing off. The anemic performance of the economy was becoming a matter of grave concern. After a little more than a decade of doubt, charged with a tinge of desperation, the electorate turned to Ronald Reagan. His administration took pride in dismantling the remnants of the New Deal.

Soon after Reagan took office, the GDP began to sink at a frightening speed that had not been experienced since the Great Depression. Although it recommenced its upward climb by the next year, the economic vigor of the Golden Age had disappeared. The economy continued to grow through the first Bush administration, except for one year of decline. Once Clinton took office, the economy began the longest uninterrupted postwar period of economic growth, although the rate of growth was relatively low until around 1995.

So, although the economy was growing, the rate of growth was fairly anemic. Even worse, the fruits of the economic growth were concentrated among the wealthiest people in the economy. This book will investigate the pathology of this growth, to see what it implies for the future of society.

A Preview of the Book

This book tells the story of the deterioration of the U.S. economy from the high point in the first decades following World War II, followed by an apparent recovery, which then set the stage for far more serious problems in the future. I will contend that the difficulties that the U.S. economy faces today reflect long-term problems that have been festering for many decades. These ills cannot be remedied by simple short-term policy adjustments.

But wait. How bad can the economy be? Certainly, for the more prosperous members of society any mention of a decline might be puzzling to say the least. Such people have prospered royally over the last couple decades. For the less fortunate, the economic problems are self-evident.

Perhaps the trajectory of real hourly wages offers the clearest indicator of the way that the economy is serving rich and poor in a different fashion. Real hourly wages in the private sector measured in 1982 dollars rose fairly steadily in the postwar period, peaking in 1973 at $8.55. As the economy stagnated, wages began to fall, bottoming out at $7.39 in the years 1993 and 1996. Real hourly wages climbed back a bit to $7.86 in 1999, still well below the 1973 high point (United States President 2000, Table B-45, p. 360).

These estimates of the real hourly wage probably underestimate the degree to which hourly wage earners have been unable to share in the modest prosperity of recent years. Under pressure from the Republican Congress, the government changed the way that it measured the Consumer Price Index. Had the earlier method of calculating the price level been used, the shrinkage of the real hourly wage would have been even more dramatic (Baker 1997).

This book will show that business interests have become so greedy that they became blinded to their own best interests. For example, they perceive that business will profit in the short run by doing anything in its power to cut wages. Based on this reasoning, business leaders are intent on following what I call "The Haitian Road to Development." When the majority of businesses attempt to cut wages, they reduce the income of their potential customers. More importantly, they cripple the labor force and thereby undermine its productivity. In the end, profits will suffer along with wages.

You can see a similar degree of ineptitude on the part of the government. During the early postwar period, fearing a repeat of the Great Depression, both business and the public supported the government's attempt to stabilize the economy. Although a stabilization policy initially helped to reduce the intensity of the business cycle, it also reduced competitive pressures. I will show that, as a result, this much vaunted stabilization policy actually impeded economic modernization, preparing the way for an economic decline. Again, a policy backfired because those in control failed to understand how the economy works.

What passes for serious concern about potential problems in the public debates is, more often than not, nothing more than a cynical manipulation of an ill-informed public. Lacking access to real information, except for that which the concentrated corporate media allows to pass through its filters, the public forms its opinions largely based on a combination of ignorance and misinformation.

Politicians use sophisticated polling techniques to identify those concerns that the corporate media successfully stir up. Then they pretend to engage in a serious dialogue about pressing issues out of concern for the common people—recall the proverbial widows and orphans—while actually using the opportunity to plead for special interests.

As the decline gained momentum, business, as well as the public at large, perceived that they would benefit by cutting taxes and limiting government activity. As a result, they helped to create a lax regulatory structure, which led to instability and chaos. Perhaps the clearest symbol of these policies was the meltdown of the savings and loan system. This inability of business leaders to recognize their own self-interest will be a recurrent theme in this book.

To cope with the drop in revenues, the government let the public infrastructure of roads and public works deteriorate enough to hobble the economy. Education suffered, further damaging productivity and profits—still another example of a policy failure.

Although business and the public oppose the government in general, they agreed that their interests would be well-served by a huge military buildup. Here too they were mistaken. These military expenditures further sap the vitality of the economy, so much so that they ultimately threaten to weaken the military itself.

Each of these policies turned out to have disastrous results. The country watched industry after industry wither, while real wages fell, and homelessness, hopelessness, and a multitude of other social and economic ills multiplied.

The Stubborn Refusal to Address the Crisis

The wealthiest and most influential members of society generally share a very different vision of the economy. Giddy with a surge of profits, stock options, and the other accoutrements of wealth and property, they could see success wherever they looked. Unfortunately, people of such prominence rarely glance in the direction of those who have not shared in the prosperity. When they do, they assure themselves that what separates them from their less fortunate brethren is their superior intelligence and work ethic. This comforting conclusion provides then with the confidence to call for a redoubling of the destructive policies that undermine both the economy and society.

This self-congratulation might be reassuring, but the resulting misinterpretation of reality is a recipe for eventual disaster. First, business and political leaders generally fail to recognize the importance of long-term processes in the economy. This lack of perspective leads them to believe that a short-term policy solution is the correct response to any economic problem. Given this mind-set, whatever improves the prospects for the next quarterly report or the next election remains uppermost in their minds.

The overblown notion of a new economy in which information overrides all other factors reinforced this emphasis on the short run. Despite the obvious importance of information, the real economy still ultimately depends on physical goods. No matter how sophisticated computers become, information cannot replace food or shelter.

The production of these physical goods depends upon investment in durable plant and equipment. Such investment decisions require a long-term perspective. In addition, inappropriate economic decisions can scar the labor force for generations.

Second, economists have saddled the world with a pervasive belief in a utopian vision of a market economy. In reality, the market is not the harmonious arrangement that abstract economic theory suggests. In particular, market economies require strong competitive pressures if they are to remain healthy.

Within the context of a market economy, the government should allow competitive forces to rid the economy of inefficient investments and management practices, while helping individuals to adjust to the dislocation that is part and parcel of a market economy. Instead, government policies protect business inefficiencies and leave workers more or less to fend for themselves when competitive forces uproot their jobs.

Although competitive pressures should be allowed to sweep away inefficiencies, you should understand that these pressures can take two forms. In the most familiar form of competition, firms can engage in cutthroat competition, which can lead to depressions, which, in turn, create widespread hardship and suffering.

I recommend a different form of competitive pressure; namely, high wages or strong environmental regulations. Increasing wages, for example, can provide the pressure necessary to coerce firms to adopt the best available technologies. Some individual firms will be unable to compete in such an environment, but other firms can emerge to take their place. Environmental regulations create similar pressures (see Perelman 1999).

My suggestion runs counter to our current economic policies. The Haitian road that the United States presently follows leads to a demoralized labor force. The road I am suggesting leads to an improved labor force capable of lifting economic productivity. I do not pretend that this road will be smooth. Market economies are by nature contradictory beasts that impose frequent hardships, but the path that I am recommending certainly is superior to the Haitian road, which threatens to destroy society unless it is reversed soon.

I do not want to give the impression that I will offer a more concrete solution to the major problems of market economies. By their very nature, markets are conflictive. Many of the current economic problems are unavoidable within the context of a market economy. Serious crises are inevitable.

Despite the inevitability of these economic crises, foolish policies are certain to make things worse. I intend to show that the current attitude toward the economy reflects an almost intentional inability to understand the nature of the economy, which all but guarantees a future fraught with disaster.

CHAPTER 1

Down the Tubes?

The Roots of Economic Mismanagement

Although the annihilation of the U.S. economy as we know it is not preordained, it is not beyond the realm of possibility. This book will explore some of the pressures that could push the U.S. economy to the point of destruction. I realize that the notion of the self-destruction of the economy is not very popular.

Certainly, few trained economists in the United States today accept Marx's contention that capitalism is inevitably destined to self-destruct. To be sure, capitalism has proved to be far more resilient than Marx had ever imagined.

The U.S. economy, in particular, stands as a stark testimony to the resilience of capitalism. In the United States, capitalism has withstood an epidemic of political and economic mismanagement. In fact, everywhere you look you will see signs of mismanagement. You will see mismanagement of the labor force, of resources, of corporate assets, as well as general financial, political, and economic mismanagement. The U.S. economy has surrendered its lead in sector after sector, especially in manufacturing. Still, even though the economy may not perform well, despite widespread mismanagement, it has avoided self-destruction.

Although capitalism has not self-destructed, it does give signs of losing its vitality, despite the recent enthusiasm surrounding the promise of high technology. In addition, many of the signs of mismanagement are, in fact, an understandable, though misguided, response to more fundamental forces.

This book will examine the underlying forces that have sapped the strength of one particular capitalist economy—that of the United States—rather than capitalism as a whole. Given the size and influence of the U.S. economy, its progressive economic fragility is interesting in its own right.

I hope that this book will also cast considerable light on the nature of capitalism as a whole. Certainly, the fate of the largest capitalist economy will exercise a significant influence on the system as a whole. Of course, just as a forest can thrive while individual trees expire, the course of the U.S. economy does not necessarily determine the future of capitalism. Nonetheless, the fate of the U.S. economy may foreshadow the future of those economies that are now rising to challenge the last remaining superpower.

The Failure of Economic Policy

The training of professional economists instills in them a belief that a market economy is naturally healthy, unless irrational policies somehow interfere with the normal functioning of the market. Given this perspective, many economists see their calling as pursuing the search for ways to root out those policies that prevent the market from doing its job. One school of economic thought, popularly associated with the University of Chicago, dogmatically insists that any attempt whatsoever to improve the workings of the market necessarily constitutes mismanagement. According to this worldview, a market economy without any government interference would naturally perform smoothly and efficiently, benefiting all concerned. Unfortunately, such an ideal, efficient economy is no more possible than a frictionless machine.

The other main school of economic thought—let us call it the "Economic Management School"—accepts that the unregulated market has some imperfections, but this school contends that a judicious dose of proper economic management can rid the economy of those imperfections without much difficulty.

I take issue with both schools of thought. Specifically, both schools of thought suffer from a flawed conception of mismanagement. The Chicago School is utopian to the extreme. Its theory might possibly work in an imaginary world in which everybody had full knowledge of what everybody else would do from now until well into the indefinite future, assuming further that everybody behaved rationally.

In a sense, the Economic Management School is only slightly less utopian than the Chicago School. It interprets market imperfections as epiphenomena—isolated problems that are unrelated to each of the other symptoms, rather than part of a systemic malaise. Accordingly, it assumes that proper management can treat these problems one-by-one and that a few simple policies will suffice to ensure the health of a market economy.

For the Economic Management School, a government that either fails to address existing market imperfections or addresses them in an improper fashion can be accused of mismanagement. The Economic Management School accepts the need for some kind of piecemeal economic management, but would have us believe that a well-managed economy with the appropriate economic controls can function about as well as the fantastic Chicago School ideal of an unregulated market.

In contrast to the Economic Management School, the Chicago School of laissez-faire economics at least recognizes the need to understand the economy holistically. It realizes that attempts to manage one part of the economy create pervasive effects throughout the economy. Hence piecemeal reforms cannot provide adequate solutions. Unfortunately, the Chicago school incorrectly draws the utopian conclusion from this realization that, left to its own devices, the market functions perfectly.

In fact, the market is far from a perfect mechanism. A careful study of the history of the U.S. economy bears out my contention. During the early postwar period, the Economic Management School was predominant. In part, you can trace their pervasive belief that piecemeal reforms could significantly improve society to the unprecedented performance of the post–World War II economy, that was mostly independent of the efforts of the Economic Management School.

You will see that the sequence of a depression followed by a wartime boom created a powerful economic momentum. Each time a new problem emerged, policy makers confidently devised new programs to cope with the problem. Each policy came with grand promises of future benefits, but what kept the economy going was its accumulated momentum.

By 1970, the momentum of the postwar boom had dissipated, leaving the economy tottering on the brink of crisis. From that point on policy initiatives lurched one way after another in a vain attempt to find a simple solution to a complex problem. Virtually all of the policies, whether they increased or decreased government involvement in the economy, proved to be dismal failures. At best, they offered a short-term patchwork solution.

This crisis discredited the Economic Management School and paved the way for the renewed ascendancy of the even more dangerous medicine prescribed by the Chicago school. Yet, as deregulation and the market came to be the watchwords of the day, the economy moved even closer to the precipice. The public became more aware that neither school was capable of rectifying the problems inherent in the economy. Economist jokes became rampant.

Fortunately, a number of factors that I will discuss later reversed the downward spiral of the U.S. economy. I suspect that these forces are not powerful enough to justify the euphoria that pushed the stock market up to unprecedented levels in recent times.

Regardless of its staying power, this recent economic upswing reduced the urgency of reevaluating the nature of recent economic policies. This opportunity for emotional relaxation was certainly most welcome, since people are loathe to recognize the hopelessness of comforting, but simplistic policy nostrums.

Indeed, many people in the United States still carry the conviction that prosperity is the norm. They are still confident that some policy—maybe deregulation, maybe some fine tuning here and there, or even a routine overhaul—suffices to get the economy running smoothly once again.

Ever hopeful, they await a new Moses to lead them into the promised land of economic prosperity. Indeed, the defining theme of the first successful Reagan presidential campaign was the promise of hope, devoid of any specifics, especially specific costs. Although Reagan retired with significant popularity, he was the exception that proved the rule. More often than not the public becomes disenchanted with its leaders as quickly their policies prove inadequate to the task.

The widespread suspicion of those with responsibility for economic policy is well deserved. They generally behave with extraordinary irresponsibility. How many leaders of business or government have been willing to acknowledge any serious problems except in an effort to win some advantage for a powerful special interest? The media have been no better. Instead of a clear analysis of the precarious nature of the current economic system, they confidently treat the public to a plethora of simplistic remedies that purport to correct the consequences of previous mismanagement, including innumerable proposals for political reform, tax reform, labor reform, each of which is every bit as insufficient to the task as all the earlier reforms.

Why should these reforms be any more effective than past reforms? Policy makers from both schools were equally confident about the efficacy of the earlier reforms that they proposed in the past. They uniformly failed to anticipate the seemingly unavoidable, unwelcome consequences of these actions. Retrospectively, the deficiencies of earlier reforms seem painfully obvious; yet time after time the public acquiesces as this cycle of mismanagement seems to endlessly repeat itself.

On closer inspection, a somewhat different picture of the policy makers' records emerges. Much of what appears as mismanagement is really the inevitable failure of any attempt to correct the deeper problems associated with a market economy with piecemeal reforms. Even policies that retrospectively appear to be based on pure stupidity often make sense in the context of the political expediency in which these policies were initially framed.

In short, a market economy embodies powerful negative forces. The majority of the population may be immune from the impact of these negative forces for extended periods of time. As a result, they have little inclination to trouble themselves with understanding the potential for a crisis. Eventually, these forces accumulate, and then erupt in a full-scale crisis that shakes the economy to its foundations.

Although economic leaders cannot exorcise these forces simply by adopting some supposedly intelligent economic policy, they can take measures that can make a crisis more manageable. Instead, however, during the comfortable times in between crises, economic leaders are more prone to convince themselves that they have somehow managed to transcend such mundane problems. In their overconfidence, they are likely to take measures that will make the next crisis even more calamitous. For example, in recent years politicians have congratulated themselves for their efforts in shredding the social safety net, which otherwise could possibly reduce the human costs of the next crisis.

Although a full-blown crisis has not yet arrived, more and more people are coming to doubt that prosperity is just around the corner. So Marx maybe was not so wrong after all. Perhaps capitalism may even be in the process of self-destructing, although the process certainly has not been nearly as rapid as Marx and many of his followers believed. Even if the U.S. economy does not self-destruct, it is due for a long and painful period of adjustment. This book is intended to provide a framework for understanding the nature of this adjustment.

The Role of Crises

At this time, I will mention an underlying thesis that runs throughout this book. Let me state it here once and let you judge for yourself based on the evidence that I will present in later chapters whether or not you accept it: Simply put, market economies require strong competition and—here is where this book deviates from the standard economic orthodoxy—strong competition breeds depressions and recessions.

I accept that market economies can survive for extended periods of time with a relatively weak level of competition. During such periods, economies can avoid depressions or even serious recessions. The first decades following World War II are a classic example. At the time, most firms in the United States were in such a strong position that the existing level of competition did not represent much more than a minor inconvenience for most firms.

Such conditions cannot last forever in a market economy. During periods when the level of competition is not very intense, competitive pressures are too weak to discipline business effectively. When economies lack the discipline of competitive pressures over an extended period of time, problems accumulate as careless and wasteful practices become more common.

Eventually, some external event—say an oil shock or a major bankruptcy—unleashes a sudden wave of competitive pressure that catches most firms by surprise. The result is often a recession or even a depression. The more time that has passed since the economy has last experienced a depression, the more vulnerable the economy will be and the greater probability that the subsequent depression will be intense.

Of course, depressions create terrible hardships, but the market has no other means of maintaining its vigor. Depressions and recessions are similar to autoimmune systems. If business is relatively strong, a moderate depression will mostly eliminate the least efficient firms and cause others to become stronger by improving their economic practices. As a result, the remaining population will consist of a higher proportion of efficient firms than before. Once this sort of depression subsides, the economy will be stronger that it had been on the eve of the depression.

If the weakness reaches a certain level, these economic crises can get out of hand and become virulent. When depressions turn into full-blown crises, they can cripple or even destroy the economy, indiscriminately sweeping away healthy firms along with relatively inefficient businesses. Instead of merely ridding the economic organism of sick and diseased elements, these crises eat away at the vital organs, threatening the very existence of the organism itself.

Unlike biological systems, where such self-consuming outbreaks are rare, market economies are likely to experience these self-destructive attacks without adequate institutional protection. I described some of these defenses in detail in an earlier book (Perelman 1999).

I know from classroom lectures and public talks that I have given that this thesis makes many people uncomfortable, probably because it challenges their comfortable belief in the possibility of perpetual prosperity. Most people do not want to think that depressions are an essential part of a market society, but present policies preclude any other means of maintaining competitive pressures.

I will show that a policy of high wages offers an alternative to depressions as a means of creating market pressures. I do not pretend that high wages are a panacea, but this policy is far more attractive than a serious depression. After all, depressions—even modest depressions—are not tidy affairs. Many people will suffer. They are wasteful. A good number of efficient firms will fall by the wayside, along with those least worthy of survival. Nonetheless, market economies require these depressions to free the system of many of the inefficiencies that made the depression occur in the first place.

Competition works like the natural fire cycle in a forest. Fires can destroy many trees, but they also clear the way for new growth alongside the healthy trees that survive the fire. Foresters attempt to prevent fires to preserve the forest, but without a fire for an extended period of time, excessive litter builds up on the forest floor. When a fire does occur, it will have such a reservoir of fuel on the forest floor that the fire can wipe out the forest altogether.

In effect, fire prevention can both enhance and threaten forest ecology. In this sense, depressions serve a vital purpose within a market economy even though they can threaten the very survival of a market economy. Both too much and too little competition can threaten market economies. In any case, one cannot hope to eliminate market pressure without erecting an alternative to a market system.

During the early postwar decades, policy makers behaved like foresters protecting the trees from the destructive fires for too long. Once more competitive pressures began to come from abroad, manufacturing jobs began to evaporate. The response was to allow labor-intensive jobs to migrate abroad, while erecting even more powerful protections in the form of intellectual property rights for high value added industries, such as Hollywood films, pharmaceuticals, and software.

Now, a substantial economic correction is long overdue, so much so that when it arrives it may threaten the very foundations of the U.S. economy.

The Challenge Ahead

Mainstream economists do not generally realize the close association between competition and depressions. Proponents of both the Chicago and the Economic Management schools mostly contend that economies can benefit from competition without enduring the inconvenience of depression. Indeed, both schools teach that depressions need not occur at all. Instead, they implicitly assume that competitive pressures are steady or do not fluctuate significantly. Consequently, they believe that competition can be effective without threatening to turn into a depression or even a recession.

This common misunderstanding of the nature of competition and crises within a market economy convinces adherents of the Chicago School to believe that mismanagement, rather than the market itself, causes crises. As a result, this school of thought generally advocates policies that reduce demand, making a recession more likely. This same misunderstanding regarding competition has induced policy makers to pursue policies from the Economic Management School to vainly attempt to vanquish the business cycle, in the manner of misguided foresters. The effect of these policies has been to diminish the strength of competitive forces, increasing the likelihood of a severe depression.

As a result of these policies, the U.S. economy no longer resembles a stripling, accustomed to the dangers and the rigors of a competitive jungle. Instead, the economy has become more like a tragic bubble-boy, who weakens daily in an atmosphere of loving care.

During the last decades of the twentieth century, industry after industry just seemed to crumble in the face of increased competition. In other sectors of the economy, industry managed to hang on, but downsizing became the order of the day. Managers prided themselves in responding to increased competition with what, at first, seemed to be unflinching determination to make "hard choices." Unions had to be broken and wages lowered. The prevailing management fashion suggested that this approach would soon pay huge dividends, but, for the most part, it merely caused the best and most experienced workers to leave, while company morale sagged.

The great success stories of the U.S. economy that the business press trumpets generally prospered because intellectual property laws shielded them from competition. Much of the rest of the traditional industrial sector withered under the competitive logic of deindustrialization.

The image of a bubble in a discussion of the economy suggests a related metaphor—that of a fragile, easily punctured object. Indeed, the decade-long attempt to shield the bubble-boy economy has so distorted the situation that society now finds itself neglecting the human inhabitants within the bubble in order to protect the bubble itself.

This tragic reversal, in which society spends billions of dollars to shore up the financial structure by scrimping on what it spends for people, cannot continue indefinitely. When Marx said that capitalism would self-destruct, he actually meant that, eventually people would see that they had no choice but to opt for a form of society that is good for people rather than for markets. So far Marx has been wrong about the nature of this choice. Instead, the postwar U.S. economy, which is the subject of this book, ended up as a market economy in which the state has protected business from market forces—leading to a feeble, bubble-boy economy, leading to rapid deindustrialization.

In recent years, the shape of the bubble has changed. The producers of primary goods, such as farmers or manufacturers of steel or automobiles, no longer enjoy as much protection from the traditional monetary and fiscal policies. Instead, they suffer from withering competition. Other sectors, such as pharmaceuticals, computer software, or the cinema, enjoy a more secure bubble than ever before. Their bubble consists of intellectual property rights protections.

This book contains no simple solutions. Instead, my prime objective is to issue a warning that, under the present regime consisting of piecemeal management often followed by thoughtless deregulation, neither the economy nor the people will prosper. With that said, let me turn to my analysis of the postwar U.S. economy so that you can judge for yourself.

The Golden Age of Capitalism

Background to the Golden Age

At the end of World War II, the United States held a seemingly unchallengeable economic position, in part due to the war. The war brought much new capital on line. It sparked innovations that gave the United States the lead in much modern technology. It left the economies of the traditional competitors of the United States in ruins.

This dominant economic strength seemed at the time to be all the more dramatic, considering that the U.S. economy had only recently emerged from the ashes of the Great Depression. In fact, the striking dichotomy between the Depression and prosperity was not at all paradoxical. Although the achievements of the postwar prosperity may seem to represent a transcendence of the failures of the Depression, in reality, the Depression did much to pave the way for the postwar recovery.

To begin with, the Great Depression set off a wave of intense competition that forced many firms to scrap outmoded plant and equipment. By 1939, U.S. firms had replaced one-half of all their manufacturing equipment that had existed in 1933 (Staehle 1955, p. 127). Although the total amount of investment during the Depression was relatively small, most of that investment was directed toward modernizing existing plant and equipment rather than adding new capacity.

Then during the war, business added still more modern equipment. This combination of modernization, together with the earlier elimination of old and outmoded capital goods left business with a stock of highly productive, modern capital. Certainly, the capital stock of the postwar United States was the envy of the world. In fact, after the war, U.S. business produced as much output as a decade before with 15 percent less capital and 19 percent less labor (Staehle 1955, p. 133).

The state of consumer demand offered an exceptional opportunity for business. Many families had deferred their purchase of expensive consumer goods for an extended period of time. For example, a good number of consumers had been unable to afford cars during the Depression. Later, during the war, the government rationed production so that the automobile plants could turn to building tanks and trucks. All the while, the stock of automobiles, as well as other consumer goods, was aging. This backlog of consumption was all the more powerful because many families had first liquidated their consumer debt and then accumulated considerable savings during the war. Consequently, a broad group of people had both the wherewithal and the desire to purchase expensive consumer goods, setting the stage for a postwar boom, while business had more than ample productive capacity to meet their demands.

In addition, financial conditions at the end of World War II were almost ideal. Business was flush with cash. The Depression had unleashed a wave of bankruptcies, which had wiped out much of the U.S. corporate debt. It had also frightened financial institutions enough to make them concentrate on high-quality investments whenever possible. At the time, banks held many of their assets in the form of highly liquid U.S. government securities. The subsequent wartime prosperity provided an unprecedented level of corporate liquidity.

In terms of international finance, the position of the United States was just as enviable. By the end of World War II, about 70 percent of world's monetary gold stock resided in U.S. vaults (Magdoff and Sweezy 1983, p. 9).

Psychological conditions following the war were also ideal. The harrowing experience of the Depression lowered expectations for the postwar economy. Many economists reasoned that, since the Depression was ended by the war, ending the war would inevitably throw the economy back into a depression once again. An economic advisor to the Secretary of Commerce wrote, " . . . in the summer of 1946, unemployment may exceed 7 million, as rising civilian employment and reductions in working hours turn out to be insufficient to absorb the additions to the labor force consequent upon the rapid discharge of workers from the armed forces" (Bassie 1946, p. 126).

A Philadelphia journalist, Joseph Livingston, surveying economists about their predictions for the near future in June 1947, found that economists were expecting prices to fall 6.64 percent during the following year (Carlson 1977). Declines of this magnitude only occur during a severe economic downturn. The public shared this bleak prognosis. In 1945, a Roper poll showed that less than 41 percent of the population of the United States believed that a postwar recession could be avoided (Wolfe 1981, p. 14).

At first, events seemed to confirm people's worst fears. The economy did decline initially, so much so that one pair of economists later labeled the moment as "The Great Depression of 1946" (Vedder and Gallaway 1991). Unlike the real Great Depression, the setback of 1946 was very short-lived, so much so that few modern economists even know about it. Instead, the massive boom that followed dominates the memory of the postwar period.

So while most economists predicted a depression, the economy proved them wrong. Prices did not fall at all. Instead, they rose at a rate of 8.09 percent, creating unfounded fears of inflation (Carlson 1977). Robert J. Gordon concluded, "Surely the greatest *economic* surprise of the first postwar decade was the failure of anything resembling a postwar depression to occur" (Gordon 1980, p. 115).

Because the healthy economic conditions of the time were so unexpected, business responded even more enthusiastically than might have otherwise been the case. Few economists at the time understood something new was afoot in the postwar period. James O'Leary was one of the exceptions. In a remarkable article, based on a paper that he delivered at the 1944 annual meetings of the American Economic Association, O'Leary gave a number of reasons why the postwar economy should prosper, but he emphasized the pent-up demand of consumers, flush with a backlog of savings. Within a short period, O'Leary's interpretation of postwar conditions became commonplace, although it largely fell on deaf ears when he first made his views known (O'Leary 1945).

The Great Depression helped to prepare the political, as well as the economic climate in which the postwar prosperity blossomed. Back in the 1920s, the dominant political posture was to trust market forces to ensure continuing prosperity. The Coolidge administration faithfully reflected the laissez-faire temper of the middle-class of the time. At the same time, his secretary of commerce, Herbert Hoover, more closely represented the real interests of big business, which understood that unregulated market forces by themselves would lead to a certain disaster. Hoover advocated a combination of pure market forces and collusion through trade associations, anticipating, in many ways, the New Deal (Perelman 1996, chapter 7).

Once the Depression struck, much of the public quickly lost confidence in laissez-faire. Economists in the United States began to read with intense interest works of an eminent British economist, John Maynard Keynes, whom we shall now discuss.

The Political Economy of the Golden Age

During the early postwar period, the experience of the Depression was still fresh in the minds of the American people, who remembered that their ordeal lasted more than a decade. They were intent on avoiding a repetition of the Great Depression at all costs. In this spirit, they realized that a multitude of smaller New Deal programs failed to get the economy rolling until the massive military buildup began.

The association between increased government spending during the war and the recovery from the Great Depression also made a deep impression on the economics profession, especially in the United States. The idea took hold that the government could effectively prevent depressions by intervening in the economy to manage the level of economic activity. Although some business leaders remained openly hostile to government intervention (Collins 1981), many others actively lobbied for a tame rendering of the new economic policy of the New Deal, recognizing its obvious benefits (Stein 1969; and Neal 1981, pp. 15–22).

During the early postwar period, many economists were becoming aware of the recent theories of John Maynard Keynes (Stein 1969; Keynes 1936). Keynes's ideas were both complicated and vague. In the United States the most common, albeit incorrect, interpretation of his work stressed that government spending was the most effective means of shoring up a weak economy (see Perelman 1989).

Although Keynes preferred productive investment, he facetiously suggested that the government could just as well bury old bottles filled with money to put people to work. One group could bury the bottles while another would dig for them (Keynes 1936, p. 129). In effect, anything that could stimulate spending enough could get the economy back on its feet.

Keynes's theory seemed reasonable enough in many respects. If both the bottle buriers and bottle diggers received money for their superfluous services, they would, in turn, spend it on goods and services. The companies that sell to them would buy from other companies, eventually bringing life to all sectors of the economy. This notion that investment sets a cumulative process in motion lies at the heart of Keynesian policy.

As the memory of the Great Depression faded with wartime prosperity, many business and political leaders became more resistant to the popular proposition that the government had the responsibility to fight unemployment in general. The fate of the proposed Full Employment Act of 1946 was symptomatic of business's ambivalence about the relative roles of the government and the market. Initially, the act promised that "every American able to work and willing to work has the right to a useful and remunerative job."

Martin Neil Baily observed that the Employment Act of 1946 "expressed the political will to avoid recession or depression" was only partially correct (Baily 1978, p. 15), since the political will extended only in so far as it left the free play of the market intact. Business may have appreciated the prosperity of the time, but they feared that a large government might interfere with their activities.

By 1946, the urgency of Depression conditions had subsided. Conservative political forces successfully whittled away at the bill. First Congress removed the word, "Full," from the original title of The Employment Act of 1946. Instead of promising full employment, Congress inserted the reminder that "it is the policy of the United States to foster free competitive enterprise" to reassure business (Bailey 1950; see also Wolfe 1981, p. 53).

Then, in the final version of the law, the forces of moderation in the Congress went even further, reducing the requirement of full employment to an intention (Santoni 1986, pp. 11–2). Robert Lekachman concluded: "Congress had carefully removed the political sting from S. 380's tail. The law merely asked the president only to prepare one more report. Congress was asked to do no more than study it" (Lekachman 1966, p. 174). The report in question was the responsibility of the president's Council of Economic, an agency that the Employment Act established.

Despite the absence of any legislative requirement, the government still seemed to behave as if this meek version of the Employment Act actually constituted a modest commitment to the principle of low unemployment. Yes, recessions periodically infected the economy, but they were relatively mild. Each time the economy threatened to go into another deep slump, a modest mix of fiscal and monetary stimuli managed to keep the economy afloat. As Milton Friedman, probably the most influential conservative economist of his time, noted, individuals and business became convinced that, "unless the recession is *exceedingly* minor, explicit action will be taken" (Friedman 1968; and 1980, p. 79).

Indeed, during the first eight years after the passage of the Employment Act, the official unemployment rate averaged below 4 percent (Editors of *Monthly Review* 1983, p. 3). In reality, this enviable record owed little to a strong commitment on the part of the government. Instead, the economy was so healthy that quite modest efforts on the part of the government sufficed to keep the economy running strong.

As the shadows of the Great Depression receded into the hazy past, leaders of business, government, and the great universities deluded themselves into believing that they had somehow mastered the art of managing the economy. When the economy temporarily slackened off during the Eisenhower years, followers of John Maynard Keynes assured the world that a renewed regimen of their policies would ensure another burst of prosperity. At the time, Paul Samuelson, perhaps the most influential of the American Keynesians, insisted that with proper fiscal and monetary policy the economy could have full employment and whatever rate of capital formation and growth it wanted (Stein 1969, p. 363).

In the words of Joseph Garbarino: "By 1955, the American economy had experienced ten years of fairly high level post-war prosperity and had weathered two minor recessions. The basis for concluding that a new economic era based on government's long-term commitment to stability and on industry's rationalized long range planning was at hand" (Garbarino 1962, p. 415).

Coming on the heels of the Great Depression, the surge in wartime demand vaulted the economy into what seemed to be an age of almost perpetual prosperity—disregarding the large numbers of poor whom the boom passed by. Indeed, during the Golden Age, everything seemed to be in place for an economy without depressions or recessions. Depression-year promises of a chicken in every pot gave way to an expectation of two cars in every garage.

Who would have guessed that, for many of the citizens of the United States, the fear of not even having a home, let alone a garage, would become a reality within a couple of decades? Who could have anticipated that we would soon add such hideous words as homelessness, rust-belt, and deindustrialization to the vocabulary?

Overconfidence and the Return of the Business Cycle

For the most part, this dream of perpetual prosperity seemed to be well within reach. Between 1947 and 1972, the average weekly earnings measured in 1977 dollars for total private nonagricultural work rose from $123 to $198 (President of the United States 1990, p. 344).

During the Kennedy administration, the government expressed a commitment to maintaining this prosperity by continuing to apply the policy tools developed during the postwar period. In light of the strong economic performance at the time, the tentative spirit of The Employment Act of 1946 gave way to an overarching confidence in the government's ability to control the economy. Walter Heller expressed this spirit, writing: "[W]e now take for granted that the government must step in to provide the essential stability at high levels of employment and growth that the market mechanism, left alone, cannot deliver" (Heller 1966, p. 9).

Indeed, the economic successes of the Kennedy years redoubled the confidence in the powers of macroeconomic management. Confidence eventually gave way to overconfidence. Economists convinced themselves that their scientific training endowed them with the ability to fine tune the economy. For Arthur Okun, one of the most influential policy economists of the time: "More vigorous and more consistent application of the tools of economic policy contributed to the obsolescence of the business cycle pattern and refutation of the stagnation myths" (Okun 1970, p. 37; and 1980, p. 163).

Even the Council of Economic Advisors, caught up in the economic utopianism of the time, reported in 1965 that: "both our increased understanding of the effectiveness of fiscal policy and the continued improvement of our economic information, strengthen the conviction that recessions can be increasingly avoided and ultimately wiped out" (cited in Wolfe 1981, p. 69).

Indeed, the performance of the economy during the first decades of the postwar period seemed to justify the confidence of the Keynesians. In terms of "growth, price and distribution . . . the first two decades after World War II may well be a close approximation to the best that in practice can be obtained from a capitalist economy" (Minsky 1982, p. 376). Not surprisingly, promoters of the new economic policy became giddy with their early successes. They enthusiastically spread the gospel of perpetual prosperity, promising the faithful that they could manipulate the economy so exactly that capitalism could supposedly proceed from now on, untroubled by the periodic crises, which had plagued capitalism in the past.

This faith in the possibility of continuous prosperity became so ingrained that, by 1967, an international conference of influential economists convened in London to discuss whether the economists had actually vanquished the business cycle forever (Bronfenbrenner 1969a). Although most of the participants remained unconvinced of the ultimate demise of the business cycle, such skepticism was far from universal.

A few economists warned that those who believed in the myth of perpetual prosperity were extrapolating from a mere two decades of experience in using their economic techniques (R. A. Gordon 1969, p. 4). This word of caution left most economists unfazed. Circles close to the center of the Democratic Party policy makers remained under sway of the idea that depressions had been conquered, once and for all (R. A. Gordon 1969, p. 4).

Most importantly, the business community largely accepted the notion that threat of a depression was a thing of the past. Investors who bet on the continuation of prosperity were more often than not rewarded for their optimism at the time. Although successful investors could content themselves with the thought that they were sensible business people who recognized sound economic propositions, they typically based their expectations on the delusion that the inevitable downturn was unlikely, if not impossible.

Optimistic expectations did seem to be capable of fueling the postwar economic boom by stimulating a vigorous investment program, which would ensure that markets would be strong enough to sustain a high level of economic activity for decades on end. In this vein, Paul Samuelson assured the readers of his 4 November 1968 column in *Newsweek* that the new Keynesian economics works: "Wall Street knows it. Main Street, which has been enjoying 92 months of advancing sales knows it" (cited in DuBoff and Herman 1972).

Shortly thereafter, the salad days of the early postwar period disappeared. The economy went into a long period of decline.

What were the unusual features that made the Golden Age so much better than the norm (Griliches 1988, p. 19)? No satisfactory answer has arisen for that question.

Markets have an intrinsic rhythm of boom and bust. After an economy runs at full throttle for a period of time, strains and pressures build up in the form of excessive speculation and imbalances due to inappropriate investments by overly optimistic firms. Such is the nature of the capitalist economy. It requires periodic recessions or even depressions in order to steady itself (Perelman 1999).

In fact, the U.S. economy has spent the majority of time during the previous century enmeshed either in depressions, recessions, or wars. Time and time again, the economy would emerge from one of these periods of turmoil, enjoy a period of prosperity, only to sink back again. Never, however, was the boom as successful as it was during the Golden Age.

The so-called New Economy promises a new Golden Age. Unlike the authentic Golden Age, wages and salaries have been stagnant or even declining for most workers. Instead, most of the boom, until the late 1990s, had been concentrated among a relatively thin stratum of society.

Postwar Decline

Economists generally have difficulty in anticipating the outbreak of an economic bust. Indeed, a few months after Samuelson published his naively optimistic 1968 *Newsweek* article, the economy entered a prolonged period of relative stagnation, although people did not realize what was happening at the time. With the benefit of hindsight, we can now recognize that many of the symptoms of decline came to light just around that time.

Although economic optimism remained relatively strong despite the deteriorating economy, social and political optimism was rapidly eroding. Two noneconomic events were especially effective in shattering the hope and confidence of the postwar period. Neither was the stuff that you would expect to read in the business pages, but, on a deeper level, both demonstrated the limits of the U.S. economy. First, the war in Vietnam made the citizens of the United States recognize the limits of their country's economic power. People in the United States were dumbfounded that a country as small and as poor as Vietnam could withstand the military might of the United States, which seemed all-powerful only a couple of decades earlier.

The Vietnam War was not merely a symptom of economic weakness. It was also a major contributor to the economic decline. I will return to this subject later. As the damage from the Vietnam War spread though the economy, political cynicism became rampant. The public lost faith in the government. The Nixon administration attempted to stem the tide of antigovernment feelings by using illegal means to stop the flow of information from the government, leading to the Watergate Scandal. In that environment, with the economy in shambles and a sizeable portion of the executive branch of the government under indictment, faith in Keynesianism and the government's ability to control the economy rapidly evaporated. Conservative economic theory became ascendant.

Wasn't the Nixon administration already thoroughly conservative? Yes, but many of their policies were quite liberal by contemporary standards. In many ways, the policies of the Nixon administration were far to the left of those enacted under Clinton. The difference was that during the earlier period, social and political activism was vigorous, forcing the Nixon administration to enact relatively progressive policies.

Behind the scenes, the Nixon administration attempted to reassert social authority by initiating the war on drugs, which was aimed at reining in the same groups that were most inclined to question authority. Although the Nixon administration was probably not able to anticipate the consequences, ballooning prison costs were a major factor in constraining state budgets across the country. With this fiscal burden, states generally limited their social programs, at the same time that Nixon's revenue sharing approach was giving them more responsibility.

Although the Golden Age was unique in the extent that it spread its gains among a broad swath of people, the racial turmoil of the 1960s reminded affluent, middle-class whites that not everybody was sharing in the great postwar prosperity. At first, the government was confident that it could extend the benefits of the Golden Age to less privileged groups of Americans. Later, as the economy slowed down, this optimism receded. Some white Americans regarded affirmative-action programs as a substantial threat—that they would have to do with less in order that African Americans could join the economic mainstream.

These two concerns—the Vietnam War and racial disharmony—were bound up with each other. During the war, nonwhite soldiers made up a disproportionate share of the combat troops and an even greater share of the fatalities. Many young white men, especially those from privileged families, found shelter in military deferments or in service safely away from the front lines.

Parenthetically, a good many of the prominent figures who avoided military service in their youth have seen the error of their ways. Now that they have reached the critical age where military service is no longer a threat, they have become among the most vocal proponents of a strong military presence. In fact, much of the optimism that remains in the contemporary United States is grounded on a pride in military strength.

The Falling Rate of Profit

The decline took a severe toll on the working people of the United States. In 1972, the average weekly earnings in 1977 dollars for total private nonagricultural work stood at $198. Since then earnings have declined dramatically, reaching $168 in 1988 (President of the United States 1990, p. 344).

In almost every respect, the United States was falling behind, while both Japan and German-led continental Europe were moving ahead in economic power.

In order to understand the nature of this deterioration of the U.S. economic position, first take account of the decline in profits. In a market economy, capitalists or the managers in their employ make the key economic decisions. Although capitalists enjoy power, perks, and other privileges, ultimately they must show a profit to succeed. So as a first approximation, you can proceed with the assumption that capitalists' single objective is to make a profit, putting aside for the moment the need to understand the economy in all its complexity.

The before-tax rate of return on fixed capital and inventories declined by more than 30 percent between 1948 and 1987 (Michl 1991, p. 271). The magnitude of this decline is dramatic enough to merit our attention, despite the undeniable limitations of the data.

Because profits are high during booms and low during recessions, we normally compare average profit rates for an entire cycle to eliminate the problem of comparing a boom year with a bust year.

Table 1.2 gives an estimate of the profit rate over the first eight postwar business cycles. Each period in table 1.2 represents a complete cycle.

The first two postwar cycles suggest a period of relative stability. Profit rates fell on the whole, but not dramatically. Next, you can see the profit rate falling substantially during the late Eisenhower years, followed by the initial Vietnam War boom. As the military buildup overheated the economy, profits subsequently deteriorated. Profit rates continued to erode until after the Reagan recession. During the final cycle, covered in the table, the profit rate recovered somewhat, approximately to where it was in 1970, but nowhere near the peaks of the early 1960s.

This growth in the rate of profits during the last cycle shown in the table does not seem to be a harbinger of the end of the decline. Profits rose in part because they had fallen so low during the previous cycle. In addition, profits rose because business was

Table 1.1 The Deteriorating Performance of the U.S. Postwar Macroeconomy

	1948–66	*1966–73*	*1973–79*	*1979–87*
Real GNP growth rate (%)	4.4	3.2	.6	2.2
Real wage growth rate (%)	2.6	2.1	0.4	0.0
Unemployment rate (ave. %)	5.2	4.6	.8	7.7
Inflation rate (ave. %)	2.0	5.1	8.9	5.2
After tax profit rate (%)	6.9	7.0	5.5	6.0
Rate of capital accumulation (%)	3.5	4.3	.5	2.8

Source: Bowles, Gorden, and Weisskopf 1989

Table 1.2 Growth in Profit Rates for Nonfinancial Corporations

Years	*Profit Rate Growth (Percent per Annum)*	*Years*	*Profit Rate Growth (Percent per Annum)*
1948–51	0.34	1965–72	–5.36
1951–55	–1.52	1972–77	–1.40
1955–59	–3.64	1977–81	–5.67
1959–65	4.01	1981–85	6.08

Source: Michl 1988a, p. 13.

able to hire workers so cheaply, not because it was able to employ them particularly efficiently. I will return to this subject later.

The Decline and Falling Profit Rates

Although many influences can affect profit rates, Tom Weisskopf has proposed a useful way of decomposing the profit rate into the product of three major factors: first, the share of profits in the national income; second, the capital stock that would be required to produce the national income if the economy were operating at full capacity; and third, the current output as a fraction of the full capacity output (Weisskopf 1979). Although economists usually identify profitability with efficiency, Weisskopf's decomposition of the profit rate reveals how the profit rate can move independently of changes in business efficiency.

At best, Weisskopf's first factor is only loosely related to efficiency. Theoretically, business could increase the share of profits in the national income as a reward for developing new and more efficient methods of producing the products that it sells; however, the profit share can change for other reasons that are unrelated to efficiency. For example, the share of wages, interest, or rent can vary because of political factors, such as tax laws or rent controls.

Since the majority of people in the United States work for their living, the largest share of national income goes to labor. Because the shares that go to interest or rents are relatively small, the rise in these nonwage shares would have to be nothing short of spectacular to compensate for the fall in real wages. As a result, the wage structure should be a crucial determinant of Weisskopf's first factor and changes in the labor market would have a significant impact on the first factor.

These changes in the wage structure may have nothing to do with efficiency. A changing political climate can allow business or labor to push the wage level one way or another, regardless of changes in efficiency. Obviously, the political tide has been moving against labor in recent decades. For example, even though the real wage has been falling, the productivity of labor has actually been growing. You might be able to credit business efficiency with increasing the productivity of labor, except that the collapse of the wage structure is far more dramatic than any productivity advances.

This combination of an increase in productivity and a decline in wages is certain to augment Weisskopf's first factor: the profit share. With falling real wages, the share of profits will grow, unless one of two conditions are met: either the productivity of labor falls faster than the real wage (which did not happen) or some other groups, such as those who earn interest, are able to gain so much that their windfall wipes out the benefits from the fall in the real wage rate.

In short, unless an erosion of the quality of labor would be responsible for the falling real wage—a notion that some economists do suggest, even though labor productivity has been growing—then the shrinking wage translates into an expansion of profits, irrespective of any efficiencies.

Tom Michl made an impressionistic calculation, which is very instructive in this regard. He estimated how much the share of wages would vary for each percentage change in the rate of labor productivity. He found that during the period 1948–1970, roughly corresponding to what we had earlier called the Golden Age of capitalism, a one percentage point change in labor productivity tended to increase the wage share by 1.21 percent, meaning that labor was able to capture rewards over and above the increases in labor productivity at the time. In the later period, labor was much less fortunate. From 1970 to 1986, the estimate fell to 0.56 percent, suggesting that labor earned only about one-half of its productivity increases (Michl 1988b).

Michl's estimates suggest that during the period in which the economic decline appeared, the share of wages in the national income began to fall due to causes that were unrelated to labor productivity. His calculations support the notion that we cannot uncritically attribute shifts in Weisskopf's first factor to efficiency during the period of the economic decline.

Weisskopf's third factor depends on the overall level of economic activity rather than business efficiency since individual business managers have little control over this factor. The policies of the federal government and the Federal Reserve Board are more important influences on the level of overall economic activity.

Only the second factor directly relates to efficiency. Weisskopf's statistical analysis indicated that the first and third factors could not explain much of the fall in the rate of profit. The second factor seemed more important.

Tom Michl made a similar diagnosis of the fall in the rate of profit. He found that, from 1948–70, an increasing share of wages rarely caused the rate of profit to fall. The exceptional years fall mainly in the late 1960s. During the 1970s, although wages did not escalate, the rate of profit declined largely as a result of increases in the price of raw materials (Michl 1991, p. 271). During the 1980s, neither rising wages nor raw materials prices could explain why profits would remain low (Michl 1988a). Instead, a deeper structural problem seemed to be at work. Something was blocking business from operating efficiently. In this book, I will attempt to identify the nature of this blockage.

You will see that, although profits are an important business incentive, the economic decline is more than a matter of dollars and cents. It works its way into the fabric of society. For example, a fall in profitability encourages firms to cut corners to protect their earnings. Under such conditions, many firms display a wanton disregard for their workers, the environment, and even their own customers.

Poverty and the Distribution of Income

Lest the decline in the rate of profit cause you to become overly concerned with the fate of the well-to-do, I should note that during the 1980s, the upper 1 percent of the families in the United States, who were already doing quite well, increased their average income by an astounding $233,322 per family, a gain of 74 percent. Indeed, more and more people were enduring poverty at the time, while the differences between rich and poor were becoming more extreme.

For example, during the 1980s, income gains for the bottom 95 percent of the families were nonexistent (Mishel and Frankel 1991, p. 25). As a result, in 1989, the share of the national income going to the upper 1 percent exceeded that of the bottom 40 percent (Mishel and Frankel 1991, p. 27). This disparity in income is all but unknown in advanced economies. It is more typical of Latin American economies.

The United States increasingly resembled a typical third world economy in other respects. Each year more and more children drop below the poverty line. In 1973, 14.2

percent of all people under 18 years of age were poor; by 1988, 19.6 percent were poor (Mishel and Frankel 1991, p. 175).

The state of labor in the United States is another clear indicator of the nature of economic decline. Table 1.3 below, shows that during the Golden Age, real hourly, nonagricultural wages steadily rose, reaching a high point in 1973 of $8.55 (all wages measured in 1982 dollars). Since then, real hourly wages have steadily declined, falling to $7.39 in 1995, thereafter to show a slight improvement.

In short, the economic decline hurt people in most walks of life, except for those at the very peak of the economy. Of course, the poorest were hurt the most, but the hardship of the decline extended even to those who were relatively well off. By 1986, an average male with a college diploma was earning 2 percent less in real terms than a similar person would have earned in 1973. Of course, a male with only a high-school degree fared even worse, earning 16 percent less than he would have in 1973 (Levy 1988, p. vii).

Some people rationalize the gross inequities in the United States with a conviction that the poor are just too lazy to get a job. In fact, a good number of the poor are physically unable to participate fully in the labor markets. For example, in 1979, the peak of the last business cycle for which we have information, the head of two-thirds of all poor families was either a person who was elderly, disabled, a student, or a woman with a child under 6 years of age. In contrast, in 1939, only one-third of all poor households fell into these categories (Danziger and Gottschalk 1986, p. 405; Levitan and Shapiro 1987).

Others tried to explain the growing inequality by unfavorable demographic changes in the United States. Such experts contend that educated white males receive more wages because they are "naturally" the most productive workers. More and more workers are young, or women, or from disadvantaged ethnic groups that earn less income.

In truth, demographic explanations are incapable of explaining such a major shift in the distribution of income. You will do better if you understand these shifts in terms of the economy-wide process of an economic decline.

The Oil Shock as a Consequence of the Economic Decline

Many people prefer to look for single causes for the decline. For example, many still believe that we can trace the economic decline to the rise in oil prices during the

Table 1.3 Real Hourly Earnings in 1977 Dollars

Years	*Real Hourly Earnings in 1977 Dollars*	*Years*	*Profit Rate Growth (Percent per Annum)*
1960	$6.79	1990	$7.52
1970	$8.03	1995	$7.39
1973	$8.55	1999	$7.86
1980	$7.78		

Source: Economic Report of the President, 2001, p. 320.

1970s. We can just as easily make the case that the conflicts arising out of the early years of the economic decline were responsible for the oil shock. I have already noted that the inability of the U.S. economy to finance the Vietnam War without severe disruption was one of the early symptoms of the economic decline.

The events growing out of the Vietnam War helped to bring on the oil shock in several ways. First, the attempt to wage war in Vietnam set off a round of inflation.

In this environment, oil reserves were a depreciating asset in a double sense. To begin with, the petroleum exporters saw the inevitable exhaustion of their oil reserves as a long-term threat to their long-term economic health. In addition, the petroleum exporters were keeping a good deal of the proceeds of their oil sales in dollar denominated bank accounts. They saw the value of these accounts falling because inflation was eating away at the value of this money (Sampson 1975, p. 251).

As a result, they had to pay more for the goods that they were importing, while the price of their principal export stagnated because oil contracts were made in dollars. For example, many oil producing countries imported wheat. Number 2, Hard Amber Durham soared in price from $2.17 per bushel in 1972 to $6.60 in 1973 (United States Department of Agriculture 1980, p. 29). Increasing oil prices seemed equitable in this light. That the price hikes coincided with the 1973 Embargo was largely coincidental (Sampson 1975, p. 252).

The Vietnam War helped to provoke the oil price increases in another way. Seeing the strains that the Vietnam War placed on the economy, Richard Nixon and his secretary of state, Henry Kissinger, proposed the Nixon Doctrine, which held that the United States would support surrogates who would carry out its policies in the third world. In this way, the United States could shift at least some of the burdens of defense onto other nations.

The job of the U.S. policeman for the Middle East fell to the Shah of Iran. Not satisfied with playing the simple cop on the beat, the Shah got swept up with illusions about his grandeur. He went on a shopping binge for sophisticated weaponry, well beyond the means of his treasury (see Hulbert 1982, chapter 3).

A number of sources report that Kissinger was acting to keep oil prices high in 1974 (Hulbert 1982, pp. 78–79). Mark Hulbert suggested that Kissinger's motives were to help the Shah afford his purchases of expensive weapons from the United States. I lean toward a different, but not mutually exclusive explanation, also rooted in the decline. During the early 1970s, the U.S. economy was increasingly unable to compete in international merchandise trade. Encouraging the Shah to keep oil prices high seemed to give U.S. industry a leg up on its rivals.

Although the United States depended on imported oil, this dependence paled compared to that of its two most important economic rivals at the time: West Germany and Japan. Increased oil prices stood to do far more damage to industry in those countries than in the United States (Castells 1980, p. 85). Certainly, the financial markets thought so. As soon as the oil prices rose in 1973, speculators began to dump their yen, marks, and francs for dollars (Tanzer 1975, p. 91).

The United States hopes for an advantage from the oil shock came to naught. Rising oil prices actually hurt the United States more than most of its rivals. The Japanese proved to be especially adept in adopting methods to cope with higher energy costs. By the late 1980s, for example, the Japanese economy could produce 2.24 times the real output for the same energy input as in 1973 (Chipello and Brauchli 1990).

In contrast, U.S. firms were all to often inclined to make do with the equipment that they had on hand, until more intense international competition eventually forced a series of devastating plant closings throughout the country. As a result, the United States was consuming about 2.5 times as much energy per person for commercial uses as Japan (Chipello and Brauchli 1990). Again, a policy that was supposed to arrest the economic decline turned out to make it more severe.

While Japanese policies were more successful in meeting the challenge of the energy shock, like all simple economic policies designed to meet one problem, they had unintended consequences. Japan used low interest rates to encourage industry to modernize. This policy was hugely successful in accomplishing its desired goal, but it also set off a speculative frenzy.

By late 1991, the total land value in Japan was estimated at nearly $20 trillion, more than 20 percent of the world's wealth and double the world's equity markets and half as large as the world's bond markets and 5 times that of the U.S. land. The land underneath the Emperor's palace in the center of Tokyo, about 3/4 of a square mile, was valued as much as all the land in California or all the land in Canada (Stone and Ziemba 1993, p. 149).

In addition, while modernizing Japanese industry also began to move a lot of its operations offshore. The Japanese built so many new factories both at home and abroad that the economy was left with an excess of productive capacity. This combination of excessive capacity together with the distortions in the economy associated with the speculation eventually hobbled the Japanese economy, which had recently been considered the marvel of the capitalist world. As of this writing, the Japanese economy has not yet recovered.

No single explanation is adequate. While some economists maintained that the oil shock was a central factor in the creating the decline, others countered that energy costs were such a small share of the total economy that they would be incapable of doing so much harm.

The Decline as a Complex Economy-Wide Process

Despite the abrupt materialization of the decline, it had been developing over decades. You can liken the process to the movement of a gigantic ship. It might not appear to be very dramatic, but it represents a powerful momentum, which is extremely difficult to reverse. This book is largely concerned with the nature of this momentum.

In general, economic theory ignores the role of momentum in the economy. Earlier economists used the example of a primitive fish market to illustrate how markets work. The fish sellers bring their catch to market. If it did not sell quickly, it would rot and lose all of its value. Buyers and sellers bargain until they find the highest price at which all the fish will be sold. Tomorrow, when the process repeats itself, the price today will be irrelevant (Thornton 1869, p. 47).

The fish market accurately reflects the simplistic theory that underlies much economic thinking. Because it inconveniently reveals the limits of economic theory, it is all but forgotten today. Add even the slightest touch of realism to this example and this brand of economic theory loses its elegant precision. For example, if fish prices remain high for a while, members of the fishing industry may choose to invest in a bigger or a better fleet. Unlike today's price, today's investment, resulting in an expanded stock of fishing capital, will have an incalculable impact over an extended period of time.

When one firm invests, it often creates favorable conditions for other firms to invest. For example, Joel Mokyr has described how the early growth of Dutch shipbuilding led to the development of rope and sail making, which led to wind-driven saw mills, which could make shipbuilding more efficient. The development of these industries gave Holland an edge in trade, which made Holland the most successful economy in the world during the seventeenth century (Mokyr 1990, p. 163).

Mokyr's depiction of the rise of the Dutch economy lacks the minimalist elegance of the classical description of an imaginary fish market, but it offers a great deal more realism. It also illustrates how economic momentum takes hold.

Nobody has an exact idea of the quantitative effects of economic momentum on specific industries, but economists do know, as Mokyr's example illustrates, that when a firm erects a new factory, other companies may emerge to service the firm. The growth of these service firms may induce still other firms to locate nearby.

In addition, the growth in demand from the investing firm may allow suppliers to enjoy economies of scale—meaning a lowering of average cost as the scale of production expands. If these resulting efficiencies lead suppliers to lower their costs, still other firms will benefit, perhaps stimulating even more investment.

Assar Linbeck uses his native Sweden as an example of the cumulative spillover of economic actions. Who could have predicted at the turn of the century that Sweden would be so successful in ball bearings, safety matches, cream separators, automatic lighthouses, telephone exchanges, and military aircraft? Sweden had no particular resource advantage that induced it to specialize in these industries. Linbeck gives a simpler answer, "Some people living in Sweden happened to take initiative," giving Sweden an advantage that lasted over a very long period (Linbeck 1981, p. 394).

Economists have long recognized how the cumulative effects of a seemingly small number of such independent decisions can combine to create a major impact. For example, in discussing why industries tend to cluster around a specific location, Alfred Marshall, who more than anyone else was responsible for the formalization of economic theory, wrote, "When an industry has chosen a locality for itself, it is likely to stay there long: so great are the advantages which people following the same trade get from near neighborhood to one another" (Marshall 1920, p. 271). Unfortunately, neither Marshall nor his successors integrated this insight into their formal theory.

Investment helps to stimulate further investment in another crucial way. When a firm invests it puts money into the hands of its employees and its suppliers. Their spending will create new markets, which will improve the potential profitability of other new investments, possibly setting off a spiral of investment (see Shleifer and Vishny 1988).

The spiral cannot continue indefinitely. After a while, this happy state of affairs will create a state of overconfidence. Some people will begin to invest foolishly, eventually causing the cumulative causation to work in reverse.

Each market economy develops its own particular pattern of spillovers within the context of boom and bust. Economic historians are familiar with the role of spillovers in a growing economy. They know less about the momentum associated with economic decline. This book explores the nature of this perverse momentum for the case of the U.S. economy.

One business's failure helps to drag another into bankruptcy. The government finds itself burdened with the damage created by bankruptcies. Besides increased obligations for welfare and unemployment benefits, the government must cover the pension plans of bankrupt firms.

Soaring government expenses, combined with declining revenues, create spiraling deficits, which raise interest rates. Where interest rates are prohibitive and investors uncertain, business will be slow to create new jobs. Yet prolonged unemployment can make workers unemployable. Certainly, it is associated with almost every measure of crime and disease, creating further demands on the government, which further adds to the demands on government.

Despite the increasing responsibilities of the government, soaring deficits lead to strong pressure to curtail public expenditures. The government responds by diminishing its commitment in crucial areas, such as education and health care, which limits the ability of the economy to produce in the future.

Historically, this process continues until the economy hits rock bottom. Hopefully, at that point, the economy bounces back and the process begins anew. This rebound is not necessarily a natural phenomenon. Often, it is associated with military adventures. In a nuclear age, that particular method of economic recovery poses obvious risks.

Economics and Oversimplification

Economists do not generally broach the subject of momentum. They are prone to ignore the complexity of economic processes. Instead, they single out a particular problem, attributing all the ills of the society to a lone cause, as I noted in the discussion of mismanagement.

This habit of reducing the focus of their work to single causes leads to serious errors in judgment. Once economic analysts commit themselves to framing the problem in terms of a single cause, they are prone to proposing to rectify the situation with a simple remedy, whether it be lower taxes or a set of measures to make workers work harder or incentives to increase savings, etc.

Such single-minded prescriptions are almost inevitably wrong-headed. By concentrating on one particular symptom of a complex process, analysts lose sight of the detrimental effects of the unexpected aftermath of their policy recommendations. They cut themselves off from the possibility of understanding how to improve the process. As a result, single-minded analysis generally deepens the overall problem rather than ameliorating it. In short, complex economic processes require systemic analysis.

This caveat regarding single remedies also extends to my recommendation of measures to boost wages. All measures must be understood in terms of the complexity of the economic process. While the promotion of high wages should be a part of the solution, it will not suffice in itself.

In part, the destructive habit of oversimplification is endemic to the discipline of economics. After all, economists purposefully developed their formal theory to allow themselves to make clear and unambiguous predictions about complex economic systems.

The key to this theory is the development of a set of unrealistic assumptions that ensure that the price system would give the proper incentives to people and firms to do what was best for society. This simplified theory is appropriate for the primitive fish market, but not for a complex, modern economy. Despite its formal elegance, this theory requires ruling out crucial aspects of the actual economic process, including the spillovers and momentum that we have been discussing.

Economists are only now beginning to think about developing models that will account for the influence of economic momentum, but this work is still in its infancy (see Arthur 1989). Rather than use sophisticated models, I will try to bring together as much as possible of the complex set of forces that are responsible for the economic decline.

Although this work will not be the first to study the contemporary economic pathologies, it will be unique in attempting to address the complexity of the problems that face the U.S. economy. Before continuing, I should confess that I have simplified my task in one respect: although the economy is a global phenomenon, I will concentrate on the case of the United States.

Resurrection?

Although momentum is an important influence on economic outcomes, it does not work in a simple, nonlinear fashion. Forces that may be obscured for a long time can build up pressure, while the seemingly irreversible momentum can weaken, causing sudden reversals.

Economists are very good at predicting the gradual changes that affect the economy over stretches of time, but their record of predicting dramatic reversals is pretty dismal. In addition, economists have no way of knowing whether minor shifts in the economy represent the beginning of some momentous change or just an interruption of a longer tendency.

The decline ended, at least temporarily in the early 1980s. The rate of profit tells the story fairly clearly. It hit a low point around 1982, and then meandered around that same level to about 1992. Then, it rose until 1997, when it fell off slightly.

This recovery was uneven, to say the least. Wages never fully recovered their 1970s peak. The distribution of income became as lopsided as it was on the eve of the Great Depression. The balance of trade for the United States has become so unfavorable that this country is now importing almost a half trillion dollars more than it is exporting.

Even so, during the late 1990s, the economy seemed to experience a resurrection, then it sputtered in 2000. Whether the more vigorous growth of the late 1990s represents an end to the decline or whether the downturn in the early years of the next decade is symptomatic of a continuation of the long period of economic sluggishness remains an open question at this time.

Summary

This book tells the story of an economy based on self-interest in which the interested parties fail to understand their own best interests. Business perceives its interest to do anything in its power to cut wages. In doing so, it reduces the income of its potential customers. More important, it cripples the labor force and thereby undermines productivity as well as the rate of profit. In contrast to the prevailing opinion about the appropriate level of wages, I will show how a high-wage policy promotes economic growth.

During the early postwar period, both business and the public supported the government's attempt to stabilize the economy. Although stabilization policy helped to reduce the intensity of the business cycle, it also reduced necessary modernization of the economy, preparing the way for an economic decline.

As the decline gained momentum, business, as well as the public at large, perceived that they would benefit by cutting back government. As a result, they helped to create a lax regulatory structure, which led to instability and chaos. The government lets the public infrastructure of roads and public works deteriorate enough to hobble the economy. Education suffers, further damaging productivity and profits.

Although business and the public oppose the government in general, they agree that their interests will be served by a huge military buildup. The military expenditures further sap the vitality of the economy, so much so that they ultimately threaten to weaken the military itself.

The buildup of the military dovetails with a program to protect the economy against depressions by maintaining demand for goods and services. Unfortunately, this policy undermines competition and weakens the economy, ultimately leading to a process of deindustrialization.

The revolution in the financial structure of the United States reinforces this process of deindustrialization, leading to an economy that is increasingly built upon low-wage service jobs. The alternative policy that I propose centers on a high-wage structure, which has traditionally been the source of the strength of the U.S. economy. Of course, in line with my earlier warning about the futility of single-minded remedies, a high-wage policy alone will be insufficient to invigorate the economy.

CHAPTER 2

The Attack on Labor Accelerates the Economic Decline

The Postwar Labor-Management Accord

During the Golden Age, social conditions on the whole were relatively harmonious, with the obvious exception of violence against blacks. In the North, racial tensions largely reflected the collision between demobilized troops and black workers who had taken industrial jobs. In the South, whites felt threatened by the inevitable dislocations that the imminent destruction of their rural, patriarchal society would cause.

During the initial years of postwar prosperity, the economy was expanding fast enough that wages could grow while profits remained high. Union leaders developed a relatively comfortable relationship with management at the time, especially within the large industrial complexes. They purged their ranks of militants and became active participants in the anticommunist crusade that was at the heart of U.S. foreign policy.

Forces were at work that would eventually undermine this implicit accord between labor leaders and capital. Although management offered workers higher wages, it also claimed the exclusive right to maintain absolute control over work on the shop floor. For example, the 1945 contract between the United Automobile Workers and General Motors included a clear "right to manage clause," which read:

> The right to hire, promote, discharge or discipline for cause, and to maintain discipline and efficiency of employees, is the sole responsibility of the Corporation except that the union members shall not be discriminated against as such. In addition, the products to be manufactured, the location of plants, the schedules of production, the methods, processes and means of manufacturing are solely and exclusively the responsibility of the Corporation. [Gartman 1986, p. 278; cited in Lazonick 1990, p. 272]

Later, when General Motors signed its agreement with the United Automobile Workers covering the period between 1948 and 1950, *Fortune,* in an article entitled, "The Treaty of Detroit," commented, "GM may have paid a billion for peace. It got a bargain." According to *Fortune,* "General Motors has regained control over one of the crucial management functions in any line of manufacturing—long-range scheduling of production, model changes, and tool and plant investment" (Anon. 1950, p. 53; see also Serrin 1974, p. 170). One estimate put the value of this newfound freedom of planning at $0.15 worth of corporate profit per hour of labor (Anon. 1950, p. 53).

Indeed, although it won higher wages for its members, the United Automobile Workers union failed to achieve any of its major policy goals in this agreement (Harris 1982, pp. 139 ff; Fairris 1990). Still, many workers, who had only recently experienced the Depression, initially found this deal acceptable.

The Breakdown of the Labor-Management Accord

Wages continued to improve well into the 1960s. Indeed, between 1966 and 1969, unemployment remained below 4 percent, allowing workers to accelerate the increases in their wages. By the early 1970s, the real value of the average weekly earnings of nonagricultural workers reached an all-time high.

Even so, many workers—especially young workers—found the organization of work alienating. They had become increasingly reluctant to accept capital's pretense of absolute control within the workplace. In General Motors's Lordstown plant, workers wrote on their machines, "Treat Me with Respect and I will give you Top Quality Work with Less Effort" (Rothschild 1974, p. 119).

Many of the younger workers also began to question the value of accumulating more and more possessions. In addition, the birth control pill allowed many workers to avoid some of the family pressures that typically had intensified the need for job security (Halberstam 1986, p. 487).

Feeling confident that they could find alternative employment, many of these young workers resisted employers' efforts at maintaining discipline. The auto "quit rate" at the time was enormous. One study found that more than half of all new unskilled autoworkers in "major northern production centers" left their job within one year (Rothschild 1974, p. 124).

Among those workers who continued their employment, absenteeism became commonplace. Ford Motor Company claimed in 1970 that absenteeism had "doubled" or "tripled" in ten years; that such average figures "mask[ed] the crippling effects often felt on a key production line" (Rothschild 1974, p. 124).

Douglas Fraser, past president of the United Automobile Workers, used to tell a story about a young employee at the Twinsburg, Ohio, stamping plant to illustrate the workers' attitude at the time. This worker faithfully labored for four days a week, but he never came for the fifth day.

The plant was loath to fire this worker because labor markets were so tight. In fact, at the time, management was on a seven-day schedule because of widespread absenteeism. Finally, the plant manager confronted the young man, demanding to know why he regularly worked 4 days a week. The worker responded, "Because I can't make a living working three days a week" (Halberstam 1986, p. 488).

Absenteeism was not the only symptom of the erosion of shop floor discipline. By 1971, the almost open use of drugs in U.S. factories became a front-page story in the *New York Times* (Salpukas 1971).

A good number of young workers even engaged in active rebellion on the job, further undermining productivity. Surely, the conduct of the Vietnam War contributed to this spirit of rebellion and a widespread disdain for authority in general. Finally, the conditions of the unions played a significant role.

Many of these workers believed that constructive attempts to create truly democratic unions, which would represent their interests, could not succeed. Without a strong union to express their concerns, they had limited opportunities to make the views felt within normal channels.

Rebellion on the Shop Floor

In this environment, workers often challenged management's authority on the job, dissipating enormous productive energies. The testimony of John Lippert, who had been a worker in General Motors's Fleetwood plant, is instructive in this regard. He described his fellow workers' vigorous efforts to slow down the assembly line (Lippert 1978). Lippert suggested the intensity of his desire to carve a bit of autonomy on the assembly line by expressing obvious pride in hurrying up his work on a few cars, in order to have 15 or 20 seconds to himself on the next car (Lippert 1978, p. 58).

Bill Watson, who spent one year in a Detroit automobile factory, offers an even more dramatic example of the lengths to which workers went to assert their independence (Watson 1971). He described how workers revolted against the production of a poorly designed 6-cylinder model car. In the process, workers and foremen argued over particular motors. Tension escalated.

After management rejected the workers' suggestions for improvements in the production and design of the product, they initiated a "counter-plan," beginning by intentionally misassembling or omitting parts on a larger than normal scale. Later, workers in inspection made alliances with workers in several assembly areas to ensure a high rate of defective motors. Workers went ahead and installed many of these defective motors, thereby requiring that management would have to go to the trouble of removing them later.

Eventually, even more complicated measures were taken. The conflict only ended during a layoff after management suddenly moved the entire 6-cylinder assembly and inspection operation to another end of the plant, presumably at great cost (Watson 1971, pp. 76–77).

In another instance, the company, intending to save money by shutting down its foundry early, attempted to build the engines using parts that already had been rejected during the year. Workers in the motor test area lodged a protest, but management hounded inspectors to accept defective motors. After motor test men communicated their grievances to other workers, they began to collaborate in intentional sabotage. Inspectors agreed to reject three of every four motors. Stacks of motors piled up at an accelerating pace until the entire plant shut down, losing more than ten hours of production time to deal with the problem. Management summoned inspectors to the head supervisor's office. Inspectors protested that they were only acting in the interest of management.

Watson's third example is the most telling of all. During a model changeover period, management had scheduled an inventory buildup, which was to require six weeks. Management intended to keep 50 people at work on the job. These workers could have earned 90 percent of their pay if they were laid off. Workers enthusiastically reacted to the opportunity, attempting to finish the inventory in three or four days instead of the six weeks.

They trained each other in particular skills, circumventing the established ranking and job classification system to slice through the required time. If workers had been given the opportunity to organize their own work, Watson claims that they actually could have completed the task in one-tenth the required time.

Management responded harshly, forcing workers to halt, claiming that the legitimate channels of authority, training, and communication had been violated. Management was determined to stop workers from organizing their own work, even when it would have been finished quicker and management would have saved money (Watson 1971, p. 80). So much for Pareto optimality!

Watson also described how workers enjoyed hose fights and even organized contests to explode rods from engines in the workplace. Watson's description communicates a sense of intense joy and exhilaration that workers felt from the opportunity to organize their own activity. Watson himself applauded industrial sabotage as "the forcing of more free time into existence" (Watson 1971, p. 80). He explained:

> The seizing of quantities of time for getting together with friends and the amusement of activities ranging from card games to reading or walking around the plant to see what other areas are doing is an important achievement for the laborers. Not only does it demonstrate the feeling that much of the time should be organized by the workers themselves, but it also demonstrates an existing animosity. . . .
>
> While this organization is a reaction to the need for common action in getting the work done, relationships like these also function to carry out sabotage, to make collections, or even to organize games and contests which serve to turn the working day into an enjoyable event. [Watson 1971, pp. 80–91]

One might argue that the managers that Watson described were unusually short-sighted; however, even when management behaves in a way that we would normally regard as intelligent, management still tries to manage; that is, managers expect to have the power to control the actions of those who fall below them in the hierarchy. This ingrained behavior would still remain, even where capitalists were not as short-sighted as those that Watson described.

The Social Dynamics of the Economic Decline

In the wake of this combination of labor rebelliousness and wartime tensions, the growth in productivity dramatically slowed and profits fell. We should not be surprised that capital would not stand by idly while workers were asserting their powers. Business was certain that strong measures had to be taken.

The business offensive against labor took many forms. Before discussing some of the more direct weapons that business used against labor, I want to turn your attention to an apparently unrelated technique that business used in its effort to gain the upper hand against labor. Specifically, I want to discuss the Civil Rights Movement. This discussion will highlight the importance of taking a broad perspective in analyzing the economic decline.

Before explaining the nature of the relationship between the Civil Rights Movement and the offensive against labor, consider the timing of the great victories of the Civil Rights Movement. I cannot accept that the movement succeeded just because a few exceptional people emerged at this particular time. Since the earliest days of slavery, strong and courageous people have stood up for the rights of African Americans.

No, the Civil Rights Movement succeeded when it did, at least in part, because economic conditions were right. Specifically, powerful interests welcomed the Civil Rights Movement, I believe, because it helped to undermine the power of labor. I do not mean that the Civil Rights Movement itself was inherently anti-labor, but it did further some interests that were decidedly anti-labor.

Certainly, the economic conditions of the time helped to reinforce the confidence of people engaged in the movement. The growing labor shortages of the 1960s were allowing many African Americans—especially those with better education—economic opportunities that had been largely denied to them before (Smith and Welch 1989). In fact, during the 1960s and 1970s, the rise in black wages was more than 10 percent higher than the gain in white wages (Smith and Welch 1989, p. 522). This modest spurt of prosperity created an optimism that eventually burst into a boundless impatience for immediate change among young African Americans (see Piven and Cloward 1971, p. 223).

Then, by the 1970s the federal government actively began to foster affirmative action. Perhaps the most seemingly unlikely instance was the Nixon administration's proposed Philadelphia Plan. The ostensible object of the Philadelphia Plan was to raise the percentage of minority group members working in six Philadelphia area construction trades (see United States Senate 1970).

What drove Richard Nixon to spearhead this first policy of affirmative action? Certainly, Nixon was no heady reformer. Indeed, he had some practical goals in mind. First, he could contain some of the demands for reform by offering affirmative action without threatening the powerful corporate interests that he represented. Even better, he could integrate African Americans into the labor force more quickly, hoping that this increased supply of employable labor would relieve the pressure for higher wages.

Perhaps best of all, the Philadelphia Plan offered the prospect of splitting two of the most powerful voices for reform. Nixon could attack the unions in the name of racial justice, thereby discrediting the unions in the eyes of liberals. Even more importantly, the Philadelphia Plan served to threaten both working-class and middle-class whites that African American progress would come at their expense. Finally, once the public forgot this obscure program, the racial animosity festered, allowing Nixon to appeal to the electorate in the Southern states, which previously had regularly voted Democratic.

Similarly, I am convinced that the government was as receptive as it was to the women's movement for equally cynical reasons. As in the case of the movement for African American civil rights, the women's movement had a long and proud history well before the dawning of affirmative-action policies. Affirmative action for women conveniently relieved labor market pressure while setting group against group.

The Decline and Social Discord

This divide-and-conquer strategy was largely successful. As the slowdown intensified and unemployment grew, many white workers would blame African Americans and women for their ills. Rather than working in unison with African Americans, Hispanics, and women, by the 1980s many white—especially white, male—workers shifted their allegiance to Ronald Reagan, who then proceeded to attack the labor movement with a vigor previously unknown in the twentieth century.

As the economy slowed down, the need for relatively unskilled workers moderated. As the labor markets accumulated an excess supply of such labor, the federal government became hostile to affirmative action and most other active measures to bring more blacks and women into better paying jobs, appealing to the worst instincts of working-class, white males. Within this increasingly acrimonious situation, working people and minorities had to bear the brunt of the economic decline. Business interests were able to cut ruthlessly into many of the gains made during the early postwar period. Today, affirmative action is all but dead. All that remains is the prospect of further losses and sacrifices until a more cooperative spirit develops.

In general, on the most superficial level, a growing economy typically fosters harmony among groups; a stagnant economy promotes social tensions. In other words, when the economy experiences a healthy rate of growth, employers can afford to be relatively generous. In addition, labor often becomes less rebellious while it enjoys an appreciable growth in its standard of living.

This generalization about harmony requires some qualification. Keep in mind, however, that the quality of life on the job is an important component of the standard of living. Once the pace of economic activity passes a certain threshold, social relations actually can become destabilized. During the Vietnam War, the U.S. economy probably exceeded that point.

In addition, even when the economy as a whole is growing at a healthy rate, economic development will be uneven. Some regions and some sectors will not share in the prosperity. Some interest groups will still try to manipulate the situation to their benefit, even when the need to do so is less pressing. Finally, at times when economic measures of prosperity may indicate an improvement, deterioration of other dimensions of the quality of life, such as the tensions associated with the hectic demands of urban life, can create discord.

Nonetheless, I would not be far off the mark by generalizing that, once the economy ceases to grow, one group can improve its situation only at the expense of other groups. Politics, as well as social and economic behavior in general, become more contentious. When an economy deteriorates, people often become disoriented and take their frustrations out in antisocial behavior.

To take an extreme example, when cotton prices fell during the early part of the twentieth century, Southern whites would lynch African Americans more frequently (Beck and Tolnay 1990; Myrdal 1962, p. 563). Today, unemployment and urban blight create an even more deadly atmosphere of violence, which is part and parcel of the process of economic decline.

When poor economic conditions persist over an extended period of time, people can come together as they get a better understanding of the roots of their problems. For example, although some people continued to follow demagogues during the 1930s, this tendency was more than counterbalanced by the growth of movements based on solid organizing and cooperation.

In conclusion, economic decline and social conflict are closely related. Although a cooperative spirit would soften the decline and probably even help to reverse it, social discord is generally associated with an economic decline.

How Business Attacked Labor

Although the war in Vietnam was part of the problem facing business, it strengthened business's position in another important respect. Vietnam represented a powerful symbol of the willingness of the government to protect corporate interests around the globe, in effect offering business an implicit guarantee that the United States would stand behind its investments abroad. This posture encouraged business to move manufacturing offshore.

The extensive use of foreign manufacturing operations is a relatively recent phenomenon. I will show later that, in earlier periods, business responded to higher labor demands by introducing technologies to make labor more efficient rather than moving in search of cheaper labor.

Why had business not taken the path of least resistance and moved its manufacturing operations to low-wage economies earlier? Two problems stood in the way: one was technical, and one political. In the first place, as Alfred Marshall noted in his classic economics text:

> The emigration of capital, with or without its owner, is obstructed by difficulties partly similar to and partly different from those which obstruct the emigration of employment. . . . [T]he tendency of capitalists in general is to prefer investments at home to investments abroad [especially because] information with regard to it is more easily obtained and more easily tested. [Marshall 1920, p. 9]

The development of modern methods of telecommunications during the postwar period largely solved the technical problem, making communication with distant lands no more difficult than placing a phone call down the street. Reports could flow into the front office from foreign operations almost as quickly as if a clerk were bringing them from an adjacent office.

The political problem still remained. How could business be assured that its investments would be safe from unfriendly treatment? Here, the Vietnam War proved to be a crucial watershed.

The Vietnam War was intended to serve as a powerful message to the world. After all, the United States had no important investments in Vietnam, yet it fought with great determination. This show of force demonstrated the resolve of the U.S. government to protect U.S. investments in the low-wage economies of Asia, just as vigorously as it had in Latin America in the past.

True, Vietnam won the war, but at a great enough cost that few nations would challenge U.S. economic military might. Given this implicit guarantee of military support throughout the globe, U.S. business confidently embarked on a policy of moving many of its operations offshore.

Even without this process of deindustrialization, business was fast getting the upper hand in the United States. Despite labor's often-defiant behavior, even during the

Golden Age, judging by the share of the private workforce under union contracts, the strength of organized labor was already deteriorating before Vietnam.

In fact, union strength had been in decline since relatively early in the postwar era. For example, the share of wage and salary workers enrolled in unions or employee associations fell from 35.5 percent in 1945 to 21.9 percent in 1980 (Adams 1985, p. 26). In 1953, a record 42 percent of all manufacturing workers belonged to unions. By 1985, only 25 percent belonged to unions (Craypo 1990, p. 4).

Some analysts contend that the decline in union strength is a natural phenomenon, reflecting changes in the mix of occupations in the U.S. economy, such as the erosion of jobs in basic industries and the surge in service jobs. This explanation appeals to common-sense. Services have been growing relative to manufacturing. Unions have more difficulty in organizing service workers than industrial workers. Of course, manufacturing employment has been in decline, at least in part, because business is moving manufacturing offshore.

Even so, while structural changes are undoubtedly important, economists tend to overestimate their significance. For example, P. M. Doyle attributed 45 percent of the decline in unionization to such structural changes (Doyle 1985). Richard Freeman and James Medoff went further, suggesting that structural changes could account for more than 70 percent (Freeman and Medoff 1984).

Jack Fiorito and Cheryl Maranto (1987) take issue with those who give excessive weight to the structural explanation of the union decline. They reject the notion that the decline in union strength could be a natural phenomenon. Instead, they make the case that business and government combined in a concerted program to render unions impotent.

Even during the Golden Age, business successfully shepherded antiunion legislation, such as the Taft-Hartley Act, through Congress. A gradual erosion of organized labor's legal rights continued until the 1980s, when the process dramatically escalated.

Soon after Ronald Reagan took office, he dramatically replaced the striking air-traffic controllers. This act clearly signaled to business that it too could play hardball with labor. In addition, the judiciary has become less favorable to unions in recent years.

The National Labor Relations Board, which has the responsibility to protect workers' rights, also has taken a decidedly antiunion stance in recent years. Even if a union eventually wins an appeal concerning unfair practices, the penalties are so slight that violating the law can be cost effective (Fiorito and Maranto 1987, p. 16).

Fiorito and Maranto cite Freeman and Medoff's own estimate that, in 1980, "one in twenty workers who favored the union got fired. Assuming that the vast bulk of union supporters are relatively inactive, the likelihood that an outspoken worker, . . . gets fired for union activity is extraordinarily high" (Fiorito and Maranto 1987, p. 15; citing Freeman and Medoff 1984, pp. 232–3).

By the late 1990s, one out of eighteen workers involved in unionization drives faced some type of punishment for supporting the union. While such retribution is clearly in violation of the law, workers must wait years and years before they can even hope for a modest remedy. The courts recently ruled that the best compensation workers should get was the lost wages minus any wages that they had earned since their termination. Such mild penalties are unlikely to act as a significant deterrent (Greenhouse 2000a).

Fiorito and Maranto highlight other antiunion tactics, such as declaring bankruptcy to make union contracts inoperative and using non-union subcontractors to replace unionized workers (Greenhouse 2000a). In short, the business offensive against labor has succeeded on many fronts.

Building on Freeman and Medoff's own observations, Fiorito and Maranto suggest a different sort of interpretation of organized labor's decline. They point to Freeman and Medoff's own conclusion that structural changes account for less than 3 percent of the declining rates of union victories in National Labor Relations Board representation elections.

Fiorito and Maranto point out that to the extent that structural forces are responsible for the decline in union representation, we would expect that the relative size of specific industries would vary, but union strength within a given industry would remain unchanged. Instead, they observe that union representation has declined unevenly from industry to industry (Greenhouse 2000a, p. 14). They also note that unions gained strength in Canada, even though the Canadian economy experienced structural changes similar to those of the U.S. economy (Fiorito and Maranto 1987, p. 14).

Unemployment and Labor Discipline

While individual firms may take advantage of the labor laws to single out particular workers, the classic method that the government uses for subduing widespread labor unrest is the imposition of restrictive economic policies to create massive unemployment. With the economy growing as fast as it did during the Golden Age, what need was there to slow the economy down? Conditions were so ideal that the economy could provide both high wages and high profits.

Alas, the Golden Age did not last forever. By the late 1960s, the economy overheated while peasant huts were burning in far off Vietnam. The sequence of a long period of relative prosperity followed by the strains of this vicious war had taken its toll. Real wages had ceased growing. Profit rates were falling. A perennial balance of trade surplus had turned into a worrisome deficit. Business began to realize that the Golden Age had ended, setting the stage for the use of the business cycle to discipline workers.

The economics profession signaled the demise of the Golden Age by electing Milton Friedman, the doyen of the Chicago school of economics, to be president of the American Economics Association. Friedman's presidential address, delivered in December 1967, offered a simplistic solution to the economic crisis. If only government would cease its efforts to guide the economy and if only the Federal Reserve System would adhere to a policy of increasing the money supply at a predetermined steady rate, all economic problems would magically disappear.

While Richard Nixon was running for president in the following year, he echoed Friedman's contention that monetary policy was the solution to all economic ills. Candidate Nixon declared inflation to be the country's number one problem.

Opinion polls did not support Nixon's view, so after his election he enlisted the Council of Economic Advisors to identify those adversely impacted by inflation. According to the chairman of his Council of Economic Advisors, Herbert Stein, "If anyone was being severely hurt, the available statistics were too crude to reveal it" (Stein 1984, p. 149; also cited in May and Grant 1991, p. 373).

In fact, a number of studies indicate that inflation does no harm to the middle or lower classes, although it does have a detrimental effect on the rich (see May and Grant 1991). None of these studies, however, attempted to analyze the role of disinflation in disciplining labor.

Indeed, when Nixon or the business leaders who supported his election complained about inflation, labor discipline was uppermost in their minds. Consequently, between 1969 to 1970, the Nixon administration engineered a short recession in order to cool the economy, a euphemism for putting labor in its place. Then, on 15 August 1971, in the run-up to his reelection campaign, President Nixon asked for wage and price controls, with a heavy emphasis on controlling wages (Blinder 1981, chapter 6). By this time, the public supported wage and price controls because many people associated rapidly rising prices with unfair wartime profiteering.

The Nixon administration's system of wage and price control, however, was not intended to limit profiteering (Blinder 1981, p. 111). Arnold Weber, a labor economist who was the director of Richard Nixon's Cost of Living Council at the time, explained the logic behind these wage and price controls, "Business had been leaning on [Nixon's economic advisors, George] Schultz and [Paul] McCracken to do something about the economy, especially wages. The idea of the [wage] freeze and Phase II [of Nixon's New Economic Policy, which began in November 1971] was to zap labor, and we did" (Anon. 1974, p. 108; see also Lazonick 1990, p. 281)

The president did not intend to harm the entire working class. Labor was shorthand for union workers. The Republicans did not expect their votes anyway.

Economists usually oppose wage and price controls because they are inconsistent with economic efficiency. They lack the flexibility to adapt to changing economic conditions. This inflexibility worked to the president's advantage. It allowed him to distort the economy to advance his immediate political objectives.

After all, Richard Nixon's focus at the time was not economic efficiency. He was far more intent on winning reelection in 1972, as demonstrated by the excesses of Watergate.

Richard Nixon clearly recognized how the economy could be engineered in other ways to further the chances of his reelection. He used his unprecedented influence over the Federal Reserve to keep the money supply growing at 7.2 percent from the third quarter of 1971 to the fourth quarter of 1972 (Blinder 1981, p. 33). Federal spending also skyrocketed just before the election. This combination was sure to provide a quick burst of economic prosperity. Coincidentally, social security benefits also rose significantly in 1971 (Blinder 1981, pp. 142–4). This massive influx of federal purchases, together with a growing money supply and wage and price controls lifted the economy. No wonder he proclaimed himself to be a Keynesian at the time, much to the chagrin of his conservative constituency (Buckley 1971).

The wage and price controls effectively ended shortly after the election in January 1973. Although these policies surely contributed to Nixon's victory, they also undermined wage and price controls by building up tremendous inflationary pressures.

Scorched Earth Economics

Social conditions also contributed to inflationary pressures. Although the union movement had been shrinking, unions were still relatively powerful. Besides, the country was in turmoil over the Vietnam War. Any all-out attack on labor would have created an electoral disaster for the Republicans. Inflation was a way of allowing workers to feel a sense of victory in winning wage increases while business could still raise prices.

The financial sector, however, unlike manufacturing and other kinds of business, could not appreciate the inflationary charade. Inflation ate away at the value of bonds. Yet during these years, the financial sector was increasing by leaps and bounds relative to the economy as a whole.

In addition, the economy was slowing down. Inflation offered a convenient target for the Republicans, who had lost the presidency to Jimmy Carter. Because of inflation, interest rates had soared. Carter eventually "fired" the head of the Federal Reserve Board by appointing him secretary of the Treasury, replacing him with Paul Volcker.

Stuart Eizenstat, Carter's domestic policy adviser, admitted that "Volcker was selected because he was the candidate of Wall Street" (cited in Greider 1987, p. 47). The installation of Volcker represented the beginning of what may be called the great capitalist restoration, which culminated in the following decades with an even harsher period of market Stalinism, which continued to ratchet up through the Reagan administration and into the second Bush administration.

Soon after Volcker took the reins at the Federal Reserve, he intentionally used his powers to tighten credit in 1979, engineering a severe recession. The Fed had done so five times before since the end of the war and the middle of the 1970s (Romer and Romer 1989, p. 135), but this one was far more severe.

Business leaders appreciated that this downturn would work to their advantage. They realized that, with soaring unemployment, labor rightfully fears the threat of termination. Under such conditions, business would be in a good position to reassert its authority on the shop floor. For this reason, business leaders welcomed the downturn because, with the end of the Golden Age, they believed that profits could only be preserved by reducing wages.

Certainly, Paul Volcker echoed these sentiments in explaining his motives for making credit scarce. He lectured the Joint Economic Committee of the Congress on 17 October 1979, "The standard of living of the average American has to decline. . . . I don't think you can escape that" (Rattner 1979). Again, economic leaders commended the Haitian path.

Listening to Paul Volcker at the time of the 1980 recession, one would easily imagine that labor was doing quite well. In truth, the real hourly wage was about 50 cents lower than it had been in 1973.

Ironically, while calling for workers to tighten their collective belt, the Fed treats itself lavishly. The *Wall Street Journal* published an article about the elegant new Federal Reserve Bank in Minneapolis. "The $100 million building sits on nine acres of prime riverfront, with a 10-story stone clock tower overlooking terraces and gardens. It will offer . . . an indoor pistol range, a fitness center and subsidized dining. The Fed's construction boom also includes the lavish new $168 million Dallas Fed and a planned $178 million Atlanta Fed" (Wilke 1996). Most of readers of the paper probably realized that a few hundred million dollars wasted on lavish office complexes was a small price to pay for the wealth that that the Fed helped to funnel from labor to capital.

This victory did not come without costs, and not just for labor. Presumably, the leadership of the Fed believed that a short recession would tame labor and then allow for a resumption of the healthy economic growth once enjoyed during the Golden Age.

Such was not the case. By that time, the economy had become more fragile. Decades had elapsed without the sort of competitive pressures that could have kept the economy strong. The inflation that Richard Nixon ignited was more virulent than the inflation that Herbert Stein had earlier dismissed as inconsequential. As a result, the downturn was far more ferocious than anybody had imagined. It was the most massive economic downturn since the Great Depression.

Even as the recession took on more terrifying proportions, Volcker still insisted on holding the course. In further congressional testimony in July 1981, he complained: "So far, only small and inconclusive signs of a moderation in wage pressures have appeared. Understandably, wages respond to higher prices. But in the economy as a whole, labor accounts for the bulk of all costs, and those rising costs in turn maintain the momentum of the inflationary process" [Volcker 1981, p. 614]. As late as January of the next year, Chairman Volcker was still unwilling to relent. He told another congressional committee:

> No successful program to restore price stability can rest on persistently high unemployment. . . . The obvious challenge is to shape our policies in a way that can permit and encourage recovery to proceed while maintaining the progress we are seeing toward greater price stability. . . . But in an economy like ours, with wages and salaries accounting for two-thirds of all costs, sustaining progress will need to be reflected in the moderation of growth of *nominal* wages. The general indexes of worker compensation still show relatively little improvement, and prices of many services with a high labor content continue to show high rates of increase. [Volcker 1982, p. 89]

Although the press saw Volcker as an almost saintly figure, untainted with the self-interest that contaminated most political figures, his recession was a disaster for the country in general, and for labor in particular. Rebecca Blank and Alan Blinder estimate that the substandard economic performance of the 1973–83 decade reduced the income share of the lowest fifth of the population by almost 1 percentage point and raised the poverty count by 4.5 percentage points (Blank and Blinder 1986, p. 207).

Of course, we cannot ascribe the recession to a single individual. Although Paul Volcker was cruelly insensitive to the hardship of unemployment, he was no more so than most business and political leaders. Certainly, business had been clamoring for the sort of policies Volcker carried out. Moreover, as I mentioned earlier, market economies require periodic corrections. Although this one was needlessly brutal, it was long overdue.

Recessions are an imperfect instrument for disciplining labor. Although business initially enjoys saving on wage costs as a result of mounting unemployment, recessionary conditions eventually prove counterproductive for business. Business generally remains insensitive to the hardships associated with recessions, at least until they reach such proportions that business also begins to feel pain. At that point, business demands that steps be taken to get the economy moving once again.

This recession was no exception. By 1982, the economy had reached the point where the recession had become painfully counterproductive in the eyes of many business leaders. The official civilian unemployment rate reached nearly 10 percent. The actual unemployment rate was considerably higher, probably about 15 percent. Still, the Federal Reserve refused to let up the pressure. Volcker saw the world from the perspective of the financial sector, which takes a more draconian view of inflation than the rest of the business community.

At this point, the recession threatened to turn into a full-scale financial panic. Only when the crisis threatened the values of the loans that the major banks had made to Mexico, did business demanded something be done to stimulate the economy. Paul Krugman put the situation in perspective, writing: "By late summer of 1982, the U.S. inflation was subsiding, but the recession seemed in danger of spiraling out of control. The sudden emergence of the Third World debt crisis raised fears of financial chaos" [Krugman 1990, p. 84]. Immediately thereafter, in order to finally bring the economy out of the tailspin of which Volcker was so proud, the Federal Reserve Board began to loosen the monetary reins and the Reagan administration resorted to deficit spending of unparalleled proportions.

A Catastrophe for Labor

Once the offensive against labor had accomplished its goal, the lack of good jobs appeared to be the major source of labor's difficulty (Harrison and Bluestone 1990). The dramatic collapse of blue-collar manufacturing industries was a major cause of this shortage of good-paying jobs.

Private service-producing industries accounted for nearly 90 percent of the job growth in the 1990s and increased their share of total nonfarm employment by more than 4 percentage points. For example, employment in home health care services rose faster than any industry during the 1990s. Childcare services, residential care, individual and family services, sanitary services, and miscellaneous, amusement, and recreation services—all typically low-paying jobs—were also among the top 20 industries in terms of employment growth during the 1990s (Hatch and Clinton 2000).

Writing toward the end of the 1980s, Bennett Harrison and Barry Bluestone found that of all new year-round jobs created since 1979, 36 percent have provided workers with less than half the real income that the average worker earned in 1973 (Harrison and Bluestone 1988, Figure 5.4). In fact, since 1986, the ranks of full-time workers earning less than a poverty wage has increased by 40 percent, to nearly 3 million workers—even as the economy has expanded by more than 30 percent (Barrington 2000).

Traditionally, relatively well-paying, blue-collar manufacturing jobs represented an important bridge that allowed families to progress from poverty to the middle class. The momentous process of deindustrialization was a major cause of the growing gulf between rich and poor in the United States.

Deindustrialization was particularly violent in specific locales. For example, manufacturing employment in the New York-New Jersey area fell by 51 percent between 1969 and 1999 (Bram and Anderson 2001). Barry Bluestone's analysis gives an even more devastating account of the human costs of deindustrialization. He used the Social Security Administration's Longitudinal Employer-Employee Data file, which contains information on 1 percent of all workers covered by Social Security, to track the fate of the workers who once ran the factories in New England. He found that in

1957, the old mill-based industries in New England employed about 833,000 workers. By 1975, 674,000 of these workers had lost their jobs (Bluestone 1988).

Bluestone's study is particularly illuminating because during this period, the New England region experienced a boom in high-tech industries, but this boom did not provide many opportunities for the displaced workers. Only 3 percent of them found their way into the new high-tech industries in the region. About 16 percent went into retail or low-wage service jobs (Bluestone 1988, p. 33).

On an even more dramatic scale, since the early 1970s, the number of people who earned their income from steel in the area around Youngstown, Ohio fell from 35,000 to 4,000 at the end of the 1980s (Lynd 1989). Since no new industry rose to take the place of the steel mills in that region, many of these unemployed workers fared badly.

The United States Bureau of Labor Statistics studied the fate of workers who had three or more years of tenure with their employers before losing their jobs between January 1983 and January 1988, due to either plant or business closing or moving, slack work, or the elimination of a position or shift, excluding those who were only seasonally unemployed. Even though the economy as a whole was expanding at the time, this survey found 4.6 million workers, who were at least 20 years old and who were displaced during this period (Herz 1990).

The Department of Labor survey found that 14 percent of these workers remained unemployed in January 1988. Another 15 percent had dropped out of the labor force altogether. The survey also reported that 30 percent of those who held full-time wage and salary jobs before and after their displacement experienced pay cuts of 20 percent or more (Herz 1990).

Many displaced workers also suffered losses of benefits. The survey found that 74 percent of the displaced workers had been previously covered by some form of health insurance at work before their termination. About one in four of these workers no longer had coverage by January 1990 (Herz 1991, p. 8). Manufacturing workers seemed to fare especially badly when management eliminates their jobs. Between 1981 and 1985, 10.8 million manufacturing workers lost their jobs. Forty percent of these workers lost their health insurance in the process (Craypo 1990, p. 9; citing Government Accounting Office 1987).

If displaced workers were to search for jobs elsewhere, they would suffer a double loss. Their new wages would be lower. They would also have to absorb the cost of moving, including the complications associated with selling homes in towns and cities where the population was leaving because of unemployment.

The desirability of the remaining blue-collar jobs also deteriorated. The quality of the opportunities for blue-collar employment depended upon an expanding manufacturing sector. For example, during the 1980s, production and nonsupervisory workers earned one-third less in industries that were growing relative to those that were shrinking. Between 1979 and 1985, expanding industries paid an average of $7.70 per hour and $257.73 per week; contracting industries, $9.93 and $402.30 (Waldstein 1989, p. 24).

Unfortunately, employment in the manufacturing sector continued to shrink during the 1990s, losing almost one million jobs, even though a massive wave of deindustrialization had already eliminated the least competitive industries during the previous decades (United States Department of Commerce, Bureau of the Census 2000a, p. 734,

Table 1230). Even within manufacturing, a growing number of administrative and supervisory personnel have been replacing blue-collar workers. By 1996, the latest date available, nonproduction workers made up about one-third of all workers in manufacturing. The average wage of this growing minority of workers was far larger than the typical blue-collar wage, so much so that the total payroll was just about equally split between the production workers and the rest of the workforce. This average is misleading however, because it includes the enormous salaries of a small number of administrators, together with the growing ranks of low-paid clerical workers.

To make matters worse, an increasing number of jobs, even in manufacturing, are staffed by temporary help agencies. These workers now account for about 5 percent of total manufacturing employment (Estevao and Lach 1999). Not infrequently, the workers who hold these temporary positions are doing the same work that they had done previously when they worked for the manufacturer directly. The company benefits from this new arrangement by saving on both wages and benefits, even though the temporary help agency takes a healthy cut from what the manufacturer pays.

Let me return to the example of Youngstown. As the collapse accumulated more momentum, arson became commonplace, since the insured value on buildings exceeded their market value. Desperate, the town turned its hopes on a minimum prison run by the Corrections Corporation of America that promised 450 jobs—not enough to make up for the losses, but still a start. The prison soon turned to housing high-risk inmates, who escaped with a frightening regularity, making the region even less desirable.

Adding Insult to Injury

During the 1980s, business in the United States tended to pay far more attention to quick financial profits rather than the long-term rewards for improving production. Given this mind-set, you should not be surprised that business generally regarded labor as a commodity to be purchased as cheaply as possible. Throughout the decade, employers seemed to be in mortal terror of making the mistake of "coddling" their workers. In reality, they had little to fear. The recession largely achieved its major goal.

Large pools of unemployed workers made business's warnings to potentially rebellious employees thoroughly credible. In the shadow of the threat of unemployment, labor's powers drastically weakened. The recession, together with the long-term process of deindustrialization, hit unions especially hard. The organized labor movement lost 2.7 million wage and salary workers between 1980 and 1984 (Adams 1985, p. 25).

Fearing unemployment, many union workers acquiesced in lower wages. A study by the Federal Reserve Board reported that, in 1981, a total of 365,000 union workers, or about 15 percent of those reaching new settlements in the private sector, accepted either first-year wage cuts or freezes. In 1982, this number rose to about 2.3 million (Gau 1984, p. 284). Wage settlements in steel, airline, and meatpacking called for initial wage reductions ranging from 10 to 20 percent (Gau 1984, p. 285). When the economy eventually recovered from the recession, labor enjoyed few of the benefits. In fact, the 1980s marked the first economic expansion in fifty years in which wages, corrected for inflation, did not increase. In addition, many workers agreed to changes in working conditions that they had previously resisted.

Real hourly take-home pay dropped by 12.5 percent between its peak in 1977 and 1995. The growth in benefits fell even faster, leaving real hourly compensation for production workers almost 14 percent lower (Nilsson 1999, p. 134). The late David Gordon of the New School aptly described this trend as a "wage collapse" (Gordon 1996, p. 20).

The difficulty of earning a living has become so extreme that the poorest fifth of the population had to rely on transfer payments from the government for over half of their income. The bulk of these people were not welfare chiselers. In fact, over 40 percent of these people worked, but their wages did not suffice to avoid falling back on welfare (Henwood 1990). The response to this situation was to blame the workers. In 1996, Congress rose up and gutted welfare entitlements, under the misleadingly titled Personal Responsibility and Work Opportunity Act, which President Clinton duly signed.

Other workers could only avoid welfare by holding multiple jobs. In 1979, 4.95 percent of all workers held multiple jobs; by 1999, 5.9 percent (Mishel, Bernstein, and Schmitt 2001, p. 255). In 1977, when the conditions for labor were considerably better, more than 33 percent of multiple job-holders said that they did so out of necessity (United States Department of Labor 1977). No doubt a higher percentage would answer similarly today.

Juliet Schor estimated that in 1987 that the average person in the United States worked 163 hours more than in 1969 (Schor 1991, p. 29). She largely attributed this trend to the need to work longer hours to compensate for falling wages (Schor 1991, pp. 79–81). She observed that production and nonsupervisory workers, who make up 80 percent of the labor force, would have to work 245 hours more each year just to maintain their 1973 standard of living (Schor 1991, p. 81).

The data on falling real wages also do not reflect the decline in the level of benefits that workers enjoy. If the wage data took account of the declining frequency of benefits such as health insurance and paid vacations, the fall in real wages would be even more dramatic.

Even with workers' benefits declining, many employers chose to do away with benefits altogether by staffing their businesses with part-time workers. For example, a trade publication, *Progressive Grocer,* reported about the industry, where part-time labor as a share of total employment has soared from 35 percent in 1962 to 60 percent in 1985: "To cut labor costs by switching to lower-paid part-timers with fewer benefits, the industry's percentage of part-timers had continually grown" (Sansolo 1987, p. 75; cited in Tilly 1991, p. 16). Because firms can hire and fire part-time workers relatively costlessly, these temporary workers shield business from the shock of market fluctuations.

The General Accounting Office estimates that contingent workers accounted for about 30 percent of the workforce in the United States in 1999, down from about 32.2 percent in 1995 (General Accounting Office 2000, p. 16). The strengthening of the economy accounted for this decline. These workers are more likely to be impoverished. For example, about 30 percent of the workers employed by temporary agencies have family incomes below $15,000 (General Accounting Office 2000, p. 20).

Although some temporary workers hope eventually to win permanent employment in their jobs, the vast majoirty do not. Most, in fact, work for very short periods of time. A senior executive of one of the largest temporary employment agencies reported that 30 percent of the agency's employees work for the agency 1 week or less,

50 percent work 1 month or less, and 70 percent work less than 2 months (United States General Accounting Office 2000, p. 24).

Even when working for the same employer for years, contingent employees often have trouble winning permanent positions. For example, in 1996 thousands of individuals whom Microsoft had classified as independent contractors even though many had worked for the company for years, finally won a court case that forced Microsoft to acknowledge their status. Microsoft had been able to deny these workers benefits by claiming that they were not actually employees of the company, but merely independent contractors.

You would not expect that contingent workers would have much reason to feel a strong commitment to their work, especially when they realize that permanent work is improbable at best. Of course, part-time jobs are not necessarily bad. Some of the part-time workers cannot accept full-time work. For example, Victor Fuchs stressed that many women, especially women with children, prefer part-time work—especially in the absence of adequate child care (Fuchs 1989). Students taking a full or nearly full load of classes also sometimes prefer part-time employment. In addition, many relatively affluent women actually prefer part-time employment, which represents the possibility of a fulfilling activity rather than economic necessity. Indeed, wives from better-off families tend to work more than those from families that earn less. Not surprisingly, these relatively affluent women tend to contribute relatively less to the family income than wives from poorer families, who typically work out of necessity (Wion 1990).

Despite the case of students or the affluent women who prefer part-time work, or even the young mothers who do not have access to adequate child-care facilities, you should be clear that workers' needs do not generally determine the growth of part-time employment. Many, if not most part-time workers would prefer full-time employment, especially because, for the most part, part-time employment pays badly. In addition, dissatisfaction among temporary employees with their work arrangements increased substantially between 1995 and 1999 (Mishel, Bernstein, and Schmitt 2001, p. 249).

In part, because of the heavy use of part-time work, many people were unable to find full-time employment. The share of the total labor force reporting involuntary part-time work increased by almost 40 percent between 1973 and 1989. What happened later is difficult to fathom because the Department of Labor changed the way it collected its data (Mishel, Bernstein, and Schmitt 2001, p. 251).

Workers who have to depend on part-time employment lead precarious lives. When hard times come, they have fewer and fewer resources on which to fall back.

Even full-time workers are reluctant to make demands on their employers because of an upsurge in job insecurity. Just think back to the earlier descriptions of the rebellious workers of the 1960s and 1970s, when labor markets were tight. When unemployment receded to comparable levels in the late 1990s, workers did not raise many demands, not even for higher wages.

The long-time chairman of the Federal Reserve Board, Alan Greenspan, famous for the obscurity of his language, was quite clear in pinpointing job insecurity as the cause of the changed relationship between workers and their employers:

> [T]he rate of pay increase still was markedly less than historical relationships with labor market conditions would have predicted. Atypical restraint on compensation increases

> has been evident for a few years now and appears to be mainly the consequence of greater worker insecurity. . . . In 1991, at the bottom of the recession, a survey of workers at large firms by the International Survey Research Corporation indicated that 25 percent feared being laid off. In 1996, despite the sharply lower unemployment rate and the tighter labor market, the same survey organization found that 46 percent were fearful of job layoff. [Greenspan 1999, p. 254]

The Disastrous Expansion of low-wage Service Employment

The low wages that predominate in the service sector are not preordained. In fact, management created many of these new service jobs in an effort to undermine the wage structure. For example, consider the growth in producer services—services that one firm sells to another. Frequently, these producer service jobs replace positions that were previously performed by workers employed by the firm itself rather than by an outside contractor.

Producer service jobs accounted for 45 percent of the total increase in service employment between 1979 and 1986. Of the 25.7 million full-time equivalent jobs created between 1967 and 1985, 26.3 percent were in producer services, compared to 22.9 percent in retail trade, 14.6 percent in health care; 11 percent in government, and 8.8 percent in consumer services (Waldstein 1989, p. 20). In the 1990s, growth in these jobs constituted only a slightly smaller proportion of the total (Hatch and Clinton 2000).

Even though workers in the producer service industry often perform the same tasks as workers who had been directly employed in the industry that now contracts out the services, their productivity often differs because of the changing work relations. For example, imagine that a factory that has just installed a sophisticated computer-aided manufacturing system. The firm could let its engineering staff set up the equipment or it could agree to let its engineering staff form a separate company, which it would hire as a consultant. In either case, all the employees would do the same work, but in one case, the engineers would be manufacturing workers; in the other, service workers. This sort of change is becoming quite common in the U.S. economy.

In the case of these engineers, they were once salaried employees. Now they have become entrepreneurs seeking maximum profits. In theory, they might work harder than ever because of the possibility of greater rewards.

For the economy as a whole, such gains from producer services do not seem to have been the rule. In fact, the soaring employment of low-wage service workers is a testimony to the low productivity of that part of the economy. If productivity had increased faster, fewer people could have performed the same work. For example, Lester Thurow, dean of the School of Management at the Massachusetts Institute of Technology, estimates that, if service productivity had grown at the same rate in the United States as it did in West Germany, service employment in the United States between 1972 and 1983 would have only increased by 3.6 million instead of the 18.7 million service jobs that the U.S. economy created during that period (Thurow 1989, p. 6).

Indeed, as Lester Thurow has pointed out, in the 1970s and 1980s, productivity in producer services had actually fallen by an astounding 1 percent per year (Thurow 1989, p. 4). The reasons for this decline in productivity are not entirely clear.

Beginning in the middle of the 1990s, productivity in general began to soar. Robert J. Gordon, an economist from Northwestern University, is very skeptical about how widespread these productivity gains actually were:

> While the aggregate numbers are impressive, the productivity revival appears to have occurred primarily within the production of computer hardware, peripherals, and telecommunications equipment, with substantial spillover to the 12 percent of the economy involved in manufacturing durable goods. However, in the remaining 88 percent of the economy, the New Economy's effects on productivity growth are surprisingly absent, and capital deepening has been remarkably unproductive. [Gordon 2000, p. 49]

Moreover, almost one-quarter of the increase in productivity reflects the unusually rapid rate of economic growth for those years (Gordon 2000, p. 54). The changing technique of measuring price indices, justified in large part by a commission on which Gordon served, created another large source of measured productivity increase (see Baker 1997). With the subsequent implosion of the dot.com sector, this rate of productivity growth may well prove to be unsustainable or even illusory.

Low-Wage Service Employment as a Drag on Productivity

One third of the growth in producer service employment came in the field of building services, reflecting, in part, a boom in the construction in office space between 1979 and 1985 (Waldstein 1989). A more important reason for hiring building service workers in recent years is the reduction of labor costs.

Imagine that you run a well-respected computer business. You would prefer to pay your janitors a low salary and avoid the responsibility of paying for the benefits that unions usually obtain. If you contract with a building maintenance firm, you avoid any responsibility for the wage rates paid by that firm. Your hands are clean. The contractor can hire undocumented workers and pay them less than the minimum wage. After all, nobody can blame you if your workers are underpaid and lack the protection of a union.

For example, according to an earlier study, service employees in France, Germany, and Japan earn wages comparable, or even superior to those of manufacturing workers. For example, U.S. workers in wholesale and retail trade earned 57 percent that of manufacturing workers; in the case of producer services, 84 percent; for consumers services, 57 percent. Only in the transport and communication sector did U.S. service workers earn more than in the manufacturing sector. Here the figure was 114 percent of manufacturing wages. For Japan, the respective figures for the four different sectors (Trade, Producer Services, Consumer Services, and Transport/Communication) were 81 percent, 133 percent, and 78 percent, and 127 percent. For Germany, the respective figures were 75 percent; 120 percent; 71 percent; 100 percent (Waldstein 1989, p. 36).

Because European service workers earn more than their counterparts in the United States, their employers take care to make them as productive as possible. In the United States, employers have relatively little reason to devise ways to increase poorly paid workers' productivity. John Legge, an Australian economist, has told me that the productivity of workers in McDonald's outlets in his country is the highest in the world because of the high wages that these workers earn.

More important, low-wage service workers get little respect for their work. Naturally, they would be less likely to put their hearts into their jobs than many other workers. Not surprisingly, the rate of growth in the productivity of service workers in the United States lags significantly behind the rates found in most advanced European countries.

The penny-wise, pound-foolish approach of hiring more and more low-wage service workers in the United States diminishes the productive potential of the U.S. economy. Individual employers are oblivious to the damage that they are inflicting on the economy. Instead, they revel in the savings that sub-minimum wage workers offer. Within this vicious cycle, those in power do not want to change and those who want to change have little or no power.

How Businesses' Defeat of Labor Impairs the Labor Force

Given the pervasive process of deindustrialization, service workers—even low-paid services workers—may be deemed fortunate compared to the long-term unemployed. Economists often refer to such periodic bouts of widespread unemployment, such as occurred in the early 1980s, as "corrections." These "corrections" impose enormous costs on the human beings who must bear the brunt of economic inactivity. Eventually, management's efforts to take command of the workplace by using unemployment to gain the upper hand lead to a series of additional costs, which are impossible to measure. To begin with, unemployment is detrimental to the future capacity of the labor force for a number of reasons. Many laid-off workers never fully recover from the shock of unemployment.

When unemployment becomes extensive, many people will just give up on the job market. Even more tragic, the job market often gives up on displaced workers. They cease being merely unemployed and become unemployable.

Given the enormous emotional impact of unemployment—especially long-term unemployment of workers lacking generalized skills—it should not be surprising that unemployed workers' earnings typically never recover after they return to the job market. For example, between 1981 and 1985, 10.8 million manufacturing workers lost their jobs. Of these 10.8 million displaced manufacturing workers, 5.1 million experienced above average durations of unemployment and eventually had to accept lower pay (Craypo 1990, p. 9; citing Government Accounting Office 1987).

The U.S. Department of Labor study of displaced workers found that 30 percent of the people suffered pay cuts of 20 percent or more (Hertz 1990, p. 31). Another study, using different data, found that the average worker who experiences involuntary terminations of any kind—not just from the elimination of a job—continues to earn 10 to 13 percent less than other workers four years after the termination occurs (Ruhm 1991). Later studies confirmed the severity of involuntary job displacement, especially when displacement hits a large number of workers simultaneously (Kletzer 1998, pp. 124–26).

Many of these displaced workers had a stable work record, which should have made them desirable employees. For example, about one-third of the displaced workers in the Department of Labor study had been employed by the same employer for 10 years or more. Of those workers, aged 55 to 64, one-third lost jobs that they held for 20 years or more (Bluestone 1988, p. 24). Unfortunately, the experience of these workers counted for little after their jobs disappeared.

As we have seen, the losses from unemployment continue even after workers return to the labor force. Many unemployed workers accept inferior jobs that do not take full advantage of their skills.

This effect of unemployment is crucial for less educated workers. In the United States, general education only provides certain basic skills. Most important job skills come with work experience. When workers fall into unemployment, they lose the opportunity to gain this experience (Hargraves-Heap 1980, p. 613). Both unemployment and downgrading interfere with the acquisition of job skills.

Economists do not understand the costs of this disruption of the acquisition of job skills very well. Economists' training teaches them to see market arrangements as conducive to an efficient allocation of resources. They interpret the switch to a less desirable job as a rational response to an economic downturn. This theory makes economists insensitive to the harsh economic costs of unemployment because it assumes that people move easily from one job to another with no difficulty whatsoever. In reality, the cost of these adjustments can be significant.

Imagine an expert machinist. The day after this worker ceases to work in her trade, she accepts employment flipping burgers without any intervening unemployment. If, after a short recession, the worker successfully returns to her original job, the traditional economic theory will not be far off the mark. The economic damage from the recession would be limited to the difference between what the worker could produce as a machinist and what the worker could produce flipping burgers during the duration of the recession, plus the difference in the acquisition of job skills during that brief period.

Now suppose that a strong upturn in the economy creates a shortage of skilled machinists, but the new machinist jobs are in a different region of the country or the new employer does not want to hire this worker only a few years before she is eligible for a pension. Consequently, the ex-machinist's job mismatch might remain permanent, creating an economic loss that far exceeds what the economists' overly optimistic vision might suggest.

The economic costs will be even higher for an extended recession, because prolonged unemployment can permanently scar its victims. In particular, when a high level of persistent unemployment causes workers to remain inactive or to take jobs for which they are overqualified, their skills will degrade (Cross 1987).

Extended unemployment often results in self-doubts, bitterness, and demoralization. Not infrequently, many workers who have remained unemployed for a long period of time will take on attitudes that make them relatively unsuitable in the eyes of their employers. Because employers are unable to identify which of the long-term unemployed have an impaired work ethic, they are understandably hesitant to hire any workers that bear the stigma of long-term unemployment (see Layard 1988; Hargraves-Heap 1980; Jackman and Layard 1991).

In part, such declines in wages represent a downgrading of workers' skills. To the extent that this downgrading occurs, the economy will never adequately utilize the abilities of these workers.

This degradation of workers' skills does not just affect the workers themselves. Alfred Marshall, author of the most influential economics text of the early twentieth century, shrewdly observed that high wages make workers' children and grandchildren more productive (Marshall 1920, pp. 2, 510, and 562). By the same token, prolonged unemployment scars entire families, not just the worker who is out of work and the spouse, but the children as well. Obviously, deaths or divorces resulting from unemployment cause children great harm. Even, when the family remains intact, the experience of watching parents suffer the indignities of joblessness damages children. Even if this harm is limited to distracting children from their schoolwork, their future productivity will likely be impaired.

Some of these unemployed workers and their children turn to crime. As a result, security costs balloon and prisons drain off needed government spending. For each one percent increase in unemployment, we can expect to see 3,300 admissions to state prisons within six years (Bluestone 1988, p. 34; and Bluestone and Harrison 1982, pp. 63–66).

Other unemployed workers internalize their predicaments, jeopardizing their health. For each one percent increase in unemployment, you can expect to see 37,000 deaths, 920 suicides, 650 homicides, 500 from cirrhosis of the liver, and 4,000 admissions to state mental hospitals (Bluestone 1988, p. 34; and Bluestone and Harrison 1982, pp. 63–66).

In conclusion, the short-term benefits to business from higher unemployment in the form of a more tractable labor force create serious negative effects that can take generations to reverse. Eventually, business itself will be harmed, in part because sales decline with consumer income; in part because business loses the stimulus to invest that a high wage rate provides—a subject that I will address in detail later. Sooner or later, profits will suffer and business will curtail investment, creating downward economic momentum.

This downward spiral leads to still more sickness and crime. The workers that business rehires when the economy turns up once again will be less productive than they otherwise would have been. Unfortunately, neither government nor business takes this long-term momentum into account when it determines its policies.

Unplanned Fiscal Costs of Labor's Defeat

Only 8.5 percent of all temporary help agency workers have employer-provided health insurance, compared to almost 60 percent of workers with standard job arrangements (Mishel, Bernstein, and Schmitt 2001, p. 249). Today, almost 45 million people lack health insurance. Moreover, workers with coverage are experiencing a significant deterioration in their benefits while generally paying more for what they do receive.

The present conditions of workers' pension plans are a scandal (Bloom and Freeman 1992). The number of firms covered by company-financed pension plans fell from 50 percent of all full-time employees in 1979 to 46 percent in 1988. For all workers, including part-time workers, the decline was more dramatic. In 1979, 43 percent enjoyed coverage. By 1988, 63 percent had no pension coverage (Bernstein 1990).

In all likelihood, an even smaller portion of workers will have pensions in the future because the continuing decline in the power of unions is a major cause of the narrowing of pension coverage (Bloom and Freeman 1992). Today, 89 percent of all unionized workers are covered, compared with 52 percent of nonunionized workers.

As unions become weaker, we can expect pension protection to deteriorate even more (Bloom and Freeman 1992).

In the 1990s, the aggregate numbers of workers covered by pensions recovered somewhat, but never recovered to the 1979 level (Mishel, Bernstein, and Schmitt 2001, p. 141).

Many of those workers who do have a pension are finding that their benefits are declining or that the plans have become considerably more risky, because firms have used pension money to finance takeovers and other speculative ventures during the past couple of decades. From 1984 to 1980, 2,000 large employers milked workers' pension plans of $22 billion (Metzenbaum 1991). Although the theft of pension-plan money is more difficult because of changes in the law, employers continue to find means to make the cost of providing pensions less expensive.

The most common change in the kind of pension coverage offered to workers is the shift from defined benefit to defined contribution plans. Under defined benefit plan, the employer accepts a commitment to provide the employee with specified benefits. With a defined contribution, the employer accepts the obligation to put aside a specified amount of money into investments every year, without any guarantee that these investments will earn enough to permit a specified pension benefit. In 1975, only 13 percent of pension plans were defined contributions; by 1997, 42 percent of all pension plans were (Mishel, Bernstein, and Schmitt 2001, p. 143).

During the 1980s, some companies declared bankruptcy as a way of avoiding their pension obligations (Orr 1998). After the government made this tactic illegal, companies still found creative ways to milk their pension funds. A *Wall Street Journal* exposé described how companies such as General Electric, Monsanto, Merck, SmithKline Beecham PLC, and Chiquita Brands transferred ownership of units in order to shed their pension obligation.

The article described how "under the tutelage of outside lawyers and consultants, companies have come to view pension surpluses as assets that, in effect, can be bought and sold at the time of a merger, sale or acquisition. Companies' ability to cash in their surpluses—a maneuver that Congress sought to deter in the past—provides a powerful incentive to pump up surplus levels by slashing benefits" (Schultz 2000).

In a promotional letter, Financial Frontiers Corp., a merchant bank in Los Angeles, exhorted potential corporate clients to "turn pension surplus into cash." The firm said in the letter that it can structure transactions enabling clients to capture as much as 70 percent of the value of their surplus (Schultz 2000).

> Companies use a range of methods for shrinking benefits. Some try to make units more attractive for sale by cutting employee medical-coverage liability. Others convert a pension plan to one that's less generous. Yet other corporations retain the pension plan for a unit being sold—which allows them to continue to invest the pension assets—but at the same time freeze the pension rights of the transferred employees. Some corporate deals include the transfer of a sizable pension-plan surplus, an amount over and above what is needed to fulfill obligations to retirees. [Schultz 2000]

General Electric was particularly successful in milking its pension plan in shedding one of its units:

> Thanks in part to its nimble shedding of employee-benefit liabilities and retention of pension-surplus assets, GE, based in Fairfield, Conn., last year reported no net expenses for pension, medical and life insurance for its 193,000 retirees and beneficiaries. Even before its recently announced plan to acquire Honeywell International Inc., which had its own overfunded pension plan, GE had a $25 billion surplus in its plan in 1999. That surplus helped the pension plan contribute $1.3 billion to operating income, which accounted for 9% of that income. [Schultz 2000]

Companies also benefit from altering their pension plans. For example, at IBM, a pension plan surplus boosted profits by less than $250 million in 2000. About a third of that amount resulted from changing the pension to what is called a cash-balance system. Profits in 1999 included $200 million from pension surpluses, with about half generated by the conversion during that year. IBM workers continue to protest the changes in their pension system (Day 2001).

Corporate pension plans are not without generosity, but the generosity is selective. The *Wall Street Journal* compared the fates of two people who both joined Florida Progress Corp. in 1989. Carolina Power & Light Co. has since acquired the company and both men have lost their jobs. One, Sonny Arnold, a 62-year-old welder-mechanic, cannot begin to draw his monthly pension of $681 for three years because he has not yet worked the requisite 15 years. Finding work to tide him over is difficult because he has asbestosis and lost much of the use of his left hand in an accident on the job.

The other, Richard Korpan, the former chief executive of the St. Petersburg company, enjoys a lavish monthly pension of $69,070, in addition to a $15.8 million severance. His pension credits him with 35 years of service, far more than his actual length of employment.

Such disparity is not at all unusual. For example, at May Department Stores Co., the liability for pensions covering 82,000 employees and retirees stood at $592 million at the end of 2000. The company also had a $147 million liability for special plans that cover fewer than 1,000 executives. In other words, almost 20 percent of the company's pension liability was for a select group of relatively few executives (Schultz 2001).

By cutting back on health insurance and pensions for workers, the corporations throw more responsibility back on the public. For example, when corporations siphon off "excess" money from their pension funds during the stock market booms, they leave these funds vulnerable once the stock market recedes.

The government is obligated to offer some protection to those workers whose pension plans are in trouble. In 1974, the U.S. Congress created the Pension Benefits Guaranty Corporation to insure defined benefit pensions, when companies go bust or close down their pension plans.

Unfortunately, like so many other parts of the government financial structure, this system stands in need of a major government bailout. Its loss in 1990 was $900 million, taking its cumulative deficit to nearly $2 billion. Among the biggest underfunded pension plans were LTV, Uniroyal, Pan Am, Continental Airlines, Bethlehem Steel, Chrysler, and General Motors. In 1990, some $8 billion worth of pensions were in serious financial trouble (Anon 1991c).

Thereafter, the pension crisis escalated rapidly. By 1991, the level of unfunded liabilities in the defined benefit pension system stood at $40 billion, $10 billion over the level of the previous year (Abken 1992, p. 1). The stock market boom of the 1990s increased the value of pension investments, substantially reducing the amount of unfunded liabilities. The Pension Benefit Guaranty Corporation reported in 1999, that its unfunded liabilities had fallen to a mere $17 billion (United States Pension Benefit Guaranty Corporation 1999, p. 37).

How much will the government do for these pension plans? How much will the declining state of medical care for the poor evolve into more general public-health emergencies that will require increased government spending?

The Haitian Road to Economic Development

Rather than face up to its own failings, business habitually attributes its woes to some external force. Business leaders continually wail about government interference (but not government subsidies), unfair foreign competition, taxes, and the like. Perhaps the most popular lament of all is the perennial complaint over excessive labor costs. This destructive state of denial reinforces the prevailing corporate preference for a policy based on the objective of a low-wage structure, which I refer to as the Haitian road to economic development.

We are told that wages must go even lower to make the economy competitive. Even though U.S. wages are now below those of the prosperous West European economies, business still chooses to relocate to the *maquilidoras* of Mexico or the sweatshops of Asia or Central America.

What level of wages would make labor competitive? Should the United States then depress wages still further—below those of Mexico? Even if wages were to continue to decline, you should be prepared to hear business leaders complain that wages are still too high for American business to compete with the Haitians. Certainly, if low wages were the key to economic success, Haiti would stand out as a role model for economic development.

But, alas, Haiti has no more succeeded than Voodoo Economics in the United States. Haiti remains the poorest nation in the Western hemisphere.

The Haitian road is most dangerous. *High* wages should be part of the solution rather than part of the problem. The provision of high wages and good working conditions are a logical part of a competitive strategy for harnessing workers' creativity to fuel high productivity. I will explore the benefits of high wages later in chapter 8.

You need only a modicum of common-sense to realize the fallacy of attempting to build an economy on the foundation of a low-wage structure. Indeed, recent history suggests the folly of this strategy. The U.S. economy grew handsomely during the early postwar period, even though wages rose continually.

In contrast, the recent erosion of real wages has certainly failed to reinvigorate the economy. After all, business has enjoyed enormous savings in wages and benefits in the past two decades. Table 2.1 demonstrates that wages have consistently lagged behind productivity in the United States since 1960. We would expect U.S. manufacturing to become more competitive if low wages were the key to development.

Instead, manufacturing has withered, especially during the past two decades, while the United States was driving wages down, supposedly to make the economy competitive. This situation explains why table 2.1 shows a pattern of increasing productivity together with a decline in wages. The elimination of unproductive capacity rather than the addition of new and more efficient plant and equipment caused the improvement in the statistical measure of productivity. A continued reliance on this source of productivity increase cannot lead to a stronger economy.

In short, low wages will not save the U.S. economy any more than they have saved Haiti. Low wages have never promoted economic development and they never will. Indeed, the experiment in emulating the Haitian road to economic development has been a dismal failure even though the leaders of this country have shown no visible interest in veering from their destructive course.

Table 2.1

Period	*Wages*	*Productivity*
All industries		
1960–9	1.5	2.3
1970–3	1.5	3.8
1974–9	0.0	1.6
1980–9	–0.9	4.0
Durable goods		
1960–9	1.3	2.7
1970–3	1.6	3.2
1974–9	0.0	1.2
1980–9	–1.0	4.7
Nondurable goods		
1960–9	1.5	3.0
1970–3	1.2	4.9
1974–9	–0.0	2.1
1980–9	–0.5	3.0

Source: Brauer 1991; citing United States Department of Commerce, Bureau of Labor Statistics, Employment and Earnings Handbook of Labor Statistics; BLS, Productivity and Costs, release March 6, 1991.

CHAPTER 3

Government and the Decline

Keynes and the Credibility of Government

During the Golden Age, the government seemed to merit the people's trust. The United States had beaten the Depression. It had just won a popular world war. Government policies seemed to be responsible for a good deal of the prosperity at the time.

Economists seemed to have discovered in their Keynesian theory the magic potion that would enable governments to deliver perpetual prosperity. To be sure, John Maynard Keynes was absolutely correct in the context of the Great Depression that massive government spending could pull the economy out of the Depression. Indeed, the war proved him to be correct.

Under the spell of this crude Keynesianism, economic euphoria became commonplace. Politicians echoed the economists' excessive claims about their ability to guide the economy to prosperity. Candidates routinely won elections by promising to end poverty and unemployment.

With the intense antipathy toward the government that prevails today, imagining a time when the government stood in a favorable light may be difficult. However, this present hostility toward the government is part of a larger cycle that has marked the attitude of the people of the United States throughout our history (Schlesinger 1986, pp. 31–43). This sequence of overly optimistic expectations and dashed hopes has repeated itself many times.

Certainly, government planning seemed capable of working wonders during World War I. By the time of the Coolidge administration, laissez-faire was in the saddle again. Once the Depression hit, many people in the United States suddenly abandoned their trust in the market, placing their hopes in the government again.

Unfortunately, although the government gave lip service to its obligation to maintain high levels of employment, its failure to take the importance of competitive forces into account contributed to the eventual process of deindustrialization.

The Dark Side of Keynesian Theory: Military Keynesianism

To many business interests in the United States, increased government spending and therefore Keynesianism itself smacked of socialism. True, Keynes himself was far from being a socialist. In fact, he saw himself as devising a strategy to save capitalism both from the ravages of the Depression and the threat of socialism, but this defense of his work could not satisfy many business interests. Once the Depression had passed, they ceased to worry about saving capitalism and turned their attention to protecting their own opportunities to make a profit.

The increasing antagonism to government involvement in the economy took the form of a virulent anticommunism, popularly associated with Senator McCarthy. Given the pervasive McCarthyism of the early postwar period, calls for increased government activity presented serious political risks at the time. Many of the leading Keynesian economists in the United States soon learned to shield themselves from the charge of socialism by restricting their calls for increased spending to military programs to assist in the fight against communism.

Unfortunately, Keynes's followers willingly distorted his theory, stripping it of all subtlety. They advocated a superficial version that proposed that all that is required to keep a sagging economy afloat is more spending, no matter what the source. Either because they succumbed to the anticommunist climate of the day or because they feared that they had no chance of stimulating through productive government spending, most of the avowed followers of Keynesian theory adopted a stunted version of their master's approach. They settled for increasing employment through military spending—an approach that became known as military Keynesianism.

In effect, then, the leading Keynesians in the United States proceeded as if they could ignore the relative merits of different kinds of spending. According to this line of thinking, spending of any kind—even wasteful military spending—stimulates the economy.

This military Keynesianism seemed to satisfy people of all stripes. Liberals could satisfy themselves that the government was acting to maintain full employment. Business relished the military contracts, without the prospect of government doing anything to reduce their business opportunities. Ultrapatriots could revel in the military superiority of the United States. And the economists would be free of any taint of socialism. The losers—those who could have benefited if the government had invested in the health, education, and welfare of the people—were largely silent.

I have difficulty believing that Keynes himself would have sanctioned military Keynesianism (Perelman 1989). Unfortunately, his theory offered few specifics to dissuade the cold warriors that acted in his name. Certainly, he failed to alert economists to the difference between military and civilian spending. Instead, his *General Theory* blandly looked at the economy as a whole.

Although Keynes preferred that the government spend its funds on productive activities (Perelman 1989), his followers took heart from his humorous aside about burying bottles, suggesting that we can disregard the question of who benefits from a particular program. What is good for one person is good for another because a rising tide supposedly lifts all ships.

Within this context, Keynes's theory evolved into a strategy to float our ships on a rising tide of military spending in the name of the sacred creed of anticommunism. Unfortunately, military Keynesianism was never a good idea for a number of reasons, which I will put off until the next chapter.

I can state here that a rising tide does not lift all ships, as the economy of the 1990s clearly proved. An economy develops unevenly. Any policy will hurt some groups and help others. Military spending is no exception in this regard. Keynesian theory turned economists' attention from the specific impact of military spending to the beneficial impacts of an increase in government spending as a whole, regardless of its intended purpose.

However, the weaknesses of military Keynesianism made it all the more attractive in some circles. Let us see why this should be so.

The Advantage of Waste

Although military Keynesianism might seem wasteful and even stupid today, during the early postwar period, military spending seemed to serve a legitimate public purpose since few people raised any doubts about its efficacy or its necessity. Indeed, military spending seemed to be one of the keys to the economic success of the early postwar period. Several decades had to pass to dispel this illusion. Later, I will show that military Keynesianism ultimately became an important contributor to the economic decline, although the nature of the impact of military spending is both complicated and controversial.

Powerful business interests were especially appreciative of military Keynesianism. Despite its calls for greater government efficiency, business generally favors something akin to Keynes's bottle-burying program over productive investment.

More productive government spending threatens business far more than truly wasteful government spending. Suppose that the government spent money on public mass transportation. The corps of companies that provide private transportation, including the automobile producers and their suppliers, as well as the petroleum companies, would let out a howl of protest because mass transportation would deprive them of profitable business. Even if they could win the bids to supply the government, changing over to a new line of business would be costly. In addition, private automobiles provide more spending year after year than mass transportation would because of the relative inefficiencies of private transportation. Business interests understandably denounce mass transportation as socialistic and even un-American.

The military does not displace existing markets. The production of a fighter-bomber or an aircraft carrier does not threaten any private seller in the same way as mass transportation might. Instead, it offers an additional market for private business. As a result, we do not hear the private sector shrieking about taxes being wasted on socialistic projects during the debates over military spending, even though the U.S. Department of Defense is undoubtedly the largest planned economy in the world.

Even as the United States inched toward World War II, business fought vigorously to prevent the government from expanding industrial capacity in strategic industries (Hooks 1991, pp. 98–110). This struggle was especially intense in the steel industry (Vatter 1985, pp. 24–27).

Once the war began, business did an about-face, calling for a rapid buildup in economic capacity. What accounts for this change? Once the war began, greater capacity was no longer a threat to its sales, because business knew that it had a guaranteed market for its output for the duration of the conflict.

During the war, the federal government invested $17.2 billion in capital goods (Hooks 1991, p. 132). Once the war ended, the government tried to transfer military plant and equipment into the private sector. Some observers have claimed that many of these military goods were of little use to the private sector. For example, a significant quantity of the machine tools used to produce military aircraft was sold for scrap (Kapstein 1990, p. 15).

Certainly somebody could have found a productive use for much of the surplus plant and equipment, but the government did nothing to promote a search for the best use. Instead, it developed procedures that impeded small business from purchasing surplus stock, lest they use this surplus capital to compete effectively with existing capital. As a result, a small group of 87 large firms accounted for two-thirds of the $17 billion worth of government plant and equipment that the government dumped (Vatter 1985, p. 65; see also Hooks 1991, p. 158).

Within this context, it appears that business purchased government surplus capital goods where it expected an expansion of capacity. It managed to get government to scrap those goods where it feared that enough capacity would come on-line to create strong competition.

As a result, much of the wartime investment was never put to good use. Hooks cites a U.S. Senate study, which reported, "Real property with a net acquisition cost of $9,277,000,000 has been declared surplus. The greater amount of this property was in the form of industrial plants. Approximately $5,479,000 worth of surplus real property has been disposed of and $1,175,000 has been realized from these sales" (Hooks 1991, p. 156).

Allowing surplus goods to be sold to smaller businesses could have made the economy stronger, although it might have inconvenienced some big businesses. Instead, big business emerged from the war with its relative position stronger than ever before while the economic potential of "surplus" military goods was squandered.

In conclusion, military Keynesianism was attractive since both politicians and economists could advocate it without risking the stigma associated with ideas that were identified as socialistic. Business profited, while the public was enjoying a higher standard of living, which did nothing to encourage it to question whether these massive expenditures could be put to better use. All seemed well as long as the Golden Age lasted.

The Political Economy of Military Keynesianism

Although military spending had brought the U.S. economy out of the depths of the Depression, many business and political leaders still accepted the pre-Keynesian notion that high government spending of any kind might unleash an unacceptable level of inflation (Etzold and Gaddis 1978, p. 384). This resistance to Keynesian thinking largely evaporated by early 1950, when high-level policy makers expected an imminent recession or even worse. They cast aside their anxiety about inflation in favor of a program of increased military spending. At the time, Paul Nitze was heading a joint State Department and Defense Department task force.

This group drafted an influential document, known as NSC 68, which became the clarion call for military Keynesianism. It proposed an escalation of the Cold War, in part, to stimulate the U.S. economy. According to this document:

> . . . there are grounds for predicting that the United States and other free nations will within a period of a few years at most experience a decline in economic activity unless more positive governmental programs are developed than are now available. [United States National Security Council 1950, p. 410]

Given the risks of a renewed depression, NSC 68 called for a massive military buildup, which could simultaneously fight recession and communism. The authors explained:

> From the point of view of the economy as a whole, the program might not result in a real decrease in the standard of living, for the economic effects of the program might be to increase the gross national product by more than the amount being absorbed for additional military and foreign assistance. One of the most significant lessons of our World War II experience was that the American economy, when it operates at a level approaching full efficiency, can provide enormous resources for purposes other than civilian consumption while providing for a high standard of living. [United States National Security Council 1950, pp. 436–7]

According to the novelist, Gore Vidal, Secretary of State John Foster Dulles was more explicit about the purpose of NSC 68. He heard Mr. Dulles predict that this policy would lead to an arms race that the Soviets were certain to lose because they were so much poorer. As a result, the Soviet economy would suffer irreparable harm (Vidal 1992, p. 88).

With the acceptance of NSC 68, military Keynesianism had won an official recognition that remained more or less unchallenged within the circles of power, except for Eisenhower's brief warning about the dangers of the military-industrial complex.

Military Keynesianism was never intended just to increase the overall economic or political power of the United States. It was expected to change the distribution of power within this society.

Military spending was attractive because it did not threaten existing markets. Increased military spending has had a more direct impact on the working people in the United States. Pumping up military spending does not simply mean an expansion of overall government spending, as crude Keynesian theory suggests. Some of the expansion of military spending comes at the expense of civilian programs.

Business obviously appreciated that military spending competed for funds with social programs. Its leaders feared that many, if not most, popular social programs undermine the work ethic.

Military Spending as Class Warfare

Because working-class people are often patriotic, military spending remains relatively popular with them. Knowing this, business interests welcome expansion of military spending, trusting that it will siphon off funds from these other programs that it opposes. In this way, business delights in inducing labor to join in an effort to undermine labor's own interests.

For example, already, back in 1949 while the country was still debating about the peace dividend of the day, *Business Week* explained to its readers why it found military spending to be preferable to social programs:

> But there's a tremendous difference between welfare pump-priming and military pump-priming. It makes the government's role in the economy—its importance to business—greater than ever.
>
> There's a tremendous social and economic difference between welfare pump priming and military pump priming. . . . Military spending doesn't really alter the structure of the economy. It goes through regular channels. As far as a businessman is concerned, a munitions order from the government is much like an order from a private customer.
>
> But the kind of welfare and public works spending that [President] Truman plans does alter the economy. It makes new channels of its own. It creates new institutions. *It redistributes income.* It shifts demand from one industry to another. It changes the whole economic pattern. That's the object. [Anon. 1949, p. 20; emphasis added]

President Truman's successors also used military spending to affect the balance of power between labor and capital every bit as much as they intended it to influence the balance of power among nations. For example, Max Frankel, Washington bureau chief of the *New York Times,* clearly expressed the strategy of using military spending to restrict social spending after the Nixon administration proposed a massive defense buildup. In discussing the trade-off between defense and social aims, Frankel observed:

> . . . the conservative dream of depriving Washington of the funds for vast new social programs is close to realization. [Increased defense commitments] for reasons that are vigorously asserted but in no sense explained or measured against the risks of frugality in other parts of the budget . . . and the two big rounds of tax cutting since 1969, in which liberal Democrats joined enthusiastically, have now left the budget $20 billion short of money that might have been invested in health or education or the cities or transportation.
>
> The President welcomes this fact and notes approvingly that current programs and current tax rates will leave only $5 billion in loose change for the budget writers of 1976—a margin that, experience suggests, will almost certainly disappear altogether. . . . For the next President, this means that there will be no special dividend for a great new initiative for either peace or prosperity. [Frankel 1972; cited in DuBoff 1989, p. 10]

The Rise of a Garrison State

The election of John F. Kennedy perhaps marked the high-water point in the general confidence in the ability of the federal government to maintain prosperity. The experience of the Kennedy administration symbolized the dominance of military Keynesianism. Kennedy was the first president to be schooled in Keynesian economic theory. According to Seymour Harris, Kennedy's economics instructor at Harvard, despite Kennedy's ambitious plans for social programs, 75 percent of the increase in government spending during the Kennedy years came from an expansion of military spending (Harris 1964, p. 197).

The Kennedy administration was infatuated with the prospects for new methods of unconventional warfare. The notion of counterinsurgency also became popular in military circles. As the military constructed new theories about fighting communism in the third world, it accumulated new weapons to carry out this mission. As a result, some parts of the military welcomed the Vietnam excursion as an opportunity to try out these weapons and these ideas. This enthusiasm for experimentation helped to ensnare us in the Vietnam quagmire.

Successive administrations in Washington convinced themselves that the United States could not afford to lose face in Vietnam. As the government got more deeply enmeshed in the insane logic of the conflict, more and more military spending became imperative. This ballooning military spending put an enormous strain on the economy.

This unquenchable thirst for military spending clashed with the economic needs of the country since the economy was already dangerously overheated. In the process, the government had to give up all hope of using the military spending as a flexible policy instrument that could be easily adjusted in light of current economic conditions.

Sometimes it seemed that no program could win support in the Congress without first demonstrating that it was essential to the national defense. The interstate highway system was, probably with good reason, seen as part of the national defense. With modern highways, the military would be able to move troops and matériel from one end of the country to the other with ease.

The School Lunch Program, established in 1946, years before NSC-68, was the classic case of the need for a military rationale to win support for a government initiative to help the civilian population. Much of the initial support for the program was due to the persuasive testimony of Major General Lewis Hershey, director of the Selective Service Commission. The general told congressional committees that, during World War II, poor nutrition accounted for an excessive number of rejections of young men by local draft boards (United States House of Representatives 1989, p. 53).

Although the military rationale occasionally does help to pass beneficial social programs, such as the School Lunch Program, the high priority given to the military has typically worked to the detriment of social programs. When military spending competes with social programs, the military usually proves victorious in the halls of Congress.

Symbolic of this state of affairs, in 1987 the Reagan administration budgeted $154 million for military bands compared to $145 million for the National Endowment for the Arts—well before that agency became controversial (Anon. 1986b). Since then the arts budget contracted to below $100 million in 1999, while the money for military bands rose. How did our priorities become so skewed?

Workers' patriotic support of military spending continues to harm their own economic interests. A number of studies have concluded that military spending creates fewer jobs than other forms of spending, although this assertion is difficult to prove conclusively (see Adams and Gold 1987; Gold 1990). The reason for the lower employment effects of military spending is due to the type of labor that defense industries hire. In part, military spending creates less employment because of the peculiar wage structure in defense industries.

For example, hourly wages in defense-intensive manufacturing industries in 1983 ran $2.80 higher then the average for all manufacturing industries (Adams and Gold 1987, p. 35). Military spending typically leads to a demand for a combination of highly paid workers (such as the scientists and engineers as well as highly paid executives and lobbyists) in private employment and low-paid government workers in the public sector (Blank and Rothschild 1985, p. 694). But the number of workers hired is small compared to other types of outlays. So, in addition to the obvious problems associated with military Keynesianism, it is an inferior form of Keynesianism in terms of its effectiveness in creating jobs.

The End of the Excessive Faith in Government Economic Management

Once the decline set in, the economy no longer seemed so manageable. Unrealistic promises of perpetual prosperity came back to haunt once overly optimistic politicians and to discredit their policies.

Now, the outrageous overconfidence of both economists and politicians might seem to be a source of amusement. By the early 1960s, they convinced themselves that they had mastered the art of steering the economy at will. Their naiveté has still not totally evaporated, although its form has changed. Conventional economists still refuse to accept that substantial declines are a normal part of the economic process. Instead, most economists continue to regard the serious recessions as unnatural. As a result, when booms turn to bust, economic and political leaders put considerable energy into assigning blame to others for any economic ills. Honest analysis has no place in such an exercise.

The decline of the late 1960s and throughout the 1970s was no exception in this respect. Pundits of all stripes bandied about innumerable simple-minded panaceas. The most favored solution was the snake oil of a market-based solution for virtually everything. Private business could do better at educating children, delivering garbage, managing the welfare system. . . . Unfortunately, as I have been arguing, no simple answers are capable of addressing the complex challenges that a modern market-based economy faces.

Moreover, the conventional wisdom frantically looked outside of the normal sphere of business for the roots of the sorry circumstances of the time, except for an occasional tirade against greedy speculators or financial interests.

Foreign powers, especially Japan, were the most convenient targets for those who wanted to assign blame. These nations supposedly competed unfairly, giving them undue advantages in competing with U.S. business. Unions were an even more popular target. The outrage against unions paled in comparison to the widespread hostility toward government—a dramatic turn-about from a couple of decades before, when the government appeared to be the economic savior.

Judging by the intensity of the antigovernment record, a casual observer could have easily imagined that the government was a determined enemy of business. In truth, for every minor inconvenience associated with government regulation, there were a host of subsidies, tax breaks, and protections that were far more valuable to business. The problem was, and still is, that the costs and benefits of government programs are not evenly distributed. The benefits, although not widely known, fall mainly into the hands of the largest and most powerful corporations, while smaller businesses tend to bear a disproportionate share of the costs. So even while the Congresses of the 1990s were so demonstrative of their zeal to cut back the role of government, they redoubled their efforts to actively support big business.

The economic decline alone might not have been enough to undermine popular confidence in the ability of the government to manage the economy. The government's actions brought some of this anger on itself. While the government kept up the pretense of an obligation to minimize unemployment and to promote social welfare, it dissipated much of its spending on military expenditures. Certainly, the conduct of the Vietnam War also did its part to cast the government in an unpleasant light.

Perhaps the straw that broke the proverbial camel's back was President Carter's famous Cardigan Sweater Speech of 18 April 1977, delivered in the midst of the energy crisis. As a candidate, the low-keyed Georgian conveyed an image of managerial competency. If anyone could manage the economy, surely he could. Yet here was the former candidate, now the president, confessing that matters were well beyond the control of government.

According to the *New York Times*'s coverage of the address, "Mr. Carter was deliberately confronting the American people with the harsh news that even in peacetime they must draw limits on their easy-going life-style if they are going to avoid 'a national catastrophe' in the long run" (Smith 1977). The next day the *Times* editorialized, " . . . the President is right, as well as brave, to press this test of Americans' willingness to behave in their long-term best interests."

Certainly, President Carter was correct in warning the people about the seriousness of the situation. Without a doubt, President Carter was courageous in calling for changes, but he was sadly mistaken if he thought that the people would appreciate his address as much as the editorial writers of the *Times* did. His popularity dramatically plummeted soon thereafter. I do not know if the American public became irritated with him because he was the bearer of bad tidings or people became indignant because he laid the blame at the doorstep of the individual citizen rather than institutions.

In any case, the public did not relish the president's challenge to confront the economic problems facing them as the "moral equivalent of war." How could politicians who had taken credit for the Golden Age now blame the public for the decline?

In one sense, the public was united with President Carter. Although they differed about whether individuals were to blame, both resisted the realization that economic contractions are endemic to a market economy.

The public went much further than the president. Repelled by President Carter's vision of the future and lured by an intensive media campaign, the popular mood laid much of the responsibility for the economic decline on the government's shoulders. Of course, this mood swing had begun earlier. President Carter himself had campaigned as an outsider who was above the standards that existed in Washington.

Swept up with this antagonism toward the government, a majority of the voting public in the United States enthusiastically embraced a new promise of eternal prosperity under a regime of laissez-faire. The seemingly preordained election of Ronald Reagan symbolized this change in the popular mood.

This reaction was not entirely irrational. As economic conditions deteriorated, people who felt the pinch looked for ways to protect themselves. Business is beyond the reach of ordinary people. After all, you cannot force your grocer to sell you food any cheaper. You cannot demand that public utilities lower their rates. Almost everything seems beyond the control of the individual, with one partial exception: the government.

Theoretically, the government is answerable to the people, who can vote public officials out of office. Indeed, President Carter met this very fate. At this point, the promise of lower taxes sounded very attractive.

The Abdication of Government from Economic Responsibility

In short, the government, in the popular mind, bore a great deal of responsibility for the economic decline. Accordingly, instead of plans for active government policies to manage the economy during difficult times, shrill calls for government policies that would improve the economy by reducing the scope of government became commonplace.

Given the growing animosity toward government, soon after the beginning of the economic decline, the tax revolt gathered momentum. The scaling back of active government policies had an undeniable appeal. By 1978, the dramatic passage of California's Proposition 13 showed how strongly people felt about cutting taxes.

The arithmetic of the tax revolt can be summed up in two obvious facts. First, the rich usually paid more taxes than the very poor. Second, when governments attempted to balance their budgets by cutting their spending, the poor were unable to protect the modest programs that improved their lives. As a result, the decline in taxes eventually translated to a transfer of income from the most needy to the most affluent. An astounding 74 percent of all the growth in income during the 1980s went to the richest 1 percent of the population. The poorest 40 percent experienced either stagnant or reduced incomes (Mishel and Frankel 1991, p. 5).

This mix of lower taxes for the rich and fewer government services for the poor was an important component of the economic decline. One measure of the impact of this transfer of income is a concept known as the net social wage, which is the difference between the benefits, which the government provides to working-class families (such as Medicaid or Social Security), and the taxes that these families paid. According to three different calculations of the net social wage, between 1980 and 1985 working-class families lost between $100 and $250 billion (Miller 1989; see also Shaikh and Tonak 1987; and Tonak 1987).

Initially, government agencies chose cutbacks for the poor as well as wage reductions and higher workloads for its employees as the first means of economizing. The typical affluent taxpayer felt little inconvenience from the initial contraction of government programs because government employees bore much of the burden of cuts.

For example, in 1970, the average municipal worker earned 2.06 times as much as the average per capita personal income in the United States. Since the average income is total income divided by the total population, including those who do not work, the average worker will earn much more than the average income. As a result, a municipal worker with a child and a spouse who was outside of the labor force enjoyed much less than the average per capita income (Henwood 1991).

Over time, municipal workers fared considerably worse. By 1980, the average municipal worker earned 1.62 times the average personal income; by 1989, 1.60. In New York City, with its expensive cost of living, the ratio declined from 1.95 in 1970 to 1.72 in 1980 to 1.57 in 1989 (Henwood 1991).

Lower wages hampered government's abilities to recruit and keep good employees. Given a staff of overworked and underpaid employees, government services became less and less satisfactory. Predictably, the regard for government services deteriorated quickly, giving rise to further resentment against the government.

Given this popular antagonism toward taxes, government agencies shifted their burdens to others whenever possible. The federal government mandated that state governments take on responsibility for a multitude of programs. State governments, in turn, legislated that local governments take on duties that had previously been the job of the states. The government typically offers a sum of money, which would have been forthcoming anyway, with the proviso that the recipient must adopt a particular set of policies, which may soak up a significant share of the initial grant.

More recently, governments at all levels have been attempting to pass their obligations on to private business. For example, rather than funding health insurance, government can pass laws requiring private employers to provide health care, or family leaves. This strategy only works when the particular benefit is so popular that public support will override the objections of business.

Perhaps the greatest abdication of responsibility occurs when the government creates a situation in which it either ignores or obscures future costs. For example, the government legislates tax cuts or the acquisition of a new weapons system. To make such policies more palatable, they phase in the program so that the bulk of the costs arise after a few years. In this way, future legislators will have to grapple with the consequences, while the current ones receive acclaim for their largesse.

For example, a Department of Energy audit in 1996 found that it faced $200 billion in unfunded expenditures for the clean up of facilities that it had polluted in the past (United States Department of Energy 1996). The Department of Defense also has littered a host of sites with expensive clean-up obligations.

The Nirvana of Deregulation

Of course, when the politicians promised tax cuts, they did not let on that they would also reduce services. Tax cuts were only supposed to eliminate the fat from government programs, especially what were supposed to be wasteful regulatory excesses. For example, Murray Weidenbaum estimated the annual cost of federal regulations to be $66 billion in 1976 (Weidenbaum and DiFina 1978; cited in Etzioni 1991, p. 387). To put this figure in perspective, keep in mind that the relaxation of regulation in the case of the savings and loans industry alone cost the taxpayers many times that amount.

Unaware of the magnitude of the decline's momentum, many economists and business leaders alike blithely promised at the time that tax cuts, together with deregulation, would effectively jump-start the stalled economy. Attractive as that strategy sounded in many quarters at the time, it actually intensified the severity of the economic decline.

Indeed, the new strategy of relying on market forces proved disastrous in almost every respect. Deregulation paved the way for the already-mentioned Savings and Loan crisis, as well as numerous environmental catastrophes and a general deterioration of the economy, not to mention the quality of life.

In addition, government service attracted fewer and fewer public-minded people. As might be expected in an age in which the distinction between rapacity and virtue disappeared, people who were intent on their own self-advancement seized upon government service as a means to promote their careers.

All to often, rather than carrying out their responsibilities, public officials used their government positions to ingratiate themselves with the very firms they were charged with regulating, in the hopes that these companies would hire them as soon as they left the government. In the process, violations of the letter as well as the spirit of the law became commonplace, further reinforcing the disrespect for the government.

Surprisingly, the more that laissez-faire undermined the economy, the more government fell into disrepute. I do not think that this unquestioning acceptance of laissez-faire will continue for long. I cannot say with certainty that people will jettison their faith in the market as suddenly as they abandoned their belief in economic management after the economic decline began, but a good number of people are now turning from the blind trust in market forces, typical of the 1980s, to a growing cynicism. The massive protests against globalization beginning in Seattle in late 1999 may signal that a more far-reaching change is already underway.

The Contraction of the Government and the Economic Decline

Conservative pundits greeted the tax cuts with delight for two reasons: First, and most obviously, the wealthy would be the main beneficiaries. Second, the sudden collapse in government revenues would create huge government deficits.

Of course, you are probably accustomed to hearing conservatives rail against huge deficits, but their real target never was the deficit, but the collection of government programs that aid the poor or rein in the harmful activities of business. You need only note how enthusiastically business embraced wasteful military spending in the early postwar period.

Milton Friedman, the godfather of conservative economics in the United States, illustrates this appreciative attitude toward the huge deficits quite well. He confessed to a gathering of so-called supply-side economists, hosted by the Federal Reserve Bank of Atlanta, "I would rather have a federal government expenditure of $400 billion with a $100 billion deficit than a federal government expenditure of $700 billion completely balanced" (Bedwell and Tapp 1982, p. 26). Later, Professor Friedman told the readers of the editorial page of the *Wall Street Journal,* whose editors have displayed a consistent antipathy toward government budget deficits, "We believe that the deficit has been the only effective restraint on congressional spending" (Friedman 1988). Recall Max Frankel's similar reasoning in welcoming the prospective increase in military spending.

Friedman was not alone in welcoming the deficit. Alan Meltzer, another noted conservative economist, commended the Reagan administration's attitude toward the deficit. He credited the Reagan administration with a policy of intentionally building up the deficit as a deliberate tactic to restrict future administrations from adopting spending programs (Meltzer 1988, p. 538; see also Alesina and Tabellini 1986). Friedrich von Hayek, Milton Friedman's only rival as an icon among conservative economists, concurred (McLemee 1995).

Ignore the moral and ethical dimensions of the enormous transfer of income and wealth from the poor to the rich that resulted from this policy. Instead, I want to draw your attention to the ways that curtailment of government activity worked to intensify the process of economic decline.

Some of the detrimental impact of these cutbacks on federal expenditures are obvious. For example, the federal government policy of curtailing public spending on nonmilitary research and development will certainly impede efforts to keep the U.S. economy competitive in later decades.

Other aspects of the restricted nonmilitary role for the government will have more subtle impacts. For instance, the combination of tax cuts for the rich together with slashing programs to help the less fortunate members of society has produced a level of inequality of income and wealth, evident to the most casual observer. The very poor are more and more coming to form a permanent underclass that is ill prepared to contribute to the economy as it now stands. As the underclass expands, it requires more government spending to build prisons and to protect the public health.

Other effects, such as the lost potential of people at the bottom of the social scale, are harder to recognize, but no less important. The corrosive effects of inequality also affect the other end of the spectrum. Certainly, the lifestyles of the very rich, surrounded by an orgy of excessive consumption, hardly offer the best preparation for a productive life. In fact, a growing collection of studies indicates that inequality is detrimental to economic growth (see Perelman 2000).

The contraction of government spending impacts on the economic decline in more direct ways. Let us now turn to the subject of public education, which offers a prime example of the dangers of cutting government spending willy-nilly.

Education, Human Capital, and the Economic Decline

Over and above their general faith in the market, economists agree on almost nothing at all. The importance of education is one of these exceptional areas of agreement. The crippling of the educational system has been an important contributor to the economic decline, which promises to create even more damage in the future.

Let me begin this discussion about public education with a brief observation about how economists approach the subject of education. Theodore Schultz earned a Nobel prize in economics, largely for his economic theory of education. According to Schultz, just as owners of machines earn profits from their equipment, a person's educational experience commands a profit when it is used productively. Schultz called this knowledge-based earning capacity, "human capital" (Schultz 1961).

The owners of this human capital are not the only ones to benefit from its existence. Society as a whole improves as a result of better education. Many economists are convinced that rising human capital is a major source of the increase in productive capacity in modern economies. For example, Edward Denison estimated that the direct effect of education on the quality of the workforce was responsible for about one-third in the total gain in productivity growth in the United States between 1948 and 1982. His estimate does not include the influence of education on improvements in technological progress, management practices, and the development of new products, all of which are important components of productivity growth according to Denison. In comparison, improved equipment accounted for only about 15 percent of the growth in productivity according to Denison's calculations (see Denison 1985).

Although economists agree that education is important, some economists contend that some of the claims made by the human capital school are overblown. Just because individual incomes tend to increase with the level of education does not prove that this income is a reward for education, which has made the person more productive.

After all, children from better off families, who will have easy access to high-salary jobs, will also be likely to get a good education. You can easily imagine a businessman who sends his son to college before taking him into his company. In this case, education has not caused the son to be affluent. Instead, this young man's social status explains both his education and his income.

In addition, many employers require college degrees, even when such training has little direct relevance to the job. Again, this practice creates a statistical illusion, making those workers with more education appear to be more productive, when, in reality, they are only better paid, but not necessarily more productive (Arrow 1973; Hungerford and Solon 1987).

Samuel Bowles and Herbert Gintis add that the educational system also devotes considerable energy to make children accept discipline that is unrelated to their ability to be productive (Gintis and Bowles 1976). Nonetheless, nobody can deny that education, training, and work experience can be a powerful force in making an economy more productive.

Despite these caveats, the performance of public education has been a serious cause for concern. For example, between 1969 and 1980, Standard Aptitude Test (SAT) scores for college-bound seniors fell on the verbal sections from 464 to 424. In mathematics, scores dropped from 493 to 476 (National Education Association 1991). Shortly thereafter, the U.S. economy entered into its long decline. Many people singled out public education as a major culprit.

The attack on public education brought together a number of disparate interests. Business saw education as a new profit-making opportunity. The financial community began to talk about educational maintenance organizations to suggest that profit-oriented schools would prosper in education much like the health maintenance organizations that took over much of the medical care in the United States. Religious conservatives saw an opportunity to indoctrinate students in what has traditionally been a more secular environment.

Finally, public education became a common scapegoat for the economic ills that captured the public interest during the economic slowdown. By 1983, the Reagan administration issued an alarmist report, entitled *A Nation at Risk.* In the best Cold War tradition, the report pronounced:

> If an unfriendly foreign power had attempted to impose on America the mediocre educational performance that exists today, we might well have viewed it as an act of war. As it stands, we have allowed this to happen to ourselves. We have even squandered the gains in student achievement made in the wake of the Sputnik challenge. Moreover, we have dismantled essential support systems, which helped make those gains possible. We have, in effect, been committing an act of unthinking, unilateral educational disarmament. [National Commission on Excellence in Education 1983]

By the 1990s, the Republican Party even campaigned on a promise to abolish the Department of Education. This stance was ironic, to say the least. If education were responsible for the decline, then certainly it deserved some of the credit for the boom of the 1990s.

As with much else in American society, racism played a role. Some attributed the lowered standards to the educational system accommodating groups of people that they deemed inferior. Blaming public education became a convenient explanation for the growing uncompetitiveness of business in the United States. And, of course, antitax groups saw an opportunity to reduce public expenditures, while antiunion forces saw an opportunity to defang a public union. While all these groups piled on, the public schools tried to cope with an increasingly difficult situation despite inadequate funding.

You might expect that teachers' salaries would have risen enormously. After all, economists mostly accept the importance of human capital. Teachers are the main bearers of human capital in the educational process. In addition, the political and economic leaders have convinced the public that high-quality education is essential for the economic health of the country.

In fact, public school teachers have long been the lowest paid professionals in the United States. According to data compiled by the American Federation of Teachers, by 1998–99, the average teacher salary had reached just over $40,000, despite the fact that the average teacher had an estimated 16.2 years of experience. In addition, already by 1990, more than 53 percent of teachers held a master's degree. An average beginning teacher made less than $27,000 in the school year 1998–9, far less than other professionals earn. For example, the average attorney made just under $70,000 in the same year (American Federation of Teachers 2000).

The Organization for Economic Cooperation and Development, an organization of the leading economic powers in the world, reported that teachers in the United States earn less relative to national income than their counterparts in many industrialized countries, yet they spend far more hours in front of the classroom. Total government spending on educational institutions in the United States slipped to 4.8 percent of Gross Domestic Product in 1998, falling under the international average—5 percent—for the first time (Wilgoren 2001).

For example, in Japan, teachers enjoy respect and high status, job security, and good pay. By law, they must be paid 10 percent more than top civil servants. They are in the top 10 percent of all wage earners (White 1991, p. 9).

Looking at the treatment of education toward the end of the 1980s, the best you could say would be that teachers fared better than the average worker (Hanushek 1986, pp. 1148–49). During the next decade, the relative position of teachers continued to erode. By 1998–99, teachers' salaries were only 12 percent higher than the annual earnings of the average full-time worker in the U.S. economy, compared to 21 percent in 1991 (American Federation of Teachers 2000). In addition, in many school districts teachers have to use their own money to supplement the meager allowance for classroom supplies.

Even though teachers' wages are embarrassingly low, society expects more and more from its school systems. Supposedly, the best method for making teachers work harder is more extensive assessment of their work by requiring their students to take innumerable multiple-choice tests.

Test Scores and the Economic Decline

The *Nation at Risk* report was not particularly unique. For a while, the fashion was to attribute the decline to a failure of the educational system. One of the major pieces of evidence that supposedly supported this theory was a fall in the scores that high-school students take to send to college admissions offices, the Standard Aptitude Test, known as the SAT.

Even if the fall in the SAT scores had preceded the economic decline by a decade, you would still have to be cautious about attributing the decline to the forces that caused the SAT scores to tumble. First, you would have to analyze what the SAT scores actually mean.

John Bishop has pointed out that college-bound students may work hard to get accepted into a good college, but business does not usually reward students for good grades. According to Bishop, young people earn the same wage with a high-school diploma regardless of their academic achievement (Bishop 1991b, p. 115). As a result, students who do not expect to advance beyond high-school have no incentive to work hard in school (Bishop 1991a, p. 237). For those students, on-the-job-training should be of greater concern.

Employers use filters other than education to screen out the workers that they want. For example, Bennett Harrison, writing in 1972, estimated that a high-school diploma increased the pay of an unskilled worker from the ghetto by about $150 per year (Harrison 1972). You may ascribe this behavior among employers either to racism or a presumption that much ghetto education is of little value. Certainly, the stressful conditions of an urban ghetto do make teaching children difficult.

In either case, this low return to education gives ghetto youth little reason to complete school, let alone succeed academically. You should not be surprised if SAT scores among disadvantaged youths should fall or even worse, that more and more of these young people simply fail to take the test at all, because they have abandoned all hope of pursuing a higher education.

In addition, some of the initial fall in the test scores actually reflected a success of sorts, rather than a failure. When a small proportion of students expected to get a college education, only a relatively elite group of high-school students took the test. As more and more students set their sights on a college education, some less prepared students began taking the test, dragging down the average score. This factor explained about one-half of the fall in the test scores (Baily 1981a).

By 1980, as a smaller proportion of students was taking the test, test scores began to improve once again, but they never reached the 1969 level. Even though the fall in SAT scores might seem to give cause for concern, you should realize that measuring educational achievement by SAT scores can be misleading. To begin with, the SAT scores may only be indicative of the educational experience of the minority of students who plan to attend college, but they are irrelevant to the majority that do not expect to pursue higher education.

More substantively, test scores are a poor indication of what students learn. By emphasizing tests, the educational system will shift attention from more important matters.

Poverty and Tests

Critics of the current educational system often make the claim that inadequate funding is not responsible for the poor performance of the educational system (Hanushek 1989). Richard Rothstein, writing in the *New York Times,* counters that while spending has increased, taking into account inflation in general, and especially inflation in textbooks and other inputs in the educational system, spending on education has not increased very much at all (Rothstein 2001a).

In addition, in more recent years, schools have had to spend enormous amounts of money on special education, while in earlier periods schools were not compelled to do so. In addition, bureaucratic requirements—often from government agencies that decry wastefulness in the educational system—have expanded enormously. As a result, the amount of buying power that goes directly into the classroom has not been increasing.

To make matters worse, the debates about the adequacy of school funding hide wildly different educational experiences. Poor children rarely got the same educational opportunities as children from more affluent families (Carnoy 1994, pp. 134–5). For example, in 1989, Chicago spent some $5,500 for each student in its secondary schools, compared to some $8,500 to $9,000 for each high-school student in the highest-spending suburbs to the north. In New York during 1986–1987, funding per student was $11,300 in the upper-middle-class Long Island suburbs of Manhasset, Jericho, and Great Neck; $6,400 in the largely working-class suburb of Mount Vernon; and $5,600 in the high-minority New York City public schools. Three years later, the figures were $15,000, $9,000, and $7,300 respectively. Although the proportionate change was equal, the absolute changes favored the already rich districts (Kozol 1991, pp. 54 and 237).

Even where poor, urban schools within a particular school district receive nearly equal funding, they must spend their resources differently. They have more need for special education, counseling, security, and so on. Teachers in those schools are generally less qualified than those in suburban schools. Teachers in schools with a large share of minority students are less likely to have a master's degree. Higher salaries would be required to attract more qualified teachers (Bracey 1998).

Suburban schools are generally newer, while inner city and, to a lesser extent, rural schools are often in a state of disrepair. As a result, the poorer school districts face higher costs of operating their physical plant than the more affluent suburban schools. For example, a General Accounting Office report to Congress noted that "one third of the nation's 80,000 public schools are in such poor repair that the fourteen million children who attend them are being housed in unsuitable or unsafe conditions" (United States General Accounting Office 1996a). Jonathan Kozol described a rather extreme instance: the Martin Luther King Junior High School in East St. Louis, Illinois, where sewage repeatedly backed up into the school, including the food preparation area (Kozol 1991, p. 21).

In California, a state often equated with perpetual prosperity, many students have appallingly limited educational opportunities. Recently, the American Civil Liberties Union filed a suit, which charged: "Many students lack textbooks of any kind. Other students must rely on illegible or incomplete photocopies provided by teachers when and if teachers have time and the individual resources to make the copies. . . . Sometimes three or four students to a book with no opportunity to take the book home and study for homework. . . . Sometimes as few as 13 percent of the teachers have full nonemergency teaching credentials. . . . Some California public schools . . . simply do not provide enough basic supplies, such as pencils, crayons, paper, and scissors" (Williams et al., v. State of California 1999).

A recent New York Supreme Court decision found "that the education provided New York City students is so deficient that it falls below the constitutional floor set by the education article of the New York State Constitution." In addition, the court also found "that State's actions are a substantial cause of this constitutional violation. . . . [T]he State school funding system has an adverse and disparate impact on minority public school children and that this impact is not adequately justified by any reason related to education" (Campaign for Fiscal Equity 2000).

Despite the extended period of growth during the 1990s, almost 20 percent of the children under 18 years old were still reported as living in families classified as poor, despite the systematic undercounting of the poor (United States Department of Commerce 2000b, Table 5; see also Murnane 1988). Rather than seeing the decline in test scores as a threat to national affluence, society would do better to interpret the low test scores as a symptom of widespread poverty.

The poor face unique educational problems. For example, the surgeon general, David Satcher, reported last May that more than a third of poor children have untreated dental cavities. Pupils taking tests with toothaches are unlikely to score as well as those undistracted by pain. "The General Accounting Office says about 10 percent of poor children have dangerous levels of lead in their blood, likely to 'cause reductions in I.Q. and attention span, reading and learning disabilities, hyperactivity and behavioral problems'" (Rothstein 2001b).

In the midst of grinding poverty, dropout rates are high. For example, about 12 percent of all poor students drop out of school (United States Department of Education 1999, Section V). Many students who do stay in school need to find employment, detracting from their education. A North Carolina study of high-school juniors found that half work, with two-thirds of those working holding jobs twenty hours or more a week. Scott D. Thomson, director of a national school principals' association, lamented that in "other nations school is considered too important for students to work" (Jacoby 1994, p. 19).

A new study by the International Labor Organization showed that American teenagers work far more than teenagers in most other countries. The study found that 53 percent of American teenagers, from the ages of 16 to 19, work in any given week. In Japan, 18 percent of teenagers aged 15 through 19 work, while in Germany, 30.8 percent of teenagers in that age bracket work. Two arms of the National Academy of Sciences—the National Research Council and the Institute of Medicine—found that when teenagers work more than 20 hours a week, the work often leads to lower grades, higher alcohol use, and too little time with their parents and families (Greenhouse 2001).

Not surprisingly, since 1988 the gap between white and black students in reading has widened somewhat at ages 13 and 17. Since 1990, the gap between white and black 17 year-old students has widened in mathematics, while the gap in science has not shrunk since 1973 (United States Department of Education 2000). In short, to the extent that test scores are a cause for concern, the blame lies less with the performance of the teachers than the resources at their disposal and the social conditions in which they work.

Political leaders have successfully convinced a good share of the U.S. public that schools should be expected to meet high standards, which means nothing more than that they be judged according to students' performance on test scores. In this environment, test scores, which are a poor indicator of learning in the first place, will be an even poorer measure, because teachers will merely concentrate on preparing students for tests rather than giving them the sort of skills that might equip them better for life.

Although I do not have any quantitative data to support my impressions, I am convinced that many of the students that I have encountered in recent decades are less prepared than the students from earlier cohorts were. I attribute this decline both to the deterioration of public education, together with the financial pressures that lead these students to work too many hours outside of school. Yes, some of the students are not working out of necessity, but rather to buy some of the accoutrements of middle-class life, but painfully large numbers of the students have no choice but to work if they are to be able to afford an education.

The Decline in Public Education as a Cumulative Process

While the decline in public education provides a cautionary lesson about undervaluing government services, you must read this lesson both carefully and critically. At the beginning of this book, I argued against the temptation to associate a single cause with a single effect. I also insisted on the importance of understanding the system as a whole. Education is also a prime example of the dangers associated with neglecting to disentangle the complex web made up of the various strands that combine to create the process of economic decline.

For example, in 1969, just as the first symptoms of the decline appeared, scores began to fall on the Scholastic Aptitude Test, which high-school students routinely take for admission to college (National Education Association 1991). Since the rate of growth in labor productivity was slowing down at the same time, some people were quick to blame the productivity slowdown on the educational system.

In fact, the cutbacks in education could not have had much immediate impact on education, just as the short run decline in educational performance (measured by the SAT tests) could not be responsible for much of a decline in productivity. Just consider the short run consequences for teachers of a cutback in spending on education. As teachers' salaries become less competitive, education will not suddenly collapse. Most teachers are dedicated to their profession. They will continue to teach and to teach well. Still, dedication has its limits. Some teachers will become demoralized enough over time that their work will suffer.

Other teachers may just quit. In fact, about 4 percent of the public sector and almost 9 percent of the private sector teaching corps leaves each year. Less than half of these departures are due to retirement, death, or some form of disability (United States Department of Education 1991b, p. 98).

Nobody should be surprised by the high attrition rates of teachers. After all, teachers typically have excellent skills that make them very employable in the private sector. Where teachers feel unappreciated or underpaid, they are more likely to move on to better-paying jobs. One study of North Carolina teachers found that, for every $1,000 increase in starting salary, a typical teacher would remain in teaching an extra 2 or 3 years (Murnane and Olsen 1990).

This turnover creates enormous costs for school districts. One study compared the estimated cost of a third-year teacher relative to their pathway to the job. A teacher with a four-year bachelor's degree in her or his subject field and master's degree in education costs about $36,500. A new teacher whose preparation was a short-term alternative certification program with some summer training was estimated to be $45,900. The difference is that 84 percent of the teachers with superior preparation remain on the job in the third year, while only 34 percent of the less qualified teachers continue with the third year (Darling-Hammond 2000, p. 18).

For a short time, this loss of good teachers can be partially buffered by college students who are already preparing for a career in teaching, although they will not have the experience of some of the departing teachers. Some of these graduates may accept jobs in the public school system, not realizing how grim their future prospects in education will be. One survey found that less than 40 percent of public school teachers were certain that they would make the same career choice if they had a chance to relive their lives (United States Department of Education 1996, p. 107). Some college students will even continue to work for teaching credentials, mistakenly assuming that the fiscal problems of the school system are temporary. So long as enough students do not recognize the threat to the teaching profession, schools will still be able to recruit some good teachers.

Over time, more and more college students will respond to the poor treatment of education by choosing other careers. For example, Scholastic Aptitude Test scores of college freshmen intending to teach was 49 points below the national average of 847 in 1991 (Putka 1991). The cumulative effect of the departure of some good teachers, the demoralization of others, along with the difficulty in recruiting good new ones will cause the quality of the teaching corps to deteriorate, but not immediately.

Just as the effects of a cutback in teachers' salaries will affect teaching over time, so too the consequences of the degradation of the teaching corps for the educational process will also be gradual. For seniors graduating from high school just after the initial cuts in educational spending, the impact should be minimal. Most of them have already formed their study habits before their senior year.

For students entering the first grade, their public school education will suffer for over 12 years before they graduate. These students will not escape the impact of a deteriorating education system. In short, you cannot blame the onset of the decline on the failure of education, measured by the pattern of SAT scores.

The Cost of Crippling Public Education

Although the erosion of the public school system was not the sole cause, it contributed to the economic decline. According to John Bishop, by the mid-1970s, the effects of the educational decline, reflected in the falling SAT scores, had time to work their way through the system. He estimated that by that time, the reduction in SAT scores reflected a setback in educational achievement equivalent to a drop of one and one-quarter grade levels per student (Bishop 1989, p. 179).

According to Bishop, if the rate of gain in the education of new high-school graduates that prevailed between 1948 and 1973 had continued, then by 1989 workers would be 2.9 percent more productive than they are today (Bishop 1989, p. 180). Consider the following example of the consequences of the crippling of public education:

> In New Jersey, all freshmen entering public colleges and universities are tested in basic skills. Of the approximately 30,000 students who took the tests in 1981, only 38 percent were fully proficient in computation at a sixth grade level, and [another] 35 percent failed to demonstrate a competence at this minimal level. Most discouraging of all, even the 7,000 students who had taken college preparatory courses in mathematics—algebra, geometry, and advanced algebra—did poorly. Only 4 percent of these were judged fully proficient in algebra and nearly two-thirds failed that portion of the test. Results for the test of verbal skills were hardly more encouraging. Of all the students who took the tests, 28 percent were rated as proficient, about 44 percent were lacking in one area (reading, vocabulary, grammar, writing) or another, and 28 percent failed in all areas. [Madison and Hart 1990, pp. 26–27]

Economists have a tendency to throw too much of the blame for economic problems on education, although poor education, together with limited possibilities for job experience, certainly can undermine productivity. Firms tell of their difficulty in finding workers with adequate skills, even during times of relatively high unemployment. The experience of Nynex, the New York telephone system, is suggestive of the sort of anecdotes about the problem. In 1987, the company had to test 60,000 applicants to hire just 3,000 employees. "There are lots of people who still want jobs, but they're dropouts who aren't qualified," said Howard Hartman, New York Telephone's director of employment (Bernstein 1988, p. 105).

The crippling of public education threatens society with a bitter irony. The initial impetus to cutting public education was the popular pressure to cut tax rates. However, money spent on public education may actually reduce tax rates in the long run. After all, more productive workers presumably produce more and thus earn more. Consequently, they will pay more taxes, lowering the tax burden for other ratepayers.

In addition, poorly educated citizens impose more costs on society. The growing number of children who fall through the cracks of the public education system are more likely to require public assistance of all sorts or to become ensnared in the criminal justice system. By 1997, the population of incarcerated people rose to an astounding two million people, the equivalent of a small nation (United States Department of Justice 2000, Table 6.1). Of course, the creation of draconian laws, especially for the mere possession of drugs, caused some of the explosion in the prison population. But then, nobody can disentangle the fear of crime and the allure of drugs from the more general breakdown in the social and economic structure.

This interplay between prisons and schools reinforces a central theme of this book. The desire to relieve the tax burden, coming at a time when the demands put on the school system were far heavier than ever, was a central cause of the deterioration of the public school system. The effort to fix one problem—the falling rate of profit—by reducing taxes, created a series of new problems that demanded even more public revenues. Everybody knows by now that prisons are far more expensive than schools. In short, the initial reduction in taxes may ultimately lead to a much higher tax rate. Such is the logic of the economic decline.

Even if society began to devote more public money to education, it would probably do so with the unreasonable expectation that the schools can improve in short order. Off-again-on-again spending policies are always inefficient. The net result might be that within a couple of years, forces advocating lower taxes will be calling for the elimination of pervasive waste.

California provided an example of the sort of unintended consequences that results from attempting a quick fix on a serious problem. Based on solid research that lower class size would benefit students, especially in the lower grades, California embarked on an ambitious initiative to decrease class size in elementary schools.

The massive and immediate way in which California undertook this reform had unintended, undesirable effects for urban school districts and their students: suburban school districts with higher pay and better working conditions were able to attract many urban teachers to fill their additional slots, leaving the urban schools with smaller numbers of experienced, licensed teachers teaching a greater number of classes and forcing them to take on large numbers of novice, inexperienced, and unlicensed teachers. To make matters worse, urban schools, already overcrowded, were much more likely to lack the space to set up additional classes. Many schools had to resort to using storage space for classrooms.

About 24 percent of California's schools have more than 20 percent of their teachers without qualifications. These schools predominantly serve the state's poorest students, those with the least academic preparation. As a result, the least prepared teachers are concentrated in the most challenging classrooms (Center for the Future of Teaching and Learning 2000).

What is needed is a more patient, long-term commitment, something entirely lacking in the current discussions about strategies for improving education. I might add that the decreasing numbers of people graduating with technical degrees seems to be another trouble spot. Mary L. Good, president of the American Association for the Advancement of Science, issued a dire warning:

> Since 1986, B.S. degrees in engineering have dropped by about 20 percent, as have mathematics and computer science. Ph.D. degrees in engineering peaked in 1996 at 6,305 and dropped 15 percent to 5,337 in 1999. Physical sciences saw similar patterns, peaking in 1994 at 3,977 and dropping to 3,582 in 1999. A large fraction of the drop was in physics, although chemical Ph.D.'s dropped as well. Mathematics and computer science also dropped, although by lesser percentages. . . . China produces over twice as many engineering graduates as we do, and Japan graduates 75% more than we do. [Good 2001]

The United States presently compensates for this deficiency by importing technically trained workers.

How the Economic Decline Reacted with the Education System

Of course, the economic decline also exacerbated the decline in education. Because of the problems associated with the decline, education was less effective than it would otherwise be.

In 1995, spending on primary and secondary students as a share of the gross domestic product was relatively low in the United States among advanced nations. Canada, Denmark, Finland, France, Netherlands, Portugal, Spain, and Sweden already ranked higher than the United States. Japan ranked quite a bit lower, both in terms of the absolute amount spent per student, and as a share of the gross domestic product (United States Department of Education 1999, Supplemental Table: Table 41–1).

International monetary comparisons are always tricky. Schools in the United States have to bear burdens that are not educational in nature because of inadequate social spending outside of education. Japan economizes in school expenses largely because of a higher student-teacher ratio, which a more cohesive society makes possible. German children have universal health insurance. French children benefit from high-quality day-care centers. Other Western nations have family leaves (Shrag 1981).

Good public transportation eliminates the need for school buses. Better health care, nutrition, children's services, and support for families could lift enormous burdens from the schools (Shrag 1981). As a result, the money spent in education in the United States is less effective in terms of delivering a purely educational function than it would otherwise be.

The rise in poverty is especially detrimental to education. Each year, the United States is becoming increasingly like a typical third-world economy. More and more children cross over the poverty line each year. Among children under 18 years of age, almost 17 percent come from families that are impoverished (United States Department of Commerce. Bureau of the Census 2000b, Table A, p. v).

Poverty creates problems and distractions that make children harder to teach. To make matters more challenging for the school system, more and more children in the school system come from non-English speaking families. In total, about one-third of all students in elementary public education in the United States are educationally disadvantaged (Levin 1989, p. 52).

These changes in the student population make the teachers' job more difficult, if not nearly impossible. Nonetheless, the public still expects more from teachers than ever before. Over and above educating students in mathematics and language skills, society calls upon schools to help in coping with drugs, teenage pregnancies, AIDS, and other social ills.

A widely circulated story reported on a 1940 survey of teachers, found that their most common problems with students were talking out of turn, chewing gum, making noise, running in halls, cutting in line, dress-code infractions, and littering. By 1980, teachers reported an entirely different set of problems. Their greatest concerns were drug abuse, alcohol abuse, pregnancy, suicide, rape, robbery, and assault (Anon. 1992a). While the actual survey seems to have been an urban legend, it rang true enough to popular perceptions to circulate widely in major publications, such as the

Wall Street Journal (26 November 1992, p. A8). No wonder our educational system does not seem to perform very well!

The complexity of the educational challenge in the midst of an economic decline made education expensive. During the long decline, the plight of education seemed understandable, but education did not seem to fare much better during the boom of the 1990s. Of course, the boom did little for the poorest members of society who are least served by the educational system. As a result, the social and economic problems that plagued the schools in the areas that the boom passed by continued to damage the educational system and the children that it was supposed to serve.

The call for privatizing the school system became stronger as the reputation of the public school system eroded. Of course, privatized schools could save a great deal of money by filtering out the more difficult children, saddling the public education system with an even greater problem.

The Deterioration of the Public Capital Stock

The deterioration of the nation's infrastructure—the name that economists give to the stock of bridges, highways, sewer systems, water systems, public transportation networks, and other publicly owned physical plant and equipment—is an important cause for concern. The passage of the famous property tax limitation Proposition 13 in California signaled the severe political difficulties that were to come. The public was convinced that, since the government wasted much of its money, curtailing taxes would eliminate waste, leaving vital expenditures intact.

George Peterson tracked the dramatic decline in public support for spending on infrastructure by following the record of state and local elections for approving bonds for infrastructural development. He found that the public only approved 30 percent of the value of all such bond issues during some years in the 1970s (Peterson 1990, p. 122).

As public resistance to taxes intensified, public officials sought to curtail spending in ways that would not create an immediate outcry. Public investment was a natural target. Although the infrastructure is of vital importance in making the economy work well, when spending on the infrastructure maintenance ceases, some time may pass before serious problems emerge. Who would notice if the maintenance on a sewer system were put off for a year or if nobody resurfaced a road?

Although the long-run consequences of deferred maintenance can be catastrophic, blame can probably be shifted to a future administration. According to one study of 42 city budgets for the period, 1978 to 1979, fiscally distressed cities routinely engaged in significantly lower capital and capital maintenance expenditures (Baumgarner, Martinez-Vazquez, and Sjoquist 1991).

Despite the growing burden put on the public infrastructure system, gross capital investment fell from 27 percent of total state and local spending in 1965 to 14 percent in 1977. In New York City, annual capital appropriations fell by nearly 70 percent between 1974 and 1978 (Bahl 1984, p. 78).

Total public net capital investment, which stood at $63 billion in 1964, fell to a mere $12 billion by 1982 (DuBoff 1989, p. 7). Since the late 1970s, public capital investment has continued to decline. Indeed, federal spending on public investment, measured as a share of total economic output, has fallen by more than a third since the late 1970s (Baker 1998).

In the mid-1960s, the ratio of nonmilitary government capital investment to gross national product peaked at 3.9 percent. By 1986, the ratio had collapsed to about 1 percent of gross national product (Aschauer 1990a, p. 9). No doubt, it is far less today, despite the capital-saving nature of modern information-processing technologies.

The divergent path of public and private capital per worker during the postwar period demonstrates the impact of this curtailment of spending on public capital. In 1950, the level of infrastructural capital per worker was around $8,500 in 1982 dollars. By the early 1970s, it had climbed to $15,000, only to fall back down to $13,000 by the end of 1987. At the same time, the dollar value of private plant and equipment per worker continued to expand from about $16,000 in 1960 to $34,000 at the end of 1987.

The Cost of Deteriorating Public Capital

As the tax revolt gained momentum, so too did the growing recognition in more enlightened circles that the condition of the national infrastructure was getting out of hand. While the public might not have noticed the immediate effects on the infrastructural system at first, years of skipping necessary expansion or maintenance eventually caused the system to fall apart, eroding the productive capacity of the economy.

Only three years after Proposition 13 passed, the Council of State Planning Agencies brought out a shocking study, entitled *America in Ruins,* which thrust the urgency of the deterioration of public works into the public eye (Choate and Walter 1981). Although this study received a flurry of attention in the press, it had little impact on public policy. Instead, the deterioration of the public works accelerated during the 1980s. Eventually, even the general public began to recognize the need for more infrastructural spending.

Despite the obvious importance of the infrastructure and the growing public support for alleviating the problem, politicians became convinced that their careers would suffer if they championed the development of improvement in the infrastructure. They only brought projects before the public that they thought would win overwhelming public support.

As a result, between 1984 and 1989, 80 percent of infrastructure bond proposals on a value basis were approved at public ballot, even though a number of states require more than a majority for approval. Since 1984, the average bond proposal commanded more than 66 percent voter approval, confirming that the politicians' excessive timidity has blinded them to a public awareness of the crisis in the nation's infrastructure (Peterson 1990, p. 122).

The longer we wait to confront the infrastructure problem, the more difficult and the more expensive our actions will be. According to the authors of *America in Ruins,* Pat Choate and Susan Walter, the 42,500 mile Interstate Highway System was deteriorating at a rate requiring reconstruction of 2,000 miles per year. They expected that the cost of maintaining the existing level of service on non-urban highways required more than $700 billion during the 1980s. One of every five bridges in the United States stood in need of rehabilitation or reconstruction. They predicted that 756 urban areas with populations exceeding 50,000 would require more than $75 billion to $110 billion over the next 20 years. According to their calculations, over $25 billion would be required to meet existing water pollution control standards. New York City alone needed more than $40 billion to repair its basic public works (Choate and Walter 1981).

After another decade of neglect, the situation had become far worse than when Choate and Walter first issued their warning. Almost a decade later, the Federal Highway Administration has estimated that 23 percent of the nation's 575,000 bridges are structurally deficient and more than 25 percent of the interstate highway has deteriorated (Malabre 1990a).

To make matters worse, the public capital stock was hit from both sides. While spending fell, the demands on the public capital stock grew dramatically, in part, because the economy expanded. For example, between 1960–5 and 1980–5, the economy grew by 80 percent although the public capital stock remained virtually unchanged (DuBoff 1989). For example, in California, capital investments declined as a percentage of the state's budget from more than 20 percent in the 1950s and 1960s to less than five percent in the 1980s. As a result, the state government of California needs to invest $82 billion to repair and maintain current structures and build new ones, over and above local government's responsibilities (Department of Finance, State of California 1998, p. 11).

Water treatment represents the sort of deficiencies associated with the decline in public capital. In the coming decades, the public will come to see that the quantity and quality of available water will be far more crucial than petroleum. Already, affluent people spend more per gallon of bottled water than gasoline.

The cost of building, operating, and maintaining drinking water and waste water facilities over the next two decades will run nearly $2 trillion, or about $95 billion a year, of which $50 billion is needed for drinking water and $45 billion for waste water. Between 1980 and 1994, federal spending on water facilities dropped 40 percent. If these projected needs are to be met, cities, states, and the federal government will have to increase the total spending by $34 billion (Water Infrastructure Network 2000). The American Society of Civil Engineers estimates that the overall cost of upgrading infrastructure over the next 5 years will be a staggering $1.3 trillion (American Society of Civil Engineers 2001).

As enormous as these costs are, they ignore other infrastructural expenses. For example, the $1.3 trillion estimate seems to ignore the cleanup costs from nuclear weapons production. As of 1996, the U.S. Department of Energy estimated that the nation would have to spend $227 billion in undiscounted 1996 dollars, which was probably an underestimate. Since then, the government has ceased keeping track of these potential costs, which could be $410 billion (Makhijani, Schwartz, and Weida 1998, p. 355).

Perhaps more ominously, the mission of the public stock has been expanding. For example, in 1964 the public gave little thought to the clean up of hazardous waste sites. Today, most people realize that even multibillion dollar budgets are hopelessly inadequate for protecting the public from hazardous wastes. The preferred solution to the toxic waste problem is to send it elsewhere. Lawrence Summers, who later became Secretary of the Treasury in the Clinton administration, famously proclaimed that poor countries were "underpolluted," meaning that since they were poor they would rationally accept the toxic wastes from the affluent societies that could afford to bribe them into poisoning their people (Anon. 1992b).

In a sense, Summers was holding the high moral ground. All too often, polluters dump toxic wastes from the affluent economies in poor countries without even offering compensation. A few years after he made his statement, a group of African countries petitioned the United Nations Commission on Human Rights to investigate this sort of abuse (Olson 1998). As might be expected, the Western nations undermined the investigation. In one notorious case, the Khian Sea left Philadelphia in August 1986, loaded with 14,000 tons of the city's incinerator ash, containing lead, cadmium, barium, arsenic, mercury, dioxin, and cyanide. After two years of trying unsuccessfully to find a place that would accept this toxic mess, in July 1998, it deposited 2,000 to 5,000 tons on a Haitian beach. Later that year, the ship appeared in Singapore mysteriously empty. In 1997, the firm agreed to retrieve the waste from Haiti, but no action has been taken regarding the rest of the cargo (Ridgeway 1998). Of course, the surreptitious dumping of toxic waste is not confined to third world nations. Sadly, it also occurs in the United States invariably in areas inhabited by poor people.

Transportation and Public Capital

Even when the threat of an inadequate infrastructure is not as dramatic as an unregulated toxic waste dump, the decaying infrastructure imposes significant costs on people and businesses. For example, the U.S. Department of Transportation reported on a dramatic increase in traffic congestion between 1982 and 1996 based on a study of traffic in 70 urban areas. The agency found that: "In 1996, drivers in [these] 70 study areas experienced an average of 40 hours of delay each over the course of the year—the equivalent of a full work week. This was 8 percent more delay than in 1990, and 150 percent more than in 1982 when the average was 16 hours" (United States Department of Transportation 1999). As sprawl continues to engulf larger areas, the rate at which the problem of traffic congestion spreads is more extreme in the previously outlying areas where traffic had been light before. The Department of Transportation analysis continues:

> The "estimated . . . total annual costs of congestion in the 70 areas reached $74 billion in 1996, $65 billion due to delay (productivity loss) and $9 billion due to wasted fuel. Costs ranged from $333 per driver in smaller cities to $936 in large cities, averaging about $629 overall. The study estimated that 6.7 billion gallons of fuel was wasted in these areas due to traffic congestion, compared with about 2.7 billion gallons in 1982." [United States Department of Transportation 1999]

In Silicon Valley, drivers lose more than 30,000 hours each day in traffic congestion (Anon 2000). That wasted time is equivalent to the working day of 3,750 workers. Because the average salary exceeds $80,000 in Silicon Valley, the hypothetical wage bill for these workers exceed $300 million. Remember, this example considers only the local effects in Silicon Valley.

Traffic delays and detours impose other unmeasured costs. John K. Mldainov, deputy commissioner of transportation for the State of New York, described the plight of the residents of Olive in Ulster County, New York. The New York City Board of

Water Supply owned an old bridge over Traver Hollow. When this bridge was declared unsafe, these people had to take a 20-mile detour. Some bought a second car. Mldainov said, "They'd drive to one side of the bridge, walk across it and pick up the second car" (Dione 1981).

In addition, the pollution from stalled or rerouted traffic threatens human health and imposes economic costs, such as damage to plants and animals. Traffic delays also impose serious costs on business.

Environmentalists might applaud inconveniences to the private automobile, which could pressure people to use public transportation as an alternative, but the public transit systems have fared far worse than the roads and highways. For example, New York City's public transit system was in such disrepair in 1980 that it stood in need of an estimated $5 billion to prevent further erosion (Anon. 1981a, p. 137). Consequently, people began abandoning the New York City subway, turning to their cars instead. As a result, in 1980, subway use fell by 2 percent. Consequently, automobile traffic to Manhattan increased by 3 percent that year. Not surprisingly, the average speed on 5th Avenue fell by 26 percent during that same year (Chall 1981).

Daniel Chall, an economist with the Federal Reserve Bank of New York, possibly because he personally experienced the inconvenience of the New York City subway system, estimated that an extra 5 minutes per trip for each subway rider in New York was equivalent to a loss of 41 million hours of work each year, or an annual average of $166 million loss per year (Chall 1981). Unpredictability adds even more to the extra cost of commuting due to the deterioration of the subway system. Chall estimated that, if commuters had to suffer two random delays of 25 minutes, one morning and one evening each week, the economic loss would be twice as large as the $166 million (Chall 1981).

I could not begin to calculate the full costs of the evisceration of the New York subway for citizens of the metropolis. Certainly, the stress and frustration from clogged streets exacts an enormous toll. The typical New Yorker must pay a considerable price for this stress. The damage to human health from increased automobile fumes must also be taken into account. Such medical costs alone could have eaten up a considerable part of short run savings from scrimping on the public transit system.

The deterioration of the subway system imposes still other costs. People who fear delays on their trips home will leave work earlier. Others will arrive later than they should. Because the absence of one worker may disrupt the work of several others, the cost to employers will significantly exceed the wage that the absent worker would have earned during the time that she or he was waiting on the subway. To cut down on the losses that the inefficient commuting system imposes on their business, some firms required that their new employees must be Manhattan residents (Chall 1981).

Chall's work lends support to Peterson's charge that politicians have failed to act on the public's desire for more infrastructure spending. Chall speculated that the delays are so frustrating that the typical subway commuters would probably prefer to have their city income taxes doubled rather than having to put up with delays in commuting (Chall 1981). Although Chall's study is more than two decades old, the New York subway system still awaits its badly needed overhaul.

Residents of New York are not alone in their dissatisfaction with their public transit. Respondents to a Census Bureau Housing Survey typically placed public transportation at the top of the list of "inadequate neighborhood services." In a 1973 survey, 36.1 percent of the owner-occupied households and 24.3 percent of the renter-occupied households reported that public transportation was inadequate to meet their needs; in 1983, the respective figures had risen to 51.1 percent and 32.9 percent (Aschauer 1990b, p. 28).

In one way or another, almost everybody pays a price for the deterioration of the infrastructure. Just as in the case of education, rhetorical flourishes about the importance on investing in the future used to abound, while the deterioration of the system continued apace.

Public capital, however, is not necessarily an unmitigated good. More often than not, state and local governments build roads to satisfy real-estate interests. These roads have promoted the blight of sprawl. The more wealthy and middle-class people flee to the suburbs, the less cities are able to support their public transportation systems, creating even more pressure to facilitate further sprawl.

Sprawl, however, undermines the ability to provide services efficiently. Sewage lines, commutes, and public-safety workers all have to traverse longer distances, creating unnecessary expenses. In recent years, wealthy people are beginning to desert the suburbs in order to take advantage of the amenities and potential efficiencies of an urban setting. Their return is not an unmixed blessing to the previous inhabitants of the cities. The resulting gentrification displaces many people and creates higher rents for those who remain.

When investment has been made in mass-transit systems, all too often the funds are concentrated in expensive systems, such as the Los Angeles subway, which serve well-heeled commuters. At the same time, most urban dwellers who rely on less flashy bus systems for their transportation see those systems fall into disrepair because of the cost overruns on the more exclusive but less economical transportation systems.

Typically, the underfunding of public transportation leads to declines in quality that cause an erosion of public support, just as the underfunding of public schools undermined considerable public support for the educational system. At times, however, the public has organized to defend its interests, as in the case of the Los Angeles Bus Riders Union, which has 3,000 dues-paying members.

Inadequate Infrastructure and the State of the U.S. Economy

Many business interests also began to recognize that the damage caused by the foolish policy of trying to economize on the national infrastructure threatened its economic position. For example, the deterioration of roadways also cut into business profits. In one case, the United States Steel Corporation depended upon a bridge that was found to be unsafe for heavy vehicles. As a result, trucks had to take a detour of almost 20 miles, increasing the company's transport costs by $1 million per year (Vicker 1981).

Some economists become convinced that the deterioration in public capital is the major cause of the economic decline. David Aschauer is the most prominent proponent of this view. Indeed, the data seems to bear him out. Figure 3.1 shows the rates of growth of labor productivity for seven nations—Japan, West Germany, France, Italy, Canada, the United Kingdom, and the United States—together with their share of their gross national product devoted to public investment (Aschauer 1990a, p. 17 and 1988a, p. 197).

The pattern in figure 3.1 is striking to say the least. Countries that devote the most to public investment show the highest rate of labor productivity growth.

Aschauer's time series data for the United States suggest that deterioration of the infrastructure alone is responsible for as much as 60 percent of the recent fall in the rate of productivity growth (Aschauer 1988a; see also Aschauer 1988b; 1989a; 1989b; 1990a; 1990b; and 1990c). Building on Aschauer's work, Alicia Munnell estimated that investing in enough public capital so that the stock of public capital per worker would grow at the same rate as the stock of private capital per work would practically double the annual growth of labor productivity to 2.1 percent (Munnell 1990). According to Aschauer's estimates, a dollar spent on public investment might be as much as four times as potent as private investment (Aschauer 1990a, p. 24).

Aschauer estimated that a $500 billion increase in the 1988 public capital stock would have boosted gross domestic nonfarm business production between 14.0 and 14.8 percent, equivalent to $479 to $509 billion. In other words, the investment in infrastructure would have almost repaid itself in a single year. In effect, this estimate assumes that all infrastructure spending expanded proportionally, even though Aschauer found that only certain kinds of infrastructure, such as roads and water-treatment plants, make a great contribution to productivity. Since this core infrastructure is what matters, the increase in the relevant capital stock would only have to be $275 billion, that the economy will return nearly $2 in output for each $1 of infrastructure investment (Aschauer 1990b, p. 34).

In 1992 soon after Aschauer's analysis was becoming more influential, Bill Clinton ran for the presidency promising massive public works investments. This objective soon disappeared as his attention turned to financial markets rather than the real economy. His attention turned instead to the objective of cutting the federal deficit. For the next eight years, the public watched the stock market soar, while ignoring the continued deterioration of public works—except perhaps when caught in a traffic jam.

Infrastructural Decline as Part of the General Decline

Although Aschauer's work did a great service by highlighting the role of the infrastructure, you have a right to be skeptical about attributing the economic decline to any single cause, whether it be the crumbling of the infrastructure, education, the military, or any other problem. In reality, the decline was the result of a complex process. No doubt, the erosion of infrastructure was an important part of the process, but it was only part.

Not surprisingly, many economists have challenged Aschauer's results. One common line of reasoning suggests that Aschauer's concern with the rate of growth of infrastructure is misleading because the need for investment in school construction and highways had been largely met by the 1970s (Tatom 1991, p. 14; Rubin 1991; and Hulten 1990, p. 105). Overcrowded schools and congested streets seem to discredit this critique of Aschauer.

Aschauer's critics have also charged that his measure of falling public capital per worker is faulty because a greater proportion of the population is now in the work-

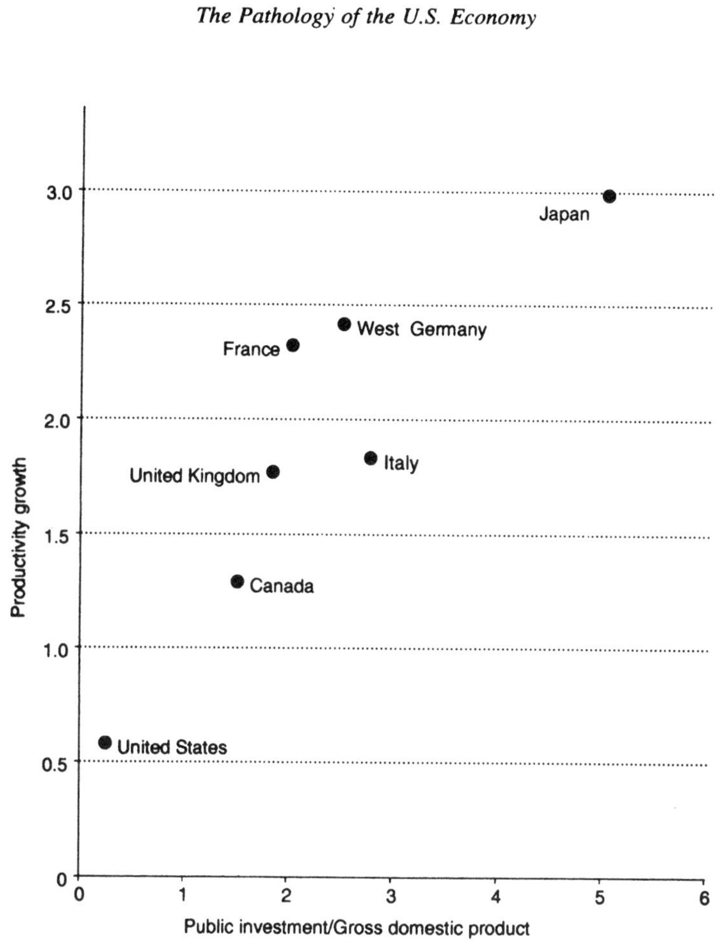

Source: Aschauer 1990, p. 17 (Economic Policy Institute)
A cross-country comparison of average annual growth rates of labor productivity with the ratio of public investment to gross domestic product indicates that, over the period 1973 – 1985, nations which invested more in their public capital stocks saw productivity gain.

Figure 3.1 Cross-country comparison of productivity growth and public investment to GDP ratio

force (Tatom 1991). Aschauer could rightly respond that private capital per worker has continued to increase despite rising labor force participation rates.

Henry Aaron centered his criticism of Aschauer on the fragility of the statistical methods that Aschauer applied (Aaron 1990). Among other things, when Aaron added the seemingly irrelevant value of the yen against the dollar to Aschauer's model, the statistical importance of public investment dropped considerably. Of course, the value of the yen was not entirely irrelevant since the decline of the U.S. economy has done much to increase the value of the yen.

Aaron massaged the model in other ways, which also diminished the estimated contribution of public investment. In this way, he satisfied himself that Aschauer had given too much weight to public investment.

In all fairness, Aschauer used standard economic procedures. Aaron's complaints about Aschauer's work could just as easily be leveled against almost any article you find in a modern economics journal. Unfortunately, we only find such critiques when an economist commits the heresy of suggesting that market solutions might be inadequate.

Aaron raised another question that Aschauer himself attempted to address: How can one know that increasing productivity might not cause public capital to rise, in effect reversing the direction of causation (Aschauer 1990b, p. 43)? Some recent papers do support Aschauer in this regard (Bougheas, Demetriades, and Mamuneas 2000; and Demetriades and Mamuneas 2000).

Even so, I believe that a broader approach is warranted, one that allows for the reverse causation as well. In that scenario, public capital augments productivity, but also the economic decline led incomes to fall, creating popular pressure for tax cuts, which, in turn, restricted spending on public capital.

The problem is that while the appeal of tax cuts is obvious, the benefits of spending on infrastructure are more vague until the system approaches a total breakdown. Once the system reaches such a crisis the cost of repair is greatly magnified. As a result, during the boom of the '90s, which left the majority of the people behind, other priorities had more popular appeal.

This broader interpretation of the infrastructure problem reinforces Aschauer's case for a massive commitment to rebuilding society's public capital stock. The stress of traffic jams and the unpleasantness of public transportation stand as stark reminders of the noneconomic benefits of public capital. Counting these amenities as part of the productivity of public capital would substantially increase Aschauer's measure of infrastructural productivity.

Future Infrastructural Needs

Arnulf Gruebler proposes that Aschauer may be altogether wrong for still another reason. Gruebler suggests that the sort of infrastructure that is falling into disrepair today may not be appropriate for the future economy. In this vein, he postulates a general theory of infrastructure, in which today's transportation infrastructure becomes tomorrow's recreational infrastructure. According to his optimistic scenario: "The horse has disappeared as a means of transportation but is presently used for recreational purposes. Former canals, riverport and dock sites become preferred leisure and residential areas, railway lines are being turned into bicycle tracks" (Gruebler 1990, p. 288). A humorous example lends some support to the idea of unexpected reshuffling of leisure and infrastructure. Princeton and Cornell were scheduled to compete in a swimming meet, but a blizzard precluded traveling. The teams agreed to race against each other without leaving their campuses. Each team swam in its home pool, while the coaches relayed information about their respective team's performances over the phone to determine the winner of each match (Anon. 1991b).

While increased information can reduce the need for transporting some manufactured goods, and bicycle tracks can improve the quality of life, modern society is far from ready to abandon all of its railway lines or highways. For example, motor freight carriage climbed at a 4.5 percent annual rate between 1960 and 1987 (Aschauer 1990b, p. 28).

True, infrastructure needs are changing. With the increasing reliance on information, many pundits suggested that a national fiber-optic system represents the national highway system of the future. Certainly, the United States would be foolish to strangle its cities with still more freeways. Nonetheless, the infrastructural problem remains a serious threat to our economic well-being.

The challenge of providing an appropriate infrastructure for the future will be all the more difficult. First, no one can predict with certainty the appropriate new forms of public capital. Second, to the extent that the public invests in creating entirely new systems, the cost will be far greater than incremental additions to the existing infrastructural system.

Unfortunately, such concerns seem to lay in the far-off future. Public officials in the United States still seem to be blissfully blind to the importance of infrastructure in economic performance. In fact, in one case, the United States government is behaving as if it believed that making foreign nations spend more on infrastructure would somehow give the United States a competitive edge.

In 1989 during bilateral trade negotiations, the U.S. government pressured the Japanese to agree to increase its spending on infrastructure (Kanabayashi 1990). In fact, the Japanese already had been spending a much greater portion of their Gross National Product on infrastructure.

In the face of pressure from the U.S. negotiators, the Japanese acquiesced, promising to spend an additional 0.8 percent of their Gross National Product on public works. To put this demand in perspective, the United States only spends about 1 percent of its Gross National Product on nonmilitary public capital. By 1993, an astounding 43 percent of the Japanese national budget went to construction projects (McCormack 1996, p. 33).

The United States negotiators may have reasoned that, if the Japanese had to spend more money on infrastructure, the Japanese saving rate would decline, making their economy less competitive. This policy would also have the added attraction of increasing the demand for imports from the United States.

Of course, this strategy could have backfired on the United States. By demanding that the Japanese devote more to public works, while the United States continued to neglect its own infrastructure, the Japanese could have guaranteed that the U.S. economy would become even more uncompetitive relative to the Japanese economy. Fortunately for the United States, the Japanese political leaders dissipated much of this infrastructure investment in providing pork barrel projects to line the pockets of various interest groups that supported the dominant political party (McCormack 1996).

The discussion of the deteriorating state of the public capital stock provides a clear perspective on the cumulative processes that play a powerful role in the economy. First, as the economy deteriorates, profits fall. In response, wages drop. People attempt to resist the decline in their economic well-being. Desperately, they search for a solution. In this case, they demand tax relief. Government responds by cutting back on investment in public capital, in the process intensifying the economic decline.

Ironically, today the public strongly supports spending on only one form of public capital—prisons to house the people who fall between the cracks of our crumbling economy. For example, the California master plan for prison construction now projects $5.5 billion in the near future expansion. Something must be dreadfully wrong when a society puts so much money into new prisons, while the average age of a school in the United States is more than 40 years old.

The Erosion of the Stock of Public Data for the U.S. Economy

In one sense, fears about the deterioration of the stock of public capital in the United States may even be too conservative. Economists now regard information and knowledge as capital. Accordingly, public information is public capital.

In its zeal for cutting back government spending of all kinds, the Reagan administration foolishly scrimped on both the quantity and the quality of economic information that the government collects and disseminates. But the savings on data collection were trivial.

For example, early in the Reagan administration, the Bureau of Labor Statistics discontinued its spot market commodity price index, which has been available to the public since 1940. In this case, Commodity Research Bureau of Analysis Corporation, a subsidiary of Bache Halsey Steuart Shields Inc. decided to maintain the index for its own use. William Jiler, head of the Commodity Research Bureau said, "I don't know how much the BLS [Bureau of Labor Statistics] is saving by dropping the index, but I figure it costs us next to nothing to turn it out—about a half hour a day of one person's time" (Stollman 1981; see also Malabre 1988).

Between 1965 and 1990, annual federal outlays for collection and analysis of statistical data fell by $4 million, or about 10 percent between 1965 and 1990 (Malabre 1990b). Another source estimated that the real resources that the U.S. government spends on the collection and processing of statistical data had remained virtually unchanged (Juster 1988). This decline continued during the Clinton administration. Spending at the Bureau of Economic Analysis, which tracks broad data such as personal income and gross domestic product, has declined by 12 percent in real terms over the past five years (Kulish 2000).

Even after the cuts, one author attempted to prove that government data is "overproduced" since few firms or even few economists are willing to spend more than $18,000 to purchase a tape from the Department of Commerce with all the raw data used to produce the Producers Price Index (Gillespie 1990). In fact, cutting back on the collection of public data may be even more destructive than curtailing investment in the infrastructure.

First of all, the cost of producing this data is increasing. As a result, the same number of dollars provides less information. Consequently, the quality of the data would be declining even if the structure economy were relatively stable. However, rapidly changing economic conditions require substantial improvements in the collection of public data. These structural changes make the deterioration of the public data stock even more severe than it would otherwise be.

For example, international transactions have become a more prominent part of the U.S. economy. In addition, service employment is becoming more important than manufacturing. This movement from the production of goods to a concentration on services makes the construction of data considerably more difficult (Stout 1989). Unfortunately, the government has failed to develop data sources that could aid in understanding such changes in the U.S. economy. To make matters worse, the Census Bureau's reports are now voluntary. Companies routinely fail to fill out these reports to save money (Stout 1989). In short, significantly more effort needs to be devoted to improving the public database if we are going to get a handle on how the economy is performing.

Many people are now coming to recognize the dangers inherent in the false economy of cutting back on vital economic data. For example, the commissioner of the Bureau of Labor Statistics at the time, Janet L. Norwood, noted that "the economy is so much more complex, you really need better data than we have ever had." In addition, Michael Boskin, head of the first Bush administration's Council of Economic Advisors, fretted that, "The quality of the statistics as a whole is a serious problem" (cited in Gleckman 1991, p. 113).

Drs. Boskin and Norwood could not complain too emphatically since some years before President Reagan had made their employer, George Bush, the person responsible for the elimination of paperwork. Indeed, Mr. Bush took great pride in the economies that he helped to introduce in areas such as the collection of public data during his tenure as vice president.

The Public Call for Improved Data

Public data serves three purposes that the budget cutters never acknowledged. First, it represents an important component of the intellectual infrastructure. Hopefully, economists' study of this data could contribute to the understanding of the economy. Second, this data assists business in making decisions. Business has to plan for an uncertain future. The quicker business can respond to new economic conditions, the more stable and more productive our economy can be.

Finally, and most important, public officials act on the basis of this data. In the words of Michael Boskin, "We make everything from budget policy to trade policy to monetary policy based on these numbers" (Stout 1989). For example, decision makers in the U.S. government adjust their economic policies according to their reading of the Department of Commerce's Index of Leading Economic Indicators, yet this data is embarrassingly flawed. The service sector, for better or worse, is coming to dominate economic activity in the United States, yet the Index of Leading Economic Indicators is relatively insensitive to conditions in services (Malabre 1990b).

One could rightly argue that the collection of data on services is maddeningly difficult. Rather than make an effort to improve its data, the Reagan administration merely eliminated important data. For example, one of the eleven components of the index is the index of initial claims for unemployment insurance. Initial claims do not give much indication of future economic trends. The government only uses this statistic because it had discontinued other labor-oriented indices, which would be a more appropriate indicator. Lacking any alternative, the Department of Commerce had to make do with this inferior statistic (Malabre 1990b).

The business press recognized the serious danger of an inadequate statistical database. They began calling for a determined effort to improve the state of the public data. For example, in a special issue of *Business Week* with the lead story entitled "Are We in a Recession?" the editors warned:

> In today's volatile economic climate, inadequate information can have a devastating effect on the decisions of policy makers, businesses, and the financial markets. It's long past time the government jettisoned economic models that lump together silicon wafers in a category of manufactured goods that is dominated by bricks and cinder blocks.

As the economy teeters on the brink of a recession, Congress should consider the extent to which the nation's economic predicament is the result of decisions made on the basis of inadequate and faulty data. It's a problem that could be fixed for a relative pittance. [Editors of *Business Week* 1990a]

The terrible state of the public data base even moved the American Economic Association, a group not known for calling for government action, to appoint a committee including representatives from business to make recommendations for improving government data collection. The committee's preliminary report concluded: " . . . the statistics now collected by the government provide a weak basis for understanding and choosing among policies, and are likely to be increasingly inadequate to meet policy needs in the future" (Juster 1988).

More than a decade passed without any improvement. In fact, the system of public data deteriorated, although the stakes may be higher than ever.

The Strategic Importance of Public Data

I can sympathize with the plight of Alan Greenspan, chairman of the Board of Governors of the Federal Reserve System, probably the singlemost person responsible for guiding the U.S. economy. The Fed's actions on monetary policy may be the most important economic decisions for determining the fate of the economy. However, monetary policy typically does not have much of an effect for about six months.

The appropriate policy must reflect the conditions of the economy six months into the future rather than what is happening right now. To make matters more difficult, the Fed does not have current data. It has to rely on data that the government collects on a monthly or quarterly basis.

Accurate prediction of the future state of the economy is impossible in any case, but with poor-quality data the probability of a serious mistake grows by leaps and bounds. Saving a few dollars on the collection of data can result in literally billions of dollars being lost as a result of public officials making decisions based on misleading information. For example, in the fourth quarter of 1989, the economy was declining at a troubling 3.1 percent; however the Department of Commerce had initially estimated that the rate of decline was about one-half as steep. After looking at the misleading Department of Commerce statistics, the Federal Open Market Committee decided not to lower short-term interest rates at a critical 27 March 1990 meeting.

According to a *Business Week* report, Federal Reserve officials insist that they received no "false signals" from the data. "And no one will ever know if the Fed would have cut rates in the spring of 1990 had it known how serious the slowdown was."

Had the Federal Reserve Board taken more prompt action, the recession might have been far less severe (Gleckman 1991, p. 112).

Today, with financial markets around the world closely linked, the Federal Reserve Board has less room for error than ever before. A miscalculation in the United States can set off problems elsewhere that can make corrective action in the United States even more difficult.

Alan Greenspan has been very clear about the importance of improving public data. He told a Senate panel in early 2000, "I am extraordinarily reluctant to advocate any increase in spending. So it's got to be either a very small amount or a very formidable argument that is involved. And I find, in this case, that both conditions are met" (Kulish 2000).

Greenspan addressed the National Association for Business Economics on 27 March 2001. The members of this group include the chief economists from some of the most powerful corporations in the country. Normally, in a talk such as this one, the audience would have expected the chairman to have discussed interest rates, productivity, or some other important economic condition. Instead, he called for the collection of better economic data. Over and above the problem that the government has provided inadequate funds for the collection of traditional data, rapid technological change was making many of these traditional measures obsolete (Greenspan 2001).

This concern on the part of Greenspan was not new. A decade earlier, he had warned, "The economy has been changing faster than our ability to measure it" (cited in Gleckman 1991, p. 112). Unfortunately, nothing had been done in the decade since he made this plea.

Greenspan's audience at the National Association for Business Economics was naturally sympathetic. The organization had already complained that a relative decline in funding for two key federal statistical agencies threatens economic data used by banks and businesses, Congress and the Fed alike (Kulish 2000). To begin with, these economists also rely on public data in advising their employers. A faulty forecast on their part could cost their corporations millions, if not billions of dollars. Even more important, a bad decision on the part of the Federal Reserve Board could throw the economy into a tailspin, causing enormous losses for their employers.

A few days after Alan Greenspan addressed the National Association for Business Economics, Richard Berner, president of the National Association for Business Economics and managing director and chief U.S. Economist for Morgan Stanley Inc. addressed the House Subcommittee on the Census Committee on Government Reform (5 April):

> CBO estimates that a mere 0.1 percentage point difference in real growth over ten years would add or take away $244 billion from cumulative projected surpluses. Sensible policy decisions require a range of forecasts or scenarios. Sensible policy decisions also must start from knowledge of the facts, and if the data on which we base those forecasts are faulty, so too will be the forecasts. And that could have grave consequences for our future prosperity.
>
> Budgets for statistical agencies, especially BEA, barely cover mandated wage escalations. Funds for research and development are sorely needed to expand the scope and improve the quality of our statistics so they remain relevant in a rapidly changing economy. [Berner 2001]

At the very moment that Greenspan and Berner were making their pleas for better data, the condition of the U.S. economy was unclear, to say the least. Greenspan himself was under attack for not having reduced interest rates enough in the face of the steep stock market selloff. A *Business Week* article published the day before his talk had observed that investors had just lost $4.6 trillion since the stock market peak (Vickers 2001).

In contrast to the United States, where firms must rely on public data for much of their information, in Japan, the government works actively to create semipublic information, which business can use, but which is unavailable to the rest of the world. The Japanese method of collecting information is extremely efficient. According to one scholar:

> the system of industrial policies in post-war Japan . . . has been a very effective means of collecting, exchanging and propagating industrial information. Government officials, industry people, and men from governmental and private banks gather together and spend much time discussing the problems of industries and exchanging information on new technologies and domestic and overseas market conditions. . . . Probably information related to the various industries is more abundant and [more] easily obtainable in Japan than in most other countries. Viewed as a system of information collection and dissemination, Japan's system of industrial policies may have been among the most important factors in Japan's high rate of industrial growth. [Komiya 1975, p. 221; cited in Vives 1990, pp. 17–18]

The false economy of cutting back on the stock of public data illustrates the foolishness of the knee-jerk call for cutting all government activities, across the board.

CHAPTER 4

The Role of the Military in the Economic Decline

The Absurd Extent of Military Spending

In contrast to the curtailment of public investment in productive infrastructure, the military has continued to grow by leaps and bounds since the Camelot days of the Kennedy administration. Today, the extent of military spending in the United States is almost incomprehensible. During the final days of the Cold War in 1990, the Military Industrial Complex was employing about 6.5 million military and civilian personnel—about one of every ten workers—in more than 135,000 factories (Melman and Dumas 1990). According to the conservative estimates of the Office of Management and Budget, national defense made up 26 percent of the fiscal 1990 budget.

Paul Murphy, an independent budget analyst, warned that these official figures are misleading. In the first place, this estimate includes the social security trust fund as part of the budget, even though it does not belong there. The Johnson administration first included it in 1969 specifically to dilute the percentage of the budget used for Vietnam. Supposedly, this budgetary manipulation was intended to give less ammunition to the peace movement. By subtracting the trust funds from the budget, national defense amounted to 32 percent of government spending. Counting military aid to foreign governments plus NASA and other military spending by related agencies brought the military's share to just over 50 percent. Murphy's estimate of the military's share of net interest on national debt in 1990 comes to $119 billion. These additional estimates bring the defense budget from $296.3 billion to $423.5 billion. Adding Veterans Administration benefits brings the defense share to a staggering 54 percent of federal spending (see Cwiklik 1990).

A detailed study by the influential Brookings Foundation calculated that the United States has spent almost $5.5 trillion (in constant 1996 dollars) on nuclear weapons and weapons-related programs between 1940 and 1998. Factoring in the costs of dismantling and disposing of nuclear weapons and disposing of and storing nuclear waste brings the total up to more than $5.8 trillion (Schwartz 1998, p. 3).

The collapse of the Soviet Union might have been expected to have allowed military spending to decline precipitously. Instead, the official Department of Defense budget fell slightly by fiscal year 2000. The official budgetary authority for national defense stood at $280.8 billion. At the same time, leading political figures from both parties called for massive increases in military spending based on fears that impoverished nations such as North Korea posed a real threat to the United States. The ease with which the United States was able to defeat the supposedly powerful Iraqi military gave lie to the myth that such countries could mount a real threat. To put current military spending into perspective, a 1999 report concluded:

> The U.S. military budget is more than nineteen times as large as the combined spending of the seven countries traditionally identified by the Pentagon as our most likely adversaries—Cuba, Iran, Iraq, Libya, North Korea, Sudan and Syria—which together spend just over $15 billion annually. [Hellman 1999]

Whether you see the military as a cancer eating away at our economy or, through the perspective of military Keynesianism, as a crutch to keep it upright, you still must confront the question—why then would our society, with so many pressing needs that remain unmet, devote such an inordinate amount of its resources to building means of destruction rather than means of production?

The Strategic Benefits of Military Power

Although this lavish military spending harms workers, military force does serve a useful function for certain groups in our society. To begin with, as I have already mentioned, the military actively supports the interests of those corporations and wealthy individuals with important stakes in the less developed nations of the world. By threatening to use massive violence against almost any political movement that might be inhospitable to the needs of business, the worldwide U.S. military presence augments profits for many individual corporations.

Certainly, judging by the history of the deployment of the military, the armed might of the United States has been directed more at third world countries than at superpowers. Frequent interventions in the third world protect U.S. markets and sources of raw materials. In the words of Ronald Reagan, "Our industries depend on the importation of energy and minerals from distant lands. Our prosperity requires a sound international financial system and free and open trading markets" (Reagan 1984, pp. 1–2; cited in Riddell 1988, p. 62).

Tom Riddell reported that according to Howard Morland, a military analyst, 37 percent of the U.S. military budget was directed to Soviet containment and another 45 percent supported U.S. military capability in the third world (Riddell 1987, p. 6). However, a substantial share of the 37 percent directed at the Soviet Union served to make the Soviets leery about lending support to third world liberation movements.

The massive military buildup was instrumental in bringing about the collapse of the Soviet Union. Although the leaders of the United States never openly admitted how harmful military spending was to the U.S. economy, it was far more destructive to the Soviet economy. Since the U.S. economy was much larger than its Soviet counterpart, the Soviets had to devote a far greater percentage of its economy to match the military budget of the United States. Already in the 1950s, political leaders in the United States realized that creating an arms race had the potential to bankrupt the Soviets. For example, Nelson Rockefeller pushed this idea while working in the State Department during the Eisenhower administration (Colby 1995, p. 274).

For a while, the Soviets attempted to build up their domestic economy while neglecting the military—hoping that they could keep that strategy secret. Once the United States developed its satellite technology in the 1960s, the Soviets could no longer afford to neglect the military (Turgeon 1996, pp. 17–18). By the 1980s, the military consumed as much as one quarter of the gross national product of the Soviet economy, where (Silk 1985; Epstein 1990; Marshall 1987, p. 484). As Judy Shelton wrote in *The Coming Soviet Crash:*

> For a while it almost looked as if Soviet claims about the efficiency of a state-managed economy would turn out to be correct. . . . After World War II, the country moved to build huge factories and construct massive dams and railroads. Projects were built to take advantage of huge supplies of natural resources and to increase manufacturing output. By the 1960s the Soviet Union was starting to close the gap with the United States—not just in terms of economic productivity, but in military armaments as well. [Shelton 1989, p. 178]

Although they did not seem to relish the need to expand their military, the Soviets felt that they had no choice. In the words of Mikhail Gorbachev:

> I shall not disclose any secret if I tell you that the Soviet Union is doing all that is necessary to maintain up-to-date and reliable defenses. This is the duty to our own people and our allies. At the same time I wish to say quite definitely that this is not our choice. It has been imposed on us. [Gorbachev 1987, p. 218]

Lou Cannon, who wrote the most solid biography of Ronald Reagan, observed, "Reagan launched a military buildup premised on the belief that the Soviet Union was too economically vulnerable to compete in an accelerated arms race and would come to the bargaining table if pressured by the West" (Cannon 2000). To make the military buildup in the United States more threatening, the United States rigged the test of the missile defense system to make it appear that it worked when they actually programmed the target missile to self-destruct (Weiner 1994).

The Soviet leader recognized the underlying basis for the U.S. stance on the arms race, noting: "United States foreign policy . . . is based on . . . the belief that the economic system of the Soviet Union is about to crumble" (Gorbachev 1987, p. 220).

Like his counterpart in the United States, Gorbachev seemed assured that the Soviets could continue to escalate their military spending without harming their own economy. Perhaps with false bravado, he bragged, "A tenth of the US investments would be enough to create a counter system to SDI (the Strategic Defense Initiative)" (Gorbachev 1987, p. 234).

The Soviet economy did not collapse. In fact, it continued to grow. However, it could not manage to match what it imagined the Strategic Defense Initiative to have accomplished, while at the same time providing for rapid economic expansion. Returning to the analysis of Judy Shelton:

> In the end, Kremlin authorities could not bring themselves to cut back on the Soviet Union's nuclear arsenal, their main claim to global status and the source of Soviet influence

> around the world. To build up the military, the other sectors of the Soviet economy were being squeezed harder and harder. Fixed capital investment was slashed, and consumer needs were give short shrift. By the early 1980s, defense was claiming more than one-fifth of total Soviet production and soaking up an inordinate proportion of Soviet economic capabilities. [Shelton 1989, p. 179]

From the standpoint of the U.S. economy as a whole, the cost of this military force far exceeds any benefits that might result from the military threat against progressive movements in the third world. For example, the military's Rapid Deployment Force was supposed to protect the supply of Middle Eastern oil. Richard Heede and Amory B. Lovins estimated that diverting the funds budgeted for supplying this operation for one year would free up enough money to develop a well-designed weatherization program capable of eliminating all Mideast oil imports (Heede and Lovens 1985).

Why bother to expend funds on the military in order to get a lesser amount in return in the form of profits? The reason is not difficult to fathom. Business pays for a relatively small part of cost of the military, but reaps the bulk of the benefits. In this respect, the military acts as a siphon to draw wealth from the country as a whole to direct it to a relatively small segment of society. The net result, is I will show, is not merely the redistribution of wealth from the poor to the rich, but a serious drain on the economy that diminishes future economic potential.

The Economic Failure of Military Keynesianism

Many experts contend that the object of this military spending is not military prowess, but the creation of a healthy economy by virtue of military Keynesianism. Some commentators revel in the notion that wanton spending on the military spending is something akin to Keynes's scheme for burying bottles: it might be wasteful, but it keeps the economy going.

Of course, all spending is not alike. For example David Aschauer estimated that $1 spent on the military increases economic output by $1. A similar investment in core public works will result in $4 (Aschauer 1990d). Still, political leaders never sold the public on military Keynesianism as such. Instead, they played on people's patriotism and implicitly promised that the government could manage the economy into prosperity.

The military did seem to be an excellent vehicle for pursuing Keynesian economic policy. Keynes himself insisted that government spending should not just grow willy-nilly. It should be flexible. When the economy falters, increased government spending should take up the slack. When the economy threatens to overheat, government spending should subside, releasing pressures that build up when the economy grows too fast. In this way, economic policy makers supposedly can guide the economy to prosperity.

From a purely political perspective, military spending seemed to be ideally suited to meeting Keynes's goal of allowing flexibility in government spending. Since military spending is less controversial than other forms of public spending, the government can quickly beef up the military when the economy threatens to sink into a recession. Once the economy needs to cool off a bit, it can reduce military spending by drawing attention to peaceful overtures from the other side.

Howard Sherman made some interesting calculations that illustrate how the government attempted to use military spending to control the business cycle in the United States. According to his calculations, in the average peacetime expansion between 1949 and 1980, military spending fell by an average 0.14 percent per month. During the average contraction, it rose 0.19 percent a month (Sherman 1983, p. 382). Although other forces do influence military spending, all in all, the evidence does suggest that the state did attempt to use defense spending to stabilize the economy (see Griffin, Wallace, and Devine 1982).

As Keynesian policies in the United States became closely entwined with the Cold War, military spending seemed to be able to accomplish what had hitherto eluded the alchemists: they seemed to succeed in changing the lead of war into the gold of business; namely profits. This formula was so attractive that long after the Cold War disappeared with the disintegration of the Soviet Union, those responsible for setting policies worked day and night to manufacture threats to the United States. Politicians and conservative think-tanks launched an intensive campaign to elevate impoverished nations, such as North Korea, dangerous rivals in order to justify an unworkable missile defense program that promised to consume hundreds of billions of dollars.

In reality, military Keynesianism was less successful than it initially seemed to be. Yes, the economy was more stable in the postwar period than before (Balke and Gordon 1989; but also see Romer 1989). How much credit does military spending deserve for this stability?

To begin with, military Keynesianism is not quite as flexible as it seemed to be. In fact, it was probably destabilizing. Although military spending is theoretically capable of kicking the economy in the right direction, the economy cannot react instantaneously. To increase military spending, government first stirs up hysterical fears, which are difficult to contain later. Even today, with the collapse of the Soviet Union, the government is attempting to convince the public that it faces a dangerous threat from impoverished nations, such as North Korea.

So, while Sherman found that military spending fluctuated with the business cycle, over the period that he studied, the time of economic expansion exceeded the time of contractions. As a result, over time military spending ballooned.

To decrease military spending, the government might try to put the public mind at ease. The government can engineer these mood swings over long periods of time, but such changes are impossible to fine tune. More often than not, overreaction will result. Overly abrupt changes in military spending will destabilize the economy—comparable to what happens in a shower when you suddenly try to make the water hotter or colder.

Certainly, military spending turned out to be far less effective as a counter-cyclical tool that it first appeared to be. To begin with, in the immediate postwar period, the economy was so strong that it was not particularly vulnerable to downturns. As a result, the economy at the time did not pose a severe challenge to military Keynesianism.

As the decline took hold, the deficiencies of military Keynesianism became apparent. For example, when Michael Edelstein included the 1980s in his analysis, he found no evidence that defense spending worked counter-cyclically (Edelstein 1990).

Robert Gordon reached a similar conclusion, a decade earlier in his analysis of the role of fiscal policy as a tool of economic stabilization. According to Gordon, "[I]n the broadest sense fiscal policy has been the most important *destabilizing* influence in the postwar economy" (Gordon 1980, p. 121). Gordon found that fiscal policy in general was not the problem. He identified the culprit as the huge swings in military spending. He explained:

> In the first postwar decade the enormous magnitude of the rise and subsequent fall in defense spending was the dominant feature of aggregated demand fluctuations, and the expansion of spending for the Vietnam War in 1965–68 destabilized the economy again. By a narrower criterion that takes defense spending as exogenous and outside the purview of discretionary stabilization policy, however, fiscal policy deserves relatively high marks in the 1947–57 decade. [Gordon 1980, p. 121]

Two economists, Valerie Ramey and Matthew Shapiro, made an even more damning finding. Most Keynesian economists would expect that increasing government spending would lead to higher wages although this particular idea does not appear in Keynes own book. So while military spending might not directly increase the welfare of workers, it should improve wages. This particular study indicated that real wages fall clearly and robustly after an increase in defense spending (Ramey and Shapiro 1998).

In short, the overall record of military Keynesianism is not a happy one. Although an intense burst of military spending did succeed in pulling the U.S. economy out of the Great Depression, the conditions created by the Great Depression made that initial success possible. Over time, as the economy became more fragile, military spending proved to be less and less capable of infusing any vigor into the economy.

The rise of military spending illustrates a pattern that recurs in this book: a remedy for an economic problem (in this case the purported cure for insufficient demand served its purpose) creates a host of other ills, which required new remedies, which, in turn, brought on new infirmities. In short, the U.S. strategy of promoting economic strength by military spending turned out to be self-defeating.

The Changing Nature of Military Spending

Some historical perspective will help in understanding why the expansion of military spending was detrimental to wages. During World War II, the Middle West was known as the arsenal of democracy. This region built military hardware with labor-intensive technology, similar to that which was used to produce automobiles and trucks. Over time, as the military technology became more sophisticated, an increasing share of the Pentagon budget went to new industries that specialized in military production.

In the process, a larger share of the defense budget went to hardware instead of wages. This trend has probably accelerated in recent years. Between 1973 and 1984, the share of spending on durable goods in defense industries rose significantly. As a result, after employee compensation as a percentage of total defense spending reached a high of 49.8 percent in 1973, it fell to 35.2 percent by 1984 (Blank and Rothschild 1985, p. 679).

James Cypher interpreted this change in mix of defense spending to be a transformation of the nature of military Keynesianism. While the initial form of military Keynesianism included low unemployment as one of its goals, this new variant, which he termed, "Redistributive Militarism," downplayed the importance of employment, focusing more and more on the profits from lucrative defense contracts (Cypher 1991, p. 609).

According to Cypher, redistributive militarism transferred income away from those in the bottom 80 percent. He concluded, "increasingly lax procurement practices . . . permitted both higher profit margins and a greater volume of business for arms contractors—thus increasing the *mass* of profits" (Cypher 1991, p. 609).

Given this new situation, military spending is now far less effective in generating jobs than earlier rounds of military spending were. William Hartung, a researcher at the World Policy Institute, has gathered a number of indications of the weakening of the effectiveness of military Keynesianism. For example, a 1992 study by the Congressional Budget Office found that if there were cuts of $20 billion per year in military purchases in the United States, only 6 out of 420 major U.S. industrial sectors would suffer reductions in output of 5 percent or more (Hartung 1999b, p. 184; citing Congressional Budget Office 1992, pp. 22–23). In fact, 9 of the top 14 defense-oriented industrial sectors were expected to break even or increase their total output, despite cuts in their defense-related orders. Four of these sectors—Aircraft (10 percent), Nonferrous Forgings (20 percent), Aircraft and Missile Equipment (13 percent), and Engineering and Scientific Instruments (21 percent)—were projected to achieve fairly impressive growth rates despite cutbacks in defense purchases (Hartung 1999b, pp. 184–85).

William Hartung discovered that 238 Congressional districts, more than half of the total, are now virtually out of the defense contracting business or on their way out (meaning that they either have less than $100 million in defense prime contracts or have lost 70 percent or more of their contracting base in the last 10 years) (Hartung 1999a, pp. 31–32). In addition, the defense industry has been busily moving jobs from regions that traditionally paid higher wages to lower-wage regions in the South and Southwest. Taken together, these clues suggest why increases in military spending might cause wages to decline.

Of course, millions of people still owe their livelihood, directly or indirectly, to military employment. If military spending were to be eliminated overnight, massive disruptions would certainly occur, probably enough to send the economy into a tailspin.

In conclusion, military Keynesianism has run its course. Even if military Keynesianism had served a purpose earlier, it now appears to be incapable of stabilizing the economy. Despite its enormous destructive potential, military spending has lost its economic punch.

The Question of Spillovers from Military Research and Development

Defenders of military Keynesianism contend that their policies have not harmed the economy. Even if military Keynesianism might have failed as an economic stabilizer, they allude to a slew of economic benefits spawned by the scientific advances that the engineers and scientists developed in the course of their military research projects. Certainly, defense spending funded many of the most important new products that we see around us today.

For example, most of the major advances in the computer industry have been products of military research (see Flamm 1988a and 1988b). One scientist from the Massachusetts Institute of Technology estimated in the late 1980s that about one-half of the $400 billion U.S. computer industry could be traced to the $1 billion that DARPA (Defense Advanced Research Projects Agency) had invested over the last 25 years. Even seemingly nonlethal computer components owed their existence to military funded research. For example, the ubiquitous computer mouse—popularly associated with the user-friendly, entrepreneurial spirit of Apple Computer—developed out of a DARPA grant to Xerox (Flamm 1988a, p. 24).

That military research and development has contributed to the development of new technologies should not be surprising. Judith Reppy of Cornell University estimated that defense projects employ 42 percent of the scientific personnel in the United States (Reppy 1985, p. 11). Considering the enormous resources that have been devoted to military research, the question about the contributions of military research should be rephrased: could these military researchers have made even more valuable contributions to the U.S. economy if they had worked on civilian projects?

In general, the answer is positive because military research is less significantly fruitful than civilian research. Reppy identified several barriers that prevent military projects from yielding benefits comparable to civilian research (Reppy 1985, p. 12).

First of all, most military projects are shrouded in secrecy. This restriction of the free flow of ideas cripples the scientific potential of military research. The major benefits from science come from communication and the cross-fertilization of ideas (Nelson 1990, p. 129). Commercial developers also want to restrict the use of their "intellectual property," but at least when they seek protection from the patent system they must reveal their discoveries (Scotchmer 1991).

Secrecy is doubly damaging because the bulk of the ultimate benefits from science come from uses that the original researchers had never envisioned. For example, the computer was initially designed as a tool to calculate the trajectory of artillery shells. Howard Aitken, one of the early pioneers in developing the computer, was confident that his invention would be of limited use. He predicted, "If it should ever turn out that the basic logics of a machine designed for the numerical solution of differential equations coincide with the logics of a machine intended to make bills for a department, I would regard this as the most amazing coincidence that I have ever encountered" (Cerruzzi 1986, p. 197).

In fact, every major corporation, as well as many small businesses, employs the computer today for the very uses that Aitken once dismissed as impractical. Computer technology became as advanced as it is today only because hackers and hobbyists, academic and commercial researchers of all kinds were free to explore the potential of this technology once it was released beyond military circles.

Regulations compound the problem of secrecy. To prevent large military contractors from using Pentagon research contracts to subsidize their civilian work, regulations require the artificial separation of large firms into military and civilian divisions. Again, this arrangement hampers the process of cross-fertilization. For instance, returning to the example of the computers, this separation would prevent people interested in office automation from becoming familiar with the work of people building specialized machines to calculate the trajectory of artillery shells.

In addition, the military usually concentrates on developing specific products rather than processes that would be applicable in civilian projects. This specificity restricts the potential benefits to other sectors of the economy. For example, military projects often require electrical components that are "hardened" so that they can continue to function during a nuclear attack. Learning to "harden" electronic components does little to help most U.S. businesses compete.

Similarly, the attempt to develop lasers to destroy incoming missiles hardly addresses a pressing consumer need. Obviously, the billions of dollars spent on missile defense will lead to some useful technologies. Considering the massive scientific energies put into this enterprise, the payoffs are not likely to be significant.

In many cases, the military objectives run counter to civilian needs. For example, the military devotes enormous sums of money to discover technologies to make its aircraft more difficult to detect. Civilian aircraft, in contrast, have no reason to want to fly undetected.

To make matters worse, many modern military products are just unsuited to the civilian sector. For example, the early jet engines that the military used had obvious civilian benefits. Once military planes entered the world of supersonic speeds, "they began to assume performance and cost characteristics that were inappropriate for the cost-conscious world of commercial travel." Similarly, communications satellites initially had great civilian spillovers, but the special requirements of contemporary military satellites are inappropriate for commercial communications (Mowery and Rosenberg 1989, p. 148). Finally, bloated military prices discourage civilian applications (Reppy 1985, p. 12).

Unfortunately, even if the United States suddenly decided to rearrange its priorities, its scientific establishment would be ill prepared for civilian research. The decades during which science has been overly committed to military missions will take its toll for decades in the future because the mind-set common to military research is inappropriate for civilian missions.

For example, the U.S. national weapons laboratories have been trying to forge an alliance with industry to develop new programs (see Carey 1990). This endeavor has not been very successful. *Business Week* editorialized:

> Naturally, lab directors are arguing fiercely that their scientists could clean up the environment, boost United States industrial competitiveness, and educate a nation. . . . But the truth is that they haven't been very adept at transferring their research, such as the expensive studies on alternative energy in the 1970s, to the private sector. . . . Let's not waste money on vague hopes. [Editors of *Business Week* 1990b]

In conclusion, although military research has paved the way for many important civilian applications, had this same research occurred outside of the military industrial complex, the benefits would have been many times greater.

In fact, today the direction of spillovers may well be reversing. The business sector is probably less dependent on advances in military technology than the military is on new civilian technological breakthroughs. If this hypothesis is true, then the gutting of the economy might eventually undermine the ability of the United States to maintain its military leadership in the world.

The Pernicious Influence of Excessive Military Spending

Even if the benefits of military research could easily spill out into the civilian sector, the military fosters a perverse institutional framework that discourages efficient use of resources. To begin with, military spending is, by its very nature, wasteful. Besides its obviously destructive objectives, military suppliers have no incentive to economize. They operate on a cost-plus basis. The more they spend, the more profits they earn. Consequently, as Seymour Melman has observed, defense contractors are geared to cost-maximizing rather than cost-minimizing (Melman 1983). Without competitive checks and balances, the military industrial complex will adhere to these cost maximizing practices (Melman 1983, p. 4).

In the words of Murray Weidenbaum, who was President Ronald Reagan's first chief economic advisor, "Military production has evolved into a business culture distinct and closed off from the normal commercial environment" (Weidenbaum 1992, p. 29). The vast majority of the attempts of leading military contractors to enter civilian markets have resulted in dismal failures (Weidenbaum 1992, pp. 29–30).

The enormous amounts of money involved in military contracts, together with the lax supervision of defense practices, invite abuse. In addition, especially in more recent times, arms suppliers have richly rewarded high-ranking military officers with generous contracts upon their retirement. Within this context, you should not be surprised by the familiar horror stories about the military spending $500 for a toilet seat.

Nonetheless, the sensational nature of these examples makes these expenses seem as if they were exceptional. In fact, all the sophisticated weaponry in the U.S. arsenal is grossly overpriced. For example, Seymour Melman once estimated that the cost per pound of a B-1 bomber was about $4,400 (Melman 1983, p. 81; also see Fitzgerald 1989), making the plane literally worth more than its weight in gold. Since that time, aircraft has gotten more expensive, while the price of gold has been relatively stable.

True, these planes had a considerable amount of sophisticated electronics, but were these really so expensive that each single pound of a B-1 bomber cost about as much to build as the retail price of a small automobile? Not surprisingly, few major military suppliers are capable of competing in civilian markets and civilian producers in the United States have become less competitive relative to competitors from other countries, where the defense industry is more modest.

The relationship between defense spending and the declining competitiveness of much of traditional industry in the United States is not hard to understand. Since the military suppliers need not worry about economizing, they have been able to attract a disproportionate share of the best and the brightest engineers. In this sense, the cost of the military buildup goes well beyond simply adding up the money that the military directly consumes, because so many of the resources that the military obtains are strategic resources, especially skilled technical labor. David Halberstam's five-year comparative study of Ford and Nissan demonstrated dramatically how the Japanese company was able to draw upon the best talents in the nation while in the United States, defense industries lured away the most promising people (Halberstam 1986, p. 726).

To make matters worse, the practices associated with doing such profitable business within the military industrial complex may contaminate other sectors of the industry, given the mobility of technical and management personnel in the U.S. economy. In this vein, Michael Edelstein concludes that the main flaw in expanded defense spending is its detrimental impact on the human element in the economy (Edelstein 1990, p. 436). Accordingly, an unbiased observer might conclude that the quality, as well as the quantity, of military spending has eroded the productive potential of the U.S. economy.

How Military Spending Might Actually Harm the Military

Since military power ultimately depends upon economic strength, sooner or later, this erosion of economic vitality can undermine the military itself. Consequently, military Keynesianism may well turn out to be a failure in terms of militarism as well as Keynesianism.

Of course, the United States still has the strongest military in the world by far, so what follows is a tad speculative. Nonetheless, the basis for this military prowess is eroding, since the cutting edge military technologies of today result from technological developments from previous decades when the United States was dominant in the commercial sector. For example, *Business Week* concluded immediately after the war against Iraq:

> The hardware doing so well in the Gulf is the product of the '70s and early '80s, when military applications were the cutting edge of technology. Now, commercial developments in high speed computers, composite wings, fiber optics, and flat-panel computer displays drive military applications. This means that the nation with the most advanced commercial uses may enjoy the greatest military spin-offs.
>
> Others worry that when high-tech manufacturing moves abroad, research and engineering with potential military use move as well. [Magnusson et al. 1990, p. 18]

The continuing emphasis on military spending in the United States allowed U.S. corporations to seek lucrative defense contracts, while abandoning the consumer sector. At the same time, Japanese corporations steadily sought to perfect their production for the consumer sector.

Yet, research and product development in the commercial sector is central to progress in military applications. For example in the low-technology washing machine market, the Japanese replaced many mechanical parts with semiconductors. This technique made their products both quieter and less expensive (Florida and Kenney 1990a, p. 117). It also gave the Japanese valuable experience in producing and designing semiconductors, so essential to a modern military.

As U.S. firms continue to abandon the consumer sector, they will progressively lose their expertise in cutting-edge technologies. The Semiconductor Industry Association, a not-disinterested party, has been quick to recognize the threat, warning, "Our international competitors are far ahead of us in developing advanced electronics applications via the consumer market segment. We as an industry, and as a country, must pull together quickly . . . before our competitors have an insurmountable lead" (Semiconductor Industry Association 1989, p. 12; cited in Florida and Kenney 1990a, p. 116).

As a result, with the continued collapse of consumer goods production in the United States, more and more of the hardware essential to new military technology will come from foreign suppliers. This arrangement poses two sets of additional problems. First, the U.S. military may not always have adequate access to these supplies when a problem arises. Second, and more important, as engineers in other nations perfect these technologies, they may well accumulate the expertise to surpass our own military engineers (Florida and Kenney 1990a, p. 116).

So in the end, military spending—at least carried to excess—may be a sure route to long run military weakness!

The Class Nature of Military Keynesianism

Excessive military spending is a cancer, eating away at the U.S. economy. Today, now that the Cold War has disappeared, the military is desperately searching for a rationale for increased spending. The military offers its services to fight the war on drugs, say in Columbia. It offers to maintain the capacity to quickly put down third world insurgencies. It presents itself as the ultimate guardian of computer security. Most of all it promises to spend a great deal of money, which we can ill afford.

Checking the expansion of military spending is no easy matter. Some groups have significant stakes in military Keynesianism over and above its effect in holding labor in check. Certainly, a small group of influential arms merchants has parlayed the naiveté, patriotism, and anxiety of the citizens of the United States into a magnificent stream of profits with the willing and able assistance of politicians who either fear being honest with the public or who directly benefit from the largesse of the arms merchants.

Military spending has many advantages for business. To begin with, as we have already noted, military spending avoids competing with private business. In addition, business generally favors military more than civilian projects, in part, because military spending tends to help business more than labor, especially in the age of redistributive militarism. Given a national fervor for a strong military presence and a guaranteed profit from the government, business has no reason not to be happy with the financial fruits of military Keynesianism.

Of course, business is not united in its support of military Keynesianism. The meat-ax approach to setting national priorities characteristic of the military contributed to the further deterioration of the economy. Only now, after decades of neglect, some progressive business leaders are coming to recognize the importance of increased spending in areas such as education.

I do not want to ignore the military's own interest in the rise of military Keynesianism. Although people commonly refer to the military-industrial complex as if the military and industry formed a homogeneous whole, the military has its own specific interests to pursue. Gregory Hooks demonstrated that the military is far more successful in pursuing its goals that do not conflict with those of business (Hooks 1991).

Certainly, the military is as generous with itself, as it is with its suppliers. Although the enlisted personnel do not live lavishly, the military tries to make everything as comfortable as possible for its constituency of high-ranking officers. Lester Thurow observed that the United States supported as many generals and admirals in the late 1980s with an army of only 2 million uniformed troops as it did in World War II with 12 million troops (Thurow 1987, pp. 339–40). Although business continually censures wasteful government bureaucracies, it has never evidenced much concern about comparable waste and corruption in the military.

Others are not so deeply wedded to military Keynesianism: for example, many liberal policy makers accepted military Keynesianism out of pure expediency. Such people hoped to avoid confronting deeper social problems. Instead, they opted for a quick policy fix that could indirectly correct some of the ills of society without stirring up the enmity of the powerful and without challenging the comfortable views of the well-indoctrinated masses.

As the economy fell into a decline, the military and the Keynesian dimensions of military Keynesianism separated. The military gained prestige while winning easy victories in Grenada, Panama, and Iraq. While the military won public favor, the economic decline soured the public on other forms of social spending. In this sense, the success of military Keynesianism in its goal of undermining social programs exceeded the wildest expectations of the early postwar leaders. Today military Keynesianism is dead; only militarism remains.

Getting a handle on the military budget represents an enormous challenge. Recent trends give little cause for optimism.

CHAPTER 5

Keynesian Policy, Monetary Policy, and the Weakening of Competition

The Logic of Keynesian Policy and Cumulative Economic Processes

In this chapter, I will look in more detail at John Maynard Keynes's doctrines, which form the theoretical base for the Economic Management School. I will show that, while Keynesian policies can stimulate the economy relatively quickly, in the long run they can also cause serious damage.

Let me begin with the positive contribution of Keynesian economic policies. Certainly, Keynes was correct in his understanding that investment can set off a spiral of economic growth. Economists do not know precisely how much cumulative economic growth will occur as a result of a new investment. Instead, they have to make rough estimates of the statistical relationship between capital investments and the size of the economy. Still, even using a crude approximation, the results are striking enough to confirm the importance of capital investments.

Lawrence Summers, who later became the treasury secretary in the Clinton administration, provided some useful evidence in a volume dedicated to Robert Solow, a famous MIT economist, who also won the Nobel prize for Economics. Summers observed that for the period 1952 to 1987, an investor who owned shares in a hypothetical mutual fund, which owned the entire corporate sector, would have earned an average return of 7.7 percent, an amount that is not far from the average accounting rate of profit of 9.6 percent for the corporate sector as a whole (Summers 1990, p. 119). He reminded his readers that Solow's own estimate of the benefit to society as a whole from capital investment was about 23 to 25 percent for the United States in 1954 (Solow 1963, p. 92).

Technically, an economist would want to look at the marginal profit rate—what a firm could earn by investing one more dollar rather than the average rate of profits. The marginal rate should be below the average rate. Similarly, an economist would want to get a handle on the rate of growth for the entire economy resulting from one more dollar's worth of investment. Unfortunately, neither the private nor the social rate of return is known, so Summers had little choice but to use average estimates as rough proxies.

Summers concluded that this discrepancy between the accounting rate of profit and Solow's estimate suggested that about half of the benefits from investment accrue to the firm that actually makes an investment in plant and equipment. The other half benefits society as a whole rather than the investing firm.

Summers interpreted this situation to mean that the average firm that invests in new capital captures about half (9.6 percent) of the fruits of the investment. Society as a whole earns about 23 to 25 percent on the same investment. Based on this line of reasoning, Charles Jones and John Williams estimated that the optimal rate of investment is four times as high as the actual rate (Jones and Williams 1998).

Why then does society as a whole benefit so much more from a new investment than does the firm that makes the investment? To begin with, new investment often incorporates new technologies. The new technologies that one plant introduces frequently become common knowledge, helping to boost productivity in nearby plants (see Paul Romer 1987; Nelson 1989).

In addition, the primary investment of one firm can create profitable opportunities for others. As a result, when one firm invests, other firms are likely to respond to the initial investment with investments of their own to supply the new demands of the initially investing firm. This pattern of new investments, incorporating new technologies, can create a cumulative spiral of investment. This wave of new investment can set off another wave of research and development, as one set of firms competes to get the business of the other firms that are investing.

Given the situation that firms earn less than one-half of the total benefits of their investments, you should expect that firms would systematically underinvest. If this hesitancy to invest could be broken and firms would invest more, business as a whole would be better off, as Keynes understood.

Unfortunately, firms will not invest as much as would be optimal for society, because each individual firm only takes its own profit into account when it makes its investment decision, ignoring the benefits that other firms reap from the cumulative spiral that investment can initiate, creating what economists refer to as a coordination failure. In other words, if each firm agreed to increase its investment proportionately, all firms would be better off. In a market economy, firms have no way of making such an agreement. Keynesian policies (meaning policies that other economists interpreted as being Keynesian rather than policies that Keynes himself advocated) were intended to break this logjam by stimulating investment one way or another.

The Contradictory Nature of the Business Cycle

At first, the logic of stimulating the economy with Keynesian policies seems impeccable, but, alas, no simple policy rule can make the market perform as well as it could if decision makers could somehow deliberately coordinate their actions. Keynesian policies are no exception. While stimulating investment has undeniable benefits, especially in the short run, Keynesian policies are beset with contradictory influences that more or less reflect the contradictory nature of the market itself.

A market is an extremely complex form of social organization, fraught with innumerable contradictions. Early economists, such as Adam Smith, revelled in these contradictions. Writing at a time when market forces were mistrusted, Smith delighted his readers by pointing out the paradox that people who followed selfish motives supposedly could benefit society as much as if they were driven by generosity.

Today, when much of society holds market forces in high repute, economists are loath to point out the destructive side of the contradictions inherent in the market. Instead, mainstream economists present markets as wholly harmonious affairs, even though the competitive forces that Smith advocated can and often do turn destructive. History shows that time and time again, economic competitiveness often becomes so intense that firm after firm withers.

Such waves of intense competition cause the process that Summers was trying to estimate to work in reverse. As one firm shrinks, others suffer from its losses. Its suppliers lose business. So do the firms that had been selling to the employees that the firm sheds. As such economic withering becomes more common, the downward momentum becomes sufficient to cause a general depression.

In short, depressions and competition are parts of the same process. Each of these parts has a twofold nature. Competition can appear benign at times, forcing firms to become more productive. At other times, the destructive side of the competitive process can spin out of control.

Similarly, depressions have a positive and a negative side. The negative side of depressions is self-evident. Depressions are terrible events that wreak havoc on a good part of society. Worse yet, depressions can persist for decades on end. In addition, in light of the earlier discussion of the cumulative nature of economic processes, depressions can permanently scar the productive capacity of the labor force and impede economic growth over long periods of time, long after the depression itself has expired.

Still, depressions also serve a positive—even a necessary—purpose within a market economy. Recall the earlier discussion about how the Great Depression too laid the groundwork for the Golden Age.

Before the Great Depression, many economists accepted the idea that depressions were a natural part of a market economy, necessary to rid industry of weak and inefficient producers. However, they never explained why this shedding process could not take place without a recession or a depression. Conceivably, new firms could continually replace the few firms that exited without a downturn in employment or production.

Today, mainstream economists studiously avoid the complexity of the competitive process by treating contradictory elements of the market as separate and unrelated forces. In particular, they treat business cycles "like tonsils, separable things that might be treated by themselves, [rather than] . . . like the beat of the heart, of the essence of the organism that displays them" (Schumpeter 1939, i, p. v).

For example, mainstream economists restrict their depictions of competition to its positive effect in spurring business to become more efficient, ignoring the destructive side of competition. Similarly, they fail to acknowledge that depressions have a positive side. Conveniently, they subsume the negative side of competition within their analysis of depressions, pretending that depressions only occur because of nonmarket influences—usually some mistaken policy decision. Acknowledgement of either the positive side of depressions or the negative side of competition is all but unknown.

Economists facilitate this habitual fragmentation of the their analysis of the contradictory forces of competition by splitting their theory into two subjects: microeconomics (how competition affects an individual firm or household) and macroeconomics (how the economy as a whole works). Economists rarely discuss how these two branches of economics are related. When they do so, they generally minimize all contradictions by pretending that economies have a magical tendency to reach an equilibrium without any mishaps along the way.

Not surprisingly, this fragmented analysis misleads economists into recommending disastrous policies. For example, most conservative economists would have the public believe that the postwar prosperity should be the norm for a capitalist society. They insist that trusting our fate to market forces would allow society to enjoy a rapidly growing standard of living without interruption because competition will automatically lead business to make the correct decisions.

Although Keynesian macroeconomics teaches that government should act to maintain sufficient aggregate demand, it still accepts that competition will lead firms to make the proper decisions within that framework. In short, both contemporary conservatives and Keynesians emphasize the positive side of competition without taking the negative side into account.

Almost all mainstream economists treat depressions as abnormal events that only occur as a result of some act of mismanagement. Conservatives and Keynesians differ only in where the blame for this mismanagement lies. In no case do they acknowledge that depressions are a normal part of the competitive process and that they have both a positive and a negative side. I will show that by assuming away the necessity of depressions, these economists recommend policies that pay no heed to the need for capital renewal.

Keynes's Heresy

Keynes delighted in posing his theory in a shocking manner. In terms of the conventional conservative economics of his day, his theory was indeed quite heretical. The full extent of Keynes's heresy went unrecognized, probably because his book was macroeconomic in nature. More importantly, despite his desire to tweak his contemporaries, Keynes's policies appeared less heretical than they were because they seemed so commonsensical given the extreme conditions that existed at the time.

You can easily understand why, given the enormous costs of the Great Depression, Keynesian policies seemed reasonable enough at first. Disregarding the excessive emphasis on military spending, the avoidance of recessions seemed to improve the immediate economic welfare of the citizenry. After all, during the Great Depression, when he was writing, competitive forces had gathered so much momentum that Keynes had good reason to doubt that the economy could correct itself and emerge from the Depression. The odds were high that popular pressure would soon cause capitalist societies to rise up and abandon the market altogether, turning to an alternative form of economic organization—either fascism or socialism.

Given this perspective, Keynes had an ambiguous analysis of competition. From a microeconomic perspective, Keynes believed that competition was good, meaning that competitive forces were effective in leading firms to make the right decision about whether to produce apples or oranges. Within a macroeconomic perspective, however, competitive forces were often incapable of producing adequate demand, causing a recession or a depression. In other words, for Keynes, microeconomic competition would lead business to produce the appropriate mix of goods and services within the existing level of demand, but the same competitive forces could lead to inadequate demand, forcing business to cut back on the overall level of output. As a result, normal competitive processes can get out of hand and throw an economy into a depression.

Without some external source of demand, competitive forces alone could be inadequate to bring production and employment back to satisfactory levels. In effect, Keynes's reasoning was similar to that of Lawrence Summers, except that Keynes went further. Rather than merely showing that markets would not create an optimal level of investment, Keynes showed how deficient investment could become pathological, leading to horrendous depressions.

Keynes did not follow through with the logical consequences of his analysis. Had he done so, he would have realized the contradictory nature of competition. On the one hand, competitiveness is essential for promoting efficiency in a market economy. On the other hand, competition can become so fierce that the economy can fall into a depression, which creates enormous inefficiencies by disrupting normal business arrangements.

Keynes was not particularly interested in pursuing a theory of competition. He was concerned about the immediate circumstances of his time. He was convinced that the momentum of the Great Depression was so strong that few managers would have any interest in expanding their productive capacity. Rather than building up their firms to weather the ongoing storm of competition, those who controlled the major companies would just let them run down instead of attempting to make their operations more competitive (Perelman 1989, pp. 18–20).

Consequently, during the Depression, competitive forces become so strong that the economy was likely to remain stagnant for long periods of time. The effect of stimulating the economy through monetary or fiscal policy, however, was to blunt competitive forces. After all, in an expanding economy business has an easier time in disposing of its products, which is another way of saying that competition has become less intense.

Knowing that the level of investment would remain weak during a depression, Keynes was intent on designing a quick means of stimulating enough investment to blunt the enormous competitive forces that the Depression had unleashed. Policies to expand demand and to shield business from competition were just what the economy needed to break out of the depression at the time. Keynes's precise policy recommendations remained exceedingly vague, but regardless of the specifics, he never doubted the need to frame measures to stimulate the expansion of investment of any kind whatsoever (Perelman 1989).

Keynes gave absolutely no indication that he was aware of the positive effects of depressions or the negative effects of competition within the context of a market economy. Instead, he took pride in his heresy and mocked the callousness of the "austere and puritanical souls [who] regard [the Depression] as an inevitable and a desirable nemesis on 'overexpansion' as they call it" (Keynes 1931b, p. 349). He complained:

> It would, they feel, be a victory for the mammon of unrighteousness if so much prosperity, was not subsequently balanced by universal bankruptcy. We need, they say, what they politely call a "prolonged liquidation" to put us right. The liquidation, they tell us,

> is not yet complete. But in time it will be. And when sufficient time has elapsed for the completion of the liquidation, all will be well with us again. [Keynes 1931b, p. 349]

Keynes's attitude is not surprising. After all, the negative aspects of depressions are so glaringly obvious and painfully tragic that people are naturally inclined to overlook the positive side of depressions, especially in the midst of the havoc of an economic crisis. Moreover, those who opposed efforts to stimulate the economy emphasized that depressions serve a positive role. Keynes would not have been inclined to grant much credence to their ideas, given the enormity of the immediate consequences of the Great Depression.

To the extent that Keynesian policies succeeded in stimulating investment, shortening or even precluding depressions, the mass of economists deemed Keynesian policies to be a success. Indeed, by the 1960s, the majority of economists in the United States embraced Keynesian policies. Recall that even the conservative President Nixon supposedly proclaimed himself to be a Keynesian.

Unfortunately in their zeal to stave off depressions, Keynes and his followers, as well as the bulk of the economists at the time, believed that appropriate government policies could effortlessly guide the economy along a path of permanent prosperity. They failed to realize the complexity of the relationship between competition and depressions.

Nobody seemed to notice that Keynesian policies, which are ostensibly designed to fight depressions or recessions by expanding demand, are more or less equivalent to a reduction in overall competitiveness.

Keynesian Policies and Replacement Investment

Keynes's success obscured the understanding of the consequences of this reduction in competitive pressures by ignoring the positive side of depressions. Keynes added to the confusion by failing to take the importance of capital renewal into account. Instead, he lumped all investment together (see Perelman 1989).

Keynes must have known that depreciation charges cover the vast majority of all investment, suggesting that replacement investment is the dominant form of investment. Still, he generally assumed that capital replacement occurs automatically when a capital good reaches a given age, regardless of economic conditions (Perelman 1989).

You might wonder why anyone should care about the distinction between replacement investment and investment in general. In fact, inadequate replacement investment was one of the keys to the decline of the U.S. economy during the late 1960s and early 1970s.

In the long run, modernization is crucial for the health of a competitive economy. In general, widespread replacement of existing plant and equipment is the key to modernization. However, modernization generally requires strong competitive pressures. As I have already noted, Keynesian policies undermined replacement by effectively limiting competitive pressures.

Economists often refer to the expansion of capacity as "capital widening." Their term for making existing capacity more efficient is "capital deepening." In effect, the concept of capital widening is meant to suggest the accumulation of more of the same sort of capital. In contrast, capital deepening suggests making existing capital more efficient rather than increasing capacity. Of course, capital widening in practice is not absolutely distinct from capital deepening. Still, economists know that firms emphasize widening during expansions. Less well-known is the extent to which firms engage in capital deepening during recessions.

Keynes's practice of ignoring the distinction between capital widening and capital deepening was appropriate to his own objective. Writing his *General Theory* in the midst of the Great Depression, he was engaged in the urgent task of finding short run measures that could prevent the capitalist system from self-destructing.

Common sense also seems to support Keynes's approach. A buoyant economy should encourage the purchase of new capital goods, which should promote economic efficiency because the new plant and equipment embody the most modern technologies. Economists and policy makers alike failed to recognize the fallacy of this common-sense approach. The root of their failure was their fragmented understanding of economic processes. To understand the nature of a market economy, you need to break through the veil of conventional economics and recognize the positive function that depressions serve as well as the negative consequences of a prolonged absence of a depression.

Specifically, during expansions, firms tend to expand capacity rather than to make the existing capacity more productive. In contrast, during depressions firms will tend to increase efficiency, often by replacing older plant and equipment with newer, more productive capital goods. In other words, what investment firms do make during slumps will frequently be capital deepening, although, as Keynes understood, hypercompetition can immobilize the investment process.

Substantial capital deepening does not generally occur during expansions. When times are good, firms prefer to concentrate their investment on the expansion of capacity rather than the replacement of existing capital goods. So, in the absence of a heightening of competitive pressures, the capital stock will age and eventually the economy will weaken.

Neither Keynes nor his followers acknowledged the importance of the downside of the business cycle. Considerations of modernization were understandably extraneous to Keynes's immediate objective of beating back the Great Depression. Certainly, the Depression had become too severe for Keynes to find much satisfaction in the knowledge that strong competitive pressures could eliminate obsolete plant and equipment. Instead, Keynes concerned himself with the immediate problem that excessive competition was immobilizing an economy.

Long after the Depression had passed, Keynes's followers continued to fail to recognize the importance of strong competition in promoting capital deepening. Several reasons contributed to the reluctance to address the downside of the continual application of Keynesian policy. First, the fragmentation of the analysis of competition described earlier obscured the connection between depressions and competition. Economists concentrated on the positive side of competition and the negative side of depressions.

Second, Keynes taught economists to focus on investment as a whole, thereby obscuring the crucial role of replacement investment (Perelman 1989). In addition, economists were disinclined to examine the role of replacement investment because they became infatuated with the undeniable short run benefits of promoting investment by stimulating the economy.

Perhaps the most important reason for ignoring the role of replacement investment was psychological. Nobody can anticipate when new technology or market conditions will make a new investment obsolete. In other words, once you allow a consideration of replacement investment, you introduce uncertainty into economic theory. This uncertainty ruins the neat and tidy theorems that economists love. As a result, economists chose to ignore reality in order to perfect their abstract theory. In the case of the study of replacement investment, this choice has proven to be disastrous.

Capital Widening Versus Capital Deepening

In this section, I will elaborate on the theory of capital deepening, a subject of the utmost importance. Consider what happens when an economy fails to engage in capital deepening over an extended period of time. A typical firm may plan to invest a great deal, convinced that demand for its product will continue to expand.

Although its investment may be substantial, management will not be likely to invest much in modernizing existing capital goods under these circumstances. After all, why divert investment funds to replace older, less-efficient plant and equipment? Even if the firm's old capital goods are only moderately profitable, they can still contribute to the firm's total earnings. Firms will prefer to use their investment funds to purchase new capital goods to expand the productive capacity of the firm without scrapping existing capital goods.

While the new capital goods are more productive than the earlier generations of installed plant and equipment, capital widening is relatively ineffective in increasing productivity. For example, a one-percentage-point increase in the growth rate of producers' durable goods leads to an estimated immediate increase in real output growth of only 0.127 percentage points (Denison 1964).

Now imagine a firm that has just emerged from a depression. Suppose that its capital stock is entirely new because it has just replaced all of its old capital goods during the depression. The firm may continue to invest in new capital goods, but now this investment will be for capital widening instead of capital deepening. One year into the expansion, the capital goods that the firm owned at the end of the depression will have aged by one year. The only new capital goods that the firm owns will be its expansion investment for that year. After two years, the firm will own a substantial amount of two-year-old capital goods, some capital goods that are one year old, and its new expansion investment for that year.

This example shows how the capital stock typically ages between the end of one strong recession and the beginning of the next. If this aging continues for too long, the economy will be likely to stagnate. In other words, without some strong market pressure, firms will continue to keep their increasingly obsolete capital goods in use, long after they should have been scrapped or even better, diverted to more appropriate alternative uses. These market pressures can come from two sides: either competitors force the firm to lower its price or suppliers will demand more for their goods and services. Since wages are typically the most important cost, higher wages are a particularly effective means to compel firms to upgrade their old capital stock (see Perelman 1999).

The aging of capital goods is not the only economic problem associated with the absence of strong competitive pressure. Where competition is lax, firms will tend to get careless, investing unwisely in plant and equipment, as well as generally adopting inappropriate business practices.

Part of the problem is psychological. During boom times, managers and investors of all kinds generally interpret their good fortunes to be the result of their own intelligence and hard work. They fail to recognize that the boom owes a great deal to the restructuring that had previously occurred when the economy was struggling during a depression or a recession. Even more ominously, they are generally blind to the fact that booms create the seeds of their own destruction.

This uncritical arrogance leads many managers and investors to overestimate their own abilities. They sink funds into foolish projects fully expecting great rewards. Without the market discipline imposed by strong competitive pressures, wasteful business practices will become increasingly common (see Perelman 1987).

To the extent that firms continue with capital widening without much capital deepening and to the extent that they continue to pursue inappropriate business practices, the economy will become increasingly vulnerable. If this process goes too far, the economy may become incapable of withstanding a severe blow. Should an oil shock occur or should foreign competition suddenly become fiercer, such an economy can swiftly collapse.

Even in the absence of the intentional application of expansionary Keynesian policies, competitive pressures will be weak during economic expansions, yet these competitive pressures are needed as an incentive to achieve efficiency, just as mainstream economics teaches. In this sense, periodic recessions and depressions act as an economic immune system. They discipline the economy by weeding out inappropriate business practices or even inefficient firms. They allow the economy to correct itself before it becomes too fragile. However, if these competitive forces become too strong, they can act as an autoimmune disease that can ravage a healthy body.

In conclusion, depressions and recessions are absolutely necessary for capitalist economies. They are a crucial phase in the process of modernizing market economies and helping to keep them efficient. Without them, the economy will eventually become weak and inefficient.

After the crisis passes, when business becomes vigorous once again, business will be in the fortunate position of enjoying a strong demand for its products together with a low production cost structure. The stage is then set for a profitable boom, such as the one the United States experienced during the Golden Age, but such expansions are destined to be temporary, not eternal, as the Keynesian theorists had imagined.

Keynesian Policies and the Aging of the Capital Stock

I want to avoid any misunderstanding. My point is not to single out Keynes or the Keynesians. All mainstream economists fail to accept the contradictory nature of market economies. All refuse to accept that markets necessarily impose pain and hardship on society. By failing to come to grips with the realities of the markets, they leave society unprepared for the inevitable.

In general, Keynesian policies are preferable to the dogmatic laissez-faire ideology of the Chicago School. Still, you must realize from the earlier discussion of the contradictory influences of Keynesian policies that policy makers are caught on the horns of a dilemma. Without Keynesian policies, firms are likely to underinvest systematically to the detriment of society as a whole. Yet, these same Keynesian policies create a long run tendency for firms to keep existing capital equipment in place rather than investing in modernization.

Policy makers find themselves in another damned-if-you-do, damned-if-you-don't situation. While Keynesian policies can increase efficiency in the short run, the same policies also impair efficiency in the long run by inhibiting the replacement of existing investments.

This dilemma is a direct result of the contradictory nature of markets, but economists have systematically avoided facing up to these contradictions. Instead, they concentrate on one side or the other of markets, leaving themselves unprepared for the consequences of the policies that they recommend. Keynesian economists were not immune to this failing, but then few economists during Keynes's lifetime were sensitive to the long-term risks of Keynesian policy.

Keynes's followers, especially those in the United States, deluded themselves into believing that their master had left them with a recipe for running an economy without contradictions. These disciples took up their master's impressionistic call and transformed it into an ambitious blueprint for permanently eradicating the business cycle.

For the Keynesians, the economist's task was to arrange policies that would steer the economy away from depressions and recessions. For the most part, they recommended that the government administer the proper dose of government spending, mostly for military purposes. In the glow of postwar prosperity, everything seemed to be going according to these economists' plan. The corrosive influence of this military Keynesianism went unnoticed. Influential economic advisors were no more aware than the typical citizen of the hidden dangers that were accumulating during the first decades of Keynesianism.

The Keynesians also overlooked the contradictory nature of expanding demand. In particular, they did not realize that the expansion of demand required weakening the forces of competition, thereby making the economy more fragile. In effect, military Keynesianism represented the worst of all possible policy mixes: it simultaneously weakened both competition and the industrial prowess of the industrial structure.

Of course, even Keynesian economists realized on an abstract level that, in a market society, competition prods business to find new and better methods of production, but they were oblivious to the converse proposition—that the absence of the pressures associated with hard times removes much of the incentive for modernization (Perelman 1989). Instead, they saw their policies in the narrow context, in which increasing demand would benefit the economy by stimulating investment.

Perhaps these Keynesians assumed that appropriate antitrust measures alone would ensure sufficient competition. At least, to the best of my knowledge, Keynesian economists gave no hint that they recognized that their policies could eventually undermine the economy by eliminating the periodic depressions that force the modernization of plant and equipment.

This failure to recognize the long run consequences of attempting to do away with recessions altogether was a serious, though understandable, blunder. During the early days of Keynesianism, this failure to recognize the necessity of downturns in a market economy was to be expected, given the enormity of the Depression. Tragically, decades after the immediate threat of the Great Depression had faded away, few economists realized the importance of depressions within market societies.

Peter Bernstein does provide some calculations that suggest how Keynesian policies protected inappropriate investments until the economic decline set in. Bernstein takes the trend in the ratio of corporate dividends to the value of the capital stock as evidence of the problem. He notes that this ratio had traditionally been fairly constant because of management's policy of paying out a fixed fraction of true capital value as dividends. This policy changed in the wake of the oil shock. Bernstein concludes:

> [This movement reveals] market and management judgments that a substantial part of stated corporate assets are worthless. . . . [As a result of this revaluation, the ratio] dropped abruptly in 1969 and . . . [has] remained depressed ever since. This suggests that many management errors have occurred during the heavy capital spending years that preceded the oil shocks of the 1970s. [Bernstein 1983, pp. 31–32]

Louis Schorsch points to the practice of the steel industry in the United States as a specific example of the sort of management errors that became obvious with the onset of the crisis accompanying the oil shock. In a well-run industry, management would concentrate investment where it could be most productive. The steel industry did otherwise. Schorsch claims that among major steel manufacturers in the United States, "without strict cost controls, investment tended to be dispersed throughout the Corporation, each plant getting its share" (Schorsch 1984, p. 36).

Once the industry began to face crisis conditions, it had to pay the price for its previous, wasteful investment patterns and the delay of scrapping. It had to expend huge amounts of money to replace and upgrade obsolete plant and equipment. As a result, the U.S. steel industry spent as much for investment between 1965 and 1979, when very little capacity was added, as it had during the previous 15 years, when capacity increased by more than one-third (Adams and Mueller 1982, p. 119).

Unfortunately, the major steel producers acted too late. US Steel, once the dominant manufacturer in the country now uses the corporate symbol, USX. The X is symbolic for it virtual demise as a major steel producer on the world market.

In conclusion, the fate of the steel industry, as well as Bernstein's data, lends support to my contention that market societies need depressions, or at least hard times. Otherwise, business will accumulate an inefficient capital stock and industry will become increasingly inefficient.

Monetary Policy and Capital Renewal

Although Keynes was mistaken in overlooking the importance of competition in fostering capital replacement, the framers of monetary policy in the United States were equally wrong in failing to recognize their own responsibility for inhibiting capital renewal. While Keynes correctly emphasized that low interest rates would promote investment, monetary authorities and financial interests favor high interest rates. In their view, money must be kept tight in order to maintain a sound financial system.

The Federal Reserve Board prides itself in its generally rigid opposition to policies that could moderate interest rates. The Fed takes the position that maintaining low interest rates threatens to create dangerous inflationary conditions. Higher rates of interest will only discourage those projects that promise a relatively low rate of profit.

The Fed has generally been successful in fighting government efforts to moderate the rate of interest, except during World War II and a very brief period thereafter. At that time, the federal government required the Fed to keep interest rates low in order to minimize the cost of financing the war, but the Fed did not do so willingly (Lucia 1983). Finally, in 1951, after a long struggle with the Treasury, the Federal Reserve Board was relieved of the obligation to keep down interest rates.

The Fed saw its 1951 accord with the Treasury as a victory for economic rationality. It contended that removing the controls on interest would not harm the economy since high interest rates would only threaten less profitable investments. Instead, by requiring firms to make investments that pay the highest rate of return, the market would discipline investors to move their capital to those activities that are the most productive.

More important, the Federal Reserve believed that the key to guaranteeing economic growth is a high level of saving. The Fed failed to distinguish between the rate of savings and total savings. John Maynard Keynes's great work, *The General Theory of Employment, Interest and Money,* showed the fallacy of this emphasis on saving. He demonstrated that, although savings rates might be higher with a higher interest rate *for a given level of economic activity,* higher interest rates are likely to lower the level of economic activity.

Keynes showed that the economic theory of the Federal Reserve led to the fallacious conclusion that a higher rate of interest automatically encourages economic growth by creating a larger pool of funds for future investment. After all, high interest rates discourage both spending and investment, so much so that total savings may fall as a consequence of raising interest rates. As a result, high interest rates can be self-defeating.

Low interest rates have a number of desirable consequences, but the Federal Reserve Board's almost pathological fear of inflation obscured these benefits. First and foremost, low interest rates reduce the cost of capital and thereby make business more willing to undertake investments, especially long-term investments. Obviously, no rational firm will want to invest in a project that will earn an expected rate of profit that is less than the interest rate.

Interest rates also affect the kind of investment that firms undertake. Later, I will discuss how high interest rates are dangerous because they actually encourage risky behavior. I will also explain how high interest rates lower the share of investment devoted to replacement investment.

A failure to understand the contradictory nature of markets was central to the Federal Reserve Board's determination to win its battle to keep interest rates high. In so doing, the Fed made a substantial contribution to the unraveling of the U.S. economy.

The resulting combination of high interest rates together with a blunting of competitive forces probably represented the worst possible policy mix. The absence of competition would ensure that firms would have little need to replace their capital goods. High interest rates would make such investments uneconomical, if not unaffordable. The following sections will explore the implications of this disastrous policy mix of high interest rates together with the relative absence of competition.

High Interest Rates and the Economics of a Short Time Horizon

All economists accept that high interest rates inhibit investment. Some, like those economists associated with the Federal Reserve Board, look with favor on this effect, assuming that high interest rates will only restrict the least efficient investments. Mainstream economists rarely realize that high interest rates will restrict replacement investment more than investment in general. I explored this subject in depth elsewhere (Perelman 1989).

While Keynes forcefully brought into public view the fallacy of trying to use interest rates to stimulate saving, no economist seemed to be capable of bringing the relationship between replacement investment and the interest rate to the attention of the world before George Terborgh, an economist employed by a machine tool builders association. Terborgh attempted to alert economists to the effect of the interest rate on replacement investment, but his work never attained the influence that Keynes's opus magnum enjoyed. Even today, few economists demonstrate an awareness of this consequence of high interest rates.

Terborgh went beyond merely showing how requiring investments to earn a higher rate of return inhibits investment. He demonstrated how high interest rates also distort the pattern of investment. I can illustrate this distortion by considering the speed with which firms expect to get their money back, known as the "payback period." James Malcomson has demonstrated that this shift in perspective is legitimate by proving mathematically that requiring an investment to earn a high rate of return is more or less equivalent to expecting an investment to repay the outlay in a short period of time (Malcolmson 1969, pp. 207–209; see also Magaziner and Reich 1981, pp. 110 and 160).

What could be wrong with creating a filter that tends to select only those investments that can repay themselves in a short time? Are not these just the sort of investments that will ensure that the economy will be run with the newest and most modern equipment?

Terborgh proved that concentrating on those investments with the highest rate of return has just the opposite effect of what you might think. Consider the following warning supplied by an industrial expert as the United States was just emerging from the Great Depression:

> The practice of expecting all new equipment to pay for itself out of savings in from one to three years, or at the very longest in five years, does not have the effect of keeping plants up to date. In fact, it often has exactly the opposite effect. . . .
>
> It is not unusual to find equipment 20–30 years old still in operation because new equipment will require from 7 to 9 years in which to pay for itself. This does not lead to low cost production. . . .
>
> The shorter the time allowed which the savings must pay for the cost of equipment, the more obsolete will be the equipment that it replaces. [Gaylord 1940, p. 52]

Terborgh, perhaps the most outspoken opponent of investing for a quick return, was even more dramatic. For Terborgh:

> A short pay-off period betokens a stodgy conservatism, willing to protect its aged mechanical assets by a Chinese wall. For the short pay-off requirement is a barrier of the most formidable character to the replacement of equipment. . . .

> The shorter the pay-off period required of the challenger, the larger the next-year advantage over the defender that is necessary for replacement. [Terborgh 1949, pp. 194–95]

Terborgh and Gaylord tried to turn their readers' attention to the fact that high interest rates discourage capital replacement. They warned that, behind the Chinese wall, to return to Terborgh's metaphor, an economy that places an excessive importance on a quick payback will gradually slip into uncompetitiveness because of a neglect of strategic investments that cannot pass the test of a high rate of return. I shall now pursue this argument in more detail.

The Economics of the Chinese Wall

Analyzing the economics of Terborgh's Chinese wall helps to throw light on an important dimension of the overall process of economic decline. The key to this problem is that the Chinese wall will be more of a hurdle for long-lived investments than for short-lived ones. Think in terms of rates of return on investment instead of payback periods. Now imagine two firms contemplating $100 investment projects that are to last two years. The first firm expects to earn at least 10 percent per year for its investments; the other, 3 percent. The first firm will reject all projects that fail to pay at least $121 after two years. The second will consider any project that returns more than $106 in two years.

For twenty-year investment projects, the disparity for the two firms is far greater. The first firm will not consider any projects that yield less than $673 in twenty years. The second needs a payoff of only $181 (Dertouzos et al. 1989, pp. 59–60). In effect, higher interest rates tend to discourage longer-term investment.

Now turn to a more concrete example to illustrate the difference between long-lived and short-lived investments more concretely. Suppose that you have an old factory that is rapidly becoming obsolete. When a machine breaks down—say a fuse burns out—fixing it can be very cheap, yet without the repair, the factory might not be able to produce anything at all.

The replacement of the fuse is a form of replacement investment, but it is very different than the reconstruction of an entire factory. It represents the minimization of replacement investment consistent with keeping the plant running.

In the case of the installation of the new fuse, even if the factory is relatively unprofitable, earning a mere $100 per year, replacing a ten-cent fuse would be a very profitable investment, representing an astounding 10,000 percent rate of return. Most people would jump at the opportunity to make comparable profits.

In contrast, building a new factory from the ground up would be very expensive. Certainly, it would earn a lower rate of return than 10,000 percent!

How does the example of the fuse square with the common-sense idea that an economy will be most efficient when all firms invest to earn the highest possible rate of return? In reality in a changing world, the strategy of investing for the highest immediate rate of return is flawed. In a competitive economy with continual technical change, a factory will become increasingly obsolete, eventually going bankrupt without replacement investment. The manager faces a paradox: a firm that can earn a rate of return of 10,000 percent on its investment (in a fuse) will eventually fall victim to new plants that earn considerably less on their investments.

Again, James Malcolmson's mathematics are relevant to the discussion. Just as the postwar economy began to peter out, he offered a theoretical proof of Terborgh's notion. He demonstrated mathematically that, when investors only put their money in investments that can repay themselves quickly—following the quick payback rule—they will invest less in long-lived capital goods than would occur in a theoretical economy in which investors had perfect certainty about the future. This distortion becomes more pronounced when capital depreciates at a high rate and when the discount rate is high (Malcolmson 1969).

In effect, keeping a patchwork of old equipment together with bailing wire and a rubber band only seems to be the most profitable use of capital. This illusion is a figment of the accountant's craft. In the previous example of our old and outdated plant, the rate of return on investment seemed to be high only because management saw the old capital as costless because its value had already been depreciated away (see Edwards 1955). Because profits are calculated on the basis of the sum of the investment outlay and current costs—and the investment outlay is nil where all the capital has been depreciated away—profits will often appear to be high in outdated operations, even when bankruptcy is near at hand. Obviously, something is amiss in this situation.

The theoretical analysis that lay behind Terborgh's warning about the economy disintegrating behind a Chinese wall dates back as far as the nineteenth-century economist, John Rae (1834; see also Perelman 1983, Ch. 6). Unfortunately, it was not widely understood then, any more than it was in Terborgh's day.

Certainly, Terborgh's metaphor did not sound very convincing to readers in the United States at the time. Despite the conventional wisdom that the economy would suffer a serious recession with the postwar demobilization, pent-up consumer demand carried the U.S. economy into the early phase of the postwar boom.

The excessive fears of recession gave way to an equally unjustified tide of confidence—if not overconfidence. After all, the United States had just won the war. Its economy was the strongest in the world. This confidence in the economy seemed to be warranted at the time. Indeed, the United States was about to enjoy two decades of unparalleled prosperity. Nobody basking in the prosperity of the Golden Age seemed to be in a mood to pay attention to Terborgh's sour note.

Today, Terborgh sounds more prescient. Because the conventional economists failed to take Terborgh's point into account, the Federal Reserve Board did not realize that raising the rate of interest would create a profound change in the type of investments that firms would undertake, encouraging firms to make short run incremental investments while discouraging them from making long run investments. The habit of expecting high rates of return compounded the decline.

This problem has an ironic overtone. The business community is in the habit of blaming much of the nation's woes on labor's expectation of a high wage. Supposedly, high wages discourage investment. In fact, as we shall see, high wages encourage needed investment, prompting firms to rebuild their factories rather than just to change blown-out fuses. High wages, in this sense, can foster competitiveness.

In contrast, the expectation of a high rate of return, rather than high wages, is a major cause of inadequate investment, just as Terborgh warned. This problem is especially severe in an economy where investors habitually expect to be able to make a quick payoff. Unfortunately, managers who attempt to act on the need to invest for the long run tend to be punished in the market place where stockholders want high dividends right away.

Managers soon learn that discretion is the better part of valor. Better to construct a Chinese wall than to build a strong economy.

The Costs of an Aging Capital Stock

Consider how the existence of an aging capital stock leads to a progressive deterioration of the economy. Anne Carter's study of the structure of industry in the United States throws some light on this phenomenon. She used a mathematical technique, known as input-output analysis, to analyze government data in order to estimate the technological characteristics for each industry in the United States in 1947.

Within this framework, Carter estimated the quantity of inputs that would have been required to produce the same goods and services that the United States produced in 1958, assuming that the economy would be using 1947 technology instead of the technology that was actually used in 1958. Although much technical change occurred during this period, according to Carter's calculations, the 1947 technology actually turned out to be superior to the 1958 technology in 14 of 76 sectors (Carter 1970, pp. 171–72).

What could explain the apparent superiority of 1947 to 1958 technologies? Ryuzo Sato and Rama Ramachandran hinted that the decline in efficiency might be related to the aging of the capital stock in these 14 industries. They noted that replacement in these 14 industries was less vigorous than in other industries (Sato and Ramachandran 1980, p. 1007). Consequently, much of the 1958 technology in these industries might simply be the 1947 technology after 11 years of operation.

What happens to an industry without significant capital renewal? Recall the earlier discussion about the nature of investment during an expansion: firms tend to install new investment alongside the old facilities instead of replacing existing investments with more efficient plant and equipment while the economy is growing. Consequently, after a long expansion, much obsolete plant and equipment operate, or at least stands ready to operate alongside modern operations. For example, in the U.S. automobile industry during the late 1960s, the productivity per employee of the top quarter plants was two and one-half times as productive as the lowest quarter (Melman 1983, p. 184; see also Hulten 1992, p. 965).

Such disparities in productivity became even more extreme during the 1970s as a result of the continued deferral of scrapping of capital goods. Over time, the absence of capital renewal operates as a drag on the economy.

For example, by the end of the Golden Age, as much as 50 percent of the railroad track in the United States is estimated to have been defective. Because of the sorry state of the railroad system, in 1976 trains had to reduce speed on more than 15 percent of the total track, sometimes to as low as ten miles per hour (Etzioni 1991, p. 384; citing United States Department of Transportation 1978, p. 15).

The aging of the capital stock helps to explain how the rate of productivity growth in the U.S. economy plummeted during the 1970s, despite widespread evidence that the rate of improvement in new capital goods had accelerated in recent decades

(McHugh and Lane 1987). In effect, the enormous accumulation of old and outdated technologies was so great that the addition of those modern technologies was unable to increase the average productivity by much.

Frank Gollop attempted to warn a congressional committee of the dangers of a long period of inadequate capital replacement. According to his description, "[T]hroughout New England, . . . you see very, very old buildings, but sometimes fairly modern equipment. The conveyor takes the product of this new equipment on floor one up to floor four. Why isn't there a new building?" (United States House of Representatives 1981, p. 471).

Gollop's question is not trivial. Frequently, different capital goods are organically related. The commitment of fixed capital to one technology often makes the adoption of later technologies less economical. More often than not, firms resist scrapping a wide range of plant and equipment to build a new "green field" operation. Instead, they tend to jerry-rig various vintages of plant and equipment together in a predictably inefficient manner. Sydney Pollard termed this practice, "patching" (Pollard 1982, p. 132).

The Economics of Patching

Now I want to return to Terborgh's paradox. Although investment in a temporary patch, such as a new fuse, seems to promise a high rate of return, continued patching will eventually result in a catastrophe. For example, Gollop noted the grave consequences that excessive reliance on patching will produce: "[I]t often postpones the introduction of new process technology. . . . Old equipment is kept in use, old methods are followed, and the advantages of new equipment and techniques are foregone with consequences for both future costs and product innovation" (House of Representatives 1981, p. 471).

Although patching is not unique to buildings, patching structures can create obvious inefficiencies over time as gradual changes in technology occur without much comparable alteration in the plant. In the end, the firm will be left saddled with an inefficient layout, which can disrupt the process of production (United States House of Representatives 1981, pp. 19 and 47; see also Schmenner 1980, p. 104).

Such cumulative obsolescence can occur relatively fast, even for structures. A survey of plants with more than 100,000 square feet in the North Central United States, which closed between 1 July 1977 and 1 September 1980, found that about half the idle plants had been constructed after 1947 (Institute of Science and Technology 1984, pp. 6–7). Of the 56 plant closings analyzed in the study, more than one-third had been demolished or abandoned or were still on the market.

Norman Robins, research manager of Inland Steel, pointed out some of the inefficiencies of working with an outmoded plant. He recalled:

> I was in the Fukuyama plant last year, and one of the most impressive things about it was the lack of truck and train traffic. Inland's plant, on the other hand, was begun in 1902 and undoubtedly was not conceived at that point in time to grow to the size that it has since become. Presently there are blast furnaces in two locations and a new one being built in a third location, steelmaking at four different locations and a great deal of material handling

> and transportation required to move steel through the finishing facilities. [Robins 1979; cited in Mueller 1984, p. 56]

Don Barnett, previously chief economist for the U.S. Iron and Steel Institute, offers another graphic example of the consequences of maintaining obsolete equipment in the steel industry. Although the Japanese steel industry was reputed to be the most efficient in the world, he calculated that the efficiency differential was limited to a small part of the overall production process. For most processes in manufacturing cold-rolled steel, the labor requirements were about equal in Japan and the United States, except for three specific processes: the production of coke, production of iron in blast furnaces, and the casting of semi-finished shapes according to his estimates for 1977 (United States Senate 1982, pp. 33–7).

In all three cases, the problem seems to be related to an aging capital stock. In the first two processes, the labor requirements were closely related to the age of the equipment utilized. In the third case, modern continuous casting technology is especially hard to install in the aged structures that are typical of the U.S. steel industry at the time of Barnett's study.

The dangers of protracted patching are so great that a number of economists have proposed that wartime destruction of a nation's capital stock ultimately gives that nation an economic advantage. I do not want to give the impression that wholesale scrapping of existing plant and equipment is necessarily an appropriate strategy. For example, in a later publication, Barnett, along with coauthor Lewis Schorsch, asserted that reluctance to invest by the steel industry might have been rational (Barnett and Schorsch 1983, p. 179). The authors contended that new greenfield plants would not significantly lower costs.

You should take the conclusion of Barnett and Schorsch with a grain of salt. Their calculations assume a much quicker write-off than is typical for the steel industry, which is notorious for its exceptional dependence on old capital (Barnett and Schorsch 1983; see also Magaziner and Reich 1981, pp. 110 and 156).

In any case, the broad picture about the aging of the capital stock in the United States does seem to be a matter of record. The United States began the postwar period with enormous advantages. As I discussed earlier, its major foreign competitors laid in ruins. The U.S. capital stock was relatively new. Business had clean balance sheets, relatively free from debt.

Under those conditions, a regime of military Keynesianism could show relatively good results for a comparatively long period of time—even in the absence of vigorous capital renewal. By the late 1960s or early 1970s, while Keynesian economists were basking in their apparent success in eradicating the business cycle, a facade of decades of prosperity had masked over the emerging weakness. In the absence of strong competitive forces, the capital stock aged and the economy weakened.

Investing for Rapid Payback During the Depression

The emphasis on a quick payback from investments predates the Federal Reserve Board's 1951 Accord with the U.S. Treasury Department. According to E. M. Richards, who was chief engineer for Republic Steel of Youngstown, Ohio, the high payoff rule was originally associated with the extreme capital rationing that became common during the Depression:

> This practice started about twenty years ago . . . but was not generally adopted by other industries until the beginning of 1932, when the extreme curtailment of all capital expenditures became almost imperative. Since then it seems to have become almost universal practice. . . .
>
> Under normal business conditions, it is felt that an improvement should pay for itself in three years or less. In a severe depression, where the conserving of cash is paramount, companies are inclined to work on the basis that an improvement must pay for itself in one year. [Richards 1933, p. 499]

In May 1930, Frederic V. Geier, a vice president of the Cincinnati Milling Machine Co. delivered a paper entitled, "Amortization of Machine Tools," to the Machinery Builders Society of New York, reporting on a questionnaire sent to 800 large U.S. manufacturing companies. He reported that none would buy equipment with a payback period of more than five years; 43 percent insisted on a two-year payback (Wagoner 1968, p. 134).

This anecdotal evidence is consistent with our limited knowledge of replacement practices during the Depression. Since the steel industry was especially uncompetitive, it felt less need than most industries to respond to competitive pressures throughout the Depression.

Note that Geier's survey includes 800 companies. This high number would include many medium-size firms. Since he merely reported the share of firms that gave a particular response, this survey probably reflects the practices of medium-size firms. Recall my earlier suggestion that in the early years of the Depression, large and relatively competitive companies, intent on maintaining their level of employment relatively steady, would have good reason to make extensive long-term investments in order to meet competition without cutting wages and employment. Richards's recollection, that the short-payback rule became common after 1932, squares with the previous discussion of the two stages of the Great Depression.

In conclusion, although the Great Depression created untold damage, it did succeed in inducing many businesses to modernize the stock of capital in the United States Unlike the steel industry, most had to adjust to strong competitive pressures during the Great Depression. Consequently, many firms weeded out much of their inefficient plant at the time.

On the Aging of the U.S. Capital Stock

During the Great Depression, almost all investment was replacement investment. After all, in the words of a report for the Committee on Recent Economic Change (1932), excess capacity stood "like masked batteries of machine guns waiting to lay down a new barrage of production whenever buying appears" (Gordon 1994, p. 36). The effect of this wave of replacement investment was dramatic. Alvin Hansen, one of the most influential American economists of the time, recalled:

> I have frequently called attention to the remarkable fact that of the 60 billion dollars of gross capital formation in business plant and equipment made in the decade 1931–1940,

> 90 percent was replacement investment. Yet even though there was relatively little net investment, the productive capacity of American industry was enormously greater at the end of the decade than it was in 1930. Better and more productive equipment was installed in place of the worn-out and discarded equipment. [Hansen 1949, p. 111]

Gustav Cassel, a famous Swedish economist, remarked that even the retrograde steel industry eventually began to modernize during the Depression: "The demolition of the old [blast] furnaces evidently took place to a larger extent in times of depression. During trade booms it was more often necessary to re-employ furnaces which had been abandoned during the depression, even if they were perhaps considered out-of-date" (Cassel 1932, p. 585). The cumulative effect of these replacements was enormous. By the end of the Great Depression, the capital stock in the United States was very new. Recall Staehle's estimate that, by 1939, one-half of all equipment that had existed in 1933 had been replaced (Staehle 1955, p. 127). In 1940, only 28 percent of all of the machine tools in the United States were ten years old or more (Noble 1984, p. 8). This state of affairs did not last long because of the absence of competitive pressures, and if Richards is correct, the increasing reliance on a short payback rule.

By 5 October 1955, *Business Week* lamented that 43 percent of all of the machine tools in the United States were ten years old or more (Phillips 1958, p. 149). The *Business Week* staff continued with its theme of the aging capital stock. Dexter Keezer, head of the McGraw-Hill Economics Department, told the *Detroit News* on 9 February 1956 that $125 billion, an amount equal to a quarter of the valuation of the existing capital stock, would be required to put the nation's industrial equipment in "first class condition" (Phillips 1958, p. 149). In 1958, Mr. Keezer returned to the subject again:

> [I]n terms of antiquity and degree of obsolescence . . . less than one third of it [has been produced] since 1950. Yet the years 1950–1958 comprise a period when rapidly changing technology has made older equipment obsolete. . . . [A] 1958 metal working tool is about 54 percent more productive than one that could be purchased in 1948. A combination of new freight cars and modern freight yard equipment can reduce operating costs up to 50 percent. New instruments that automatically direct the flow of chemical (or other raw material) processes can often reduce costs enough to pay back the cost of the controls in one year. These savings are rarely possible in older plants. [Keezer 1958, p. 23; cited in Baran and Sweezy 1966, p. 96]

Business Week was not alone. Angus Maddison speculated in 1964 that the U.S. capital stock had aged more than its European counterparts (Maddison 1964, p. 93).

The U.S. capital stock seems to have continued to age long after Keezer had issued his warning. Unfortunately, much of the data on the age of the capital stock is relatively impressionistic. The usual economic data bases do not help very much in getting a fix on the degree to which the capital stock consists of obsolete plant and equipment (see Miller 1990; Perelman 1989, p. 109). However, the machine tool sector provides more reliable information.

Seymour Melman noted that only 31 percent of machine tools in use in the United States in 1976–8 were ten years old or less (Melman 1983, p. 6). In the U.S. automobile industry in 1978, 76 percent of the machine tools were ten years old or even older (Melman 1983, p. 184).

An international comparison of the age of equipment in the machine tool sector of the major capitalist nations indicates that aging of capital goods still might be a greater problem in the United States than elsewhere.

The steel industry also showed dangerous signs of aging. Given the lack of competitiveness, which has characterized the U.S. steel industry, we should not be surprised about the aging of the capital stock in that industry. By 1979, 33 percent of steel production facilities were more than 20 years old; 12 percent dated back more than 30 years (Melman 1983, p. 189; see also Barnett and Schorsch 1983, esp. p. 91).

Although good data on the age of capital goods for the economy as a whole do not exist, the evidence is fairly conclusive that a smaller and smaller portion of investment funds have been devoted to the acquisition of long-lived capital goods. Economists usually attribute this phenomenon to high interest rates, the degree of economic uncertainty, or taxes. In contrast, I have been emphasizing the absence of strong competitive pressures during the Golden Age. Later I will turn to another strategic factor in the aging of the capital stock: low wages.

More recently, the concentration of investment in information processing has caused the age of capital equipment in the United States to fall very rapidly. This type

Table 5.1 Age Distribution of Machine Tools in the United States (percentages)

Year	*Under 10 Years Old*	*10–20 Years Old*	*More than 20 Years Old*
1963	36.0	43.3	20.7
1968	35.6	41.0	23.4
1973	32.9	38.7	38.4
1976–8	30.5	35.2	34.2

Source: National Machine Tool Builders Association 1982–1983, p. 259.

Table 5.2 International Distribution of Machine Tools Ages (percentages)

Country and Year	*Under 10 Years Old*	*10–20 Years Old*	*More than 20 Years Old*
US '76–'78	31	35	34
W. Germany '77	37	37	26
UK '76	39	37	24
Japan '73	61	21	18
France '74	37	33	30
Italy '75	42	30	28
Canada '78	47	35	18

Source: National Machine Tool Builders Association 1982–1983, p. 259.

of capital creates a different sort of problem: because this technology depreciates so rapidly, much of its value disappears in a couple of years, unlike a building, which can hold considerable value for decades on end.

The Short Payback Period and the Decline in U.S. Competitiveness

Some years ago, Martin Weingartner came to the defense of the quick payback rule (Weingartner 1969). He argued that a quick payback could make sense for the individual firm by providing flexibility. Just think of the risk that a firm faces when it commits itself to an expensive investment in a durable capital good, especially when that good has a purpose that is specific to the firm. In the words of John R. Hicks, "an entrepreneur by investing in fixed capital gives hostages to the future" (Hicks 1932, p. 183). Keynes himself amplified this point, speculating:

> Investment based on genuine long-term expectations is so difficult to-day as to be scarcely practicable. . . . Furthermore, an investor who proposes to ignore near-term market fluctuations needs greater resources for safety— . . . a further reason for the higher return [expected from long-term investment]. [Keynes 1936, p. 157]

Keynes's observation is important. Writing in the midst of the Great Depression, Keynes was pointing out that excessive risk (at that time stemming from the heightened competitive pressures of depression) would destroy the confidence required to allow firms to invest in expensive long-lived capital goods.

Consider the central problem that Keynes faced. Now think of the short payback rule as a partial withholding of investment. Under this rule, firms will only commit to those investments that promise an immediate return. Given the uncertainty of economic conditions, each firm might rationally refrain from investment, but when all firms choose to do so, the economy as a whole suffers. So too do the individual firms that refused to invest. Had they been able to work out a common agreement to invest, these same firms would have benefited.

My analysis of replacement investment takes the discussion one step beyond Keynes. I have already shown that, although the quick payback rule allows individual firms to maintain their flexibility, the short payback rule also condemns an economy to eventual uncompetitiveness, because the short payback rule effectively rules out extensive replacement investment.

Indeed, some authorities attributed Japan's economic success during the 1970s and 1980s to the low rate of return required to justify investment projects to be adopted in that nation (Leontief 1981; and Magaziner and Reich 1981, p. 160). For example, U.S. companies expect to earn their money back in 4.5 years; Japanese firms, in 12 (Magaziner and Reich 1981, p. 351). With the collapse of the Japanese bubble, financial pressures are causing the Japanese to behave comparably to their counterparts in the United States.

The reasoning of Bernard Butcher, vice president of Dow Chemical, illustrates the destructive logic behind the quick-payback rule. He explained why his firm avoids building new plants from the ground up by saying, "These incremental expansions don't cost much and *you don't have to be thinking in terms of three years from now*" (cited in Naj 1988; emphasis added).

The devastating consequences of this strategy of piecemeal investment might not appear for years. For example, although industrial buildings do not physically decay very fast, they become obsolete after an extended policy of minimum alterations in plant. After a sequence of several such changes, the poor layout of the plant will eventually undermine productivity (Institute of Science and Technology 1984, p. 19).

A short payoff criterion will be self-reinforcing. The restriction of long-lived investment eventually leads to lower profits although the rate of profit may be higher. For instance, in the earlier example of the replacement of a fuse you saw this combination of a relatively small total profit with a very high rate of profit. As the profit base shrinks, business will find itself with fewer funds than it would otherwise have. Given this shortage of investable funds, business will set its sights on a still shorter payoff period.

A short payback criterion may even encourage business to put off needed maintenance, the costs of which will not be felt until some time in the future. For example, a *Wall Street Journal* article concerning the takeover of Cities Service by Occidental Petroleum reported:

> [I]n the worksheds and offices nearby, Cities Service roughnecks talk of the changes. Spare-parts inventories and preventative maintenance have been reduced, they say. As aging underground pipes in the oil field's water injection system fail, geysers of water sometimes shoot 20 to 30 feet into the air. "We replace the section that's broken and wait for the next one to blow," a worker explains. [Rose 1984]

I am grateful to this anonymous worker for providing us with a telling metaphor for the economy as well as his workplace: We [try to] replace the section that's broken and wait for the next one to blow.

Crisis and Competition in the U.S. Economy

By the time the problems associated with an obsolete capital stock came to light, the crisis had already gathered substantial momentum. Unbeknownst to the leaders of the U.S. economy, fundamental forces were at work, which were altering economic relations. The balance of power between labor and capital, as well as the balance between the United States and the rest of the world, was shifting.

At first, the crisis appeared in the form of what seemed to be unique and seemingly unrelated incidents. Given this mind-set, relatively simple and direct measures seemed to be appropriate. For example, when the government finally recognized that foreign competition was becoming a serious problem during the 1970s, it merely attempted to moderate the force of foreign competition by stimulating the economy with monetary and fiscal policy.

Unfortunately, domestic business enjoyed only part of the benefits of this attempted stimulus. A substantial part of the demand stimulus encouraged the purchase of imported goods, providing foreign producers with an even stronger beachhead in the United States.

The government also attempted to blunt the force of foreign competition through trade agreements, but these too proved to be an inadequate solution. Nor could devaluing the dollar stem the tide of foreign imports.

The dramatic oil shocks that rocked the economy during the 1970s should have immediately jolted business into realizing the seriousness of its situation, but they did not. Once again, the leaders of the U.S. economy attributed economic ills to external events. The popular mood created an image of evil Arabs who were supposed to have caused much of problems of the times.

Eventually, in some quarters, the combination of the oil shock and the military defeat in Vietnam, together with the heightened political and economic militancy of the period, brought on a delayed recognition of the gravity of the new state of affairs. In this context, the hideous neologism, "deindustrialization," became a common term in economic and business circles. This expression did have the advantage of suggesting a generalized, although incompletely understood, force. It evoked a mood in which simple measures would no longer appear to be inadequate.

Still, most of the business community, as well as the economics profession, failed to realize the consequences of the decade-long blunting of the forces of competition. When the oil shock hit the U.S. economy, it revealed or at least it began to reveal, what could no longer be entirely hidden: a substantial portion of the capital stock in the United States consisted of obsolete plant and equipment, which could no longer add much to the productive potential of the economy.

Within this context, some economists noted that the oil shock literally wiped out the value of a substantial portion of the capital stock of the U.S. economy. They reasoned that many capital goods, installed during a period when low energy prices prevailed, were designed to take advantage of inexpensive energy (Baily 1981a; and 1981b; see also Gibbons 1984; and Klein 1983, p. 54). As energy prices rose, a good deal of this equipment suddenly became economically inefficient and its value diminished accordingly.

You might expect then, that newer capital goods, which would be optimized to take advantage of the cheap energy prices that prevailed at the time of their purchase, would be far more vulnerable to the energy shocks. Instead, firms that owned more recent vintages of capital goods performed much better during the energy shocks of 1973–4 and 1979–80 (Sakellaris 1997).

This outcome suggests that something more than energy efficiency was involved; that the newer equipment offered a more generalized form of efficiency. My interpretation is that before the Golden Age had come to an end in the late 1960s competition had been relatively light. In an environment, old and relatively obsolete capital goods could still turn a profit, albeit less than or modern equipment. Once the economy turned sour and competition stiffened, much of this updated capital became uneconomical (Perelman 1999).

Using a different line of reasoning, Ernst Berndt, an economist from MIT, also discounted the importance of the oil shock. He contended that, because energy prices represented a relatively small fraction of manufacturing costs, they should not be a major determinant of the level of productivity in the U.S. economy (Berndt 1980). Robert Pindyck and Julio Rotemberg challenged Berndt's reasoning (Pindyck and Rotemberg 1983). Naturally, I prefer my own explanation.

Still, I believe that we should always be careful about attributing the decline to any single cause. I remain convinced that the surge in oil prices in the 1970s was symptomatic of other far-reaching changes in the political economy of the United States and the rest of the world (Wolfe 1981; and Bowles, Gordon and Weisskopf 1983).

The Overhang of Phantom Capacity

Even the massive oil shock proved to be insufficient to cause management in many industries to recognize that its capital stock had become inappropriate until the crisis threatened to get out of hand. For example, Robert Gordon and John Veitch noted that the airlines did not ground their 707s until four years after the second oil shock (R. J. Gordon and Veitch 1984, p. 19).

As usual, the steel industry provided another excellent example of the inability of management to realize the importance of keeping the capital stock in good order. Some of its "dinosaur" steel plants took longer to retire than the relatively new 707s did (R. J. Gordon and Veitch 1984, p. 19). Conditions became so desperate in the steel industry that, despite its belated attempts at modernization, a substantial portion of the U.S. steel capacity still had to be scrapped. Between 1977 and 1984, the industry abandoned 25 million short tons of capacity—16 percent of the industry total (Anon. 1984).

Paul Davidson referred to such obsolete capital goods as "fossils of many past investment errors" (Davidson 1972, p. 135). I prefer the term, "phantom capacity," because these obsolete capital goods give an appearance of a productive potential that does not exist, except within an environment of lax competition.

The people of the U.S. economy paid a high price for the errors of their leaders, who imagined that they could build a solid economic structure on a foundation of old and obsolete capital stock. As I have been insisting, over time, absence of strong competitive forces led U.S. business to allow its capital stock to age almost without interruption until the Volcker recession, which briefly reinvigorated competition during the early 1980s.

The absence of competition explains this buildup of phantom capacity. As the economy took on more and more of this phantom capacity, it became more fragile and less able to withstand shocks. I referred to some evidence of this growing economic weakness in discussing the respective calculations of Tom Michl and Thomas Weisskopf, mentioned in the first chapter. Both suggested that the capital structure seemed to become less efficient as the decline progressed.

In general, however, when the government stands by and lets a depression or a recession occur, government leaders count on hard times to drive labor costs down. This recession was no exception. I have already noted the single-minded approach of Paul Volcker during this recession. Rather than trying to develop policies to make the economy as a whole competitive, he chose to single out labor as the culprit and to make workers bear the burden of adjustment. Indeed, the hard times of the 1980s seem unique, because of the extent to which labor was almost alone in absorbing the shocks to the system, while business was left relatively unscathed. This approach minimized the urgency to renew the capital stocks.

When an economy slows down, unemployment generally increases before most businesses feel the pinch. When the slowdown reaches that level, business typically calls upon the government to get the economy moving again. Despite the best efforts of the government, the economic slowdown typically accumulates enough momentum to make business become serious about efficiency, but by the time the Volcker recession hit, business was quite vulnerable.

Had the resulting Volcker recession been allowed to run its course, the results would have been disastrous for U.S. business as well for labor. The once robust U.S. economy had become relatively fragile. Most industries in the United States would have had difficulty surviving the competitive forces that are an integral part of a healthy capitalist economy. In effect, the more Keynesian policy succeeded in taming the business cycle, the weaker business became.

No one can tell how much of a shock business can absorb. Once the Volcker recession had done its job of taming labor, the government leaders realized the magnitude of the competitive forces that it unleashed. The Federal Reserve Board loosened its monetary controls and the Reagan administration began a more vigorous regimen of military Keynesianism than any of its predecessors had ever imagined.

The Elimination of Phantom Capacity

In contrast to the experience of the earlier downturns of the postwar period, the shock of the recession of the early 1980s was severe enough to force business to scrap considerable amounts of obsolete plant and equipment, even though the government moved to cut short this recession. This statement remains at the level of generality because accurate data on the scrapping and upgrading of installed plant and capital do not exist. Economists can only infer how much of this scrapped plant and equipment constituted phantom capacity and how much phantom capacity still remained.

One shred of evidence about the effectiveness of the recession in eliminating phantom capacity concerns a measure that economists use, called, "the capacity utilization ratio." This measure is intended to indicate how close an economy is operating to its optimal level of production. During the 1950s, annual capacity utilization rates exceeded 85 percent in five years; in the 1960s, six years; in the 1970s, only two years. In the first four years of the 1980s, annual capacity utilization failed even to reach 80 percent (President of the United States 1990, p. 351).

Although some of this trend may be explained by fluctuations in the business cycle, I am convinced that gradual accumulation of phantom capacity is a major cause of the declining frequency of peak-capacity utilization rates. Let me explain.

Economists theorize that production costs per unit decline as a firm increases its output up to a point near full capacity. This reduction of average costs occurs because fixed costs are spread over a larger output. Eventually, as output expands further, the firm reaches a point where average costs increase because the plant runs up against difficulties in expanding output. For example, it might have to pay overtime wages or machinery might break down from overuse.

I have been making the case that, beginning in the late 1960s, with the onset of the economic decline, competitive forces have been on the upswing due to greater foreign competition. If that hypothesis is correct, you might expect to find a diminution of the tendency for prices to rise well before the economy begins to reach full capacity. As we noted in the previous paragraph, as competition increases, prices should not begin to accelerate until the economy reaches a point near full capacity.

You should expect that, as competitive forces increase, the capacity utilization rate for any particular firm would have to come closer and closer to 100 percent before prices would begin to rise. Presumably, the same tendency would work for the economy as a whole. In fact, the opposite tendency seems to have been at work. During the mid- to late-1960s, prices did not begin to accelerate until the capacity utilization rates reached the mid-80s; in the mid- to late 1970s, by contrast, prices began to accelerate at only about 80 percent of capacity (Woodham 1984).

Why should prices begin to increase at a lower capacity utilization rate during the late 1970s? I attribute this trend to the existence of phantom capacity. During the early postwar period the government shielded the U.S. economy from strong competitive forces. Over time, more and more capital goods ceased to be very productive, falling into the category of phantom capacity. Management could prevent phantom capacity from becoming a larger share of the capital stock by a commitment to replacement investment, but throughout the postwar boom, management gave little indication that it had much of an inclination to maintain a healthy capital stock.

According to this scenario, a substantial portion of the reported capacity of the U.S. economy would constitute phantom capacity. Suppose that phantom capacity represented 5 percent more of the reported productive capacity in the 1970s than it did in the 1960s. I suspect that this number is a substantial underestimate. In that case, other things being equal, during the 1970s, prices would begin to rise when the capacity ratio stood at about 80 rather than as it did in the mid-1960s when a capacity ratio of near 85 was the point where prices would escalate.

If, however, competitive pressures were stronger in the 1970s than in the previous decade, the ability of business to raise prices must have receded. As a result, the same degree of cost pressure—as indicated by the capacity utilization rate—would have translated into a smaller increase in prices. This logic indicates why the increase in phantom capacity as a share of reported capacity might be even greater than 5 percent.

In the wake of the strong recession of the early 1980s, business scrapped considerable phantom capacity. From that time on, prices began to accelerate at a higher capacity utilization rate than before, although, of course, other explanations are possible (e.g., McElhattan 1985).

Creative Redeployment of Old Capital Goods

Although the continued inappropriate use of old capital goods in outmoded production processes results in a progressively weakening economy, society can still deploy older capital goods productively. Words of caution about the dangers of inappropriate use of capital goods remain tautological without any definition of the term, "inappropriate." Given the almost universal condemnation of the investment practices of the steel industry, the Barnett and Schorsch analysis of the futility of investing in modern steel industry capacity suggests how almost any hypothesis about capital obsolescence is subject to dispute.

Just because capital goods are old does not mean that they are obsolete—even though they may be obsolete for their current use. With care and ingenuity, innovative managers can turn old capital goods to new uses for which they are absolutely appropriate. Indeed, many old capital goods are quite suitable to uses for which they were not necessarily designed. For instance, in my own neighborhood, farmers commonly use old tractors, which they consider to be uneconomical for plowing and harvesting, to carry irrigation pipe.

Given this perspective, the fact that many of the plants studied in the survey of plants in the North Central United States stood idle or even no longer existed did not demonstrate the absolute absence of an economic potential. Instead, the underutilization of these plants stood as a bleak testimony to a failure to recognize that potential.

For example, one group of analysts combined a detailed architectural study of old industrial buildings with relevant economic analysis to investigate the possibility of alternative uses for such buildings. These analysts were not recommending patching. They were suggesting a complete redeployment of the factory. The same characteristics that made these buildings obsolete for their initial uses might make them ideal for others.

For example, some of these buildings were abandoned because they were multistoried, making them inappropriate for an assembly line process. Yet a multistoried layout can well suit the gravity feed and batch milling of pharmaceutical powders (Institute of Science and Technology 1984, p. 19). Indeed, many old industrial plants near Boston now house some of the prestigious high-technology companies that had sprung up in the region.

In fact, with enough ingenuity such plants can even successfully accommodate traditional smokestack industries. For instance, General Motors profitably renovated its half-century-old Baltimore manufacturing plant with a 1,500 person retrofit team using a winding roller-coaster-like assembly line (Zaslow 1985, p. 9c).

Where old capital stock becomes inappropriate for a particular use, specialists often cannibalize it, selling off individual components for alternative uses. Creative redeployment can significantly upgrade the value of capital stock even for sophisticated multinational corporations. For example, in 1961, "Lockheed Aircraft Corporation's outer space research [was] . . . depending to a large measure on a 52-ton generator that formerly fed power to the inner reaches of Boston's subway system" (*New York Times,* 3 June 1961; cited in Waterson 1964, p. 91). This 40-year-old generator, used "on such projects as Agena B satellite vehicles and advanced versions of Polaris ballistic missiles" cost about one-tenth as much as a new unit (Waterson 1964).

In an example of ingenuity that might seem obvious in retrospect, Williams Cos., the largest transporter of natural gas in the United States, converted some of its obsolete natural gas pipelines into an underground corridor for fiber-optic cable. In doing so, it saved itself the need to purchase right of way and dig trenches. In areas where the pipelines were still in use, the above-ground cable was still protected since contractors rightly feared disturbing the cable for fear of explosion. "The next best thing to being inside a pipeline," Mr. Williams says, "is to be alongside a pipeline" (Pentzinger 1988).

Williams Cos. eventually became the fourth-largest U.S. telecommunications service after AT&T, US Sprint, and MCI (Pentzinger 1988) before it sold these assets off to WorldCom in 1995. Now that its noncompete agreement has expired, it has embarked on a massive program to build a massive fiber-optic network alongside its pipelines.

In a humorous example of creative deployment, when British Telecom tried to scrap its ubiquitous and much-loved red, cast-iron pay-phone booths, public opposition was widespread. The company relented. It then came up with the idea of installing microtransmitters on top of each box to use them as sites for wireless base stations (Krause 2001).

When the military cut back on its aerospace expenditures in the 1980s, General Dynamics sold a wind tunnel to Micro Craft, which rents it for $900 an hour to businesses such as bicycle helmet designers and architects who wish to gauge air flows between buildings (Douglass 1994). In a more recent example, Iridium invested $5 billion in a satellite phone system. After only six months of operation, the company folded in what was one of the largest bankruptcies in history. The company proposed to crash its 70 satellites into the oceans, until the military breathed life into the system by offering a two-year $72 million contract (Chang 2000; Nelson 1998).

While this system has proved to be of limited use as a communication network, it seems to be ideal for measuring the electrical currents in the upper atmosphere. This information might seem to be esoteric, but the flow of charged particles from the sun fluctuates a great deal. When these auroral currents are active, they can disrupt radio signals, damage power grids and puff out the Earth's atmosphere to drag down satellites (Chang 2000). In the end, the investment in Iridium might well have turned out to be a good use of resources, even if the original investors may not have benefited.

These examples are worth mentioning only because this sort of creativity, which is common in a traditional environment, is so rare among modern corporations. With the exception of Iridium, they also serve as a reminder that references to the aging of the capital stock do not necessarily refer to a chronological age of plant and equipment. I have only been using the term "aging" as a shorthand expression to refer to the economic dangers that occur when an economy relies on old plant and equipment for *inappropriate* uses.

In conclusion, the utilization of old equipment may just as well signify creativity as an economic failure. The Lockheed generator and the Williams Cos. pipeline discussed above represents excellent examples of such creativity.

The Elimination of Productive Capacity

While you might applaud the elimination of phantom capacity, the cleansing of the economy comes at a high cost. To begin with, when firms shut down factories or go out of business altogether, innocent people bear much of the burden. Workers and their families suffer. So do people who count on the business of the plant or of the laid-off workers. To make matters worse, plant closings are typically clustered in economic crises, when the unemployed have the least opportunity of finding alternative employment.

Ideologues of laissez-faire counsel us to trust in market forces. People are supposed to believe that when the crises cut a swath across the economy, the efficient firm that falls will be the exception that proves the rule.

The evidence from the economic decline suggests a less sanguine understanding of crises, suggesting that crises are not precise affairs. Instead, they attack both sick and healthy firms (Perelman 1999).

During the early postwar period, prosperity in the United States was synonymous with manufacturing. As profits fell and wages rose during the decline, businesses throughout the United States began to shed much of their domestic manufacturing activity. This turn of events came as a shock. Few, if any observers, realized that the foundation of the manufacturing system in the United States was crumbling beneath their feet as the capital stock aged during the comforting prosperity of the Golden Age.

Part of the problem was the growing penetration of imports, but deindustrialization can occur in a closed economy without any exports or imports. Hanns-Joachim Rüstow has convincingly shown how easily competitive pressure can create a destructive wave that indiscriminately engulfs a growing portion of the capital stock.

The key to Rüstow's theory is the enormous productivity differentials between older and newer capital goods. Rüstow's data suggest that newer capital goods are commonly four to five times more productive than many of the older capital goods (Rüstow 1978, p. 413; Rüstow 1967).

Normal competitive processes can become so powerful that they force industry to lower prices. Some less efficient factories cannot continue at that price level. As firms scrap their weakest operations, they lay off workers. These unemployed workers have to reduce their consumption causing competition elsewhere to become even more intense. The least productive remaining operations in many industries then become vulnerable and eventually they too fall out of use, leaving another layer of unproductive plants ready to suffer the same fate. This downward momentum can create a cumulative downward spiral of prices and production leading toward an economic collapse.

Once this process begins, markets generate no inherent force to reverse the downward course, striking efficient as well as inefficient firms. Rüstow's model demonstrates why this pattern of deindustrialization is a normal outcome in a market economy.

The Big Question

Keep in mind that strong competitive pressures can produce two different outcomes. In a healthy economy, competition can lead to capital deepening. In a fragile economy, it can result in a cumulative deindustrialization.

Economists typically make confident pronouncements about the inevitability of one outcome or the other. In truth, economists lack any scientific method for determining whether or not a particular economy is destined to collapse.

Few examples of a thriving laissez-faire economy exist. A review of the course of British history indicates that from the seventeenth century on, a series of imperial conquests supported British development. Certainly, the leaders of the American Revolution believed so, as did Irish and Indian nationalists.

Once the United States freed itself from its bonds with England, it refused to trust its future to market forces. Instead, the government developed a system of tariffs, bounties, subsidies, and grants of monopolies to foster economic development. More importantly, the economic strength of the society rested on the products of slaves rather than a system of free markets.

The election of Andrew Jackson in 1828 represented a challenge to this system of government market controls. Much of the success of his administration came from his policy of expelling Native Americans from their land to make way for more cotton production. Once his vice president, Andrew Van Buren, succeeded him, the economy suffered a severe depression.

Within a couple of decades, the Republican party was formed with the intent of protecting domestic industries and artificially promoting development. The Civil War created strong demand for domestic products. With this stimulus, as well as the generous federal grants to the railroads, the economy flourished. Giant industrial developments emerged, employing the most modern technologies.

The productive capacity of these new industries eventually overwhelmed the purchasing capacity of the U.S. market by the 1870s. As cutthroat competition became commonplace, bankruptcy became commonplace as well. The resulting depression was as severe as the Great Depression of the 1930s.

Industry banded together to protect itself. Companies formed trusts, cartels, and monopolies. Government leaders as well as most economists applauded their efforts. In fact, the American Economic Association was founded in order to provide a platform for anti-laissez-faire ideas (Perelman 1996).

This mistrust of the market lasted until World War I broke out. After the war, the United States elected Calvin Coolidge, its most laissez-faire president since Andrew Jackson. Soon thereafter, the Great Depression swept across the economic landscape.

This brief survey of the history of market economies does not offer much hope that competitive forces will automatically restore economic health. Competitive forces can and do ravage the economy from time to time. Inevitably, this pattern will repeat itself.

CHAPTER 6

Finance, the Falling Rate of Profit and Economic Devastation

Finance and the Momentum of the Decline

In this chapter, I will investigate the contribution of financial forces to the economic decline. Although most economists hold that financial institutions are designed to channel resources into productive activities, they do not necessarily do so. Indeed, the financial pressures associated with a decline can lead investors to withhold their funds from productive activities while they dissipate their funds in investments of the most wasteful sort.

The ease of discovering opportunities for producing useful goods and services fluctuates with the state of the economy. While an economy prospers, opportunities for productive behavior may abound, but over time some capitalists, seeing how others have prospered, overreach themselves, getting caught up in their own overconfidence. Generally, after a boom has persisted for a while, more and more capitalists become swept up with this general feeling of optimism. Lacking strong competitive pressures, managers become profligate with the resources of their firms. They also foolishly sink money into losing projects. The cumulative effect of their eventual disappointments finally reverses the economic momentum, leading to a recession or even a depression.

In short, a boom provides some incentives to invest in productive activities. Over time, the same conditions that led to productive investment become perverted and lure people into wasteful economic practices.

A depression also leads capitalists in two different directions. Depressions create forces that can lead to renewed prosperity. For example, as an economy sinks lower and lower, capitalists' expectations eventually recede. Moreover, as bankruptcies wipe out old debts, business may have an easier time turning a profit. In addition, many capitalists require less profit to make them feel successful after a prolonged recession. Finally, during a depression, firms shed obsolete capital goods and find ways to modernize their methods of production.

As a result, many economists conclude that recessions naturally contain the seeds of their own recovery. Consequently, they should not last very long or become very severe. Some little accident, say a good harvest or a new invention, can swiftly turn their pessimism to optimism, sending the economy on an upward course once again.

Most people reject these economists' easy confidence about the self-correcting nature of a recession. The popular belief that war is necessary to shake an economy out of a depression reflects an intuitive understanding of the difficulty of reversing the downward momentum of an economic decline. Is this popular view something more than a common economic superstition or is it grounded in reality?

Keynes demonstrated long ago that popular opinion might be closer to the truth than conventional economic dogma. With a particular mix of conditions, an economy can easily become stuck in a stagnant position rather than responding with a round of capital renewal. We can take Keynes's argument one step further, arguing that the existing financial incentives may not just be insufficient to take the economy back to prosperity; they may actually reinforce the decline.

Once an economy begins a downward spiral, firms try to cut costs in ways that impair their long-term efficiency. Not all businesses respond to the depression by attempting to modernize their operations. Some merely try to milk their businesses of slight profits while letting them fall into disrepair. In addition, workers suffering long-term unemployment lose some of their job skills (see Cross 1987). If this unemployment persists too long, unemployed workers may become unemployable. This general deterioration of both the productive system and the workforce contribute to a further decline in the rate of profit. Consequently, once the economy falls into one of these perverse patterns of stagnation, then indeed only a dramatic event, such as a war, may be capable of moving the economy onto a different course.

I shall now discuss other ways in which an initial fall in the profit rate, which normally accompanies a recession, can contribute to a further decline in the rate of profit.

Falling Profits and Rising Interest Rates

Profits are the most important incentive in a market economy. A combination of forces responsible for setting the stage for the economic decline, including the prolonged absence of strong domestic competition, the aging of the capital stock, pressure of strong international competition, as well as the reaction to the poor treatment of labor, resulted in a precipitous fall in a rate of profit at the end of the Golden Age.

As the rate of profit falls, most capitalist agents must make adjustments. Unfortunately, these adjustments can exacerbate the decline. To begin with, a fall in the profit rate for the producers of goods and services makes them more dependent on credit. This situation allows financial interests to gain more power relative to the rest of the economy.

Some businesses, as well as individuals, will be highly indebted no matter what economic conditions are. In general, just before the end of a boom, the extent of this leveraging will be at a peak. Those entities need a certain cash flow in order to stay afloat because they have substantial outstanding obligations to service their debt. A temporary reduction in profits threatens to push the highly leveraged into bankruptcy.

The difference between their needed cash flow and their profits is not that great, even in good times. Such is the nature of leverage. Consequently, a small swing in profit margins suffices to cause these investors to suffer irreparable losses.

Since profits, in general, fall during recessions, most investments will earn less during these periods than they did when the economy was more prosperous. For these investors, the failure to earn as much profit as they expected triggers a desperate search for funds no matter how much interest they have to pay.

These investors reason that, if only they can weather the storm, the return of good times will allow them to salvage at least some of their positions. William Zeckendorf, a bankrupt real-estate tycoon, once expressed the spirit of such times, exclaiming: "I'd rather be alive at 30 percent interest than be dead at 3 percent" (cited in Gordon 1999, p. 287).

Even those firms that have adequate cash flow to service their debt feel financial pressure from a falling rate of profit because they ordinarily use some of their profits to finance investments. As the average rate of profit falls, many firms lack the financial resources to cover much of their investment needs.

Recall the earlier discussion in chapter 5, where I maintained that heavy competitive pressures force firms to renew their capital stocks in an effort to remain competitive. Not all firms have the option to renew their capital stock—only those with access to finance. During the severe recessions, banks generally restrict credit to their most important customers, fearing loss of their business when good times return. Consequently, the companies that tend to renew their capital when competition stiffens are the largest businesses. Once the economy begins to expand again, the competitive position of the small companies will be even more disadvantageous.

In short, firms are likely to become dependent on borrowed money when the rate of profit falls. To make matters worse, with the fall in the rate of profits, the availability of internally generated earnings—a major source of investment funds—shrinks. This rise in the demand for credit coinciding with a drop in the supply of available funds can put upward pressure on real interest rates.

All these forces taken together contribute to a perverse situation: as profits fall, investors can demand a higher rate of profit on their money. Because the cost of money is escalating, firms become disinclined to commit their funds to any project that fails to promise a high rate of return. All these forces combine to reinforce the conditions that made the rate of profit decline in the first place.

Profits are falling, yet investors are looking for a rate of profit that is so high that it precludes all but a very few capital investment projects. This situation parallels the earlier discussion of the paradox of the Chinese wall.

The Falling Rate of Profit and Increasing Risk

While the economy is prospering, many investors can find what seems to be relatively safe investment opportunities that promise to return what they consider to be a reasonable rate of profit. When the economy sinks into a recession and average profits fall, the majority of investors will typically become less optimistic. They will respond to the deteriorating economic conditions by cutting back on their investment and just holding on until the economy improves.

The highly leveraged investors discussed earlier will behave differently. We can compare these investors to a gambler at a racetrack. All but one race has been already run. Imagine that the gambler has run up substantial debts. The gambler needs to win a certain amount of money to pay off the bookie.

Suppose that the gambler feels relatively confident that a particular horse stands a good chance of winning. The gambler expects that placing money on that horse can provide the required amount of money if the horse wins the race. As the time of the race approaches, more and more people come to agree with the gambler. As the odds on the horse become more unfavorable, betting on it will no longer pay enough money to satisfy the gambler's need. The only way the gambler can win enough money will be to bet on a horse that seems to have a lesser chance of winning.

In this example, the gambler shifts to a more risky investment in order to meet the objective of a fixed reward objective. A minority of investors behaves similarly. These investors shift to more and more risky investments in order to maintain the possibility of obtaining the same level of rewards. Because of the greater level of risk these investors take on, a higher share of them will fail, intensifying a sense of economic desperation and fueling the decline.

The proportion of investors who behave like the unfortunate gambler will depend upon a complex set of circumstances. The greater the pressure of debt repayment, the more investors will feel compelled to opt for more risky investments. If this tendency to increase risk becomes common enough, it can compound the likelihood of an economic decline.

A falling rate of profit is associated with a parallel tendency toward increasingly speculative investments. After all, a successful speculation can bring rates of return many times more than what a firm can earn from building a new factory. Moreover, the investor can earn these speculative profits quickly rather than waiting for years as would be the case in building a factory. Consequently, as profits from traditional manufacturing declined, investors devoted an increasing share of the national resources to speculation rather than productive activities.

The dismantling of the regulatory system that used to protect the financial markets has reinforced the increasingly speculative nature of the U.S. economy. Next, I will discuss the financial system and the nature of that regulation.

What Banks Ideally Do

Take a moment to consider the role of banks. Most people think of banks as moneylenders, but they do not exactly lend money. At least, they do not generally lend their own money in the way a pure moneylender would. Instead banks lend other people's money, but they do not just lend other people's money. For the most part, they lend money that the banking system creates by giving credit to borrowers.

People give banks their money to let them lend it out because they believe that banks can place this money more effectively than they could do themselves. Although the banks charge a higher rate than they give their depositors, banks promise depositors a fixed return and the right to withdraw funds almost at will. Banks then lend these funds to borrowers for long periods of time—for years or even decades.

If some adversity should make the borrower unable to repay the loan, the bank still has to obligation to honor its debt to the depositors. In effect, the bank shields depositors against uncertainty. John Maynard Keynes summed up this arrangement, explaining that "the banking system . . . interposes its guarantee between its depositors who lend it money, and its borrowing customers to whom it loans money wherewith to finance the purchase of real assets" (Keynes 1931a, p. 151).

Ideally, banks can lower the risk of lending money out for the long term while borrowing for the short term because of bankers' superior efficiency in making loans. In part, bankers can be efficient because they enjoy economies of scale. They can pool large amounts of money together, simplifying the business of borrowing money. Instead of a giant borrower having to go to the trouble of soliciting a few dollars here and a few dollars there, it can go to a bank and borrow significant amounts of money on the spot.

Bankers' supposedly superior knowledge of the business of lending money represents a much more important source of potential efficiency in lending money. You or I might have difficulty in evaluating the creditworthiness of a corporate borrower. We might not understand the intricacies of its business or the soundness of its books. Bankers specialize in ferreting out crucial information about such subjects. Armed with this specialized knowledge, banks are willing to accept the risk of borrowing short and lending long.

Given the advantages that a bank enjoys in the business of lending funds, depositors are willing to deposit their money into the bank rather than lending money directly. The banks repay them a portion of the money that they earn from lending it out. The rest of the banks' earnings, over and above their operating expenses, provide the bank with profits.

In reality, the banking system is not quite as neat and tidy as this idealized version. To begin with, individual depositors have no guarantee that the bank is a safe place for their funds. If depositors lack the wherewithal to evaluate the creditworthiness of the typical corporation, how can depositors judge the creditworthiness of banks that lend money to such borrowers?

Bankers traditionally attempted to reassure their depositors by exuding a sense of trust. They would conduct their business in solid-looking buildings. They would dress conservatively. Still, the individual depositor would have no way of penetrating that facade until it was too late.

Once people come to doubt the efficiency of any particular banker, they will rush to withdraw their deposits. This reaction is dangerous for the bankers, because they have most of their money tied up in loans, which will not be repaid until sometime in the future. Relatively few depositors can quickly strip the bank of all of its cash.

If a run hits a single bank, it can borrow from other banks to tide it over until confidence returns. When people become skeptical about the health of banks in general, such temporary borrowing becomes impossible. The history of the nineteenth and early twentieth century is replete with frequent runs on the banking system.

Even the Federal Reserve System, which was supposedly capable of supplying banks with sufficient funds to stop banking panics, was unable to stem the tide when it faced its first serious panic during the Great Depression. The government had to close the banking system to keep depositors from withdrawing all their funds.

On the Regulation of the Financial System

Once the Great Depression set off a wave of bank runs, the government saw no alternative to insuring the deposits of small investors as part of the Glass-Steagall Banking Act of 1933. In addition, the Federal Reserve Code contained a provision, known as Regulation Q, which prohibited banks from offering interest on checking accounts and limited the rate of interest paid on savings deposits. Savings and loans could pay a slight premium over what banks could offer under Regulation Q. Typically, economists regarded Regulation Q as an unnecessary intrusion into the banking system, although it made sound sense.

Even Adam Smith, the patron saint of laissez-faire—certainly an economist who was not known to favor active intervention in economic affairs—observed more than two centuries ago, that putting a ceiling on interest rates could benefit society. He explained:

> If the legal rate of interest . . . was fixed so high as eight or ten per cent., the greater part of the money which was to be lent, would be lent to prodigals or projectors, who alone would be willing to give this high interest. Sober people, who will give for the use of money no more than a part of what they are likely to make by the use of it, would not venture into the competition. A great part of the capital of the country would thus be kept out of the hands which were most likely to make a profitable and advantageous use of it, and thrown into those which were most likely to waste and destroy it. When the legal rate of interest . . . is fixed but a very little above the market rate, sober people are universally preferred, as borrowers, to prodigals and projectors. [Smith 1776, II.iv.15, p. 357]

In other words, when interest rates are high, the people who borrow are likely to be those who are speculating on risky projects.

More recently, Joseph Stiglitz and Andrew Weiss added a valuable institutional insight to Smith's observation. They noted that selling credit differs from selling other goods. When merchants sell shoes, they expect to be paid in full. In contrast, banks do not receive their payments until a later time once the debt becomes due. As a result, they face a risk of default. Lacking full information about the credit-worthiness of their potential customers, banks fall back on a variety of screening devices, including the interest rate that consumers are willing to pay.

The logic of the insight of Stiglitz and Weiss flows from the realization that the borrower who is willing to pay an extremely high interest rate typically has a greater than average chance of being a poor risk (Stiglitz and Weiss 1981). Stiglitz has also observed that a higher interest rate can actually encourage a borrower to take more risks (Stiglitz 1987, p. 18).

In light of this situation, Stiglitz and Weiss, writing during the dawn of financial deregulation, when interest rate regulations were still more or less in effect, assumed that banks would not necessarily lend to those who offered to pay the highest return. Instead, they would ration credit to the most creditworthy customers, thereby protecting the integrity of the banking system.

Dr. Smith was correct in his analysis, but Regulation Q was incapable of maintaining the soundness of the banking system since banks soon found a way to circumvent it. After all, from the banker's perspective, Regulation Q limited the growth potential of the banks because other borrowers, especially the government, generally paid higher rates of interest.

Indeed, large depositors could usually earn more interest buying Treasury bills than they could by depositing their money in banks. Unfortunately, as competition in the banking sector heated up, forcing banks to pay more for their money, banks ceased to behave in line with the theories of Stiglitz and Weiss. Instead, they actively sought out those who would pay the highest rates. The results were predictably disastrous.

The Circumvention of Bank Regulation

During the 1960 recession, as the rate on Treasury bills fell, the banks saw an opening. Since the rewards from purchasing government securities were no longer so much higher than placing money in banks, the large banks tried to entice major corporations and other large depositors to place their money in the banks. Toward this end, First National City Bank invented the Certificate of Deposit. The bank offered to pay between a quarter and a half a percent above the going Treasury bill rate. Moreover, it created a market in which corporations could buy and sell their CDs if ever they needed cash in a hurry (Mayer 1974, p. 200).

Soon, CDs were everywhere. During the early 1960s, California thrifts attempted to attract as much money as possible to meet the demands of the California building boom by offering interest rates that were a tad higher than the going rate. They even advertised these rates in East Coast newspapers.

The banks and thrifts did not seem to realize that these moves, which were profitable in the short run, eventually would make them more vulnerable. Under an effective Regulation Q, banks would mostly serve depositors who were satisfied with low rates of return. These depositors would not quickly shift their funds around in search of the highest interest rate. Such depositors would offer banks a stable base.

Remember that this stable base was important because banks have to commit funds for a long period of time. If depositors remove even a relatively small portion of their funds from a bank, they can drive it to insolvency. Once banks come to depend upon interest-sensitive depositors, they have to continue to offer a high rate of return to keep their depositors.

This need to pay a high interest rate requires the banks to earn a high rate of profit, in effect transforming them from conservative institutions into something resembling Adam Smith's prodigals and projectors. The evidence of this vulnerability was not long coming.

Remember that the CDs were attractive, only because the Treasury bill rate was depressed in 1960. As Treasury bill rates rose between 1962 and 1966, the Fed systematically raised the maximum interest rates that banks could pay under Regulation Q so that the CD rates remained under the maximum that Regulation Q permitted. By 1966, when the Vietnam War had begun to fuel inflation, which raised the rate of interest on Treasury bills well over the permitted rates (Mayer 1990, pp. 34–35).

California savings and loan banks soon learned about the danger of depending on hot money. In 1966, Franklin National Bank began advertising CDs of $1,000 denominations, carrying an interest rate higher than the legal maximum on savings accounts. Within a month, Franklin had sold $420 million worth of CDs. So much of this money came from the California thrifts that these withdrawals nearly ruined these thrifts (Mayer 1990, p. 204). Once the crisis passed, the industry forgot any lessons that it might have learned from the experience.

Franklin National Bank, however, soon returned to the vortex of financial instability (see Wolfson 1988). In 1972, Fasco International purchased 21.6 percent of Franklin, bringing the bank into the vast and complex international empire of Michele Sindona, a shadowy figure with ties to the Vatican, International intelligence agencies, and right-wing extremists. Sindona had looted about $15 million from Franklin, according to a criminal indictment (Wolfson 1988, p. 96).

Under Sindona's direction, Franklin suffered significant losses speculating in bonds and foreign currencies in 1973 (Wolfson 1988, pp. 76–8). By May 1974, national bank examiners criticized the soundness of loans equivalent to 62 percent of its total capital (Spero 1980, pp. 71–72). Soon thereafter, Franklin, once the twentieth largest bank in the U.S., became insolvent.

The regulators of the financial system failed to learn the lesson of the failure of Franklin National Bank. To begin with, Franklin could appear to be sound, even after it had experienced crippling losses, because it posted fictitious profits on transactions with some of Sindona's European banks (Spero 1980, pp. 81–82). In addition, because of Franklin's dependence on volatile, interest-sensitive accounts, it had an inducement to invest in speculative transactions that could turn a quick profit.

The dealings of the Franklin National Bank were atypical at the time. Nonetheless, the rest of the banking system was coming to resemble Franklin National Bank more and more. For example, at the end of World War II, banks in the United States were extraordinarily healthy. Banks primarily held relatively riskless Treasury bills. By 1984, the commercial banks held only 13.0 percent in government financial assets and an additional 30.0 percent in the assets of other U.S. government agencies (Minsky 1986, pp. 71 and 74).

The dangers of increased risk were even more extreme for the savings and loan industry. Although Franklin disappeared, the savings and loan problems did not. Depositors continued to search for the highest possible returns. Withdrawals threatened savings and loan banks because they had frequently committed themselves to 30-year mortgage loans. Many competed by offering higher interest rates on CDs of their own. This strategy was self-defeating since they could not increase the rates on their existing home loans.

Although the original purpose of the savings and loan banks was to promote home ownership, the government responded to their difficulties by allowing them to engage in the same sort of speculative practices that bankrupted Franklin. Government officials reasoned that only the higher profits from risky behavior could save the industry.

The lifting of regulatory oversight opened the door to a torrent of fraud and financial abuses. With the collapse of the markets for junk-bonds and commercial real estate, the thrift industry approached bankruptcy. The rest of society could not avoid the maelstrom that the savings and loan crisis caused. So-called zombie thrifts, which were on the verge of bankruptcy, offered incredibly high rates for CDs to stave off their inevitable fate. This practice significantly raised interest rates. For example, one study estimated in 1990 the federal government had to spend an extra $73 to $266 billion just to compete for funds with the zombies (Shoven, Smart, and Waldfogel 1992).

The eventual costs of the fiasco came to almost $500 billion (see U.S. General Accounting Office 1996b). Because of the vast sums of money that the bailout consumed, the government curtailed spending on health, education, and infrastructure.

New Dimensions to Speculation

The speculative investments of banks suggest a further dimension to the undermining of the regulatory structure of the banks. The Federal Reserve requires that banks keep a specified portion of their loans in reserves, either as cash or as deposits with the Federal Reserve Bank. For the banks, these reserves partially represent a loss of earning potential. Yes, they know that they need to set aside some money to take care of a few unusual withdrawals, but not nearly as much money as the Federal Reserve requires.

When banks get access to money through CDs, they do not have to set aside reserves the way they do with ordinary deposits. They have developed other, even more elaborate ways of raising money without any reserve requirements. When banks speculate in such risky investments with volatile money, the financial system becomes fragile.

Even more dangerously, banks can take on speculative risks without the need to have immediate access to cash by taking on commitments that do not appear on their balance sheets. Many banks do not have to hold reserves to tide them over if this sort of speculation turns sour.

For example, Franklin speculated on the fall of the British pound, the French franc, and other foreign currencies relative to the dollar. When the dollar fell instead during the first quarter of 1974, Franklin lost $33 million (Spero 1980, p. 86). Today, Franklin's dealings are small potatoes. Consider the example of Citicorp. At the end of 1990, it held $1.2 trillion worth of outstanding contracts in futures, forwards, swaps, and options on interest rates and foreign exchange alone, up from $980 billion the previous year, and 6 times its assets. Its credit risk exposure on these contracts was $24.5 billion, up from $14.1 billion, the year before (Anon. 1991a). Citicorp was already strained by its holdings of bad loans. Had the company experienced a run of bad luck in those speculative holdings, its net worth could quickly have turned negative. Although Citicorp's speculative banking ventures did not pan out, it struck a gold mine in its credit card business, which carried it over the hump (Manning 2000).

In this speculative environment, small events can push a couple of banks into insolvency, weakening confidence in the others, leading ultimately to a panic of the first order. In the ensuing melee, the public at large, rather than the banking system, carries most of the burden.

Finance and the Decline of U.S. Manufacturing

These financial excesses did not arise spontaneously. The fall in the rate of profit was the driving force in the financial revolution, which, in turn, reinforced the effect of the falling rate of profit by accentuating the insidious process of deindustrialization.

First, let me put the financial system into perspective. During the Golden Age, most individual investors favored blue chip stocks, which they held for long-term appreciation. Similarly, institutional investors behaved conservatively, perhaps because of the lingering memories of the aftermath of the excess that preceded the Great Depression. As late as 1952, commercial banks, mutual savings banks, and insurance companies held over 69 percent of all outstanding U.S. corporate bonds. Life insurance companies alone held 58 percent of all outstanding U.S. bonds, but only 1.5 percent of U.S. corporate stocks (Lazonick 1989; citing Goldsmith 1958, pp. 224–25).

Over time, institutional investors became the dominant traders in the U.S. stock exchange. They began to hold an increasing share of the nation's equities. As profits from industrial activity declined, institutional investors attempted gain an edge by quickly shifting their funds around in terms of short-term profits. Since they turned their holdings over so quickly, institutional investors accounted for a disproportional amount of stock purchases and sales.

In 1960, institutional investors owned 17.2 percent of the value of the shares and accounted for 24.3 percent of the volume of trading on the New York Stock Exchange. After 1960, these powerful financial institutions became more aggressive. Mutual funds led the search for higher yields. Rather than hold their funds in a stock that promised significant long-term growth, the mutual funds attempted to shift their funds about rapidly in anticipation of short-term movements in the market. Their initial success led pension funds to follow a similar strategy.

By 1982, institutional investors owned 24.3 percent of the value of all shares and accounted for 83.8 percent of the volume of trading. The turnover of shares on the New York Stock Exchange rose from 12 percent in 1960 to 54 percent in 1985. Trades of over 10,000 shares increased from 3 percent in 1965 to 52 percent in 1985 (Lazonick 1989; citing Light and Perold 1987, p. 108).

This new breed of institutional investor is too impatient to wait for long-lived capital investments to turn a profit. *Business Week* published a survey of the average turnover time for stocks. The average share in Priceline.com was sold every four days. Even the most stable stock that it found, General Electric, turned over in less than three years (Byrne 1999).

If, at any time, management fails to show a healthy rate of return, these money managers can threaten to organize a corporate takeover to oust management. Corporate executives, fearful of this threat, must struggle to keep profits high. Andrew Sigler, chief executive officer of Champion International and chair of the Business Roundtable's Corporate-Responsibility Task Force, dramatically explained how this change in the investment climate affected corporate investment strategy. He declared: "The problem is deciding who the hell the corporation is responsible to. I can't ask my shareholders what they want. 75 percent of Champion is owned by institutions, and my shareholders change so fast I don't even know who they are. We're owned by a bunch of index funds. Who votes for an index fund? Some damn mathematical formula votes your stock" (cited in Sloan 1985). The late Hyman Minsky went so far as to identify this stage of development, money-manager capitalism (Minsky 1990).

Even when managers realize that longer-term investment projects are in the best interest of the company, they understood that the stock market would only reward those who made the next quarterly earnings report as favorable as possible. Managers who invested for the long term could cause a decline in their company's stock and even perhaps their own dismissal.

Within this environment, managers cannot invest in the sort of long run project that could improve the economic health. As a result, profits eventually suffer, intensifying the pressure for more short-term financial gains.

The Falling Rate of Profit and Capital Renewal

Earlier, I discussed how strong competitive pressures are essential in inducing firms to renew their capital. Falling profits inevitably accompany increased competition, yet, here I am making the case that falling profits have undermined competitiveness.

You should not be surprised at this apparent paradox. Throughout this book I have shown how economic categories such as competition and depression have a contradictory nature. The notion of profits is also fraught with contradictions, preventing one from making any simplistic pronouncements about the influence of the falling rate of profits.

Some whole industries will indeed wither under the strain of intense competition and financial pressure. Some firms will rise to the challenge, developing improved competitive practices.

Generalizations about how firms will respond to the decline are difficult, but the broad outlines of one change in the financial structure makes optimistic outcomes less likely. During the Great Depression, many banks viewed their relations with their clients as long-term affairs. Doing what they could to help their clients—at least their most important clients—through the hard times would ensure profitable future business relation once the depression had past.

Within the current financial structure, the relationship between firms and their creditors is decidedly short-term. Banks no longer have any reason to give special treatment to individual businesses. Even if the current managers would feel a sense of gratitude, management changes so fast that this good will can become worthless in short order.

As a result, banks now aim for the highest possible short run return. Consequently, they are less likely to finance renewal of the capital stock. In addition, many firms are too saddled with debt to be able to consider investing for the long term.

Corporate management, stymied from investing in their firm's future, often joined with the institutional investors in actively seeking quick financial returns. They found that they could acquire assets cheaper by buying other firms than by investing in their own productive capacity.

The government undermined capital renewal by abandoning all pretense of an effective antitrust policy as part of its fanatical pursuit of deregulation. As a result, firms became virtually free to speculate in the takeovers of other firms rather than making their own lines of business more efficient. In this sense, industry began to resemble a division of the financial sector.

Douglas Dowd pointed out a riveting statistical tendency that suggests an explanation of the increasingly financial emphasis of the economy: "Corporate profits were more than ten times as high as net interest in 1949; more than five times in 1959; more than two-and-half times in 1969; a quarter more in 1979; in 1989 and since corporate profits have been less than net interest" (Dowd 2000, p. 183).

The Inefficiency of Corporate Takeovers and Leveraged Buyouts

During the 1980s, an immense wave of corporate takeovers swept across Wall Street. Of the 100 largest mergers and acquisitions on record prior to 1984, 65 occurred between 1981 and 1983 compared to only 11 before 1979. During 1981–84, 45 takeovers involved more than $1 billion (Varian 1988, p. 3).

In the 1990s, billion dollar takeovers became almost commonplace. Mergers amounted to a record of about $3.48 trillion in 2000, but takeovers in the 1980s remained unique in one respect. Time after time, a small group of takeover specialists accumulated fabulous fortunes through leveraged buyouts. The takeover artist would offer stockholders much more money than their stock was worth on the open market. This offer would be contingent on the firm selling high-yield junk-bonds to finance the purchase. After the completion of the deal, the typical firm would be left with a huge debt (see Bruck 1989).

For a while some of the largest firms were immune from the pressures of money manager capitalism. Lacking either the confidence or the pressure to invest in productive projects, they would sit on large accumulations of cash, waiting for the right opportunity. For example, the editors of *Business Week,* in commenting on a 1985 story about Exxon's massive cash surplus, worried, "The sight of so many companies sitting on bags of cash they cannot find profitable use for raises some distressing questions about the vitality of the U.S. economy" (Cited in Magdoff and Sweezy 1985, p. 11).

Business Week was justified in its concerns. Why, with so many unmet needs in society, could the major corporations not find anything useful to do with their cash hoards?

Eventually, the takeover movement reached such proportions that even managers of the largest corporations took measures to restructure their corporation in much the same way that the takeover would have done by buying back stock and taking on debt.

Michael Jensen proposed that this accumulation of debt was in the public interest. According to his argument, the paid managers who normally run large corporations do not have their stockholders' interest at heart. They use the corporate resources for their own personal aggrandizement. Given their comfortable situation, without some outside pressure, they fail to take measures that would make the firm efficient. For Jensen, "the debt created in a hostile takeover (or takeover defense)" means "that it cannot continue to exist in its old form" because it "creates the crisis to motivate cuts" (Jensen 1988, p. 30).

In other words, the takeover would push the firm to the edge. The firm would then have to struggle to earn enough cash to cover its debt payments. Should it fail to do so, creditors would compel the firm to declare bankruptcy. Given this necessity to be efficient, managers would rise to the challenge, making the firm competitive.

Jensen's theory has some merit. Certainly, corporate management in the United States had a poor record on many counts. Managers often used corporate resources to finance corporate jets, boats and limousines, elegant offices, and corporate retreats that did little to contribute to corporate efficiency. In this respect, Jensen is no doubt correct.

The question remains, did the corporate restructuring make management more efficient? To begin with, consider Jensen's notion that the creation of a crisis atmosphere will be conducive to greater productivity. As Amitai Etzioni noted, "A large body of research shows that under stress people's decision-making becomes less rational" (Etzioni 1988, p. 73).

Consider the case of Exxon again. After all, Jensen often used the petroleum industry as his prime example of the benefits of restructuring. In this case, he might have difficulty reconciling his theory with the actual outcome (Jensen 1988, p. 33). According to a writer for the *Wall Street Journal,* Exxon's workers were stretched thin, but not necessarily in a manner that was conducive to efficiency. Several fires broke out in the company's largest refinery in Baytown, Texas because Exxon was too tight-fisted when it came to winterizing pipes against freezing, even though they were warned beforehand (Sullivan 1990).

In fairness, I should note that some of Exxon's negligence predated its restructuring. In New York City, where a pipeline ruptured, local and federal officials charged that Exxon was negligent and irresponsible in ignoring a faulty leak detection system for 12 years (Welles 1990).

Many observers believe that restructuring was ultimately responsible for Exxon's most famous mishap, the tragic oil spill of the Exxon Valdez. Alaskan officials allege that Exxon's systems for training and monitoring employees were ineffectual. The company's own tanker captains complained of heavy crew cutbacks and other unsafe operating procedures. Numerous former Exxon executives claim that Rawl's cost cutting system, as one put it, "created an accident prone system" (Welles 1990, p. 75).

The Unproductive Labor Dissipated in Corporate Takeovers

This wave of corporate takeovers did not come cheap. For example, in 1984, the three investment banking houses involved in the Gulf-Socal merger earned a total of $63 million for their efforts (see DuBoff and Herman 1989, p. 123). The *Wall Street Journal* predicted that, if Texaco's $9.89 bid for Getty Oil would be successful, four investment-banking firms would be expected to share a record $47.1 million in fees. The largest single fee was expected to go to Kidder, Peabody, and Co., which was slated to receive $15 million for advising the Sarah C. Getty Trust. Salomon Brothers, which declined to confirm it, was slated to receive a reported $4 million. First Boston was Texaco's advisor. For 79 hours work, it was to receive $10 million or $126,582 an hour (Anon. 1983).

As time went on, the merger fees grew apace. By 1988, Campeau's $6.6 billion bid for Federated Department Stores produced $200 million in fees. "It's called the Wall Street Fair Employment Act of 1988," said a lawyer involved in the deal (DuBoff and Herman 1983, p. 123; citing Labaton 1988).

Lawyers have also fared quite well from the boom in corporate takeovers. The *Wall Street Journal* recently reported that one in nine U.S. lawyers was a millionaire in 1986 (see Gray 1986). Of course, not all these lawyers owed their wealth to takeovers, but a good number did. For example, the firm of Wachtell Lipton earned $20 million in just two weeks advising Kraft on its $12.9 billion attempt to take over Philip Morris Cos. This works out to about $5,000 an hour assuming virtual round-the-clock work by a couple of dozen lawyers (Adler and Cohen 1988).

Individuals who handled the finances of takeovers also prospered. In 1987, over and above his normal salary and the millions and millions of dollars that he earned using inside information for trading on his own account, Michael Milken received a bonus from Drexel Burnham Lambert amounting to an astounding $550 million (Stewart 1991, p. 208). Some commentators noted that this bonus exceeded the profits that McDonald's, the 65th largest corporation in the U.S., earned at the time (Abelson 1989). Such huge merger fees naturally induced financial agents to go to great lengths to construct mergers and takeovers.

Young people understood that even lesser figures in the financial world still earned astronomical amounts. For example, a well-placed Wall Street employee could make several hundred thousand dollars within a couple of years after graduating from college. In light of the enormous amounts of money changing hands, highly educated, young people directed their energies and ambitions to participating in speculative activities rather than productive activities. For example, 40 percent of the 1986 graduating class of Yale applied for a job at First Boston Co. (Lewis 1989, p. 24)!

Of course, we need to give our youth more constructive incentives. Countries with a high share of engineering college majors grew faster than those who train their youth as lawyers and financial experts (Murphy, Shleifer, and Vishny 1991).

Financial Capital Versus Industrial Capital

Even where financial restructuring was not an issue, the need to raise profits enough to satisfy money managers proved to be another important factor in promoting deindustrialization. In this environment, when U.S. firms attempted to turn their cash to a profitable use, more often than not they neglected productive investment, thereby reinforcing the decline.

Rather than attempting to make plants more productive, managers often took the easy road of shutting them down. Indeed, a good deal of anecdotal evidence suggests that a number of plant closings were related to what seems to be a sharp increase in the expected rate of return on existing plant and equipment, rather than a competitive crisis. For example, during a prenegotiation meeting between General Electric and the representatives of workers at its Fort Edward capacitor facility in 1982, "local management announced that while heretofore 9 percent profit had been considered satisfactory, GE nationally was then insisting that all of its facilities show at least a 12 percent profit margin in the future" (Bloch 1983, p. 30).

David Broderick, chairman of the board of United States Steel, told a Pittsburgh audience that the huge Dorothy Six operation would not be worth saving unless it were able to earn 18 to 20 percent profit each year (Morse 1985, p. 175). Barry Bluestone and Bennett Harrison cite a similar example:

> The Herkimer [New York] plant, producing library furniture, had been acquired by Sperry Rand in 1955. The plant had made a profit every year except one through the next two decades, and yet Sperry Rand decided to close the plant [in part because it] was not yielding a 22 percent profit on invested capital. That was the standard used by this conglomerate management in determining an acceptable rate of return on its investments. [Bluestone and Harrison 1982, p. 151]

The 1977 annual report of Genesco, Inc. provides further evidence of increased corporate profit requirements: "In all cases, the ultimate consideration was: 'Does this operation have the potential to produce a 25 percent pre-tax return on assets employed'" (cited in Bluestone and Harrison 1982, p. 151).

The behavior of Genesco and Sperry Rand might increase measured profits and even productivity. By eliminating all but the most profitable operations, the average performance of the residual divisions may be higher. Indeed, deindustrialization has raised measured productivity. In fact, the 10 percent decline in manufacturing employment accounted for an estimated 36 percent in the recorded improvement in labor productivity in the U.S. between 1979 and 1986 (Dertouzos et al. 1989, p. 31).

Like the quick payback rule, deindustrialization might raise the profit rate while depressing total profits if the process were confined to a single country. Because firms such as General Electric can shift their operations from one economy to another, they need not experience any adverse effects from deindustrialization. For the multinational sector, profits as well as profit rates can increase.

No wonder deindustrialization seems to be a fact of life in the midst of the economic decline! The long run consequences of this pattern of cutting back investment altogether in the face of stepped up competitive pressures rather than investing in capital deepening presents a frightful prospect for the U.S. economy. If too many firms begin to follow the same strategy, they can create a cumulative downturn, which can hurt just about every business.

A third factor also increased the momentum of deindustrialization. Many firms threaten to shut down in an effort to coerce labor into accepting lower wages or reductions in employee benefits (as we saw before). Such threats are effective only to the extent that they are credible. Occasionally, firms must actually follow through with their threatened shut-downs in order to make workers comply with the demands that the firms make.

Business Week denounced this tendency to increase productivity by shutting down plant and equipment, instead of making it more efficient. It called such behavior, "slash-and-burn cost-cutting." It cited Stephen S. Roach of Morgan Stanley and Co., who warned that it is a "really dangerous . . . recipe for total capitulation of market share" (Pennar 1991).

This pattern of deindustrialization reverberated throughout the economy. The U.S. is now importing more and more of its manufactured goods, such as automobiles and consumer electronics. On an aggregate level, the U.S. share of world manufacturing exports fell from 17.1 percent in 1966 to 11.7 percent in 1986, a drop of more than one-third, suggesting that the leaders of the economy were foolishly trudging along the road to ruin (Epstein 1990–1991, p. 33).

Later, as the U.S. strengthened its intellectual property laws, its share of world manufacturing exports stabilized at about 13 percent. This rebound did not so much reflect manufacturing expertise as the power of the U.S. to coerce other nations to respect its version of intellectual property. Perhaps, the pharmaceutical industry is the most notorious example of this phenomenon. Wielding the power of intellectual property laws, until very recently, this industry has been demanding about $15,000 for the most effective regimen for holding AIDS at bay, even in Africa, where the disease is running rampant and the average income is only a few hundred dollars per year.

The industry's extortionate demands become even less defensible when you realize that most of the research that made these medicines possible came from public agencies rather than the pharmaceutical companies.

Unproductive Labor and the Hobbling of the Corporate Sector

Although the takeover movement proved to be a bonanza for the financial and legal sector, the Herculean efforts to change the structure of corporate ownership did nothing to enhance the productive capacity of the economy. Instead these shenanigans dissipated much of the remaining vitality of the productive sectors of the economy.

Certainly, excessive amounts of money went to financial transactions or legal maneuvering rather than productive investment. Texaco's failed takeover of Getty Oil, mentioned above, is a case in point. Penzoil sued Texaco, claiming it had a prior agreement with Getty. Between 1984 and 1988, Texaco and Penzoil waged an intense legal battle. Penzoil eventually won. The court initially awarded it a judgment that was worth more than $10 billion, but the ultimate settlement was a paltry $3 billion. Even so, an enormous amount of resources was dissipated in the process.

Not unexpectedly, the value of Penzoil's stock rose and Texaco's fell, since Texaco had to give so much money to Penzoil. What is noteworthy was the imbalance in the movements of the respective stocks. The fall in Texaco's value exceeded the rise in Penzoil's. The combined value of the stocks in the two firms fell by about $21 billion.

Could the legal fees consumed in this struggle explain this loss? Probably not. Texaco's legal fees accounted for about $250 million, but the after-tax cost would be only $165 million (Cutler and Summers 1988). The combined productive capacity of these two firms shrunk so much because management squandered so much time and energy in legal maneuvers rather than devoting their resources to make their firms more efficient.

The direct financial costs and the dissipation of talent associated with the assembling of these financial deals were but a small part of the damage created by the wave of mergers, takeovers, and leveraged buyouts. This speculative frenzy left many corporations saddled with so much debt that they could no longer function effectively, despite Michael Jensen's belief that this debt would spur efficiency.

Perhaps nothing typifies the perverse association between the financial sector and the decline in manufacturing than the relationship between Burlington Industries and the great investment-banking house, Morgan Stanley. Asher Edelman, a famous corporate raider, was threatening to take over Burlington, the largest textile company in the United States. Morgan offered to rescue Burlington, which it then purchased for $2.2 billion (Anders 1990).

Morgan itself put up only $46 million of the total cost. Bank loans and later junk-bond offerings provided the rest. In return, Morgan got all of the Class A voting stock and control of the company. In the first 50 days of owning the company, Morgan collected $87 million in fees, almost double what it paid to gain control.

Morgan charged $29 million for "advising" Burlington on how to be bought by Morgan. Morgan got $8.24 million for underwriting $12.5 million of junk-bonds in Burlington. Its fees equaled 4 percent of the value of the acquisition, well above the 3.02 percent that was the average charged for floating junk-bonds. Of course, Burlington could not complain. After all, Morgan controlled the board of directors.

For the first two years after the buyout, Burlington laid off 900 headquarters workers and sold 20 businesses to help repay its debt. The divestitures generated $1 billion in cash, which Burlington used to pay down debt. The workforce ultimately shrunk from 44,000 in 1986 to 27,000. Consequently, the company ceased to be the leader in the textile industry.

Faced with dissatisfaction from Burlington's management, Morgan devised an Employee Stock Ownership Plan (ESOP) to put stock into workers' hands. The plan required that Burlington pay $175.3 million in dividends to its equity holders, chiefly

Morgan. Morgan's dividend of $56 million equaled more than half of the bank's entire 1989 third quarter dividend. Although Morgan profited from this transaction, it added another $212.5 million junk-bond debt on the textile company, making Burlington's total debt reach $1.6 billion.

The ESOP plan purchased 2.9 million worth of total outstanding Class A voting stock, 36 percent of the total outstanding. Wilson Ellis, an Atlanta banker who helped create the ESOP, said that Morgan Stanley insisted that the ESOP pay $50 per share, five times what Morgan had paid for the stock only two years earlier. After a month of "aggressive negotiation" the plan agreed to purchase the stock at $37.80 a share.

Morgan relied on the appraisal firm, Houlthan, Lokey, Howard, and Zukin, to help it determine a fair value for the stock. This same firm had aided Morgan in appraising Burlington in 1987 when it purchased the company at $10 per share. Presumably, the appraisers felt that Morgan had magically added substantial value to the firm. Soon after the formation of the ESOP, the same appraisal firm valued the employee's stock at $14.62, less than half the price the employees paid 14 months earlier. Again, Morgan's association was so valuable, once it distanced itself from the firm, the value of the stock plummeted.

The Morgan affair left Burlington in shambles, but Morgan Stanley profited handsomely. All in all, Morgan Stanley collected $176 million from the captive textile company, including more than $120 in investment-banking fees and another $56 million in a special dividend. In addition, the company collected a windfall on its sale of the stock. Quite a return on its initial investment of $46 million!

Financial Services and Unproductive Labor

Even though everybody hates paperwork, we keep doing more and more of it. Most people consider paperwork to be unavoidable. In contrast, the corporate sector enthusiastically concentrates its attention on profiting by unproductive paperwork, while shutting down its factories. These financial manipulations consume an enormous amount of time and energy. Just consider the quantity of paper that has to be shuffled to complete one of the epidemics of giant corporate takeovers, which swept over the U.S. during the 1970s and 1980s.

In the case of Dupont's $7.5 billion takeover of Conoco, First New Jersey National Bank had the responsibility of overseeing the deal. W. E. Buchsbaum, DuPont's vice president for finance, said that First Jersey was beset with "great, great volumes of paperwork" and "a lot of mismatches between what people said they would tender and the stock certificates that have arrived." The result: the bank worked from 9 A.M. till midnight. The work overflowed into the bank cafeteria. On weekends, 16 branch managers and some people from DuPont had to work on the paperwork for this transaction (Anders 1981).

Had some government regulation required the same quantity of paperwork, statements of outrage would pepper the business press. Political candidates would campaign with anecdotes about the imposition of excessive paperwork. Instead, such transactions were held up as examples of capitalist efficiency.

The upsurge in this sort of financial transaction was a consequence, as well as a cause, of the economic decline of the U.S. economy. As the decline took hold, we saw that people, as well as firms, turned to speculation rather than producing useful goods and services because they saw relatively little promise from productive activities.

The wave of corporate takeovers that occurred during the 1970s and 1980s caused only part of the explosion of financial transactions. Much of the unproductive financial work is unrelated to corporate restructuring. Increasingly fewer people in the United States perform work that results in useful goods and services. Just look at the Yellow Pages of your phone book under the headings of real estate. Compare the number of firms on these pages with the number of places that are employing people who are engaged in the production of useful goods and services.

Fred Moseley lays the bulk of the blame for the falling rate of profit on the escalation of unproductive labor and unproductive investment (Moseley 1991). He estimates that a little more than one half of the workers in the U.S. economy in 1980 were doing productive labor (Moseley 1988; see also Wolff 1987). This estimate is conservative on two counts. First, all evidence suggests that the share of unproductive labor has been increasing over time (see Dawson and Foster 1981).

Moseley himself estimates that the ratio of productive to unproductive labor rose by about 70 percent between 1950 and 1980 (Moseley 1988; see also Moseley 1991, p. 113). The increasing pace of deindustrialization of the 1980s obviously accelerated the trend. By 1987, Moseley calculates that the ratio had almost doubled its 1950 level (Moseley 1991, p. 121). I know of no indication that this trend toward an increasing share of unproductive labor is tapering off.

Second, much of the productive labor is actually used to produce goods and services that are used for activities that are unproductive. For example, even though paper workers are productive, their work is dissipated unproductively when paper is consumed up in the course of corporate takeovers. A goodly number of paper workers or people assembling computers, through no fault of their own, end up assisting in the production of more paper work rather than contributing to our standard of living.

Christopher Niggle illustrates the growing importance by analyzing the growth of financial services in the U.S. economy. He notes that the ratio of the book value of financial institutions to the Gross National Product of the U.S. was 78.4 in 1960. In 1970, it was still only 82.9. By 1984, it reached 107.4 (Niggle 1988, p. 585).

Niggle suggests a second ratio to demonstrate the enormous growth of the financial sector: the ratio of financial institutions' assets to the assets of nonfinancial institutions. In 1960, this ratio was 0.957, meaning that the financial and the nonfinancial sectors were about equal. By 1970, the financial sector had overtaken the nonfinancial sector, boosting the ratio to 1.094. By 1983, the dominance of the financial sector had driven the ratio to 1.202 (Niggle 1988, p. 585).

Finally, Niggle reports the growing size of the part of the economy known by the acronym, FIRE, which stands for Finance, Insurance, and Real Estate. In 1960, the FIRE sector represented 14.3 percent of the Gross Domestic Product of the U.S.; in 1980, 15.1 percent. The 1983 share of the FIRE sector was 16.4 percent, meaning that within these mere three years the relative importance of the FIRE sector grew by more than it had in the previous 20 years (Niggle 1988, p. 585).

Just consider the explosion in transactions in the stock market. In 1960, 766 million shares were traded on the New York Stock Exchange. In 1987, 900 million shares changed hands in the average week. Lawrence Summers, who later became Secretary of the Treasure and then president of Harvard, along with his wife, Victoria, a lawyer, calculated that more shares were traded on the lowest volume day in 1987 than in any month in 1960. More shares were traded in the first 15 minutes of 19 and 20 October 1987 than in any week in 1960 (Summers and Summers 1989).

The stock market represents a relatively small share of all financial speculation. Speculators trade many different types of assets. For example, they buy and sell derivative securities, such as stock futures, which provide the rights to buy or sell stocks at a set price a specified time in the future. Organized markets in such derivative securities did not even exist in 1970. The Summers' article calculated that the value of trades in stock futures exceeded that of the trades in stocks themselves. Trade in the New York Stock Exchange averaged less than $10 billion per day; government bonds, $25 billion; daily trade in foreign exchange averaged more than $25 billion. Trade in index options equaled that of stock futures (Summers and Summers 1989).

How much do all these transactions cost? According to the Summers' article, the combined receipts of the firms on the New York Stock Exchange was $53 billion in 1987—an enormous sum, considering that the total income for the entire corporate sector in the U.S. at the time was only $310.4 billion. Beside these direct costs, corporations whose stock is traded in organized markets devote much time and energy to efforts to influence the markets. For example, chief executive officers of major corporations commonly spend a week or more each quarter just telling their corporate story to security analysts. In addition, both individuals and firms spend a great number of resources monitoring their portfolios, acquiring information about securities or making investment decisions. If these supplementary costs are one-half as much as direct payments to security firms, then the cost of operating the securities markets was greater than $75 billion (Summers and Summers 1989).

Since the Summers article appeared, finance has continued to expand. The article itself is symbolic of this expansion. Not long after this article appeared, Lawrence Summers accepted a job as the number two person in the U.S. Treasury Department, and later rose to become secretary of the Treasury. His concern about the wasteful nature of finance soon disappeared, illustrating on a personal level the ability of the financial sector to swallow up like a black hole everything in its vicinity.

Notice how the various symptoms of the decline reinforce each other. The falling rate of profit produces the pressure for deregulation and lax government regulation as well as a scramble for higher and quicker returns from investments. These factors perversely combine to create an environment in which corporations put more energy into shuffling paper than producing useful goods and services.

The commitment of an increasing portion of economic energies into unproductive channels makes the decline more severe, putting more downward pressure on the rate of profit. Here again you can see a problem (excessive paperwork) resulting from other problems, such as deregulation, which itself is a response to still another problem—the falling rate of profit.

The new regime of intellectual property rights has currently reversed the downward trend in profit rates, but in doing so it creates other problems, including the stifling of scientific and technical progress. On a purely economic level, it will eventually create an enormous imbalance between the ability to produce and the people's capacity to consume, laying the groundwork for still another economic crisis.

Tracking the Elusive Profit Rate

I have already alluded to the fall in the rate of profit, but it is more serious than table 1.2 in chapter 1 indicates. However, despite the pervasive importance of profits, economists have no precise method for measuring them. Even worse, economists cannot measure either of the two numbers—total profits and total capital—the ratio of which determines the rate of profit.

Let me begin with total profits. Ultimately, economists get their estimate of profits from reports that accountants prepare (see Fisher and McGowan 1983). Unfortunately, accounting is far from an exact science. Accountants can adopt a number of different procedures for calculating profits. Obviously, they will choose the method that is most beneficial to their clients.

In an economy where taxes depend on profits, firms profit by keeping the books in a way that makes their earnings appear to be as small as possible. For example, accountants can choose different ways to depreciate their capital goods. Large firms, perhaps because they can afford more sophisticated accounting personnel, typically adopt accounting methods that make their profits appear smaller than they would be if these large firms used the same accounting methods that smaller firms do (Salamon 1985, p. 497). Accountants also have to keep in mind how the books will appear to investors and lenders.

All these considerations will distort accounting measures of profit. These complications pale beside a more serious complication: time. Accounting profits indicate merely how much the firm earned in the most recent period. In general, a firm's profits today depend on actions that it took in the past. In the case of long-lived capital goods, investments made many years ago may influence profits today. In this sense, profits are backward-looking, but backward-looking profit rates give us only part of the picture.

In particular, policies that maximize immediate profits might be detrimental to the long run health of the firm. For example, no firm would engage in research and development if it were trying to increase its current accounting profit. After all, research and development might not pay off for years and years.

As a result, economists use a conception of profits that is forward-looking. They argue that, to be successful, a firm must try to earn a stream of profits over an extended period of time in the future (Jordon 1989; Fisher and McGowan 1983). Economists think in terms of what they call, "the discounted present value of profits." These profits are forward-looking.

Economists calculate the discounted present value of profits by adding up this year's profits plus a fraction of next year's expected profits plus a smaller fraction of the following year's expected profits, et cetera. The decreasing fractions reflect the fact that money tomorrow is worth less than money today.

Of course, these expected future profits are impossible to measure. To begin with, they depend on what will happen in the future. In addition, economists have no scientific method for choosing the appropriate fractions to use in discounting those future profits. As a result, when I talk about profits, I am stuck with data that has glaring inadequacies.

Similar problems complicate coming to grips with the measurement of the capital invested, the second number used in the calculation of the profit rate. Even if someone knew exactly how much every firm has spent for its capital—and nobody does—he or she would have to add together old and new buildings and equipment of all kinds. Over time this stuff wears out and/or becomes obsolete. Some depreciates quickly. Some does not. No adequate method exists to take account of the complexity of the depreciation process.

Consider what has been happening with computer prices over the last few decades. The original purchase price of a typical ten-year-old microcomputer is many times what a comparable system would cost today. So economists develop formulae to tell them how much of its original value a three-year-old computer retains today. These formulae are very crude and very rigid. For example, they assume that all office machinery (not just computers) will depreciate at some preordained rate.

To make matters worse, accurate calculation of depreciation must take into account what will happen in the future. Notice that these formulae are predetermined based on past accounting practices. They ignore the fact that changing economic conditions or a shift in technology can dramatically alter the value of capital in unexpected ways.

Consider a company that began making slide rules just before pocket calculators first became inexpensive. The market values of the capital owned by the slide-rule firm would probably depreciate relatively slowly—perhaps in line with the formula—until people began to realize that the factory's product would be obsolete. Suddenly much of its capital stock would be worthless, except for what it could bring in scrap. Nonetheless, according to the depreciation formula, this capital still would retain considerable value.

All economists recognize the inadequacies of this method of handling the data, but it is all we have to work with so far. Hopefully, the innumerable errors will average out, but economists have no reason to believe that they will. The data may be reasonably good in stable economic conditions, but they will be of substantially less value in turbulent periods. For this reason, you have to be wary of relying on the usual economic measures during times of rapid transition.

I am convinced that the strong competitive pressures that are sweeping across the U.S. economy are wiping out a good part of the existing capital values. If so, contemporary measures of the rate of profit might be overstated.

The Dual Nature of the Profit Rate

The lure of future profits helps to determine economic conditions by serving as an incentive to guide business behavior. Both investors and managers know that, to the extent that capitalists succeed in taking advantage of economic opportunities, they will enjoy comfortable profits. Conversely, the profits that firms collect today are, at least in part, a consequence of general economic conditions. Keynes correctly emphasized that to a large extent, the previous profit-seeking actions of all other capitalists taken together determine general economic conditions.

So the firm acts as an individual agent, but must adapt to the collective action of all other agents. This particular dualism often causes markets to move along destructive paths. An ideal economic system would include a feedback mechanism capable of signaling economic agents that their actions are either socially beneficial or socially harmful. Markets contain no such feedback mechanism.

Individual capitalists only take their own profits into account when they make an economic decision. They have no reason to consider the indirect effects of their actions on overall economic conditions, nor whether these effects will be socially beneficial or not.

Of course, subjective feelings will influence some of what people consider to be socially beneficial. Products, which provide enjoyment for one party, often inconvenience another. We can think of any number of examples. Another person's smoking, loud music, or fast cars can make life less pleasant for many others.

Still, as a rough approximation you can say that, to the extent that capitalists do pursue socially useful activities, the market leads to desirable outcomes. To the extent that capitalists direct their energy into channels that are socially wasteful or even destructive, society is the loser.

We can identify some economic activity that leads to no social gains. For example, speculation is a wasteful activity. For the most part, my speculative gains are only possible if you or somebody else experiences a corresponding speculative loss (although some economists make the questionable assumption that speculators perform a useful service by absorbing risk for those who wish to avoid it).

Although people cannot all agree on which particular firms are behaving in a positive or a negative manner, you can assume that if firms predominately are acting productively then people's lives are more likely to be better off than if they are making wasteful decisions.

CHAPTER 7

Deindustrialization and the Rise of the Service Economy

Postindustrial Vision

Should you be concerned about the elimination of manufacturing jobs and the rise of service employment in the United States? In the past, economists as far apart as Karl Marx and Adam Smith regarded services as decidedly unproductive. Recently, the attitude toward services has shifted. Despite the prevalence of low-wage service employment, some modern economists welcome the replacement of manufacturing employment as a positive development.

Of course, the category of services, as such, has no fixed meaning. In fact, the service industry is not really an industry at all. Instead, it is a catchall category that includes all businesses that do not fall within the established industrial categories (see Hill 1977).

Even if you knew what services were, you would still have difficulty identifying service workers. In general, you can count workers as service workers if they work for a company that supplies a service. For example, a person writing an owner's manual in an automobile factory is an industrial worker. A person writing a program for a computer software company is a service worker. Since the program is recorded on a floppy disk or a tape, both the automobile manual and the program take on a physical form. Both the manual and the program can help the purchaser make better use of a piece of hardware, yet the statistics count only one of these workers as a service worker.

This approach to counting service workers becomes more problematic when jobs shift from one sort of business to another. For example, manufacturing firms can make arrangements to contract for services that their own employees would otherwise perform. For example, unionized companies commonly contract with businesses that hire minimum-wage employees to do janitorial work rather than pay union wages to workers in their direct employment. Still, by any measure, the service sector has indeed expanded by replacing manufacturing in the United States.

I can identify three different classes of writers who find the replacement of manufacturing by services to be benign. The first group welcomes deindustrialization because it supposedly heralds the dawn of a new postindustrial, service-oriented stage of economic development. The second group says that the previous examples of deindustrialization constitute nothing more than a collection of isolated incidents; that deindustrialization is not occurring or, if it is, it only represents a normal rearrangement of economic worldwide activity. In either case, you have no reason to worry. The third group contends that what appears to be deindustrialization may be nothing more than a normal, but long overdue cyclical correction, which is clearing away obsolete and inefficient capital stock.

First, I will turn to the theory of a postindustrial economy, which has permeated popular culture (Bell 1976; Toffler 1990; see also Frankel 1987). This theory holds that the United States will inevitably retire from manufacturing and specialize in the creation of intellectual property and the performance of sophisticated services, while the less developed economies do the less rewarding work of building the material goods that people in the advanced economies enjoy.

These writers are correct in so far as they point out the obvious fact that service work has been displacing manufacturing. With rates of profit in domestic manufacturing operations sagging, firms in the United States have been expanding their investment in service industries, rather than investing in manufacturing.

Although the meaning of the service sector as a whole is fuzzy at best, these theorists of postindustrial society write as if service employment were synonymous with highly skilled professional work. In this sense, the postindustrial visionaries correctly grasp that a society cannot build a successful economy on a strategy of low wages. Their mistake is to delude themselves into proceeding as if the majority of the new service jobs were professional service jobs, rather than low-wage, dead-end service jobs, which neither draw upon nor develop workers' skills.

The Hollow Economy and the Dangers of Postindustrial Utopianism

Given the ever-greater reliance on low-wage service employment, you can dismiss out of hand the unrealistic, utopian vision of postindustrial society. The U.S. economy will not prosper simply by moving beyond manufacturing, yet a number of major businesses are behaving as if the United States can build a future on a service economy. According to *Business Week:*

> In industry after industry, manufacturers are closing up shop or curtailing their operations and becoming marketing organizations for other producers, mostly foreign. . . . The result is the evolution of a new kind of company: manufacturers that do little or no manufacturing are increasingly becoming service oriented. . . . In contrast to traditional manufacturers, they are hollow corporations. Unchecked, this trend will ultimately hurt the US economy. [Anon. 1986a, p. 57]

The *Business Week* report pointed to Lewis Galoob Toys, Inc., a corporation significant enough to be listed on the New York Stock Exchange, which has only 115 employees. Everything depends on contracts with other corporations. Nike is depicted in similar terms. *Business Week* cited Raymond E. Miles, dean of the School of Business Administration at the University of California, Berkeley, "What you'll have is a switchboard instead of a corporation" (Anon. 1986a, p. 64). The *Business Week* article concluded: "By shifting production overseas or shopping abroad for parts and components, US companies are whittling away at the critical mass essential to a strong industrial base" (Anon. 1986a, p. 60). *Business Week* also cited a warning by Jack D. Kuehler, senior vicepresident of International Business Corp., who warned that U.S. companies will gradually become less adept at understanding how new technology can be exploited and eventually "lose the ability to design" (Anon. 1986a, p. 61).

Complacency about this trend could lead to grave problems. The concentration of unskilled service jobs promises to accelerate the process of deindustrialization. In the long run, professional service jobs are not a substitute for manufacturing. If anything, professional service jobs are the result of successful manufacturing activities.

For example, when Britain was a major industrial power, British banks were preeminent. Similarly, U.S. banks were world leaders during the ascendancy of U.S. industry. The same phenomenon occurred in the Far East. At one point, seven of the ten largest banks were Japanese. Only one U.S. bank, the then-wounded Citibank, ranked among the ten largest banks worldwide (Glasgall 1988). In fact, the delinking of Japan's now-crippled banking sector from domestic manufacturing probably contributed to the vulnerability of the Japanese banking system.

Because few U.S. banks had the size to compete in the global market for financial services, they closed about 100 foreign branches between 1985 and 1990 (Mandel and Bernstein 1990, p. 62). Since then, banks in the United States have grown both through consolidation and through integration with other parts of the financial sector. While this new evolution has given U.S. banks more leverage relative to the rest of the world, it may also have made the domestic financial sector more vulnerable.

The Electronics Industry in the Age of Postindustrialism

The direction of the semiconductor industry represented an even more ominous threat to the U.S. economy. With the exception of Micron and Texas Instruments, U.S. producers had more or less abandoned the market for memory chips by 1985 (Macher, Mowery, and Hodges 1999, p. 251). Many innovative semiconductor companies avoided any involvement in fabricating their products. Instead, these so-called fabless companies farm their production out to factories, which they refer to as foundries. By the year 2010, fabless producers are expected to control 40 percent of the world's chip production (Macher, Mowery, and Hodges 1999, p. 249).

Most state-of-the-art foundries are in Asia, especially Taiwan (Macher, Mowery, and Hodges 1999, p. 268). Even the companies that do produce semiconductor wafers in the United States more often than not send them abroad to factories that test them and package them into a form in which they can attach to a circuit board.

The move toward fabless corporations poses a serious danger for the U.S. semiconductor industry. In the process of manufacturing for U.S. firms, these foreign foundries gain a great deal of expertise. Before they can begin production for the U.S. contractors, these firms must develop the expertise in transferring the technology from blueprints to the production equipment. They must also develop an understanding of product specification, machinery, and the engineering required to assist with manufacturing setup and quality control (Florida and Kenney 1990a, p. 135). These tasks require considerable sophistication.

After years of subcontracting out their manufacturing, the U.S. semiconductor industry had been gradually losing touch with the manufacturing process by the 1980s. As a result, the industry has had to establish manufacturing partnerships to gain access to state-of-the-art production technologies. Even Intel was not immune from the symptoms of a lack of hands-on experience. At one point *Business Week* reported that: "Intel had to call in Malaysian experts from its Penang factory to help set up the chip assembly line at an automated chipmaking factory it started building in Arizona three years ago. None of its US employees had that expertise any longer" (Anon. 1986a, p. 62).

The semiconductor industry is famous for groups of employees with strategic information defecting to begin their own firms. Fortunately for Intel, the Malaysian experts were still in its employ at the time. Had these Malaysian experts followed the example of the U.S. counterparts, the lack of manufacturing experience might have wounded Intel.

Some time ago, Intel established a joint venture with NMB Semiconductor to market the Japanese company's memory chips and to acquire NMB's production technology for use in Intel's manufacturing. A top Intel executive said, "One big thing we get out of this is to have them help us with automated factories" (Florida and Kenney 1990a, p. 135).

Similarly, Advanced Micro Devices sold one of its Texas factories to Sony for $55 million. As part of the deal, Sony promised to upgrade the plant and use it as a base to teach AMD executives and engineers about Japanese production technology (Florida and Kenney 1990a, p. 135).

Despite the lagging productivity of the U.S. semiconductor industry, the industry continues to hold its own. Intel, the giant semiconductor firm, manufactures still many of its own chips, although two of its five wafer production facilities are abroad. It does license others to produce chipsets, which connect the PC to the rest of the computer through the system bus. Advanced Micro Devices, like Intel, still prospers although most of its wafer production capacity is abroad.

Why can't the offshore companies that now produce these chips develop their own products to compete with the companies in the United States? While the U.S. corporations have devoted considerable resources to producing new processors, both they and the United States as a whole have been neglecting investment in basic research that can lead to a fundamental breakthrough.

Moreover, as people elsewhere learn to manufacture semiconductors, they can also learn to design them. In the words of a *Harvard Business Review* article:

> [B]usiness cannot design in a vacuum. It cannot exploit new technologies if it has no chance to apply them. . . . The fact is, design and manufacturing are linked. A company that subcontracts its manufacturing to foreigners will soon lose the expertise in design and the ability to innovate because it won't get the feedback it needs. [Markides and Berg 1988; cited in Kenney and Florida 1990a, p. 134]

In fact, the Taiwanese Semiconductor Manufacturing Company now produces more semiconductor wafers than Intel (Anon. 2001; and Magee 2000a). In addition, the company developed the technology to produce 0.13 Micron semiconductors before either Intel or AMD (Magee 2000b).

Some experts warned that even the seemingly invincible U.S. software industry might suffer the same fate as the U.S. automobile industry (Cusumano 1991, p. 5). According to Michael Cusumano, "Toyota had 50 percent more efficiency [than the U.S.] in 1965, but the cars were terrible." He predicted that the same would occur in software (Schlesinger 1990).

Offshore competitors began to apply the same techniques to software production that made their automobile manufacturing so efficient. Japanese programmers could produce 50 to 70 percent more code than U.S. programmers with one-third to one-half as many errors based on a sample of 40 large U.S. and Japanese computer systems (Cusumano 1991, p. 53). Countries such as India are making great strides in catching up to the United States in developing software, although they are still behind.

Based on the problems described above, the long-term prognosis for the U.S. semiconductor industry might not seem to be optimistic. Presently, intellectual property rights rather than technological prowess represents the main defense of the giant U.S. semiconductor firms.

Intellectual Property and High Technology

Although deindustrialization threatened to debilitate high-technology sectors, such as semiconductors during the 1970s, happily for the dominant players in the U.S. semiconductor industry, these industries managed to avoid falling prey to competitive forces. Yes, the production techniques of other nations, such as the Taiwanese semiconductor industry, are superior to those of their U.S. counterparts.

The key to success in the semiconductor industry lies outside of manufacturing expertise. This industry has successfully found refuge from intense competition that had wounded most of the more basic industries by enforcing its intellectual property rights. According to one industry insider, James Koford of LSI Logic, "Silicon Valley and Route 128 are worlds of intellectual property, not capital equipment and production. Most of the employees of U.S. high technology live in southeast Asia" (cited in Florida and Kenney 1990b, p. 237). Some, like George Gilder, applaud this arrangement, arguing that these companies will maximize their profits by specializing in the design of computer chips (Gilder 1989).

Both the government of the United States and industry leaders realized that a wave of deindustrialization threatened to sweep away the semiconductor industry along with many other important sectors of the economy. Here is the explanation of the situation published by the Federal Reserve Bank of Philadelphia:

> When it became clear they [the United States semiconductor industry] could no longer dominate Japanese firms on the basis of production technology alone, American firms attempted to consolidate their comparative advantage in research and development. To do this, they would have to find ways of reducing their competitors' ability to reverse-engineer their products. To that end, American companies began to lobby Congress to increase intellectual property protection for their semiconductor designs. In 1984, Congress created a new form of intellectual property right, called mask rights, especially tailored to address the needs articulated by the industry. [Hunt 1999, pp. 19–20]

During this period, both Texas Instruments and National Semiconductor were tottering on the verge of bankruptcy. Irving Rappaport, former vice president and associative general counsel for intellectual property national semiconductor recalled:

> I'm not exaggerating when I tell you that National Semiconductor was only weeks away from bankruptcy in late 1990. . . . All the papers had been signed before it was decided to continue the business and give licensing a more aggressive push. And without a doubt if, patent fees bought us valuable time in which to complete our restructuring process. For a while there, in fact, three-quarters of our revenues came from patent licenses. [Rivette and Kline 2000, pp. 125–26]

Texas Instruments struck first, filing a suit against eight Japanese and one Korean semiconductor company, accusing them of infringing semiconductor patents. The settlements yielded the company more than $600 million in payments according to a 1990 report. The company became so aggressive in seeking royalties that by 1992, it earned $391 million in royalties, compared to an operating income of only $274 million (Warshofsky 1994, p. 111). Other companies are even more successful. For example, the 2000 Annual Report of IBM announced that the firm had earned more than $1.5 billion in income in 2000 from its intellectual property portfolio.

This new legal framework allowed some of the most important high-technology sectors of the economy to become a perverse kind of service sector. Rather than directly providing services, they merely demanded payment for their intellectual property.

The software industry has managed to sail along, more or less unfazed by the phenomenal growth of places such as India, which exports about $6 billion worth of software (Joseph 2001). While the Indians fear competition from the low-wage Chinese programmers, they do not pose much of a threat to the dominance of the U.S. industry. Again, their holdings of intellectual property make them virtually unassailable.

Services and High Technology

Although I believe that manufacturing is an essential part of a successful economy, I do not mean to suggest that the service industry is inherently either bad or inherently unproductive. The fate of an economy will depend more upon the precise mix of spillovers and linkages associated with the industries that it retains rather than the proportions of manufacturing and services.

If you want to analyze the impact of the growth of the service economy, you must take account of the specific services that are performed as well as the context in which they are performed. For example, I have already suggested that service productivity growth has been more rapid in countries such as Germany, Japan, and France, where services are paid more relative to manufacturing than they are in the United States.

Historically, concern about services was not based on the low productivity of service jobs. Instead, economists singled out manufacturing jobs because of the nature of the effects of manufacturing employment on the rest of the economy. They believed that manufacturing was more desirable than services because manufacturing jobs appeared to promote the further growth of manufacturing jobs as well as service employment, while services did not appear to induce manufacturing jobs to grow to the same degree.

For example, the bicycle industry, which was centered in the Detroit area, created a pool of skilled workers and suppliers that gave this region a head start in developing the automobile industry. As the automobile industry evolved, it spawned a multitude of suppliers, including suppliers of services. Few service industries created such "agglomeration economies" (Malecki 1991, p. 84), since—at the risk of violating my warning about generalizations on this subject—services tend to be so labor-intensive.

Despite the labor intensity of many services, the U.S. economy has been devoting more and more of its capital stock to services rather than industry. In part, this trend reflects the increasing relative size of the service sector. In addition, some service sectors, such as telecommunications, have become very capital intensive.

At the end of 1948, over 80 percent of the net stock of private nonresidential structures and equipment was used in agriculture, mining, construction, manufacturing, transportation, and public utilities—what economists call, the "primary sector" (Magdoff and Sweezy 1990, p. 5). Harry Magdoff and Paul Sweezy, two of the most astute observers of the economy pointed out that, between 1978 and 1988, the net stock of manufacturing capital rose 21 percent. The net stock of capital used in finance rose by an astounding 80 percent (Magdoff and Sweezy 1990, p. 8; see also Magdoff and Sweezy 1985). For example, I understand that Wall Street is the number one customer of Sun Microsystems.

By the end of 1988, the net stock of private nonresidential capital found in the primary sector represented less than 50 percent of the total net stock of private nonresidential equipment and structures. Not unexpectedly, the relative position of each of these primary industries declined steadily throughout the past few decades, in part, because the capital investment, which could have made these industries more productive, went to the service sector (Magdoff and Sweezy 1990, p. 5).

Figure 7.1 compares the change in capital per worker in the manufacturing sector with that of the service sector between 1960 and 1985. The top line shows the slow increase of the capital per worker in manufacturing between 1960 and 1985. The middle line indicates the doubling of the capital intensity in the service industry. The bottom line represents the ratio of the capital intensity in manufacturing relative to that of services over the same period. In 1960, the typical manufacturing worker worked with 2.65 times as much capital as the typical service worker. By 1908, the ratio had fallen to 1.47. The overall message of the graph is that, although most service jobs are found in the stagnant low-skill, low-wage economic backwaters, a minority of service jobs is absorbing an enormous share of capital resources.

Besides generating the demand for auxiliary suppliers, investment in manufacturing seems to be particularly advantageous, because it creates spillovers of knowledge, such as I described before. The companies that benefit from this new knowledge need not be in the same industry. For example, large Japanese companies use microelectronic innovations to develop cutting-edge consumer electronic goods. They then apply these same innovations from consumer goods to high-technology products. For example, they used the technology for watchman televisions to improve the displays for laptop computer displays (Florida and Kenney 1990a, p. 145).

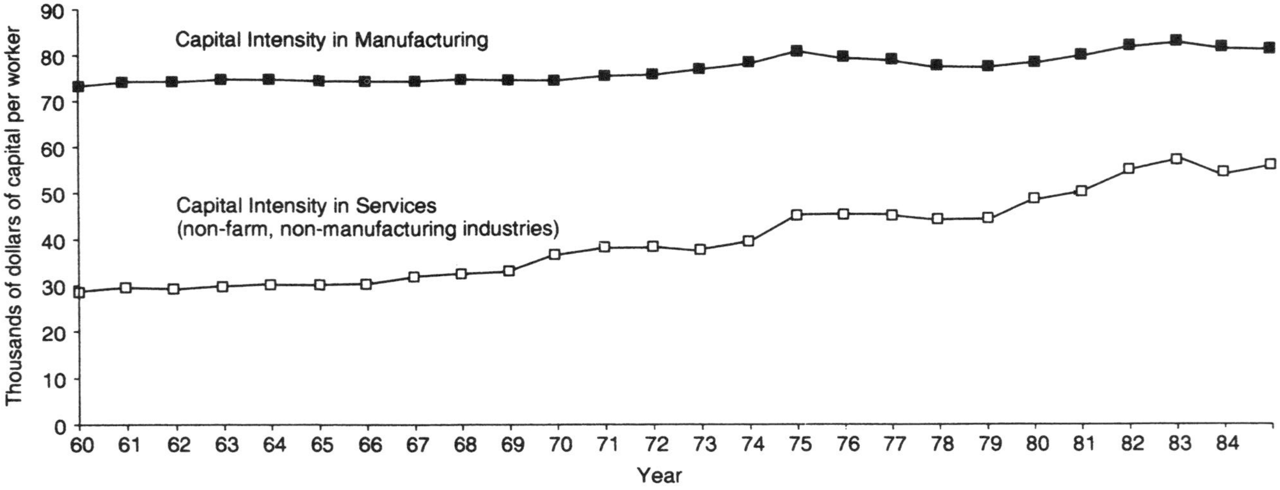

Notes:
Employment data in thousands.
Data listed under services is less government sector.
Fixed Nonresidential Private Capital: Millions of 1982 dollars.

Sources:
U.S. Department of Labor. 1989. Employment and Earnings, Vol. 36, No. 9 (September), p. 43, Table B-1 'Employees on Nonagricultural Payrolls by Major Industry, 1937 to Date.'

U.S. Department of Commerce, Bureau of Economic Analysis.1987. Fixed Reproducible Tangible Wealth in the United States, 1982 – 1985 (Washington, D.C.: U.S. Government Printing Office), pp. 166 – 7.

Figure 7.1 Capital intensity in services and manufacturing

This sort of spillover explains why economists find a close correlation between machinery investment and economic growth, while other forms of investment do not seem to be capable of driving economic growth (DeLong and Summers 1991; DeLong 1992).

The Demand for Services and the Proximity to Manufacturing

In making the case that manufacturing jobs are more advantageous than service jobs, I am implicitly introducing proximity into the argument. Proximity is relevant because services generally use less specific tools than manufacturing does. For example, typewriters may not differ much from office to office, but manufacturing frequently requires quite specialized equipment. The more specialized the equipment, the more valuable close contact with suppliers will be. For this reason, manufacturing is more likely to spawn new employment than services.

I suspect that even service industries using high technology generally require more generic manufactured inputs than manufacturing industries do. For example, companies that produce fiber-optic cable may not have to tailor them closely to the particular needs of the firms that purchase them. If this is the case, for the producer of fiber-optic cable that intends to sell to one of the great communications companies of today, the cost of maintaining close connections with this handful of giant communications companies would not be great, so long as these companies could provide unambiguous specifications for the fiber-optic cable that they purchase.

Unlike the example of the early Detroit automobile industry, an expansion of services in one city may be less likely to create many new jobs in the vicinity, especially now that the economy is more global in scope. Consequently, spillovers from services are not necessarily contained within a specific region.

If the potential benefits from spillovers from manufacturing accrue to all firms in an industry, regardless of their location, whether a particular manufacturing process occurs in Detroit or Dakar should be a matter of indifference. While Japanese firms produce the watchman, U.S. firms could easily apply this same knowledge to the production of laptop displays if proximity did not matter.

Unfortunately, the current Japanese dominance in laptop displays suggests that proximity is indeed important. The fact that the same firm produces both the laptop display and the watchman is not an issue here as I mentioned earlier in the discussion of the semiconductor industry. The linkage could just as easily connect separate firms in a given locale rather than two divisions within the same firm.

Theoretically, services as well as industry could create spillovers of information, as well as other linkages. For example, the growth of communications services necessitates a corresponding growth in the production of goods, such as fiber-optic cables or satellites. In addition, the growth of modern communications services allows for a greater delocalization of economic activity.

In this sense, manufacturing jobs still might have an advantage over services in terms of stimulating a particular region, since manufacturing typically requires a wider array of complementary inputs than services do. Nonetheless, any generalization about this relationship should be taken with a grain of salt.

In the case of other service industries that are more typical than fiber-optic communications, suppliers that are in close proximity to their potential customers may very well have a competitive edge. Even so, the growth of such an industry is unlikely to provide the same degree of beneficial spillovers that manufacturing has traditionally provided.

While the previous examples suggest the importance of manufacturing, they should also serve as a reminder of the pitfalls in generalizing about the nature of services. At the very least, one should be careful about blindly asserting that service jobs are more or less productive than other types of employment. Some services can be highly productive. Other service work is unproductive, or at least, not particularly productive.

Even to the extent that the postindustrial utopians are correct about an ever-greater demand for highly trained, professional service work, the future may not be as rosy as they have predicted it to be. I feel certain that people in the United States have good reason to be worried about the sort of services that are becoming dominant in the U.S. economy. Although some services can be both capital-intensive and highly productive, the bulk of service jobs are in low-wage sectors, such as food service, retailing, and nonprofessional health-care work.

Does Deindustrialization Exist?

At last, I am ready to address the other two theories that dismiss concerns about deindustrialization as alarmist. Let me begin with the theories of those economists who dismiss the reality of deindustrialization altogether. These commentators insist that manufacturing is not decreasing at all. They take heart in the fact that U.S. business still employs about the same number of people in manufacturing as it did in the late 1960s, although substantial changes have occurred during this period (Lawrence 1983).

In part, this controversy revolves around semantics. The term "deindustrialization" unfortunately conjures up a misleading image of an economy without any manufacturing whatsoever. Obviously, manufacturing has not entirely disappeared from the United States.

Although, one must be careful not to overstate the extent of deindustrialization, nobody can deny that the cumulative impact of plant closings throughout the nation has been devastating to many of those most directly affected. Today, the region that once represented the core of this manufacturing prosperity has been popularly known as the Rust Belt for several decades. Although some high-tech centers have emerged in this region, other areas have been left behind.

Still, those who are skeptical about the existence of deindustrialization are partially correct. Although manufacturing employment peaked in 1979, it has indeed remained relatively steady. At the same time the relative importance of manufacturing employment has fallen considerably, because total employment in the country has expanded by more than 80 percent since 1979. As a result, manufacturing employment as a share of total employment has fallen from almost 30 percent to about 14 percent between 1969 and 1999 (United States President 2000, Table B 44, p. 368). Indicative of the declining importance of production workers, the Bureau of Labor Statistics of the United States Department of Commerce found that by 1983, the United States employed about one sales worker for every production worker (Bils 1990).

Similarly, those skeptics, who question the existence of deindustrialization, are correct that government data actually did show that manufacturing as a share of total domestic output remained relatively steady between 1973 to 1985, but I must put this fact in perspective. The share of manufacturing has remained steady even though the amount of labor involved has steadily declined, in part because the average manufacturing worker is so much more productive than the typical service worker.

However, these same skeptics fail to take account of the fact that the government data are misleading because they overstate the share of manufacturing in the aggregate economy, because they fail to account for the imports used in production. Instead, the government merely tallies the final output of the manufacturing sector (see Mishel 1988).

This procedure is unwarranted because manufacturing in the United States is relying more and more on imported inputs. Consider the example of the automobile industry. Suppose you want to use the government's measure to test for deindustrialization in that industry. During the 1960s, an automobile produced in the United States consisted largely of domestically built parts. Today, an automobile assembled in the United States contains an enormous number of imported parts.

If the number of cars produced remained constant, you would find no evidence of deindustrialization because the government data would just count the value of final product, the car, as a measure of manufacturing activity in the economy. In reality, the car represents considerably less domestic manufacturing than it did when the parts were produced domestically.

Other data also indicate a decline in the domestic content of U.S. manufacturing—meaning the value of work performed in the United States as share of the total value of a typical manufactured item. For example, finished goods are an increasing share of U.S. imports, while their share of exports has remained virtually unchanged (Hickok 1991, p. 27).

The failure to account for the falling domestic content of manufacturing in the United States masks the ongoing process of deindustrialization. As a result, the government data may not show that manufacturing activity has been shrinking even though, in reality, it has been declining.

Now let me discuss a position that some economists have taken, that deindustrialization may well exist, but it does not necessarily represent the failure of American corporations. Recall how the Vietnam War paved the way for an exodus of business from the shores of the United States. First to leave were labor-intensive industries, such as textiles and footwear. Based on the success of these pioneers, heavier industry followed suit. Business no longer had to respond to higher wages with better technology; it would suffice just to leave in search of cheaper wages.

While manufacturing in the United States receded, U.S. multinational firms lost no ground whatsoever. Instead, they maintained their share of world markets. In fact, foreign affiliates of U.S. multinationals actually *increased* their share from 8.0 percent to 9.8 percent between 1966 and 1986 (Epstein 1990–1991, p. 33; see also Kravis and Lipsey 1989).

The outsourcing of production is far more important than the production of foreign affiliates. Consider the magnitude of the 200 largest corporations worldwide. Their combined sales exceed the combined economies of all countries minus the biggest ten. Their combined sales are 18 times the size of the combined annual income of the 1.2 billion people (24 percent of the total world population) living in "severe" poverty (Anderson and Cavanagh 2000).

While the sales of these behemoths are the equivalent of 27.5 percent of world economic activity, they employ a miniscule 0.78 percent of the world's workforce. The jobs provided by these corporations are not necessarily desirable positions. For example, Wal-Mart, a company notorious for union-busting and widespread use of part-time workers to avoid paying benefits, accounts for a full 5 percent of their combined workforce (Anderson and Cavanagh 2000).

The pattern suggests that, what appears as deindustrialization is part of a larger strategy in which multinationals reduce their investment at home, while they increase their investment abroad (Epstein 1990–1991, p. 36; see also Kravis and Lipsey 1988). Robert Reich notes, "Overall, the evidence suggests that the U.S. companies have not lost their competitive edge over the last 20 years—they've just moved their base of operations" (Reich 1990, p. 55). For example, today 40 percent of IBM's employees are foreign and the percentage is increasing (Reich 1990, p. 55).

In addition, Reich might have observed that corporate ownership is becoming diffused. In the process, U.S. multinational corporations become truly multinational, losing their identity as U.S. firms and becoming stateless entities whose influence rivals that of many existing nation states.

Once again, I should mention that our current adherence to the Haitian path will not prevent further deindustrialization from the denationalization of the corporate sector. Originally, a prime purpose of this denationalization was to take advantage of cheap labor, but this process has evolved since then. Today, corporate refugees from the United States do not just seek out low-wage economies. Many of the advanced corporations locate their affiliates to take advantage of superior training that students get in other countries.

The example of IBM reminds us of the fallacy of a low-wage strategy. For example, IBM-Japan has 18,000 employees, enjoys annual sales of $6 billion, and is one of Japan's largest exporters of computers. Texas Instruments employs over 5,000 people in Japan to make advanced semiconductors, almost half of which are eventually exported to the United States (Reich 1990, p. 54).

Is Deindustrialization the Rule in Market Economies?

Finally, I want to turn to a different question regarding deindustrialization: specifically, can one take comfort in the idea that the current wave of deindustrialization simply represents the elimination of a backlog of phantom capacity? Alternatively, might deindustrialization be nothing more than the normal response of an economy to a sharp increase in competitive pressures?

Common-sense, as well as earlier chapters indicates that any healthy economy certainly needs a mechanism to shed outmoded and obsolete productive capacity. Now ask yourself, what incentive do individual firms have to engage in this process?

Ideally, normal competitive pressures should induce firms to modernize. Unfortunately, modernization is easier said than done. To scrap a piece of equipment that could still be put to work constitutes a capital loss for its owner. At best, it could be sold for a relatively small amount on the second-hand market. As a result, in the absence of strong competitive pressures, firms generally have insufficient reason to pare away much inefficient plant and equipment. Under normal conditions, they will attempt to keep their plant and equipment in operation as long as possible, so long as their business is expanding.

For this reason, as I have shown, a market economy requires periodic downturns in order to generate enough competitive pressure to rid itself of old and outmoded plant and equipment. This purgative process should be part of the normal life cycle of capitalism; otherwise, an excessive buildup of phantom capacity will accumulate, eventually undermining the health of the economy.

Despite the necessity of competition for a healthy economy, competition does not occur without substantial costs. Markets impose great hardships on innocent bystanders. Plant closings are an obvious example.

Political leaders often attempt to protect business from the harsh consequences of competitive processes. Although such policies may turn out to be counterproductive in the long run, those who call for protection do not do so out of sheer stupidity. Instead, they often want to shield people from the disruptive actions of markets.

I would go so far as to say that in the United States, military Keynesianism was not so much designed to protect the "free market" from communism; the more basic goal of military Keynesianism was to shield firms and people from the threat posed by unregulated markets. True, in the process, military Keynesianism weakened the U.S. economy in the long run: without the competitive pressures that military Keynesian suppressed, firms had little incentive to replace outmoded capital goods. Economists should have foreseen the eventual economic atrophy, which people called deindustrialization. This process has now proceeded so far that people take it for granted. As a result, one rarely hears the word "deindustrialization" anymore.

Economists might have been slow to come to grips with deindustrialization because of the complexity of the competitive process. Competitive pressures are not constant over time. When competition becomes more intense, many businesses shrink or even expire. When competitive pressures become even more intense, they will annihilate both efficient and inefficient production units.

Although deindustrialization and the ideal cleansing process of a "normal" business downturn both rid the economy of old and obsolete plant and equipment, you should take care to distinguish between the two phenomena. Although sharp increases in competitive pressures might cause the economy to recede temporarily, economists' ideal of a business downturn does not lead into an outright collapse. Instead, the ideal business cycle produces short setbacks embedded within a long run process of economic growth. In contrast, deindustrialization is a long run trend, rather than a normal phase in the business cycle.

Of course, the shedding of particular industries is a normal part of long-term economic growth; so too is a gradual shift from the production of basic goods to a growing emphasis on services. Deindustrialization, however, represents an unprecedented acceleration of this normally evolutionary process. Perhaps, the closest antecedent would be the abandonment of manufacturing in Great Britain before it went into decline.

In both the ideal economic downturn and deindustrialization, most firms do not attempt to renew their industrial capacity. Instead, they attempt to increase productivity merely by eliminating less profitable plant and equipment. In the context of an ideal economic downturn, this paring of industrial capacity is a temporary phenomenon, which soon corrects itself.

You may recall the earlier discussion about the extent to which firms did renew the capital stock during the Great Depression. I do not have any firm evidence to back up my suspicion, but I believe that the firms that did renew their capital tended to be the largest and most powerful. Whether or not they were the most efficient, they were unique in having access to credit.

The net effect of this process of renewal, then, was that the big companies got bigger. Many other businesses either failed or disappeared through mergers and takeovers. Once the depression subsided, the typical industry had fewer competitors and less competitive pressure. Because of this more concentrated economic structure, an even greater crisis would be required to compel capital renewal in later years.

The long decline that followed the Golden Age differed from the Great Depression in one important respect. During the Depression, the major capitalist economies began to look inward. International trade was in retreat. During the long decline, globalization was accelerating. In this environment, competitive pressure was less effective in coercing economies to modernize their plant and equipment. Instead, they could economize by shifting their production to low-wage economies.

Many of the largest corporations—the same type of companies that renewed their plant and equipment during the Great Depression—were in the forefront of those businesses that were moving their production operations offshore during the long decline.

As a result, the corrosive process of deindustrialization stubbornly ate away at the very foundations of the economy for an extended period of time. Such a force might even turn out to be irreversible. In this sense, I feel confident in asserting that a healthy economy does not deindustrialize—unless you accept the vision of the postindustrial utopia in which all jobs are service jobs.

In a more recent book I explored the possibility that market economies suffer from a congenital tendency toward convulsive deindustrialization (Perelman 1999). Rüstow's analysis also suggests that, in the normal economic structure in which great disparities of productivity exist between the most and the least efficient plants in an industry, that economic downturns will naturally evolve into collapses.

While waves of competitive pressure may have promoted economic modernization in the past, they did so with considerable support from the government. You might note that the behavior of political leaders when a market economy experiences a crisis, suggests that they believed that the market would be incapable of recovering on its own. After all, why should the government act to cushion the blow if the problem is temporary?

Of course, the economy might have recovered on its own in a relatively brief period of time. In my opinion, it would not be likely to do so. Happily, the world has not had much opportunity to learn about the ability of a market economy to recuperate from a serious depression without government intervention.

Debates over Deindustrialization

Relatively few economists have addressed the question of whether downturns are necessary for the economic health of a market economy or if they tend to self-destruct. Most of our knowledge of the nature of slumps comes from scholars who have analyzed the historical conditions of specific economic crises.

For example, the experience of the Great Depression does not offer a great deal of hope for believers in the free market. The downturn began in 1929. Despite energetic actions by the U.S. government, the Depression did not end until World War II commenced, after more than a decade of economic hardship. In this respect, military Keynesianism seemed at the time to be necessary to the long-term survival of capitalism in the United States.

Mainstream economists often disregard the history of economic crises. Instead, they generally build theoretical models, which either assume that downturns need not occur at all or purport to prove that they could not occur in the absence of some nonmarket force. More often than not, members of this school of thought lay the blame for crises entirely at the foot of government for naively interfering with natural economic forces.

These free market ideologues argue that once some nonmarket force makes an economy experience a downturn, then market forces alone suffice to bring the economy back to health; that government intervention, which they believe had originally caused the problem, can only make things worse. Economists build their models of the robustness of the market on unrealistic assumptions that bear little relationship to the real world. These economists tend to ground their theory more on faith instead of realistic observations of actual economic events.

Among those heretical schools of thought, which do attempt to study the nature of economic slumps, we find widely divergent views. Although Keynes devoted much energy to devising a theoretical analysis of slumps, he was relatively uninterested in studying how economies would go into a depression. His concern was that an economy would remain in a depressed state for an extended period of time, not that the Depression could set off a continuing downward spiral. In contrast, Marx believed that economics crises would eventually spell the end for capitalism. Although this part of his work remained sketchy, it was very advanced for its time (see Perelman 1987).

Still, we cannot know with certainty which side is correct until we are willing to experiment by standing aside and allowing the economy to go into a free fall during some future recession. We do know that competitive pressures seem to have a built-in tendency to drive down both prices and profit rates. Firms will attempt to protect themselves by cutting wages by a greater extent than the reduction in the prices of the goods that they sell.

Investment and Taxes

As the decline became more pervasive, a growing number of economists and public officials came to accept the reality of deindustrialization, without using that specific term. They recognized that, given the floundering state of the U.S. economy, saddled with an aging and increasingly uncompetitive capital stock, something had to be done.

The Reagan administration thought that it had the answer: a program of massive tax cuts, bolstered by a strong commitment to deregulation. The administration convinced the American public that tax cuts would unleash the enormous potential of the entrepreneurial spirit of American business.

According to this scenario, reducing taxes would create a stronger economy, which would help everybody, even the tax collectors. Supposedly, with a larger tax base, total taxes would rise despite falling tax rates. In the long run, we would have more money to spend on infrastructure, education, and government services by enacting tax limitations.

In reality, taxes are a horribly inefficient instrument for stimulating basic industry. Despite its long-standing claim that excessive taxes remove much of the incentive to invest in plant and equipment, business is surprisingly insensitive to the generous tax provisions that are designed to promote investment (see Neild 1964). For example, the U.S. government has to give business an estimated $2 of immediate tax benefits to induce it to increase its investment by a single dollar (Eisner and Chirinko 1983).

To make matters worse, because U.S. business fears risking its money by investing in long-lived capital goods, much investment will be used for making money through finance rather than providing useful goods and services. For example, the Wall Street manager for Sun Microsystems expected to sell $70 million worth of computer workstations in 1991, triple the level of two years ago (Anders 1991). These systems are especially attractive to traders who want to devise new programs for extracting profits from the financial markets.

Nonetheless, the Reagan administration passed the 1981 Economic Recovery Tax Act, which dramatically cut business taxes, ostensibly to encourage investment. Indeed, business seemed to respond to the tax cut just as the Reagan administration had predicted. It increased investment in producers durable equipment by 42 percent between the second quarter of 1982 and the fourth quarter of 1984 (Bosworth 1985, p. 1).

Upon further reflection, this investment record turned out to be less impressive than it appeared to be at first sight. In 1982, the economy was emerging from the worst recession of the postwar period. Indeed, a study by the Federal Reserve Bank of New York found that modifications of the business tax code accounted for only about one-fifth of the 1983–84 increases (Sahling and Akhtar 1984–85).

Consideration of the actual composition of the investment goods leads to even more skepticism about the effectiveness of the tax incentives. Harry Magdoff and Paul Sweezy noted that investment in manufacturing capacity accounts for barely 10 percent of the total of what the government counts as capital investment (Magdoff and Sweezy 1985, p. 3). In fact, between 1979 and 1985, an astounding 93 percent of all of the growth in investment was confined to only two categories of goods: office equipment (such as computers) and transportation equipment (largely automobiles leased by business) (Bosworth 1985, p. 4).

In fact, the new tax law did not deserve much credit for the investment in office equipment. The 1981 tax law actually made investment in computers less attractive (Bosworth 1985, p. 4). In addition, the category of office equipment includes personal home computers, some of which should be classified as consumer goods.

Even if we assume that the new tax code spurred the investment in office equipment, it did little to make the economy healthier. To begin with, much of the office equipment was used to take advantage of the new opportunities made possible by the deregulation of the financial sector. In other words, a considerable portion of this office equipment helped to erect junk-bond empires and to steer the Savings and Loan system toward disaster.

In addition, productive businesses often installed office equipment to eliminate jobs rather than to expand production. Theoretically, this office equipment could have made business more productive. The resulting gains in efficiency could have stimulated general economic activity. Unfortunately, the massive infusion of office equipment did little or nothing to make management more efficient.

Much of the investment in transportation equipment did little to help the economy since it merely reflected the growing practice of leasing automobiles to take advantage of the tax laws. Leasing becomes attractive when the tax break to the automobile-leasing company is generous enough to allow it to make a profit, after passing some of the savings on to its customers.

When an individual purchases a car, the government counts the car as a consumption expenditure. In contrast, the government includes leased automobiles as investments, regardless of whether they are leased for private or business uses (Sahling and Akhtar 1984–5). Although the tax laws affected the profitability of leasing, this practice did not contribute much to economic efficiency.

Of course, debating whether or not the tax laws stimulated investment suggests that the key to economic progress is investment. Yes, new investment can benefit future economic activity, but investment is not the be-all and end-all of economics.

Economists understandably tend to think of progress in terms of investment. After all, training in economics infuses students with a spirit of thoroughgoing Calvinism. It indoctrinates students to believe that economic growth comes entirely from sacrifice, hard work, and saving. In truth, economic growth springs from two other far more important sources: the natural wealth of the planet and the creativity of the people who inhabit the planet.

Creativity Again

The Reagan administration expressed no doubts that the mix of tax cuts and deregulation would create an environment in which the creativity of the American people would flourish, thereby assuring that the U.S. economy would regain its competitiveness. No one noticed a problem with the deteriorating public capital stock. No one seemed concerned about the dangers of curtailing spending on education. The magic of the marketplace would solve all existing problems.

In one sense, the Reagan administration was not far off the mark. True, the tax cut never sparked the burst of investment that was supposed to revitalize the U.S. economy. Yes, the erosion of the public capital stock crippled the economy and public schools failed to prepare children for the future. Still, the Reaganauts were correct in pointing to the spirit and creativity of the people as the hope for the economy.

The mistake of the Reaganauts was to accept that greed, and greed alone, could rouse the spirit and creativity of the people. Yes, self-interest plays a role in motivating people to act, but a sense of a broader social purpose is more effective than greed in spurring creativity.

CHAPTER 8

High Wages, Enlightened Management, and Economic Productivity

High Wages as a Defense Against Deindustrialization

This book has tried to make the case that government policy makers are caught on the horns of a dilemma. Market economies have an inherent tendency to create strong pulses of competitive pressures, which can drive the economy into crises. Governments have a range of policy options to counteract the threat of economic collapse under competitive pressures. First, they can attempt to prevent competitive pressures from gaining strength. Military Keynesianism represents an excellent example of this strategy. Governments can also change the legal structure, allowing firms to collude to inhibit competition. All such measures, as I have shown, will eventually weaken the economy, although perhaps not as much as unbridled competition will.

When many firms attempt to maximize profits by cutting wages, markets will contract, making firms fearful about making investments. This process combines with the phenomenon, which Rüstow described: strong competitive pressure leads to the ongoing elimination of the weakest firms without a corresponding creation of a comparable quantity of new and more efficient firms. Other firms may attempt to reduce wage costs by shifting their operations abroad to low-wage economies.

This combination of forces drives the economy toward deindustrialization. For example, the recent experience of the U.S. economy with its falling real wages and runaway shops certainly conforms to the pattern of deindustrialization that Rüstow's theory suggests.

Without some sufficiently strong offsetting influence, affluent market economies may have an inherent tendency toward deindustrialization. When the financial pressures of highly leveraged firms reinforce this tendency toward falling wages and deindustrialization, the economy will have a tendency to go into violent convulsions.

One avenue does exist that allows strong competitive pressures to coexist with an expanding market: gradually raising the level of real wages. Bhaduri and Marglin provide a suggestive model that shows how increasing wages can fuel economic growth (Bhaduri and Marglin 1990). I tried to elaborate on this line of thought in an earlier work (Perelman 1999).

Although wage growth may be an effective countermeasure to prevent the tendency toward deindustrialization, protecting wages is no easy matter. Unfortunately, market economies have no inherent tendency to make real wages expand, especially when competition is strong. For example, I will show that even though the U.S. government attempted to persuade corporations to resist the temptation to cut wages during the onset of the Great Depression, it ultimately failed.

Although higher wages may benefit business in general, an individual firm will profit—especially in the short run—from a reduction in its own labor costs, providing all other employers continue to pay higher wages. Business rarely recognizes the benefits of higher wages. Instead, business tends to believe that it has a powerful incentive to curtail wage growth. If government wants to make sure that firms do not cut wages when competitive pressures intensify, it must somehow impose regulations (such as minimum-wage laws) or change the legal structure (for example, to foster the growth of unions).

Admittedly, devising effective legislation to ensure growth in wages is no easy matter, even in a closed economy without any international trade. In an open economy in which exports and imports are significant, protecting the wage level may be all but impossible without international coordination or protectionism.

As things stand today, firm after firm is attempting to circumvent what it sees as the high wage levels in the United States by moving its manufacturing operations abroad. If the U.S. economy is to be able to perform well, it needs some mechanism to protect itself from this natural tendency to depress wages when the economy is in retreat.

The Two Faces of Management-Labor Relations

Most economists are ill-prepared to come to grips with this tendency to depress wages because they habitually fall into the trap of oversimplifying the multifaceted nature of the labor-management relationship. This failing has been no less dangerous than the disregard for the two-sided nature of competition and depressions.

As a first step in addressing the complexity of the labor-management relationship, I will highlight one important dualism in this relationship: the financial perspective versus the production perspective.

The financial perspective presumes that labor is a passive participant in the production process, indistinguishable from any other inert, raw material that business purchases. Within this perspective, when employers buy labor as a commodity, the workers need only contribute their physical presence and superficial obedience.

This interpretation of the labor-management relationship is consistent with the world as seen from the firm's account books. Indeed, business has the object of shoring up its financial health, in part, by purchasing all inputs as cheaply as possible. In this respect, business justifiably treats labor as a commodity like any other—to be purchased as advantageously as possible.

In terms of the process of physically producing goods and services, labor takes on an entirely different appearance. On the shop floor and in the office, business must pay close attention to the specific details of labor's activities. In this respect, employers expect more than just the bodily presence and superficial obedience of their workers. Herein lies the essence of this other face of management-labor relations.

In evaluating the production process, some employers recognize that they will profit when workers feel obligated to exert themselves and perhaps even to bring creativity and ingenuity to their work. Some employers even call upon their workers to excel, but nobody exerts himself or herself to the utmost without a strong desire to do so—certainly not people who feel that their employer regards them as nothing more than a mere commodity to be bought as cheaply as possible.

How then should employers cajole or entice their workers into performing their tasks as well as possible relative to the wages that they earn? Employers have a wide range of options for managing labor at their disposal. At one extreme, business can resort to the threat of punishment for unsatisfactory work. Workers under this sort of regime soon realize that, if they fail to perform adequately, they will be rendered unable to feed themselves and their families. Under a regime based on strict discipline, business practices are consistent with the financial perspective.

This method has several drawbacks. First, in a prosperous economy, workers have the option of finding alternative employment if they lose their jobs. Second, while a heightened anxiety can admittedly increase work effort, it also impairs the performance of skilled tasks (Fenoaltea 1984).

In short, this system of threats can only be effective for tasks that are easy to monitor and that require a minimum of care (see Fenoaltea 1984). Resentful workers will always find ways to withhold effort or even to sabotage the business where they work. As Eugene Genovese has shown, not even slave owners were able to achieve absolute dominance over the workplace, even though the technical complexity of the slave's responsibilities was relatively limited (Genovese 1976).

At the other extreme, employers can attempt to instill a spirit of cooperation, in which workers identify with the interest of their employer. Employers have various options for eliciting this cooperation. They can reward workers financially for good work or they can appeal to the workers by offering them an exciting challenge. For example, in his award-winning book, *The Soul of a New Machine,* Tracy Kidder depicted the zeal with which engineers for Data General competed to develop a new computer (Kidder 1981).

Most of all, if employers want to use the carrot to elicit effort rather than to rely on the proverbial stick, they will have to treat workers with respect. You should not be surprised that sticks are far more popular than carrots in management circles in the contemporary United States, despite the occasional rhetorical flourishes that might suggest otherwise.

After all, the allure of treating labor as a commodity is self-evident. Using punishment to control the labor process is devilishly simple to administer, even though it is relatively ineffective, and possibly even counterproductive, except for anything but the crudest sort of labor. In contrast, while the use of incentives can be extremely effective, incentives are exceedingly difficult to administer.

Of course, no firm relies exclusively either on threats or on positive incentives. In effect, employers choose a mix of these two seemingly contradictory sets of incentives. The employer promises to reward workers to make them perform their jobs well or even take pride in their work. They appeal to the workers' ambition and self-respect.

Because employers have no assurance that the bargain will create the desired attitude in their labor force, employers also tell the workers that they are entirely dispensable.

Employers convey the message—perhaps even intentionally—that no individual worker is anything special. Should any employee fail to satisfy the employer or ask for too much money, then the employer stands ready to fire that worker and hire another, who presumably will do a better job.

In this sense, the employer's message is essentially antagonistic. Yet, in appealing to the workers to put a great deal of themselves into their work, the employers' message conveys cooperation and a mutuality of interests.

The Internal Politics of Management-Labor Relations

Finding the proper mix of threat and incentive is no simple task, but the employer must somehow make these two essentially contradictory messages coherent. Coherence is all the more elusive because of the subtlety of the labor-management relationship.

Workers evaluate the specific combination of signals within any employment relationship in terms of an unstated norm of "fairness." When workers perceive employers as fair—when they feel that they are treated with respect—they respond accordingly.

Both labor and management attempt to control the labor process. From this perspective, workers are active agents, with goals of their own and with the ingenuity and creativity to accomplish these goals, at least in part. If an employer violates the workers' norm of fairness, the employees will seek redress by withholding their cooperation.

These disgruntled workers often go to great lengths to exercise some control over the labor process, even when they have no expectation of wringing any concessions from management, often with dire consequences for the firm. Michael Burawoy attempted to come to grips with the depth of the tensions between labor and management by interpreting the workplace as an "internal state" (Burawoy 1979, p. 11). Within this state, each party—labor and management—has certain unspecified powers.

Indeed, the idea of exercising some control over their activity, even when that control is nothing more than the disruption of the labor process, can be a source of pride and even delight to workers. In fact, workers, who might not be inclined to work harder for monetary rewards, sometimes go to great lengths just to assert their independence vis-à-vis management.

For example, Burawoy described a piecework machine shop that produced parts for truck engines, where workers transformed the incentive system into a game to relieve their boredom. Within this game, these workers developed a complex equilibrium with inspectors. If an inspector challenged them by rejecting articles with marginal tolerance, workers would retaliate by turning out scrap after the first piece was rejected, making the inspector look bad. Underlying their game was a need to relieve boredom rather than any economic motives (Burawoy 1979, p. 89). Workers sometimes attempted to produce as much as 140 percent of the norm. They resisted producing any more than 140 percent only because they feared an upward revision of what the employer would expect of them.

These workers could have turned their creativity to making the plant more productive, but to do so would not have done much for their self-respect. When this cynical creativity becomes general, the economy as a whole will become less competitive within the world economy.

Because management typically adheres to the financial perspective of labor-management relations, it is unable to comprehend how much it loses by failing to tap workers creativity. Academic authorities—especially economists—do not offer much guidance in this regard. Burawoy rightfully charged that, "Political economy has conspired in a separation of economics and politics, never attempting to theorize a politics of production. Production has both ideological and political effects" (Burawoy 1979, p. 7).

In many cases, management attacks labor in order to wring economic concessions from the workers. In many other cases, the financial perspective leads management to display an insensitivity that can push workers to turn their creativity to disruptive ends. Harley Shaiken writes of an incident that illustrates the importance of according adequate respect to the workers:

> A familiar sight in most shops is an engineer walking in with a stack of blueprints to ask the worker if a particular job is feasible. The machinist carefully studies the prints, looks at the engineer, and says, "Well, it can be tried like this but it will never work." Grabbing a pencil, the machinist marks up the print and, in effect, redesigns the job based on years of experience. . . .
>
> [In one shop, when] management initiated a campaign to strictly enforce lunch periods and wash-up time, the judgment of some machinists began to fade. About this time a foreman dashed up to the shop with a "hot" job. . . . Anxious to get the job done quickly, the foreman insisted that the machinist run the lathe at a high speed and plunge the drill through the part. Under normal circumstances the machinist would have tried to talk the foreman out of this approach but now he was only too happy to oblige what were, after all, direct orders. The part not only turned out to be scrap, but part of the lathe turned blue from the friction generated by the high speed. The disciplinary campaign was short-lived. [Shaiken 1985, pp. 19–20]

Shaiken's vignette illustrates business's ultimate dependence on labor's cooperation. Once labor withdraws this cooperative spirit, business is in trouble. Observing a similar situation, Shoshana Zuboff captured the subtle ambivalence of the management labor-relationship, noting that "obedience fed by cynicism became a form of revenge" (Zuboff 1988, p. 273).

Not infrequently, employers implore their workers to excellence, but this excellence is of a particular kind. Management expects workers to perform to their utmost according to the directives that it gives them. Workers are unlikely to display such unthinking excellence. Even if they were, it would be impossible unless the employer were able to anticipate all contingencies in advance. Shaiken's vignette suggests how difficult it would be to "pre-program" workers for their tasks. Instead, an efficient workforce must be able to find some satisfaction in the work it performs.

The Advantage of a Cooperative Policy Toward Labor

The need to tap workers' creativity is especially crucial in highly advanced technological systems, where management depends on labor in developing the best possible methods of production (see Glyn, Hughes, Lipietz, and Singh 1990, p. 89). Unfortunately, relatively few employers adequately acknowledge the degree of skill involved on the job.

Instead, employers prefer to attempt to coerce labor into absolute obedience with the threat of unemployment. By compelling obedience through coercion, management stifles the creativity, which is central to the successful functioning of modern industry. This approach does serious harm to the economy. As Richard Walton, an expert on progressive pay schemes, has observed:

> Especially in a high wage country like the United States, market success depends on a superior level of performance, a level that, in return requires the deep commitment, not merely the obedience—if you could obtain it—of workers. And as painful experience shows, this commitment cannot flourish in a workplace dominated by the familiar model of control. [Walton 1985, pp. 77–78; cited in Glyn, Hughes, Lipietz, and Singh 1990, p. 89]

In contrast to the United States, Japanese firms were extremely successful at tapping the knowledge of their workers. For example, the average worker in a Toyota plant gave 31.8 suggestions in 1983. Of these, 96 percent were accepted (Kaplinsky 1988, p. 460). Now that recent financial pressures are causing the Japanese companies to adopt a more "American" business style, I suspect that this sort of response is becoming a source of nostalgia.

The Japanese approach was not novel. In fact, during the late nineteenth century foreign observers associated this approach with the United States. For example, British industrialists visiting the United States realized that worker involvement was an integral part of the success of the U.S. economy. An industrialist, A. Mosely, head of one of the many delegations of British industrialists that visited the United States at the beginning of this century, reported:

> One point that has struck me with enormous force, as I believe it has all the delegates, is the close touch and sympathy between master and man, which is carried a step further in the enlistment of the men's good offices to improve factory methods. Suggestions are welcomed, the more so because the American manufacturer has realized that it is not the man sitting in the counting-house or private office who is best able to judge where improvements can be made in machine or method, but he who attends that machine from morning to night. . . . In short, the man feels that the work of his brains will handsomely benefit himself. Is it any wonder, therefore, that American machinery is continually changing and improving, that the evolution of methods is ever and rapidly going on? . . . As a rule the British employer hardly knows his men, seldom leaves his office for the workshop. [Offer 1989, p. 124]

A cooperative labor policy can and will make an economy healthier. Nonetheless, treating labor with respect and rewarding workers to encourage productivity is not a panacea, which can permanently rid the economy of crises. Moreover, the inevitable extended bouts of unemployment, typical of a market economy, will work to embitter workers. Still, within the bounds of a market economy, a cooperative labor policy is about the best rule to follow. The alternative is the Haitian road to development.

The Economy of High Wages

Business often complains that high wages are the root of many of the ills of the U.S. economy. Presumably, the economy could prosper if only we could maintain low enough wages. Such reasoning is absolute nonsense.

Low wages ensure *low,* not high productivity. In fact, the United States historically enjoyed a high rate of productivity growth just because wages in the United States exceeded those of the rest of the world.

Economists usually turn this analysis around. From the very beginning of their introductory economics classes, most students learn that high productivity causes high wages rather than the other way around. The conventional theory is correct insofar as a group of workers with an especially valuable skill can command a high wage rate, but it explains only part of the wage-productivity relationship. This section analyzes the other side of the coin: that higher wages can result in greater productivity.

Because the expression, "the economy of high wages," has a long and distinguished lineage, dating from the late nineteenth century, we will continue to refer to high wages. Moreover, I will not lead you astray in this discussion by treating high wages in terms of a commonsense understanding of what high wages means, although you will see that what constitutes high wages has a subjective component.

I want to explore several means by which high wages can benefit an economy. To begin with, high wages stimulate demand.

Second, the increasing demand associated with high wages helps to create what economists call, "economies of scale," a term that refers to the savings that high volume producers enjoy. As these economies of scale develop, firms can afford to pay higher wages, augmenting demand still more. Here again we have an example of cumulative causation.

Third, high wages encourage employers to develop improved technologies to save labor. In this vein, one writer described high wages as a "productivity whip" (Streeck 1992, p. 40). Unlike the pressure of price competition, the whip of high wages forces firms to economize without constricting the demand for goods and services (see Perelman 1999). Indeed, it expands demand as the previous point indicated.

Fourth, high wages stimulate workers to be more productive. A number of studies show that workers respond to higher wages by contributing more effort to the jobs (Akerlof and Yellen 1986).

Finally, to the extent that high wages promote investment in new technologies, workers often respond to the challenge of working with new techniques by developing their own skills and abilities. Shoshana Zuboff's work offers dramatic examples of this response by workers in a variety of environments (Zuboff 1988).

Despite the numerous economies of high wages, one must be careful not to treat the subject dogmatically. For example, high wages will not necessarily create economies of scale in all economies at all times. Imagine a small country in a crowded region of the world with cheap transportation and relatively free trade, say Luxembourg. If wages rise there, employers could conceivably move to a neighboring country to take advantage of cheaper labor costs—although in this particular example such an exodus has not occurred.

In addition, much of the extension of demand is likely to be dissipated in imports. In a massive nation, such as the early United States, which was geographically isolated from much of the rest of the industrialized world and which was largely protected from foreign competition by high tariffs and duties on imported goods, high wages worked magnificently. To the extent that improvements in transportation and communication make the economy more open, the benefits of high wages are less assured.

In addition, the benefits of high wages partially depend on the ability of business to discover new labor-saving technologies, which will ultimately promote competitiveness. No guarantee exists that the new methods of production that business develops will be so efficient that firms will be able to more than compensate for a higher level of wages.

Despite such qualifications to the theory of high wages, maintaining a healthy rate of wage growth offers a far more promising outcome than attempting to compete by depressing wages.

Efficiency Wages

I want to explore in more detail the notion that high wages can improve the human element in the production process. I cannot do much better in this respect than to cite Alfred Marshall, the author of the leading textbook on economics during the first quarter of the twentieth century. Marshall wisely observed:

> [I]t was only in the last generation that a careful study was begun to be made on the effects that high wages have in increasing the efficiency not only of those who receive them, but also of their children and grandchildren. In this the lead have been taken by Walker and other American economists; and the application of the comparative method of study to the industrial problems of different countries of the old and new worlds is forcing constantly more and more attention to the fact that highly paid labour is generally efficient and therefore not dear labour. [Marshall 1920, p. 510]

This statement is interesting in several respects. First Marshall's reference to children and grandchildren—to which I will return later—indicates how high wages can changes workers' character so profoundly that the benefits will carry over to their children and grandchildren. This phenomenon is relevant to the earlier discussion of the contemporary crisis in education in the United States.

Secondly, Marshall's uses of the term "forcing" serves as a reminder that most business people and economists still resist the notion that "highly paid labour is generally efficient and therefore, not dear labour," although, as I shall discuss later, some larger firms are more aware of the benefits of high wages.

Finally, Marshall knew that the United States paid higher wages than anywhere else and that its economy was the most powerful in the world. As a result, he could mention without any need for further comment that the American economists were the pioneers in discovering the beneficial influence of high wages.

Marshall's words suggest that the technical competency that accompanies high wages becomes contagious. In the first place, high wages allow other family members and even friends to become acquainted with modern technologies. Just as children acquire computer skills through video games today, during the Golden Age, many children honed their mechanical abilities by fixing up old cars.

The transmission of skills does not depend only on learning through consumer goods. Workers who take pride in their work will share their experiences with other workers, on and off the job. In this way, expertise will permeate society.

Given these important pathways through which high wages induce workers to develop their abilities, individual employers will reap only part of the spillovers from the high wages that they pay. They will be willing to pay only for the direct benefits they receive from their expenditures on wages. They will not take the indirect benefits into account. In terms of economic theory, this situation creates an insufficient incentive to pay high enough wages.

To make matters worse, many employers fail to realize that high wages can improve the quality of their workers' output. In this sense they will not even take into account all the direct benefits that they can reap from paying their workers more.

Of course, some employers had understood the benefits of high wages, even long before the writers that Marshall cited. For example, in 1835 a British writer, Andrew Ure, posed a question about the subject to a number of authorities. He asked "how with . . . surplus hands the wages of fine spinners can be maintained at their present high pitch?" Ure reported:

> One of the best informed manufacturers made me this reply: "We find a moderate saving in the wages to be of little consequence in comparison of contentment and we therefore keep them as high as we can possibly afford, in order to be entitled to the best quality of work. A spinner reckons the charge of a pair of mules in our factory a fortune for life, he will therefore do his utmost to retain his situation, and to uphold the high character of our yarn." [Ure 1835, p. 336; cited in Marglin 1990, p. 15]

Lamentably, we have forgotten much since the days of Ure.

The Tradition of the United States as a High-Wage Economy

The historical record of the U.S. economy does suggest that business did indeed manage to create new technologies fast enough to make prices fall, even in the face of rising wages.

Certainly the rapidity of technical change struck most observers of the early United States. For example, the renowned French visitor, Alexis de Tocqueville, reported:

> I accost an American sailor, and I inquire why the ships of his country are built so as to last for a short time; he answers without hesitation that the art of navigation is every day making such a rapid progress that the finest vessel would become almost useless if it lasted beyond a certain number of years. [de Tocqueville 1835, II, p. 420]

H. J. Habakkuk wrote an entire book about the positive effect of high wages on technical change in the United States during the nineteenth century. According to Habakkuk: "The Secretary of the Treasury reported in 1832, that the garrets and outhouses of most textile mills were crowded with discarded machinery. One Rhode Island mill built in 1813 had by 1827 scrapped and replaced every original machine" (Habakkuk 1962, p. 57; and the numerous references he cites).

The anticipation of early retirement of plant and equipment in the United States was so pervasive that manufacturers in the United States built their machinery from wood rather than more durable materials, such as iron (Strassman 1959, p. 88).

Throughout the nineteenth century, commentators continued to echo de Tocqueville's observation that technology in the United States was designed to be short-lived (Schoenhof 1893). For example, in the late nineteenth century, the U.S. secretary of state commissioned Joseph Schoenhof to inquire into the effects of high wages on the competitiveness of business in the United States. Schoenhof concluded:

> the employer of labor is . . . benefited by the inevitable results of a high rate of wages. . . . [T]he first object of the employer is to economize its employment.
>
> Manufacturers introducing a change in manufactures have a machine built to accomplish what in other countries would be left to hand labor to bring about. Machinery, used to the limit of its life in Europe, is cast aside in America if only partially worn. [Schoenhof 1893, pp. 33–34]

The Cornell economist, Jeremiah Jenks asserted: "No sooner has the capitalist fairly adopted one improved machine, than it must be thrown away for a still later and better invention, which must be purchased at a dear cost, if the manufacturer would not see himself eclipsed by his rival" (Jenks 1890, p. 254; cited in Livingston 1986, p. 39).

This pattern of rapid capital renewal made the manufacturing capacity in the United States the envy of the world. By the turn of the century, exports from the United States were inundating Europe, much the same as Japanese exports were displacing manufacturing in the United States during the 1970s and 1980s. Just as people in the United States today tried to discover the secret of Japanese ascendancy in popular books, English readers pored over alarmist books with titles, such as *The American Invaders* (1901), *The Americanization of the World* (1901), or *The American Invasion* (1902) (Wright 1990, p. 652).

By the late nineteenth century, rapid technical change had brought productivity in the United States to such a high level that the rationale for high wages shifted from the first reason to the second and third.

High Wages and Protectionism

The early case for high wages rested on the notion that high wages (together with protectionism) would stimulate the demand for new industries, helping them grow and mature, and eventually to benefit from economies of scale. The new emphasis stressed greater substitution of capital for labor and the promotion of a more productive labor force.

In fact, leading protectionists, such as David Wells, became eventually so confident about the competitive position of the U.S. economy that they abandoned their previous advocacy of protective tariffs and called for free trade (Wells 1885). Wells and his school were certain that the highly paid U.S. labor force could easily out-compete what they regarded as pauper labor in the rest of the world.

Where Ure's previously cited informant made the case for high wages in terms of "the high character of our yarn," writers in the United States were more likely to discuss the association of high wages with a high character of the worker. For example, Wells observed: "High wages, then, are the normal result of low cost, and low cost is the normal result in turn of intelligence, conjoined with good machinery, applied to great resources for production" (Wells 1885, p. 138).

Wells's insight has been lost on most business people in recent decades. Today, they seem to be infatuated with the narrow financial perspective on the complex relationship between labor and capital.

Wells noted that wages in England's cotton industry were from 30 to 50 percent higher than in France, Belgium, and Germany. He observed that an English cotton operative received more wages in a week than a Russian in a month. Yet the continent demanded protection against English labor (Wells 1885, p. 137).

Gregory Clark published an extensive survey of this relationship between high wages and British competitiveness in an article entitled, "Why Isn't The Whole World Developed? Lessons from the Cotton Mills" (Clark 1987). Although British wages were less than those earned in the United States, they were high relative to the rest of the world. According to Clark, compared with Manchester, hourly wages on the Continent ranged from less than 25 percent as high in Prussia to 47 percent in Rouen (Clark 1987, p. 142).

In 1911, 140 years after the first cotton mills and despite an enormous wage cost disadvantage, 40 percent of all factory spindles were in England. Another 22 percent were in the United States and Canada. Low-wage countries had only 39 percent of all spindles worldwide (Clark 1987, p. 143).

Clark reported that in 1910, one New England cotton textile worker was equivalent to 1.5 British or 2.3 German workers. Compared to lower-wage economies, the difference was phenomenal. New England textile operatives tended six times as much machinery per shift as workers in the Greek, Japanese, Indian, or Chinese textile industries (Clark 1987, p. 150).

A Test of the Theory of High Wages

During the period immediately following World War I, Well's vision was widely shared. At the time, business, especially small business, took great pains to crush unions and root out "subversives," suggesting that this willingness to pay high wages was not driven by some humanitarian instinct. Nonetheless, business understood the wisdom of the notion that high wages could augment profits. For example, Herbert Hoover told an audience on 12 May 1926:

> The very essence of great production is high wages and low prices. . . . the acceptance of these ideas is obviously not universal. Not all employers . . . nor has every union abandoned the fallacy of restricted effort. . . . But . . . for both employer and employee to think in terms of the mutual interest of increased production has gained in strength. It is a long cry from the conception of the old economics. [cited in Barber 1985, p. 30]

Hoover's reasoning was that sufficiently high wages would eliminate the appeal of unions; that high wages would make labor feel that its interests were at one with those of business. The key to the high-wage policy of the 1920s was the restriction of immigration—although the restrictions drew upon xenophobic emotions as well as economic realism. Thomas Nixon Carver, a famous Harvard economist exclaimed:

> To be alive today, in this country, and to remember the years from 1870 to 1920 is to awake from a nightmare. Those were the years when our ideas were all but obscured by floods of cheap laborers upon whose cheap labor great fortunes were made, and by floods of abuse because we were not instantaneously solving all the social and economic problems these newcomers were inflicting upon us. Those were the years of slums and

> socialist agitators, of blatant demagogues and social legislation. [Carver 1925, pp. 261–2; cited in Barber 1985, p. 30]

For both Hoover and Carver, the degree of the appeal of the socialist agitator was an excellent indicator of the low level of intelligence of the worker. Limiting immigration and raising wages would expand the intelligence of the American worker, which, in turn, would increase productivity. Stripped of their racial and political biases, Carver and Hoover were correct about the outcome of cutting back on the supply of low-wage workers.

The average number of immigrants fell dramatically, from 856,000 in 1910–15 to 356,000 in 1915–30. The decrease in male immigrants was even more extreme, falling from 584,000 to 217,000. Yet, this decline in this major source of unskilled labor coincided with a rise in the demand for manufactured goods (Oshima 1984, p. 163).

Standard economic theory suggests that curtailing immigration will create a shortage of unskilled workers relative to skilled workers. To some extent, migration of workers from agriculture compensated for the curtailment of immigration, but only to a degree.

One would expect that the wages of unskilled workers would rise relative to the wages of skilled workers. Nothing of the kind occurred. Instead, employers invested in an enormous quantity of machines, so much so that the wages of unskilled labor fell 8 percent compared with 3 percent for skilled workers between 1920 and 1929 (Oshima 1984, p. 164). In the process, output per hour of work increased by 48 percent during this same period (Jerome 1934, p. 5; see also Dumenil, Glick, and Rangel 1987). Given this phenomenal increase in productivity, personal consumption expenditures for manufactured goods climbed from $11 billion in 1912–1921, measured in 1929 dollars, to $17 billion, 1922–31, again measured in 1929 dollars (Oshima 1984, p. 163).

Falling Wages During the Great Depression

Even with the onset of the Great Depression, a substantial portion of big business refrained from cutting wages, fearing that a wave of decreases in wages would set off a downward spiral that could spin out of control. In the words of Jacob Viner: "the Hoover Administration became apostles of the . . . doctrine that high wages are a guarantee and an essential of prosperity." At the beginning of the depression, Hoover pledged industry not to cut wages, and for a long time large-scale industry adhered to this pledge (Viner 1933, p. 12; cited in O'Brien 1989, pp. 724–25).

Many firms, especially large firms, were in agreement with President Hoover, convinced that cutting wages would only intensify the crisis. As a result, during the early years of the Depression, wages remained surprisingly steady. In fact, hourly wages in manufacturing declined only about 2 percent by January 1931, 17 months into the downturn (O'Brien 1989, p. 720). Since prices were falling during the first years of the Depression, the buying power of the hourly wage was rising.

Rather than cutting wages, firms employed their workers for fewer hours (Bernanke 1986; Sherman 1981). In some industries, the total number of hours worked dropped by more than 50 percent, far more than the drop in the numbers of workers employed. Bernanke estimates that changes in the average number of hours worked per week contributed nearly as much as changes in employment to variations in the earnings of labor over the course of the Depression (Bernanke 1986, p. 82).

Herbert Hoover recalled with pride that the American Federation of Labor noted that in the depression of 1921, 92 percent of firms reporting to the Bureau of Labor Statistics cut wages; in 1931, only 7 percent did so (Hoover 1952, p. 46). In part, this stability of wages was illusory since firms often dismissed the least-paid workers and shifted foreman to working on the shop floor. As a result, the wages that an individual earned declined while average wages may remain unchanged (Lebergott 1990; see also Jensen 1989). Even so, the relative stability of wages was remarkable.

Large firms' initial reluctance to cut wages substantially dampened the intensity of the initial contraction in the United States. Large employers, committed to maintaining a steady level of wages, would be likely to turn to capital renewal as the obvious strategy to make their operations more efficient. Such investment would have helped to buffer the shock of the Depression.

As I have already shown, this capital renewal was far from insignificant. Think back to Staehle's estimates about the extent to which firms renewed their capital stock during the Depression. His calculations underestimate the extent of capital renewal since they only begin in 1933, after the wage collapse was underway.

The pattern of intensity of research and development offers more evidence of emphasis on modernization during the Depression. Although we might expect to find a curtailment of research and development during a depression, such was not the case. Many large firms also responded to the crisis by intensifying their research and development. In fact, the value of industrial research and development expenditures, adjusted for inflation, actually increased during the Great Depression and fell during the war (United States Department of Labor 1989).

Large corporations' willingness to refrain from cutting wages for a long time after the onset of the Depression was remarkable, but it was not enough to stave off the contractionary forces that eventually overwhelmed the economy. You can best understand the inevitability of the collapse in light of the interplay between the differing situations of large and small business operations.

Large firms had a number of advantages over small firms. Let me mention only two. To begin with, many large firms enjoy economies of scale. Second, during the Great Depression, banks tended to ration credit to their most valued customers, which tended to be the large firms rather than their smaller counterparts (Hunter 1982). As a result, small firms were less able to invest than large firms were (see Calomiris and Hubbard 1990; Fazzari, Hubbard, and Peterson 1988). Presumably, this lack of access to credit precluded many small firms from competing through modernization. Given their circumstances, many small firms had little choice but to lower wages.

The large manufacturing firms tend to achieve their economies of scale by creating relatively inflexible, capital-intensive production structures that can only operate efficiently at high levels of output. In contrast, although small manufacturing firms have higher costs, they are more agile and are better able to absorb fluctuations in demand. In general, the output of small firms tends to be more unstable than that of large firms (Mills and Schumann 1985; and Carlson 1989).

Now consider the differential impact of a depression on large and small firms. Under depression conditions, the output of small firms will fall to a much greater extent than their larger counterparts. Since small-scale firms are more labor-intensive, they will experience more pressure to cut wage costs, especially since the depression will hit them harder than the large manufacturing firm.

Wages only began to collapse around October 1931. The result bore out big business's initial fear of the impact of wage cutting, since soon thereafter the Depression moved into a far more serious phase (O'Brien 1989, p. 720). At this point, with firms laying off workers and shutting down factories, the inclination toward capital deepening would be likely to be far weaker than it would have been during the initial phase of the Depression. Think back to Richards's observation that the short-payback rule became common after 1932 as anecdotal evidence of this weakening of the intensity of capital renewal at the time (Richards 1933). Unfortunately, I know of no database capable of confirming or refuting my hypothesis about the pattern of capital renewal.

Mitigating Factors

The Great Depression wreaked havoc on society, especially after wages began to collapse, but the immediate effect of the Depression was not as destructive as it might have been. Fortunately, many large corporations did not abandon their longer-term perspective all at once. Having superior access to credit, many large corporations took advantage of the situation to make some use of their excess capacity by redirecting production into new industries.

The dean of U.S. business historians, Alfred Chandler, offered numerous examples of firms that responded to the crisis brought on by the Depression by expanding the scope of their operations. In an early work on the subject, he wrote:

> It took the economic pressure created by the slowing down of the economy in the 1920s and its miserable performance in the 1930s to turn these technically sophisticated enterprises to the new strategy of expansion. Precisely because these firms had accumulated vast resources in skilled manpower, facilities, and equipment, their executives were under even greater pressure than those of the smaller firms to find new markets as the old one's ceased to grow. . . . During the Depression General Motors moved into diesels, appliances, tractors, and airplanes. Some makers of primary materials, particularly aluminum and copper, turned to consumer products like kitchen ware and household fittings, while rubber firms developed the possibilities of rubber chemistry to compensate for declining tire sales. In the same period food companies employed their existing distribution organizations to market an increasing variety of products. [Chandler 1969, p. 275]

Later, Chandler wrote: "In the 1930s, as the depression in farming contracted the agricultural equipment market, International Harvester began to produce construction equipment, trucks, and other commercial vehicles" (Chandler 1990, p. 603).

Although such diversification might occur at any time, Michael Gort found statistical evidence that, among the large firms that he studied, it was more frequent during the Depression than at other times (Gort 1962). Gort's data may even understate the importance of the impetus that the Depression gave to diversification.

The Dissipation of the Residual Momentum of High Wages

As wages began to decline, the wisdom of an economy of high wages fell into oblivion. Nonetheless, high wages continued to work to the benefit of the U.S. economy throughout the first half of the twentieth century and into the Golden Age even though economic and political leaders ceased to believe in the economy of high wages.

Consider the relative prices of labor and capital. For example, from 1939 to 1947, average hourly wages of industrial workers in the United States increased by 95 percent, compared with only 39 percent for the prices of machine tools. In fact, some authors have singled out high wages as the key to the success of the Golden Age (see Glyn et al. 1990, p. 57).

The era of high wages did not continue indefinitely. It came to an end in the mid- to late 1960s, just as the first signs of the economic decline began to appear. Seymour Melman uses the relative growth of wages and the average prices of metalworking tools to track this phenomenon. During the Golden Age, wages rose much faster than the prices of metalworking tools, sparking a great deal of investment. Then, from 1965 to 1977, when the productivity collapse first became apparent, the average prices of metalworking tools rose by almost the same amount as wages. During the latter part of that period, the ratio became even more unfavorable to labor. Between 1971 and 1978, wages increased 72 percent. In comparison, the prices of machine tools rose 85 percent (Melman 1983, pp. 3–5).

In fact, each year after 1975, the index of capital costs grew more than the index of unit labor costs (Melman 1983, pp. 3–5 and 168). In the case of the agricultural sector, the ratio of farm labor costs to machinery costs explained a substantial portion of the rise in the investment in tractors (Kislev and Peterson 1982).

As real wages fell in the advanced capitalist countries during the late 1960s and 1970s, business reduced the real value of the equipment with which it supplied the average worker, just as you would expect (Schmid 1981). From 1950 to 1965, business expanded its capital stock by two percentage points more than the growth in total hours. After 1965, the capital stock growth rate exceeded the rate of growth in hours by only 1 percent (Kopcke 1980, p. 26).

As the Golden Age came to a close, the business and political leaders of the United States were all but unanimous in calling for an economy of low wages—a certain recipe for economic disaster. Indeed, average hourly earnings, measured in 1982 dollars, fell from their 1973 peak of $8.55 to $7.86 in 1999 (United States President 2000, Table B 45, p. 360). As might be expected, manufacturing continued to decline.

High Wages in an International Context

High wages can benefit developing countries as well as advanced countries. For example, Arghiri Emmanuel even went so far as to identify imperialism as a process that unfairly kept wages high in the developed countries (Emmanuel 1972). Here is his capsule summary of British relations with India:

> Britain exchanged her cotton goods for Indian cotton and gained from this exchange the means of paying high wages to her workers. The day when India took up weaving . . .

> Britain changed her approach. She began to exchange her cotton yarn for Indian cotton and Indian fabrics. Then India started to produce her own yarn. So now Britain exchanges her looms and spindles for Indian fabrics, still obtaining the wherewithal to pay her workers high wages. [Emmanuel 1972, p. 146]

According to Emmanuel, "there is not a single example where high wages have not led to economic development" (Emmanuel 1972, p. 124). Although Emmanuel is prone to overstate his case, there was more than an element of truth in his analysis. Certainly, he is far closer to the truth than those who advocate low wages. Of course, if real wages rise too quickly, profits can collapse, but a steady rise in wages is probably an essential element of a competitive economy.

In reality, an economy can enjoy the benefits of high wages even when it pays wages considerably below the norm for other parts of the world. The recently developing, low-wage nations of Southeast Asia constitute a case in point. In countries, such as these, which begin with a poor agricultural population, industrial workers may consider themselves to be earning high wages during the initial stages of development, even when their wages are a pittance by the own standards of the more affluent economies. Industrial wages continued to grow in these nations until the Asian Crisis of 1997, in part, due to the economies of high wages. This pattern of rising wages served these economies well, although now, they, like Japan, have begun to conform to the management norms of the United States.

Over time, these workers will revise their notion of high wages. As a result, wages must continue to increase at a relatively brisk rate. If they do not, workers may turn to political activism to bring their wages in line with their evolving norms of fairness.

For example, the Korean government long used savage repression to keep wages in check. Once the Korean government suddenly reduced the level of repression in 1988, wages soared. For example, at Lucky-Goldstar, wages doubled from 1988 to 1990 (Nakarmi 1991). Not surprisingly, profits fell considerably, but given a bit of time to adjust to these higher wages, advances in technology might have more than compensated firms for their higher wage costs.

Instead, the Korean government, like many others around the world, began to follow the advice of the International Monetary Fund. They opened up their financial system to the world market, leaving them vulnerable to the Asian crisis.

Had wages in this region continued to rise, within a few decades, these poor, but perhaps subjectively high-wage countries would have evolved into what might objectively be considered high-wage countries.

Surprise! Unions Can Promote Productivity

Now that the theory of efficiency wages that Herbert Hoover espoused has fallen from view, the popular press has conditioned the public to associate high wages with the scourge of unionization. This ominous force has supposedly sabotaged the health and welfare of the U.S. economy in more ways than we can count.

In fact, unions play, at worst, an ambiguous role in the economy. True, to protect the welfare of their members, unions have created numerous work rules that impede productivity, but many of these work rules also serve valuable purposes, often protecting workers' health and safety.

Conversely, unions have promoted productivity in important ways. To begin with, by raising wages, unions have prodded employers to devise new and improved, labor-saving methods of production, just as the theory of efficiency wages suggests. The precise impact of this "productivity whip" will not be obvious, since many nonunion firms will also eventually adopt these new techniques. Consequently, the spread of these techniques will appear to be part of the general pattern of industrial progress.

Even so, economists consistently find that workers in unionized firms are more productive than workers in comparable nonunion companies, despite the impact of union work-rules. For example, Richard Freeman and James Medoff concluded that the detrimental effects of union work rules on efficiency tend to be very small (Freeman and Medoff 1984, p. 12). They uncovered "striking new evidence on what unions do to productivity" (Freeman and Medoff 1984, p. 163). They called their results "striking" because they were able to conclude, "In sum, most studies of productivity find that unionized establishments are more productive than otherwise comparable nonunion establishments" (Freeman and Medoff 1984, p. 169).

Freeman and Medoff are not alone in regarding unionization to be consistent with high productivity. For example, Steven Allen estimated that union work rules increase typical office building costs by about two percent (Allen 1986a). Allen found that union productivity, measured in square feet of floor space completed per hour worked, was at least 30 percent higher than nonunion productivity.

In the construction of school projects, union productivity was equal to nonunion productivity measured by the number of workers required to build a project. Measured in terms of value-added, union productivity was 20 percent higher then nonunion productivity (Allen 1986b). Allen also found that union projects produce 51 percent more square footage per hour than nonunion projects (Allen 1988a). After reviewing the literature concerning the relationship between unions and productivity, Allen concluded that most studies find that union workers are more productive than nonunion workers in comparable establishments (Allen 1988b).

Unions even make teachers more productive. For example, students from schools with a unionized environment score about 4.7 percent higher on their college entrance exams than their counterparts from a nonunion environment (Register and Grimes 1991).

In fairness, we cannot conclude that unions necessarily cause this increase in productivity. In part, unions may be an effect, rather than a cause of high productivity. In other words, firms that are highly productive may be forcing workers to exert themselves beyond what the employees consider to be fair. Indeed, as Tibor Scitovsky noted, in the West in general, workers who felt exploited and resentful frequently turned to unionization in an attempt to create a defensive force to match the force of their employers (Scitovsky 1990, p. 144).

Several authors have built on generalizations, such as Scitovsky's, to reach the conclusion that workers tend to join unions in situations where the work demands are high (FitzRoy and Kraft 1987; and Duncan and Stafford 1980; 1982). According to this line of reasoning, workers are not more productive because they belong to unions. Instead, they belong to unions because their work environment forces them to be more productive.

Freeman and Medoff also lend support to the notion that unions may be the effect, in part, rather than just the cause of high productivity. They concluded that unionized workers in the U.S. express less satisfaction with their jobs than nonunion workers, but are less willing to quit, presumably because of their superior wages (Freeman and Medoff 1984).

Although the extent to which unions are the cause or the effect of higher productivity is unmeasurable, the superior efficiency of unionized teachers lends support to the notion that unions do indeed promote productivity. A school administration might treat teachers poorly or deny them adequate resources, but such policies would not be likely to make students learn better. You would have to stretch your imagination quite a bit to see how policies that improve students' test scores would drive teachers to join unions.

In any case, unions can be advantageous to employers for several reasons. To begin with, unions can be a boon to employers, especially large-scale employers, who would otherwise have difficulty in recruiting employees to work on weekend and overtime shifts (Allen 1987, p. 352).

Besides raising wages and helping with the mobilization of the labor force, unions can benefit employers by changing workers' feelings about their situation. Freeman and Medoff build on Albert Hirschman's notion of the importance of voice within an organization. According to Freeman and Medoff, without unions, many workers would lack a voice in the large, faceless corporation.

With a voice, workers can take more satisfaction in knowing that they can make management know how they feel. Without a voice, workers would be reduced to making their negative feelings felt by exit, causing employers to bear the expense of costly employee turnover.

Japan offers some suggestive material regarding the role of unions in giving workers a voice. Japanese unions are company unions. Japanese employers only turned to unionization after a period of intense labor militancy. Workers might be reluctant to cast their lot with company unions, which do not take a particularly adversarial position toward business. In order to make these unions more credible, Japanese firms first offered lifetime employment (Kenney and Florida 1988, p. 128). In the process, Japanese firms soon realized that offering the workers more respect and better working conditions induces better performance (Scitovsky 1990, p. 144).

Although Freeman and Medoff found that unions generally promoted efficiency, they do not always do so to the same extent. At times, unions can even become counterproductive. Freeman and Medoff blamed these periods of a negative association between unions and productivity on shifts in labor-management relations, but they did not elaborate on this hypothesis (Freeman and Medoff 1984, p. 168). Presumably, Freeman and Medoff mean that when labor-management relationships deteriorate, unions can assist workers in resisting management.

Although many students of labor-management relations recognize the benefits of unions, business has been slow in coming around to this position. Instead, it comforts itself by blaming problems on others—on the government, on foreigners, and whenever possible on unions. This stance may be comforting, but it is also self-defeating.

How Good Management Can Prod Labor to Work Hard

To the extent that unions can force improvements in labor-management relations, they will make workers more productive. Of course, enlightened management on its own without the intervention of unions can and sometimes does take actions, which improve the relations between labor and capital.

For example, Tom DeMarco and Timothy Lister, report on what they called the Coding Games War, a test that they organized for programmers between 1984 and 1986. They included 600 program developers from 92 companies. Each employee was measured on his or her ability to design, code, and test a medium-size program. The investigators found that pleasantness of the office work environment closely correlated with performance. Developers in the top quartile were 30 to 50 percent more likely to say that their workspaces were acceptably quiet, private, and spacious compared with those in the lowest quartile (DeMarco and Lister 1987, p. 49). The best programmers seemed to work in an atmosphere of independence. Instead of attributing good programming to stringent monitoring, DeMarco and Lister suggest that the best programmers migrate to those companies that provide the best work environment (DeMarco and Lister 1987, p. 49).

In general, recent experience has shown that workers who are given detailed rules and are more closely monitored experience less job satisfaction and are less motivated and place more importance on external rewards, such as compensation (Deci, Connell, and Ryan 1985; cited in Akerlof and Yellen 1987). The famous Hawthorne experiments also seemed to indicate that workplace democracy can increase job satisfaction and work effort, although some recent work has questioned these results (see Drago 1986).

Harvey Leibenstein suggests that Japanese employers have turned this principle to good effect. He recalled:

> Recently I spent six months in Japan and visited some large firms. In all cases I inquired about the way in which employees were monitored. The managers were extremely sensitive to the idea and convinced me . . . that no monitoring by superiors was attempted. Promotions, by and large were a consequence of age and duration of employment. Here we have examples of some highly . . . efficient firms who did everything possible to avoid monitoring. The managers were aware that such practices were carried out in the U.S., but these were practices that they assiduously chose not to use, despite the fact that at some earlier period they were tried by some Japanese firms and dropped. [Leibenstein 1983, p. 838]

Unfortunately, the attitude that Leibenstein found in Japan is exceedingly rare in the United States. In fact, now it is probably rare in Japan as well.

The tennis-shoe industry provides another clue about how a high-wage strategy could work. This industry is notorious for relying on sweatshop labor, pushed to the limits by ruthless subcontractors. Nike led the way in this tactic, first making shoes in Japan to cut back on labor costs, then moving a lot of its production to Korea, then to Indonesia, and finally to China—always in search of the cheapest labor.

In contrast, New Balance pays workers $14 an hour to produce its shoes. Its domestic labor costs are still higher than in its Chinese factories, where labor costs are a mere 40 cents an hour, but the difference is only $2.70 per shoe. If productivity in the American factories were still higher than in China, the labor costs per shoe would be $44. New Balance is able to keep the labor costs roughly in line by installing sophisticated machinery (Bernstein 2001).

Low Wages and the Structure of Deindustrialization

Rüstow's model highlights what conventional economics obscures: the importance of the structure of the capital stock. If an economy were somehow to develop without severe disruptions, you would expect the amount of new investment to exceed the amount of disinvestment. You would not expect to see only the very least efficient plants scrapped or turned to more appropriate ends.

Unfortunately, economists know very little about the specifics of disinvestment, to a large extent, because economists have an almost pathological aversion to analyzing this subject. A. Lamfalussy, head of the Bank for International Settlements, has observed in this respect, "Disinvestment is a necessary corollary to growth." He continued:

> Theoretical economists over the last fifteen years have been so busy analyzing growth that they seem to have forgotten that, even assuming fairly rapid expansion, growth in one industry may occur at the expense of another, so that growth in one field may be associated, indeed is likely to be so, with decline in others. This neglect is based on the implicit assumption that there is little to be said about declining industries. [Lamfalussy 1961, p. xiv]

Even Lamfalussy confined his remarks to disinvestment within the context of declining industries, whereas Rüstow reminds us that disinvestment is also an important part of growing industries as well because economic growth itself is a source of disruption.

Unlike Rüstow, most economists build models in which the rate of growth is a smooth and regular process. The motivation of their models is a desire for mathematical simplicity rather than realism.

Why should market forces cause an economy to shed a constant percentage of its capital stock each year? Whey should the excess of the rate of new investment relative to the rate of disinvestment constitute another fixed percentage?

Take another look at Rüstow's model and ask yourselves: why should the economic process proceed tranquilly? Rüstow's model calls upon his readers to ask another, more difficult question: if disinvestment does occur irregularly, what market forces stand in the way of disinvestment accumulating so much momentum that it destroys an economy?

Further, Rüstow's model warns of the danger of a disinflationary disinvestment process getting out of hand. In other words, normal competitive processes can become so powerful that they force industry to lower prices. Some firms cannot continue to operate at that price level. As these firms exit their industries, they make competition become even more intense, creating a cumulative downward spiral leading toward a Haitian road to economic development.

Because conventional economic models either treat capital goods as a whole or assume that each good depreciates away at a regular rate, they are ill equipped to address the important questions, which Rüstow's model poses. As a result, economists regularly assume that the dangers of a competition-induced disinflation are nonexistent. Unfortunately, they arrive at this conclusion without even seriously considering the question.

In this book, I have been arguing that the ignorance of the conventional economists puts them in a frame of mind that leads them to promote policies that block the process of reinvestment. In this respect, they compound the danger of an economic collapse, but, of course, the possibility of a collapse exists irrespective of their policies.

I have suggested an alternative route to disinvestment: augmenting wages—what I elsewhere called "simulated competition" (Perelman 1999). High wage pressures can cause less efficient firms to depart, but the increased purchasing power of higher wages can create a wide enough market to accommodate new firms with enough of a market to allow them to create even more efficient production methods. In the process, some other plants will fall by the wayside, but other new and more efficient plants will take their place.

In the beginning of this book, I argued that I knew of no single economic panacea. The U.S. economy has experienced the failure of both regulation and deregulation, of both Keynesian and anti-Keynesian policies. Still a policy of high wages does have some promise. Wage growth is consistent with expanding profits, so long as wages do not accelerate too rapidly, although I know of no measure that could ensure that wages would remain within the necessary bounds.

I can say for sure that the experiment with a low-wage economy has proven to be a disaster. Factories disappeared. Homelessness became almost commonplace. Virtually every social pathology multiplied. A high-wage economy certainly could do no worse.

Creativity and Economics

Although economic models assume some sort of efficiency or optimality, economies, like people, rarely work to their full potential. You can catch a glimpse of this potential during periods of emergencies when people respond to broader social purposes than just greed. For example, consider how the economy behaves during wartime. Robert Lucas estimated the average level of economic efficiency by calculating the trend of the ratio of output per unit of capital in the United States between 1890 and 1954. He found that, at times, for instance during depressions, the actual output per unit of capital fell below his trend line. At other times, the actual output per unit of capital exceeded the trend line.

Lucas discovered that during the war years, 1944 through 1946, the output per unit of capital surpassed the trend line by more than 20 percent. At no time, before or after, did the U.S. economy match this remarkable performance or even come near it (Lucas 1970, p. 154).

This achievement is extraordinary because, during this period, many of the most qualified workers were in the military rather than on the shop floor. The workers who replaced them had considerably less experience on the job. Because of decades of discrimination, the black workers who came from the South to work in Northern factories had much less education than the workers that they replaced. Similarly, many women without much experience working for wages effectively "manned" the assembly lines.

Conventional economic theory suggests that industrial efficiency should have suffered dire consequences from this reliance on a supposedly less qualified labor force, yet Lucas shows that nothing of the sort happened. Instead, productivity soared.

Of course, people are accustomed to expecting productivity to increase during wartime. In part, the military Keynesians were correct that war stimulates demand. Lucas himself attributes some of the marvelous performance of the wartime economy to the use of overtime in industry.

While increased demand and overtime might have been a factor in stimulating the economy, another important force was at work: war makes people pull together. War creates a sense of urgency. As a result, powerful ideals motivated the people who labored in the factories in the United States during the war to do their best to help in the struggle against fascism. Such ideals were more compelling than greed for most workers.

Eventually, the consensus frayed around the edges. Workers became frustrated seeing their sacrifices unmatched by their employers, who were enjoying unparalleled profits. As a result, toward the end of the war, strike activity began to pick up. Even so, the spirit of community was sufficiently strong to produce high levels of productivity.

The wartime experiences of Japan and Germany offer an even more powerful illustration of the ability of people to overcome adversity. Jack Hirshleifer reports that ten days of bombing raids during July and August 1943 destroyed half the buildings in Hamburg. Yet, within five months the city had regained up to 80 percent of its productive capacity (Hirshleifer 1987, pp. 32–33).

On 6 August 1945, the U.S. Air Force dropped an atomic bomb on Hiroshima. The next day, electric power service was restored to surviving areas. One week later, telephone service restarted ((Hirshleifer 1987, p. 34).

No doubt the Germans and the Japanese also worked overtime to rebuild their economic capacity, but even trebling the average workday would not have sufficed to accomplish what they did. Their success in reconstructing their economy required enormous creativity and ingenuity.

You can usually see more intensive development of new technologies during periods of crisis. Ordinarily, the typical large corporation is timid about exploring new ideas, yet the same people, who typically display little creativity within the confines of the large corporations, make great scientific breakthroughs under the urgency of war.

The development of the computer is a case in point. The U.S. scientific community developed the computer in relatively short order. True, the scientists who participated in this project had no idea of the ultimate potential of the computer. Recall Howard Aitken's firm dismissal of the commercial potential of the computer. Their intention was merely to create a tool to calculate the path of artillery shells more quickly.

Nonetheless, this limited goal spurred them on to important discoveries that revolutionized modern technology. In contrast, even after the microcomputer technology had proven itself, IBM saw no reason to consider changing its reliance on mainframe computers.

Under intense pressure from a few engineers who were more farsighted than upper management, the company finally agreed to produce a few microcomputers. Nonetheless, the company officially predicted that it would sell only about 250,000 microcomputers over the five-year life cycle of the product (LaPlante and Scannell 1989).

On some level, IBM must have realized the potential of the microcomputer. For example, developers of the original PC line chose the 8088 chip rather than the more powerful 8086 because the corporate headquarters would never allow the computer to be built with the 8086, which might threaten the existing IBM line of computers (see Chposky and Leonisis, 1988, pp. 23–4).

The contrast between the innovative spirit of the pioneers of the computer industry and the marketing mentality of modern-day multinational corporations could not be more striking. No wonder so many political leaders become bored by peace and enamored with war!

Creative Destruction and Destructive Creativity

Joseph Schumpeter, one of the greatest economists of the twentieth century, proposed that large corporations are ideally suited to leading the way in innovations. For Schumpeter, the giant corporations clear the way for progress by developing new products and processes that make huge swaths of the economy obsolete. Schumpeter described this process as "creative destruction" (Schumpeter 1950).

Some giant corporations in the United States may indeed have grown large by virtue of creative destruction, but, in general, once these organizations have reaped their initial rewards they become lethargic dinosaurs that are destructive of creativity. Just recall IBM's attitude toward the microcomputer.

War can sometimes energize these beasts for a while. This destructive creativity gives the illusion that military spending promotes innovation. It does not. Instead, the urgency of the war effort changes people's mind-set. The people who contribute their creativity to the war effort see themselves as serving a higher purpose, however misguided they might be. In addition, corporations sometimes loosen the bureaucratic mold during emergencies, offering their researchers more latitude.

Our challenge should be to develop creative channels through which people can contribute to more noble goals than the slaughter of their fellow humans. We need to find a way to make people feel the same sense of urgency when a child goes to bed hungry as they do when a flag suffers a supposed indignity. We need to feel as much pride in our smart students as our smart bombs.

CHAPTER 9

Is There a New Economy?

Market Dreams

In the mid-1990s, after decades of enviously watching Japan's success, while languishing under a sub-par performance, the U.S. economy began to enjoy a sudden burst of productivity, while the Japanese economy sputtered. On a purely financial basis, this robust development had actually already begun in the early 1980s. For example, the Dow Jones Industrial Average stood at 884 in 1982, about the same as it was back in 1971. By 1999, it was just shy of 10,500. The rise of the technology-heavy NASDAQ index was even more dramatic. In 1971, the index was at 107. By 1982, it had grown to 189. By March 2000, it had exploded, going beyond 4,800.

Giddy with the success of the stock market, pundits began predicting that the stock market would soon reach even more fanciful levels. Publishers marketed books with titles such as *Dow 36,000* (Glassman and Hassett 1999), *Dow 40,000* (Elias 1999), and *Dow 100,000* (Kadlec and Acampora 1999).

Investors were so confident about the future that they even took the huge losses that companies absorbed as a sign that their stocks were even more valuable. During 2000, "the more money a company lost, the better its stock did, while the more money a company earned, the worse its stock fared. Think of Amazon.com, iVillage, and Priceline, all of which took pride in the amounts of money they were spending" (Morgenson 2001). Presumably, the willingness to lose money represented a strong statement by management that it was confident of the prospects of future success.

In another sign of gullibility, a study in the *Journal of Finance* found that merely announcing the change in the name of a stock to an Internet related.com name produced cumulative abnormal returns on the order of approximately 125 percent for the ten days surrounding the announcement day (Cooper, Dimitrov, and Rau, forthcoming). Yet, so long as investors can expect everybody else to be foolish, foolish behavior can be profitable.

Corporations joined in this speculative frenzy paying outlandish prices to buy up other firms. In the middle 1990s, MFS Communications Co. laid telephone lines around major cities that would allow long-distance companies to bypass the Baby Bells. By the time of the telecommunications reform in 1996, the company had networks in most of the big cities in the United States. WorldCom agreed to buy MFS for a staggering $14 billion, only slightly less than what SBC had paid for Baby Bell Pacific Telesis Group earlier that year:

> The figure that stuck out for every would-be telecom entrepreneur was that WorldCom paid more than six times the value of the assets MFS had put in the ground. . . . The math was simple. You didn't need to build a business. You just needed to raise money, put telephone lines in the ground, and you could make a bundle. Some giant would pay you a multiple of every dollar you invested. The MFS model seemed to work for the next couple of years. In 1997, WorldCom bought another competitive upstart called Brooks Fiber for about $7 billion, or nine times the company's assets in the ground—the property, plant, and equipment. [Elstrom 2001, p. 105]

In effect, the telecommunications industry began a bidding war for virtually anything that could carry a signal. When the bubble burst, the industry collapse proved to be a calamity for its suppliers as well. One company, Cisco, had to write off an astounding $2.25 billion worth of inventory in Spring 2001.

The excessive acquisition binge was not confined to telecommunications. The Fabless Semiconductor Association recently made note of a flurry of mergers and acquisitions in the semiconductor industry that occurred in 2000:

> For example, Intel bought communications chipmaker Level One for $2.3 billion. That works out to $3 million for each Level One engineer. PMC-Sierra paid $2.3 billion for Quantum Effect Design Inc., which amounts to $23 million for every QED engineer. Broadcom bought NewPort Communications Inc. for $1.2 billion, or $17 million per engineer. FSA Executive Director Jodi Shelton says, "Now the challenge is for them to integrate all of these companies." [DeTar 2001]

Nobody seemed to pay attention to the few skeptical voices while the market was soaring—not even when Warren Buffet, whom many regard as the most astute investor in the country, issued a warning. Buffet left no room for misinterpretation. He scornfully compared the soaring values to a "chain letter," in which early participants reap rich rewards at the expense of those who follow, but still virtually nobody listened (Miller 2000).

Indeed, many companies even made a high percentage of their profits from betting on their own stocks. For example, in the third quarter of 1998, the computer maker, Dell, earned $3.1 billion by speculating in puts and calls on its own stock. The company reported an earnings total of $2.5 billion during the same period, meaning that its nonspeculative earnings were negative (Raymond 1999).

In addition, many of the most successful companies were actually incurring losses, while reporting spectacular profits. This legerdemain involved the failure to report the cost of stock options. A company would reward its most important employees with huge stock options in lieu of larger salaries. When the employees eventually cash in the option, the company has to purchase the stock to give to the employees. For example, in 1998, Microsoft declared a profit of $4.5 billion; however, if the company had accounted for its outstanding options, it would have made a loss of $18 billion (Anon. 1999).

Deceptive accounting, together with the undeniable technological achievements, led investors to believe that they could enjoy unrealistically high profits. They bid up the price of the stock market. As stock prices surged people were reluctant to exercize their options much before their expiration date. Companies reported more profits because of their successful bets on their own shares. The higher profits led to even higher stock prices, creating the classic recipe for a stock market bubble.

On 5 December 1996 in an otherwise staid speech, Alan Greenspan used the term "irrational exuberance" to describe the behavior of stock market investors. The market dropped precipitously, but then soon recovered its upward path (Shiller 2000, p. 3).

Despite the huge gains enjoyed in the financial markets, during the first decade of the boom, most nonfinancial economic indicators were not particularly robust. Although dramatic technological advances that appeared virtually everywhere, productivity remained sluggish. Nobel prize-winning economist, Robert Solow, famously wrote, "You can see the computer age everywhere but in the productivity statistics" (Solow 1987, p. 36). Economists commonly used the term "productivity paradox" as a shorthand expression of Solow's observation.

Here was a technology capable of performing with extraordinary efficiency, yet overall productivity seemed unaffected. Shortly after Solow pointed out the productivity paradox, Paul David, an unusually perceptive economic historian from Stanford, suggested that the introduction of computers would turn out to be like the earlier introduction of electricity. Even though manufacturers had begun to get electricity in their factories at the beginning of the twentieth century, this new technology did not improve productivity for another 20 years.

According to David's explanation, the manufacturers initially failed to tap the technical potential of electricity. They merely replaced their steam power with electricity. These old, steam-driven plants had depended on a central power source that would drive a series of shafts and belts that would drive machinery throughout the factory. This indirect system of providing power wasted considerable energy and space, while cluttering the factory in a way that interfered with the production process.

Only later, did they redesign their factories so that they could take advantage of the capacity to distribute smaller electrical motors throughout the factory. At that point, technology began to take off. David predicted that something similar would happen with computers (David 1990).

Around 1995, David's prediction seemed right on target. Productivity finally began to take off. The excitement about the new technology soon registered in the stock market. Between 1995 and 1999, while the Dow Jones Industrial Average more than doubled from 4,493 to 10,465, the more technologically-oriented NASDAQ was even more frenzied. That index almost trebled, from 925 to 2,728 during this period.

While Paul David's analysis suggested that computer technologies could create dramatic improvements in productivity, it also suggested that such improvements were not exactly revolutionary: in the past other technologies had also created spectacular increases in productivity. For example, the telegraph represented a much greater improvement in the speed of communication than the Internet did.

One writer even dubbed the telegraph, "The Victorian Internet" (Standage 1998). Prior to the telegraph, information had moved at the speed of railroads and ships. The telegraph moved information at unbelievable speeds. This information saved innumerable lives since it allowed railroad operators to become aware of trains coming in the opposite direction. Even more so than in the case of the Internet, the main beneficiaries of the telegraph were financial brokerage houses (Field 1998). Enthusiasts at the time even credited the telegraph with transformative powers, much like those of the Internet:

> Presence is not essential to mass suggestion. Mental touch is no longer bound up with physical proximity. With the telegraph to collect and transmit the expressions and signs of the ruling mood, and the fast mail to hurry to the eager clutch of waiting thousands the still damp sheets of the morning daily, remote people are brought, as it were, into one another's presence. [Ross 1908, p. 63; cited in Ewan 1996, p. 71]

Intellectual Property as a Defense Against Competition

One major factor in the productivity increase was unrelated to technological improvements. The government of the United States strengthened all of the institutions that protected intellectual property rights—patents, copyrights, and trademarks. By granting corporations the protection of intellectual property, the government shields their products from competition.

This approach created a two-tiered economy in which producers of basic goods earn relatively low profit rates in markets characterized by strong competition, while those companies shielded by intellectual property protection tend to earn high profits in markets with limited competition. Under this regime of strong intellectual property rights, companies that sell pharmaceuticals, films, and software generally prosper, while those that produce steel or cars or agricultural products earn relatively low profits in highly competitive markets.

To a large extent, this new regime of strong intellectual property rights was a response to the declining health of the U.S. economy. As manufactured goods poured into the United States, government leaders agonized about finding ways to increase exports. Strengthening intellectual property rights seemed to be an ideal strategy for promoting exports from the United States. The most powerful multinational corporations in the United States took advantage of this climate and energetically lobbied for even stronger intellectual property rights (Granstrand 2000, pp. 39 and 53; Ryan 1998). A valuable journalistic study of the subject described the change in the perception of intellectual property:

> . . . as a flood of imports washed away millions of domestic manufacturing jobs, attitudes toward patents and their role in the economic equation began to change. The interests of industry and labor coalesced in the search for viable weapons in the fight against foreign competition. The election of Ronald Reagan further shifted the mood toward protection of intellectual property. The major philosophical argument against patent protection—that it was inherently monopolistic—was no longer politically or, even more to the point, economically correct in an era of increasing trade competition. The policy of using antitrust laws against companies that refused to license their patent technologies was reversed by the Justice Department. [Warshofsky 1994, p. 8; see also R. Hunt 1999, p. 19]

In 1986, six months before the Punta del Este meeting launching the Uruguay Round of the General Agreement on Tariffs and Trade, the chief executive officers of 12 corporations, representing: Bristol-Meyers, CBS, Du Pont, General Electric, General Motors, Hewlett-Packard, IBM, Johnson and Johnson, Merck, Monsanto, and Pfizer formed the Intellectual Property Committee. The result was profound: "The IPC, in conjunction with its counterparts in Europe and Japan, crafted a proposal based on existing industrialized country laws and presented its proposals to the GATT Secretariat. By 1994, the IPC had achieved its goal in the Trade Related Aspects of Intellectual Property (TRIPs) accord of the Uruguay trade round. . . . In effect, twelve corporations made public law for the world" (Sell 1999, pp. 169 and 172).

Domestic law also changed to enhance intellectual property rights. The history of the semiconductor industry exemplifies this trend toward changing the legal structure to aid firms in gaining a competitive advantage from intellectual property rights rather than from developing an edge in productive capabilities.

As late as 1981, Roger S. Borovoy, vice president and chief counsel for Intel Corporation declared, "In the electronics industry, patents are of no value whatsoever in spurring research and development" (Anon. 1981b). A recent study published by the Philadelphia branch of the Federal Reserve System describes the dramatic transition that came soon after Mr. Borovoy's evaluation of the important of the patent system to his industry:

> Within the U.S. semiconductor industry, reverse-engineering was a well-established practice. But by the late 1970s, American firms objected to similar behavior by Japanese firms when they began to increase their market share in the more standardized products, such as computer memory chips. The level of competition eventually became so intense that, by the mid 1980s, most American companies abandoned these segments entirely.
>
> When it became clear . . . [the United States semiconductor industry] could no longer dominate Japanese firms on the basis of production technology alone, American firms attempted to consolidate their comparative advantage in research and development. To do this, they would have to find ways of reducing their competitors' ability to reverse-engineer their products. To that end, American companies began to lobby Congress to increase intellectual property protection for their semiconductor designs. In 1984, Congress created a new form of intellectual property right, called mask rights, especially tailored to address the needs articulated by the industry. [Hunt 1999, pp. 19–20]

Soon thereafter, Texas Instruments sued eight Japanese and one Korean semiconductor company, accusing them of infringing semiconductor patents. The settlements yielded the company more than $600 million in payments according to a 1990 report. Texas Instruments became so aggressive in seeking royalties that by 1992, it earned $391 million in royalties, compared to an operating income of only $274 million (Warshofsky 1994, p. 111).

In addition to making the administrative arm of government more sympathetic to the rights of intellectual property, the judicial system, with vigorous support from the legislative side, also moved to embrace intellectual property rights more warmly. In 1982, the Federal Courts Improvement Act established the Court of Appeals for the Federal Circuit as a central patent appeals court to streamline the litigation process and create a judicial body for appellate review of the patent infringement decisions of the lower courts (Warshofsky 1994, p. 9).

This court has been very sympathetic to the claims of patent holders. Previously, the percent of patent challenges that were ending invalidation had been on the rise. The proportion increased from roughly 60 percent in the 1950s to more than 70 percent in the 1970s, suggesting a possible tightening of standards (Scherer 1980, pp. 155 and 449). The new court, in a stunning reversal, now upholds patents 80 percent of the time (Warshofsky 1994, p. 9).

The Corporate Payoff from Intellectual Property

This trend toward upholding a larger share of patents comes at a time when the scope of patents has broadened at an unprecedented rate. For example, in recent years, the patent system has begun granting claims for computer software, life forms, and even business practices. When moving into such previously uncharted terrain, a growing number of questionable proposals would be expected to come up for consideration. Nonetheless, the proportion of patents approved has continued to increase.

Each year, the government of the United States moves to strengthen intellectual property rights still further. Patents now last 20 years instead of 17, despite the fact that high technology typically becomes obsolete in less time than ever before. In addition, a new law has recently transformed many types of copyright infringement into criminal offenses.

At the time of this writing, furthering the powers of domestic holders of intellectual property in the international marketplace is one of, if not the highest priority of the government of the United States. The creation of the World Trade Organization in 1995 symbolized this expanding role of intellectual property. The forerunner of the World Trade Organization, the General Agreement on Trade and Tariffs, had the mission of liberalizing trade in goods. The World Trade Organization, in contrast, encompassed trade in intellectual property.

From the standpoint of exports alone, this emphasis on intellectual property proved highly successful. In 1947, intellectual property comprised just under ten percent of all U.S. exports. By 1986, the figure had grown to more than 37 percent. By the early 1990s, the best estimate was that intellectual property accounted for well over 50 percent of exports from the United States (Warshofsky 1994, p. 6).

In 1999, U.S. exports in the form of royalties and licensing revenue alone exceeded $37 billion—topping aircraft exports or telecommunications equipment. Moreover, the trade surplus in intellectual property—the exports minus imports—is running at about $25 billion annually, and growing (National Science Board 2000). IBM alone says its worldwide licensing revenue exceeded $1 billion last year (Wysocki 2000). These figures exclude payments for physical goods, such as computer chips, which also embody intellectual property.

Intellectual property goes well beyond high technology. Jack Valenti, chairman and chief executive officer of the Motion Picture Association told the Committee on Ways and Means Subcommittee on Trade of the U.S. House of Representatives:

> The U.S. copyright-based industries, which include the motion picture, sound recording, computer software, and book industries, were America's number one export sector in 1996. These industries together achieved foreign sales and exports of $60.18 billion, surpassing every other export sector, including automotive, agriculture and aircraft. The U.S. filmed entertainment industry alone earned about $12 billion in foreign revenues in 1997, 40 percent of the total revenues earned by the U.S. film industry. [Valenti 1999; based on Siwek and Mosteller 1996]

While these revenues are impressive, outside of the benefits to the large, transnational corporations, the future implications of stronger intellectual property rights are ominous. While exports have grown impressively, despite the declining performance of manufacturing in the United States, imports have soared, leaving the U.S. economy with the largest balance of trade deficit ever recorded. On a deeper level, the question remains whether this newest method of limiting competition will, in the long run, prove to be as self-defeating as the earlier techniques of protecting business from competitive forces.

The profitability of intellectual property rights ultimately rests on the power of the state to compel enforcement. In a globalized economy where the bulk of intellectual property rights is held in a handful of nation states, those states that hold intellectual property must be able to wield power internationally to insure that the rest of the world complies with their laws regarding intellectual property.

The rest of the world, in contrast, has little to gain by paying the inflated rents demanded by holders of intellectual property rights. So ultimately, the enforcement of these intellectual property rights depends upon the military power that a country can project upon the rest of the world.

The full weight of its power is brought to bear against all evildoers who would dare to create knock-offs of a Disney cartoon or a Nike swoosh. In the words of Thomas Friedman, perhaps the most enthusiastic proponent of globalism at the *New York Times:*

> The hidden hand of the market will never work without a hidden fist—McDonald's cannot flourish without McDonnell Douglas, the designer of the F-15. And the hidden fist that keeps the world safe for Silicon Valley's technologies is called the United States Army, Air Force, Navy and Marine Corps. . . . Without America on duty, there will be no America Online. [Friedman 1999, p. 373]

Lest the skeptical reader dismiss Friedman's clever phrasing as nothing more than a rhetorical flourish, consider the words of William Cohen, the secretary of defense in the Clinton administration. In February of 1999, upon his arrival in Seattle—a city that a few months later became a symbol of resistance to the policies that he was sent to advocate—to speak to the employees of Microsoft, the secretary told reporters, "I will point out that the prosperity that companies like Microsoft now enjoy could not occur without having the strong military that we have" (Burns 1999).

Thomas Friedman and William Cohen expressed what is probably the central thrust of the foreign policy of the government of the United States. I suspect that the response of the U.S. government to Saddam Hussein would have been far more severe had he engaged in counterfeiting such intellectual property rather than merely invading a neighboring country.

Associating the protection of intellectual property with national defense might seem far-fetched, however, I am convinced that much of the defense of intellectual property is equally preposterous. Consider one more piece of evidence. Recent history demonstrates fairly conclusively that the government of the United States signals a high priority for any policy initiative by associating it with national security. In the case of such intellectual property, the Clinton administration raised the stakes to an even higher level by invoking the threat of terrorism.

An unsophisticated reader might wonder how the counterfeiting of corporate logos and the like might threaten the life and limb of citizens of the most powerful nation on the face of the earth. Apparently, the government has let it be known that it is seriously concerned that people counterfeiting T-shirts and ripping off logos might actually be raising funds for terrorists (Light 1996). Naturally, the government has no choice but to use every power available to it to prevent such dangerous activities.

Reality Check

The increasing profits associated with these holders of intellectual property rights spurred the soaring stock prices, which in turn created an atmosphere of enormous optimism. Just about anybody who got into an Internet business expected to get rich. Indeed, many did, but most of the wealth went to the very richest. Even within the most affluent group in the United States, the Forbes 400, annually surveyed by *Forbes Magazine,* the bulk of the wealth went to the wealthiest.

Arthur Kennickell, senior economist and project director of the influential Federal Reserve Survey of Consumer Finances, surveyed the distribution of wealth within this select group and reported:

> Between 1989 and 1995, most measures of the wealth of the wealthiest people grew fairly modestly in real terms: The minimum wealth level in the Forbes 400 group grew 3 percent, total wealth of the group grew 10 percent, the number of billionaires rose 14 percent, and the average wealth of the top ten grew 79 percent. However, the data suggest that in recent years there has been a distinct jump in the level of wealth among the wealthiest families. From 1995 to 1998, the total amount of net worth accounted for by the Forbes 400 rose in real terms from about $379 billion to about $740 billion (a 95 percent increase); the number of billionaires rose from 97 to 191 (a 97 percent increase). Although these changes might be taken to imply that similar changes occurred at the same time all across the broader upper end of the net worth distribution, the data also indicate that the largest gains were at the very top, and they tapered off at lower levels even within the Forbes group. In particular, while the maximum level of wealth and the average of the top ten members of the list increased 270 percent, the minimum level of wealth needed to qualify for the Forbes list rose by a somewhat more moderate 39 percent increase. [Kennickell 2000]

As the wealthy bid property away from the less fortunate, the term "affordable housing" became a tragic oxymoron for all but the most affluent. Housing prices became so high in Silicon Valley, a family of four scraping by on $53,100 a year or an individual earning less than $37,200, was officially poor according to federal housing officials. Indeed, the median price for a house in Silicon Valley, $410,000, was more than twice that for the rest of the country (Nieves 2000a).

While almost unimaginable wealth flowed to some of the residents of this seeming dot.com paradise, average incomes for the lowest fifth of Valley households actually fell during most of the 1990s (Bernstein 2000, p. 80). In the words of Amy Dean, the energetic director of the American Federation of Labor - Congress of Industrial Organization's Silicon Valley office: "Unfortunately, the New Economy is looking a lot like an hourglass with a lot of high-paid, high-tech jobs at the high end and an enormous proliferation of low-wage service jobs at the bottom" (cited in Greenhouse 2000b).

Less than 30 percent of the households in Santa Clara County could afford to buy a house. In San Francisco, rents were even more unaffordable. There, the median price of a home was close to $500,000, a price that only 11 percent of the city's 750,000 residents could afford (Nieves 2000b).

While the great surge of wealth directly benefited a relatively small number of people, the stock market began to soar. Within this environment, investors enthusiastically funded a huge number of ludicrous business plans with no real prospects of success. Many of the new companies compounded the problem by using nontraditional accounting methods.

Alas, this euphoria was not permanent. The NASDAQ, which had reached 4,800 only a short time before, suffered a meltdown, falling below 1,640 by April 2001. By late March 2001, an estimated $4.6 trillion worth of value had evaporated (Vickers 2001).

The *Wall Street Journal* reported that about 80 percent of the Bay Area Web firms were expected to fail, threatening to wipe out some 30,000 jobs. Great swaths of office space in the Bay Area suddenly became vacant (Muto 2001a). Home prices in the region also fell rapidly (Muto 2001b).

What Conclusion?

Looking at the economy from the perspective of the last half of the 1990s, you might be tempted to interpret the long postwar decline as an aberrant interruption in the long ascent of the U.S. economy. Viewing the same period from the perspective of the long decline, and you could be equally justified in interpreting this burst of productivity and growth as a relatively unimportant period given the history of the long decline.

Similarly, using an even wider lens for viewing history suggests even greater grounds for uncertainty. Over the last of 600 years, the center of capitalist development has shifted from Italy, which developed many of the tools of modern commerce, to Spain and Portugal, which led the way in the Imperial conquest. Then, Holland assumed the lead by inventing many of the modern techniques of finance and trade. Next, England wrested the lead from Holland by combining naval might with a commercial empire, while ruthlessly taking the traditional means of support from the poor, leaving them no choice but to work for wages.

Challengers rose up and then fell back again. For example, France tested England's leadership any number of times, but never quite succeeded. Similarly, during the 1970s, Japan seemed like it might have developed the institutional capacity to pass the United States.

None of these nations were able to understand fully the limits of their own potential nor the strengths of the rivals that eventually displaced them. The ambivalent relationship between Japan and the United States in recent years suggests how nations both overestimate and underestimate their rivals.

The English writer Lytton Strachey once observed: " . . . ignorance is the first requisite of the historian—ignorance, which simplifies and clarifies, which selects and omits, with the placid perfection unattainable by the highest art" (Strachey 1918, p. v). We owe our ignorance to our times as well as our own personal defects. I cannot pretend to have rid myself of my own ignorance, but I am painfully aware of the failures of those before me who have adopted a tone of arrogant certainty in making predictions about the future.

The U.S. economy today, mired in debt and facing a horrendous balance-of-trade deficit, may somehow find a way out of the problems that keep accumulating. I do not think so, but I cannot say with certainty.

I do not mean that the economy will never enjoy a spurt of rapid growth again. In all likelihood, the economy will experience a number of such periods in the future. However, over time, the accumulations of problems and contradictions will eventually catch up with the economy. At that time, quite likely, some presently unnoticed contradiction will sneak up on an unsuspecting economy. When and how, I cannot say.

Again, as I mentioned in the introduction, perhaps the best an economist can do is to tell an interesting and coherent story in the hope that it can help people to understand the economy better today and to assist other people who will tell even better stories in the future.

References

Aaron, Henry J. 1990. "Comments on Aschauer." In Alicia H. Munnell, ed. *Is There a Shortfall in Public Capital Investment? Proceedings of a Conference Held in June 1990,* Conference Series No. 34 (Boston: Federal Reserve Bank of Boston): pp. 51–63.

Abelson, Alan. 1989. "The Rise and Fall of the King of Junk." *Barrons* (3 April): p. 1.

Abken, Peter A. 1992. "Corporate Pensions and Government Insurance: Deja Vu All Over Again." *Economic Review of the Federal Reserve Bank of Atlanta,* Vol. 77, No. 2 (March/April): pp. 1–16.

Adams, Gordon and David Gold. 1987. *Defense Spending and the Economy: Does the Defense Dollar Make a Difference?,* Defense Budget Project at the Center on Budget and Policy Priorities (Washington, D.C.).

Adams, Larry T. 1985. "Changing Employment Patterns of Organized Workers." *Monthly Labor Review,* Vol. 108, No. 2 (February): pp. 25–31.

Adams, Walter and Hans Mueller. 1982. "The Steel Industry." In *The Structure of American Industry,* edited by Walter Adams (New York: Macmillan): pp. 73–135.

Adler, Stephen J. and Laurie P. Cohen. 1988. "Even Lawyers Gasp Over the Stiff Fees of Wachtell Lipton: Firm's $20 Million Bill to Kraft for Two Weeks of Work Sets New Legal Standard." *Wall Street Journal* (2 November): pp. A1 and A5.

Akerlof, George A. and Janet L. Yellen. 1986. *Efficiency Wage Models of the Labor Market* (Cambridge: Cambridge University Press).

———. 1987. "Rational Models of Irrational Behavior." *American Economic Review,* Vol. 77, No. 2 (May): pp. 137–42.

Alesina, A. and G. Tabellini. 1986. "A Positive Theory of Fiscal Deficits and Government Debt in a Democracy." NBER Working Paper No. 2308 (July)

Allen, Steven G. 1986a. "Union Work Rules and Efficiency in the Building Trades." *Journal of Labor Economics,* Vol. 4, No. 2 (April): pp. 212–42.

———. 1986b. "Unionization and Productivity in Office Building and School Construction." *Industrial and Labor Relations Review,* Vol. 9, No. 2 (January): pp. 187–202.

———. 1987. "Can Union Labor Ever Cost Less?" *Quarterly Journal of Economics,* Vol. 52, No 2 (May): pp. 347–73.

———. 1988a. "Further Evidence on Union Efficiency in Construction." *Industrial Relations,* Vol. 27, No. 2 (Spring): pp. 232–40.

———. 1988b. "Productivity Levels and Productivity Change Under Unionism." *Industrial Relations,* Vol. 27, No. 1 (Winter): pp. 94–113.

American Federation of Teachers. 2000. Teacher Salary Home Page. <http://www.aft.org/research/salary/home.htm>

American Society of Civil Engineers. 2001. *The 2001 Report Card for America's Infrastructure* (8 March). <http://www.asce.org/reportcard/>

Anders, George. 1981. "DuPont Deal Puts a Strain on Agent Bank." *Wall Street Journal* (25 August): p. 25.

———. 1990. "Captive Client: Morgan Stanley Found A Gold Mine of Fees by Buying Burlington." *Wall Street Journal* (14 December): pp. A1 and A6.

———. 1991. "Computers Bypass Wall Street Middlemen and Stir Controversy." *Wall Street Journal* (28 August): pp. A1 and A4.

Anderson, Sarah and John Cavanagh. 2000. *The Top 200: The Rise of Global Corporate Power* (Washington, D.C.: Institute for Policy Studies).

Anon. 1949. "From Cold War to Cold Peace?" *Business Week* (12 February): pp. 19–20.

Anon. 1950. "The Treaty of Detroit." *Fortune,* Vol. 62, No. 1 (July): pp. 53–55.

Anon. 1974. "Did Controls Flunk Their First Peacetime Test." *Business Week* (27 April): pp. 106–117.

Anon. 1981a. "State and Local Government in Trouble: Special Report" *Business Week* (26 October).

Anon. 1981b. "The Patent Is Expiring as a Spur to Innovation." *Business Week,* Industrial/Technology edition (11 May): p. 44 C.

Anon. 1983. "For 4 Days' Work, $126,582 an Hour." *Wall Street Journal* (17 January): p. 33.

Anon. 1984. "The Worldwide Steel Industry: Struggling to Survive." *Business Week* (20 August).

Anon. 1986a. The Hollow Corporation: The Decline of Manufacturing Threatens the Entire U.S. Economy." *Business Week* (3 March).

Anon. 1986b. "No Comment." *Monthly Review,* Vol. 38, No. 2 (June): p. 19.

Anon. 1991a. "American Investment Banking: Beyond the Balance Sheet." *The Economist* (11 May): pp. 74–8.

Anon. 1991b. "Swimming on Line One . . ." *Sports Illustrated* (28 January): p. 28.

Anon. 1991c. "American Pensions: Gray Peril." *The Economist* (11 May): pp. 78–9.

Anon. 1992a. "Public School Problems: 1940 vs. 1980." *CQ Researcher* (11 September): p. 797.

Anon. 1992b. "Let Them Eat Pollution." *The Economist* (February 8–14): p. 66.

Anon. 1999. "Share and Share Unalike." *The Economist* (5 August).

Anon. 2000. "A Squeeze in the Valley." *The Economist* (5 October).

Anon. 2001. "Europe's Fab-Tool Growth Will Top Other Regions In 2001, Says *Dataquest.*" *Semiconductor Business News* (14 January). <http://www.siliconstrategies.com/story/OEG20010112S0003>

Arrow, Kenneth J. 1973. "Higher Education as a Filter." *Journal of Public Economics,* Vol. 2 (July): 193–216.

Arthur, W. Brian. 1989. "Competing Technologies, Increasing Returns, and Lock-in by Historical Events." *The Economic Journal,* Vol. 99 (March): pp. 116–31.

Aschauer, David Alan. 1988a. "Is Public Expenditure Productive?" *Journal of Monetary Economics,* Vol. 23, No. 2 (March): pp. 177–200.

———. 1988b. "Government Spending and the 'Falling Rate of Profit.'" *Chicago Economic Perspectives: A Review From the Federal Reserve Bank of Chicago,* Vol. 13, No. 3 (May/June): pp. 11–17.

———. 1989a. "Public Investment and Productivity Growth in the Group of Seven." *Chicago Economic Perspectives: A Review From the Federal Reserve Bank of Chicago,* Vol. 13, No. 5 (September/October): pp. 17–25.

———. 1989b. "Does Public Capital Crowd Out Private Capital?" *Journal of Monetary Economics,* Vol. 24, No. 2 (September): pp. 171–89.

———. 1990a. "*Public Investment and Private Sector Growth: The Economic Benefits of Reducing America's 'Third Deficit'*" (Washington, D.C. Economic Policy Institute).

———. 1990b. "Why is Infrastructure Important?" In Alicia H. Munnell, ed. *Is There a Shortfall in Public Capital Investment? Proceedings of a Conference Held in June 1990.* Conference Series No. 34 (Boston: Federal Reserve Bank of Boston): pp. 21–50.

———. 1990c. "Public Spending for Private Profit." *Wall Street Journal* (14 March): p. A16.

———. 1990d. "Is Government Spending Stimulative?" *Contemporary Policy Issues,* Vol. 8, No. 4 (October): pp. 30–46.

Bahl, Roy. 1984. *Financing State and Local Government in the 1980s* (New York: Oxford University Press).

Bailey, Stephen Kemp. 1950. *Congress Makes a Law: The Story Behind the Employment Act of 1946* (New York: Columbia University Press).

Baily, Martin Neil. 1978. "The Effectiveness of Anticipated Policy." *Brookings Papers on Economic Activity,* No. 1: pp. 11–60.

———. 1981a. "Productivity and the Services of Capital and Labor." *Brookings Papers on Economic Activity,* No. 1, pp. 1–50.

———. 1981b. "The Productivity Growth Slowdown and Capital Accumulation." *American Economic Review,* Vol. 71, No. 2 (May): pp. 326–31.

Baker, Dean, ed. 1997. *Getting Prices Right: The Debate over the Consumer Price Index* (Washington, D.C.: Economic Policy Institute).

Baker, Dean. 1998. *The Public Investment Deficit: Two Decades of Neglect Threaten 21st Century Economy.* Economic Policy Institute Briefing Paper (Washington, D.C.: Economic Policy Institute).

Balke, Nathan S. and Robert J. Gordon. 1989. "The Estimation of Prewar Gross National Product: Methodology and New Evidence." *Journal of Political Economy,* Vol. 97, No. 1 (February): pp. 38–92.

Baran, Paul A. and Paul M. Sweezy. 1966. *Monopoly Capital: An Essay on the American Economic and Social Order* (New York: Monthly Review Press).

Barber, William J. 1985. *From New Era to New Deal: Herbert Hoover, the Economists, and American Economic Policy, 1921–1933* (Cambridge: Cambridge University Press).

Barnett, Donald F. and Louis Schorsch. 1983. *Steel: Upheaval in a Basic Industry* (Cambridge, MA: Ballinger).

Barrington, Linda. 2000. *America's Full-Time Working Poor Reap Limited Gains in the New Economy* (Washington, D.C.: Conference Board.

Bassie, V. L. 1946. "Consumers' Expenditures in War and Transition." *Review of Economic Statistics,* Vol. 28, No. 3 (August): pp. 121–9.

Baumgarner, Mary, Jorge Martinez-Vazquez, and David L. Sjoquist. 1991. "Municipal Capital Maintenance and Fiscal Distress." *Review of Economics and Statistics,* Vol. 73, No. 1 (February): pp. 33–39.

Beck, E. M. and Stewart E. Tolnay. 1990. "The Killing Fields of the Deep South: The Market for Cotton and the Lynching of Blacks, 1882–1930." *American Sociological Review,* Vol. 55 (August): pp. 526–38.

Bedwell, Donald E. and Gary W. Tapp. 1982. "Supply-Side Economics Conference in Atlanta." *Economic Review of the Federal Reserve Bank of Atlanta,* Vol. 57, No. 5 (May): pp. 25–35.

Bell, Daniel. 1976. *The Coming of Post-Industrial Society* (New York: Basic Books).

Belous, Richard S. 1989. "How Human Resource Systems Adjust to the Shift toward Contingent Workers." *Monthly Labor Review,* Vol. 112, No. 3 (March): pp. 7–12.

Bernanke, Ben S. 1986. "Employment, Hours, and Earnings in the Depression: An Analysis of 8 Manufacturing Industries." *American Economic Review,* Vol. 76, No. 1 (March): pp. 83–109.

Berndt, Ernst R. 1980. "Energy Price Increases and the Productivity Slowdown in United States Manufacturing." In *The Decline in Productivity Growth* (Boston: Federal Reserve Bank of Boston): pp. 60–89.

Berner, Richard B. 2001. "Testimony." United States House of Representatives Subcommittee on the Census Committee on Government Reform, 107th Congress (5 April).

Bernstein, Aaron. 1988. "Where the Jobs Are Is Where the Skills Aren't." *Business Week* (19 September): pp. 104–8.

———. 1990. "In Search of the Vanishing Nest Egg." *Business Week* (30 July): p. 46.

———. 2001. *Business Week* "Low-Skilled Jobs: Do They Have To Move?" (26 February).

Bernstein, Peter L. 1983. "Capital Stock and Management Decisions." *Journal of Post Keynesian Economics,* Vol. 6, No. 1 (Fall): pp. 20–38.

Bernstein, Aaron. 2000. "Down and Out in Silicon Valley." *Business Week* (27 March): pp. 78–92.

Bhaduri, Amit and Stephen Marglin. 1990. "Unemployment and the Real Wage: The Economic Basis for Contesting Political Ideologies." *Cambridge Journal of Economics,* Vol. 14, No. 4 (December): pp. 378–93.

Bils, Mark. 1989. "Selling versus Producing in Market Fluctuations." *Carnegie-Rochester Conference Series on Public Policy* (Autumn).

Bishop, John H. 1989. "Is the Test Score Decline Responsible for the Productivity Growth Decline?" *American Economic Review,* Vol. 79, No. 1 (March): pp. 178–94.

———. 1991a. "Docility and Apathy: Its Cause and Cure." *Educational Reform: Social Change or Political Rhetoric,* Samuel Bacharach, ed. (New York: Allyn Bacon): pp. 234–58.

———. 1991b. "The Productivity Consequences of What is Learned in High School." *Journal of Curriculum Studies,* Vol. 22, No. 2: pp. 101–26.

Blank, Rebecca and Alan Blinder. 1986. "Macroeconomics, Income Distribution and Poverty." In Sheldon Danziger and Daniel Weinberg, eds. *Fighting Poverty: What Works, What Doesn't* (Cambridge, MA: Harvard University Press): pp. 180–208.

Blank, Rebecca and Emma Rothschild. 1985. "The Effect of United States Defense Spending on Employment and Output." *International Labour Review,* Vol. 124, No. 6 (November/December): pp. 677–97.

Blinder, Alan. 1981. *Economic Policy and the Great Stagflation* (New York: Academic Press).

Bloch, Ed. 1983. "Trade and Unemployment: Global Bread-and-Butter Issues." *Monthly Review,* Vol. 35, No. 5 (October): pp. 28–34.

Block, Fred L. 1977. *The Origins of International Economic Disorder: A Study of United States International Monetary Policy from World War II to the Present* (Berkeley: University of California Press).

Bloom, David E. and Richard B. Freeman. 1992. "The Fall in Private Pension Coverage in the United States." *American Economic Review,* Vol. 82, No. 2 (May): pp. 539–45.

Bluestone, Barry. 1988. "Deindustrialization and Unemployment in America." *Review of Black Political Economy,* Vol. 17, No. 2 (Fall): pp. 29–44.

Bluestone, Barry and Bennett Harrison. 1982. *The Deindustrialization of America: Plant Closings, Community Abandonment, and the Dismantling of Basic Industry* (New York: Basic Books).

Bosworth, Barry P. 1985. "Taxes and the Investment Recovery." *Brookings Papers on Economic Activity,* No. 1: pp. 1–45.

Bougheas, Spiros, Panicos O. Demetriades, and Theofanis P. Mamuneas. 2000. "Infrastructure, Specialization and Economic Growth." *Canadian Journal of Economics,* Vol. 33, No. 2 (May): pp. 506–22.

Bowles, Samuel. 1989. "Business Ascendancy and Economic Impasse: A Structural Retrospective on Conservative Economics, 1979–87." *Journal of Economic Perspectives,* Vol. 3, No. 1 (Winter): pp. 107–34.

Bowles, Samuel, David M. Gordon, and Thomas E. Weisskopf. 1983. *Beyond the Wasteland: The Democratic Alternative to Economic Decline* (Garden City, NY: Doubleday).

Bracey, Gerald. 1998. "The Eighth Bracey Report on the Condition of Public Education." *Phi Delta Kappan,* Vol. 80, No. 2 (October): pp. 112–20.

Bram, Jason and Michael Anderson. 2001. "Declining Manufacturing Employment in the New York-New Jersey Region: 1969–99." *Current Issues in Economics and Finance* (Federal Reserve Bank of New York), Vol. 7, No. 1 (February).

Brauer, David. 1991. "The Effect of Imports on U.S. Manufacturing Wages." *Federal Reserve Bank of New York Quarterly Review,* Vol. 16, No. 1 (Spring): pp. 14–26.

Bronfenbrenner, Martin, (ed.) 1969a. *Is the Business Cycle Obsolete? Based on a Conference of the Social Science Council Committee on Economic Stability* (New York: Wiley-Interscience).

———. 1969b. "Summary of the Discussion." In Bronfenbrenner (ed.) 1969a, pp. 505–59.

Bruck, Connie. 1989. *The Predators' Ball: The Inside Story of Drexel Burnham and the Rise of the Junk Bond Traders* (New York: Penguin).

Buckley, William F., Jr. 1971. "Are You a Keynesian?" *National Review,* Vol. 23 (9 February): pp. 162–3.

Burawoy, Michael. 1979. *Manufacturing Consent* (Chicago: University of Chicago Press).

Burns, Robert. 1999. "Post–Cold War Worries: Cohen to Call for Strong Military in High-Tech Visit." Associated Press (18 February). <http://www.abcnews.go.com/sections/us/DailyNews/cohen990218.html>

Byrne, John A. 1999. "When Capital Gets Antsy." *Business Week* (13 September): pp. 72–76.

Calomiris, Charles W. and R. Glenn Hubbard. 1990. "Firm Heterogeneity, Internal Finance and 'Credit Rationing'." *The Economic Journal,* Vol. 100, No. 399 (March): pp. 90–104,

Campaign for Fiscal Equity, Inc., et al., Respondents, v. State of New York et al., Appellants. 2000. Supreme Court of New York, Appellate Division, First Department, 271 A.D.2d 312; 706 N.Y.S.2d 411. <http://www.courts.state.ny.us/CFE10.pdf>

Cannon, Lou. 2000. *President Reagan: The Role of a Lifetime* (New York: Public Affairs).

Carey, John. 1990. "Can U.S. Defense Labs Beat Missiles into Microchips?" *Business Week* (17 September): pp. 84–92.

Carlson, Bo. 1989. "Flexibility and the Theory of the Firm." *International Journal of Industrial Organization,* Vol. 7, No. 2 (June): pp. 179–204.

Carlson, John A. 1977. "A Study of Price Forecasts." *Annals of Economic Social Measurement,* Vol. 6, pp. 27–56.

Carnoy, Martin. 1994. *Faded Dreams: The Politics and Economics of Race in America* (New York: Cambridge University Press).

Carter, Anne P. 1970. *Structural Change in the American Economy* (Cambridge, MA: Harvard University Press).

Carver, Thomas Nixon. 1925. *The Present Economic Revolution in the United States* (Boston: Little Brown).

Cassel, Gustav. 1932. *The Theory of Social Economy,* 2d ed. tr. S.L. Barron (New York: A. M. Kelley, 1967).

Castells, Manuel. 1980. *The Economic Crisis and American Society* (Princeton: Princeton University Press).

Center for the Future of Teaching and Learning. 2000. *The Status of the Teaching Profession In 2000: An Update to the Teaching and California's Future Task Force.* <http://www.cftl.org/documents/2000complete_report.pdf>

Cerruzzi, Paul. 1986. "An Unforeseen Revolution: Computers and Expectations, 1935–1985." In *Imagining Tomorrow,* edited by Joseph J. Corn (Cambridge, MA: MIT Press).

Chall, Daniel E. 1981. "The Economic Costs of Subway Deterioration." *Federal Reserve Bank of New York Quarterly Review,* Vol. 6, No. 1 (Spring): pp. 8–14.

Chandler, Alfred D. Jr. 1969. "The Structure of American Industry in the Twentieth Century: A Historical Review." *Business History Review,* Vol. 63 (Autumn): pp. 255–98.

———. 1990. *Scale and Scope: The Dynamics of Industrial Capitalism* (New York: Alfred A. Knopf).

Chang, Kenneth. 2000. "New Assignment for Satellite System." *New York Times* (19 December).

Chipello, Christopher J. and Marcus W. Brauchli. 1990. "Japan Has Greatly Boosted Its Resistance to Oil Shocks." *Wall Street Journal* (9 August): p. A7.

Choate, Pat and Susan Walter. 1981. *America in Ruins: The Decaying Infrastructure* (Durham, NC: Duke University Press).

Chposky, James and Ted Leonisis. 1988. *Blue Magic: The People, Power and Politics Behind the IBM Personal Computer* (New York and Oxford: Facts on File Publications).

Clark, Gregory. 1987. "Why Isn't The Whole World Developed? Lessons from the Cotton Mills." *Journal of Economic History,* Vol. 47, No. 1 (March): pp. 141–73.

Cohen, Stephen S. and John Zysman. 1987. *Manufacturing Matters: The Myth of the Post-industrial Economy* (New York: Basic Books).

Colby, Gerard with Charlotte Dennett. 1995. *Thy Will Be Done: The Conquest of the Amazon: Nelson Rockefeller and the Evangelism in the Age of Oil* (New York: HarperCollins).

Collins, Robert M. 1981. *The Business Response to Keynes, 1929–1964* (New York: Columbia University Press).

Committee for Economic Development. 1987. *Children in Need: Investment Strategies for the Educationally Disadvantaged* (New York: Committee for Economic Development).

Congressional Budget Office. 1992. *The Economic Effects of Reduced Defense Spending* (Washington, D.C.: Congressional Budget Office. February).

Cooper, Michael, Orlin Dimitrov, and P. Raghavendra Rau. 2001. "A Rose.com by Any Other Name." *Journal of Finance* (forthcoming).

Cowherd, Raymond G. 1977 *Political Economists and the English Poor Laws: A Historical Study of the Influence of Classical Economics on the Formation of Social Welfare Policy* (Athens: Ohio University Press).

Craypo, Charles. 1990. "The Decline of Union Bargaining Power." In Bruce Nissan, ed. *U.S. Labor Relations, 1945–1989* (New York: Garland): pp. 3–40.

Cross, Rod. 1987. "Hysteresis and Instability in the Natural Rate of Unemployment." *Scandinavian Journal of Economics,* Vol. 89, No. 1: pp. 71–89.

Cusumano, Michael A. 1991. *Japan's Software Factories: A Challenge to U.S. Management* (Oxford: Oxford University Press).

Cutler, David M. and Lawrence H. Summers. 1988. "The Costs of Conflict Resolution and Financial Distress: Evidence from the Texaco-Penzoil Litigation." *Rand Journal of Economics* Vol. 19, No. 2 (Summer): pp. 157–72.

Cwiklik, Robert 1990. "Serious Money." *The Nation,* Vol. 250, No. 15 (16 April): p. 524.

Cypher, James M. 1991. "Military Spending After the Cold War." *Journal of Economic Issues,* Vol. 25, No. 2 (June): pp. 607–16.

Daly, A., D. Hitchens, and K. Wagner. 1985. "Productivity, Machinery and Skills in a Sample of British and German Manufacturing Plants." *National Institute Economic Review,* No. 111 (February): pp. 48–61.

Danziger, Sheldon and Peter Gottschalk. 1986. "Do Rising Tides Lift All Boats? The Impact of Secular and Cyclical Changes on Poverty." *American Economic Review,* Vol. 76, No. 2 (May): pp. 405–410.

David, Paul. 1990. "Computer and Dynamo: The Modern Productivity Paradox in a Not-Too-Distant Mirror." *American Economic Review,* Vol. 80, No. 2 (May): pp. 355–61.

Darling-Hammond, Linda. 2000. *Solving the Dilemmas of Teacher Supply, Demand, and Standards* (New York: National Commission on Teaching and America's Future).

Davidson, Paul. 1972. *Money and the Real World* (New York and Toronto: John Wiley).

Dawson, Michael and John Bellamy Foster. 1991. "The Tendency for the Surplus to Rise, 1963–88." *Monthly Review,* Vol. 43, No. 4 (September): pp. 37–50.

Day, Kathleen. 2001. "IBM Workers Continue to Fight Pension Changes Proposal at Shareholders Meeting." *Washington Post* (18 April): p. E 1.

Deci, Edward L., James L. Connell, and Richard M. Ryan. 1985. "Self-Determination in a Work Organization." (mimeo).

DeLong, J. Bradford. 1992. "Productivity and Machinery Investment: A Long-Run Look, 1870–1980." *Journal of Economic History,* Vol. 53, No. 2 (June): pp. 307–24.

DeLong, J. Bradford and Lawrence H. Summers. 1991. "Equipment Investment and Economic Growth." *Quarterly Journal of Economics,* Vol. 106, No. 2 (May): pp. 445–502.

DeMarco, Tom and Timothy Lister. 1987. *Peopleware: Productive Projects and Teams* (New York: Dorset House).

Demetriades, Panicos O. and Theofanis P. Mamuneas. 2000. "Intertemporal Output and Employment Effects of Public Infrastructure Capital: Evidence From 12 OECD economies." *The Economic Journal,* Vol. 110, No. 465 (July): pp. 687–712.

Denison, Edward F. 1964. "The Unimportance of the Embodiment Question." *American Economic Review,* Vol. 54, No. 1 (March): pp. 90–4

———. 1985. *Trends in American Economic Growth, 1929–1982* (Washington, D.C.: Brookings Institution).

Department of Finance. State of California. 1998. *Capital Outlay and Infrastructure Report, 1999* (Sacramento, CA). <http://www.dof.ca.gov/HTML/capoutly/capout.pdf>

Dertouzos, Michael L., Richard K. Lester, Robert M. Solow and the MIT Commission on Industrial Productivity. 1989. *Made in America: Regaining the Productive Edge* (Cambridge, MA: The MIT Press).

DeTar, James. 2001. "Is The Cost Of Engineers Getting Out Of Hand?" *Investor's Business Daily* (19 April): p. A4.

Dione, E. J. 1981. "Many Billions Necessary to Restore Public Works, Albany Aides Say." *New York Times* (13 October): p. B1.

Douglass, Elizabeth. 1994. "Light At The End Of The Wind Tunnel." *San Diego Union-Tribune* (23 October): p. I1.

Dowd, Douglas. 2000. *Capitalism and its Economics: A Critical History* (Pluto Press).

Doyle, P. M. 1985. "Area Wage Surveys Shed Light on Decline of Unionization." *Monthly Labor Review,* Vol. 105, No. 9 (September): pp. 13–20.

Drago, Robert. 1986. "Capitalism and Efficiency: A Review and Appraisal of the Recent Discussion." *Review of Radical Political Economy,* Vol. 18, No. 4 (Winter) pp. 71–92.

DuBoff, Richard. 1989. "What Military Spending Really Costs." *Challenge,* Vol. 32, No. 5 (September/October): pp. 4–10.

DuBoff, Richard B. and Edward S. Herman. 1972. "The New Economics: Handmaiden of Inspired Truth." *Review of Radical Economics,* Vol. 4, No. 4 (August): pp. 54–84.

———. 1989. "The Promotional-Dynamic of Merger Movement: A Historical Perspective." *Journal of Economic Issues,* Vol. 23, No. 1 (March): pp. 107–33.

Dumenil, Gerard, Mark Glick, and Jose Rangel. 1987. "Theories of the Great Depression: Why Did Profitability Matter?" *Review of Radical Political Economy,* Vol. 19, No. 2 (Summer): pp. 16–42.

Duncan, G. C. and F. P. Stafford. 1980. "Do Union Members Receive Compensating Wage Differentials?" *American Economic Review,* Vol. 70, No. 3 (June): pp. 355–71.

———. 1982. "Do Union Members Receive Compensating Wage Differentials? Reply." *American Economic Review* Vol. 72, No. 4 (September): pp. 868–72.

Editors of *Business Week.* 1990a. "We Need to Repair our Economic Compass." *Business Week* (13 August): p. 128.

Editors of *Business Week.* 1990b. "It's Time to Shrink the Weapons Labs." *Business Week* (17 September): p. 164.

Editors of *Monthly Review.* 1983. "Unemployment: The Failure of Private Enterprise." *Monthly Review,* Vol. 35, No. 2 (June): pp. 1–9.

Edelstein, Michael. 1990. "What Price Cold War? Military Spending and Private Investment in the US, 1946–79." *Cambridge Journal of Economics,* Vol. 14, No. 4 (December): pp. 421–37.

Edwards, Edgar O. 1955. "The Effect of Capital Depreciation on the Capital Coefficient of a Firm." *Economic Journal,* Vol. 45, No. 260 (December): pp. 654–66.

Eisner, Robert. 1991. Infrastructure and Regional Economic Performance: Comment." *New England Economic Review* (September/October): pp. 47–58.

Eisner, Robert and Robert Chirinko. 1983. "Tax Policy and Investment Models in Major U.S. Macroeconomic Models." *Journal of Public Economics,* Vol. 20, No. 2 (March): pp. 139–66.

Elias, David. 1999. *Dow 40,000: Strategies for Profiting From the Greatest Bull Market in History* (New York: McGraw-Hill Professional Publishing).

Elstrom, Peter. 2001. "Telecom Meltdown." *Business Week* (23 April): pp. 100–10.

Emmanuel, Arghiri. 1972. *Unequal Exchange: A Study of the Imperialism of Trade* (New York: Monthly Review Press).

Epstein, David F. 1990. "The Economic Cost of Soviet Security and Empire." In Henry S. Rowen and Charles Wolf, Jr. 1990. *The Impoverished Superpower: Perestroika and the Soviet Military Burden* (San Francisco: Institute for Contemporary Studies): pp. 127–54.

Epstein, Gerald. 1990–1991. "Mortgaging America: Debt, Lies, and Multinationals." *World Policy Journal* (Winter): pp. 27–59.

Estevao, Marcello and Saul Lach. 1999. "Measuring Temporary Labor Outsourcing in U.S. Manufacturing." National Bureau of Economic Research Working Paper No. W7421 (November).

Etzioni, Amitai. 1988. *The Moral Dimension: Toward A New Economics* (New York: The Free Press).

———. 1991. "The Socioeconomic View of Redevelopment." *Review of Political Economy,* Vol. 3, No. 4 (October): pp. 373–92.

Etzold, Thomas H. and John Lewis Gaddis. 1978. "NSC 68: The Strategic Reassessment of 1950." In Thomas H. Etzold and John Lewis Gaddis, eds. *Containment: Documents on American Policy and Strategy, 1945–1950* (New York: Columbia University Press, 1978): pp. 383–855.

Ewan, Stuart. 1996. *PR: A Social History of Spin* (New York: Basic Books).

Fairris, David. 1990. "Appearance and Reality in Postwar Shopfloor Relations." *Review of Radical Political Economy,* Vol. 22, No. 4 (Winter): pp. 17–43.

Fazzari, Steven, R. Glenn Hubbard, and Bruce Peterson. 1988. "Investment, Financing Decisions and Tax Policy." *American Economic Review,* Vol. 78, No. 2 (May): pp. 200–5.

Fenoaltea, Stefano. 1984. "Slavery and Supervision in Comparative Perspective: A Model." *Journal of Economic History,* Vol. 44, No. 3 (September): pp. 635–68.

Field, Alexander J. 1998. "The Telegraphic Transmission of Financial Asset Prices and Orders to Trade: Implications for Economic Growth, Trading Volume, and Securities Market Regulation." In Alexander J. Field, Gregory Clark, and William A. Sundstrom, eds. *Research in Economic History,* Vol. 18 (Stamford, CT.: JAI Press): pp. 145–84.

Fiorito, Jack and Cheryl L. Maranto. 1987. "The Contemporary Decline of Union Strength." *Contemporary Policy Issues,* Vol. 5, No. 4 (October): pp. 12–27.

Fisher, Franklin M. and John J. McGowan. 1983. "On the Misuse of Accounting Rates of Return to Infer Monopoly Profits." *American Economic Review,* Vol. 73, No. 1 (May): pp. 82–97.

Fitzgerald, A. Ernest. 1989. *The Pentagonists* (Boston: Houghton Mifflin).

FitzRoy, Felix R. and Kornelius Kraft. 1985. "Unionization, Wages and Efficiency: Theories and Evidence from the U.S. and West Germany." *Kyklos,* Vol. 38, No. 4, pp. 537–54.

———. 1987. "Cooperation, Productivity, and Profit Sharing." *Quarterly Journal of Economics,* Vol. 52, No. 1 (February): pp. 23–35.

Flamm, Kenneth. 1988a. *Creating the Computer: Government, Industry, and High Technology* (Washington, D.C.: The Brookings Institution).

———. 1988b. *Targeting the Computer: Government Support and International Competition* (Washington, D.C.: The Brookings Institution).

Florida, Richard and Martin Kenney. 1990a. *The Breakthrough Illusion: Corporate America's Failure to Move from Innovation to Mass Production* (New York: Basic Books).

———. 1990b. "High-technology Restructuring in the USA and Japan." *Environment and Planning* A, Vol. 22, pp. 233–52.

Frankel, Boris. 1987. *The Post-Industrial Utopians* (Madison: University of Wisconsin Press).

Frankel, Max. 1972. "The Budget: Defense vs. Social Aims." *The New York Times* (25 January): pp. 1 and 18.

Freeman, Richard B. and James Medoff. 1984. *What Do Unions Do?* (New York: Basic Books).

Friedman, Milton. 1968. "The Role of Monetary Policy." *American Economic Review,* Vol. 58, No. 1 (March): pp. 1–17.

———. 1980. "The Changing Character of Financial Markets." In *The American Economy in Transition,* edited by Martin Feldstein (Chicago: University of Chicago Press): pp. 78–86.

———. 1988. "Why the Twin Deficits Are a Blessing?" *Wall Street Journal* (14 December): p. A14.

Friedman, Thomas L. 1999. *The Lexus and the Olive Tree* (New York: Farrar Straus & Giroux).

Fuchs, Victor R. 1989. "Women's Quest for Economic Equality." *Journal of Economic Perspectives,* Vol. 3, No. 1 (Winter): pp. 25–41.

Garbarino, Joseph. 1962. *Wage Policy and Long Term Contracts* (Washington, D.C.: The Brookings Institution).

Gartman, David. 1986. *Auto Slavery: The Labor Process in the American Automobile Industry, 1897–1950* (New Brunswick, NJ: Rutgers University Press).

Gates, Paul W. 1960. *The Farmer's Age: Agriculture, 1815–1860* (New York: Harper and Row).

Gau, Robert S. 1984. "Union Settlements and Aggregate Wage Behavior in the 1980s." *Federal Reserve Bulletin* (December): pp. 843–56; reprinted in Ben Bernanke, ed. *Readings and Cases in Macroeconomics* (New York: McGraw-Hill, 1987): pp. 280–300.

Gaylord, W. W. 1940. "Don't Expect All New Equipment to Pay Out in Three Years." *Factory Management and Maintenance,* Vol. 98, No. 2 (February): p. 52.

Genovese, Eugene D. 1976. *Roll, Jordan, Roll: The World the Slaves Made* (New York: Vintage).

Gibbons, Joel C. 1984. "Energy Prices and Capital Obsolescence: Evidence from the Oil Embargo Period." *The Energy Journal,* Vol. 5, No. 1 (January): pp. 29–44.

Gilder, George. 1989. *Microcosm: The Quantum Revolution in Economics and Technology* (New York: Simon and Schuster).

Gillespie, Stephen. 1990. "Are Economic Statistics Overproduced?" *Public Choice,* Vol. 67, No. 3 (December): pp. 227–42.

Gintis, Herbert and Samuel Bowles. 1976. *Schooling in Capitalist America: Educational Reforms and the Contradictions of Economic Life* (New York: Basic Books).

Glasgall, William. 1988. "The World's Top 50 Banks: It's Official—Japan Is Way Out Front." *Business Week* (27 June): 76–8.

Glassman, James K. and Kevin A. Hassett. 1999. *Dow 36,000: The New Strategy for Profiting from the Coming Rise in the Stock Market* (New York: Times Books).

Gleckman, Howard. 1991. "Washington's Misleading Maps of the Economy." *Business Week* (3 June): pp. 112–3.

Glyn, Andrew, Alan Hughes, Alain Lipietz, and Ajit Singh. 1990. "The Rise and Fall of the Golden Age." Stephen A. Marglin and Juliet B. Schor, eds. *The Golden Age of Capitalism: Reinterpreting the Postwar Experience* (Oxford: Clarendon Press): pp. 38–125.

Gold, David. 1990. *The Impact of Defense Spending on Investment, Productivity and Economic Growth* (Washington, D.C.: Defense Budget Project).

Goldsmith, Raymond W. 1958. *Financial Intermediaries in the American Economy since 1900* (Princeton: Princeton University Press).

Good, Mary L. 2001. "21st Century Science and Technology: The Role of the United States: Leader, Viable Competitor or Follower." Presentation to be American Association for the Advancement of Science annual meeting (San Francisco, 15 February). <http://www.ualr.edu/~codept/goodtext.html>

Gorbachev, Mikhail. 1987. *Perestroika: New Thinking for Our Country and the World* (New York: Harper and Row).

Gordon, Colin. 1994. *New Deals: Business, Labor, and Politics in America* (Cambridge: Cambridge University Press).

Gordon, David M. 1996. *Fat and Mean: The Corporate Squeeze of Working Americans and the Myth of Managerial Downsizing* (New York: New Press).

Gordon, John Steele. 1999. *The Great Game: The Emergence of Wall Street as a World Power, 1653–2000* (New York: Scribner).

Gordon, R. A. 1969. "The Stability of the U.S. Economy." In Bronfenbrenner (ed.): pp. 3–35.

Gordon, Robert J. 1980. "Postwar Macroeconomics: The Evolution of Events and Ideas." In *The American Economy in Transition: A Sixtieth Anniversary Conference,* edited by Martin Feldstein (Chicago: University of Chicago Press): pp. 101–62.

———. 2000. "Does the 'New Economy' Measure Up to the Great Inventions of the Past?" *Journal of Economic Perspectives,* Vol. 14, No. 4 (Fall): pp. 49–74.

Gordon, Robert J. and John M. Veitch. 1984. "Fixed Investment in the American Business Cycle, 1919–83." National Bureau of Economic Research Working Paper No. 1426 (August).

Gort, Michael. 1962. *Diversification and Integration in American Industry* (Princeton: Princeton University Press).

Granstrand, Ove. 2000. *The Economics and Management of Intellectual Property: Towards Intellectual Capitalism* (Edward Elgar).

Gray, Patricia Bellew. 1986. "Parties, Polls and Pejoratives: Lawyers Meet." *The Wall Street Journal* (13 August): p. 25.

Green, Alison and David Mayes. 1991. "Technical Inefficiency in Manufacturing Industries." *The Economic Journal,* Vol. 101, No. 406 (May): pp. 523–38.

Greenhouse, Steven. 2000a. "Report Faults Laws for Slowing Growth of Unions." *New York Times* (24 October).

———. 2000b. "Janitors Struggle at the Edges of Silicon Valley's Success." *New York Times* (18 April): p. A18.

———. 2001. "Problems Seen for Teenagers Who Hold Jobs." *New York Times* (29 January).

Greenspan, Alan. 1997. "Statement Before the Committee on Banking, Housing, and Urban Affairs, U.S. Senate (26 February)." *Federal Reserve Bulletin,* Vol. 83, No. 4 (April): pp. 254–9.

———. 2001. "The Challenge of Measuring and Modeling a Dynamic Economy: Speech Delivered to the Washington Economic Policy Conference of the National Association for Business Economics, Washington, D.C. (27 March).

Greider, William. 1987. *Secrets of the Temple* (New York: Simon and Schuster).

Griffin, Larry J., Michael Wallace, and Joel A. Devine. 1982. "The Political Economy of Military Spending: Evidence from the United States," *Cambridge Journal of Economics,* Vol. 6, No. 1 (March): pp. 1–14.

Griliches, Zvi. 1988. "Productivity Puzzles and R&D: Another Nonexplanation." *Journal of Economic Perspectives,* Vol. 2, No. 4 (Fall): pp. 9–21.

Gruebler, Arnulf. 1990. *The Rise and Fall of Infrastructures: Dynamics of Evolution and Technical Change in Transport* (Heidelberg: Physica Verlag).

Habakkuk, H. J. 1962. *American and British Technology in the Nineteenth Century: The Search for Labour-Saving Inventions* (Cambridge: Cambridge University Press).

Halberstam, David. 1986. *The Reckoning* (New York: William Morrow).

Hansen, Alvin H. 1949. *Monetary Theory and Fiscal Policy* (New York: McGraw Hill).

Hanushek, Eric A. 1986. "The Economics of Schooling: Production and Efficiency in Public Schools." *Journal of Economic Literature,* Vol. 14, No. 3 (September): pp. 1141–77.

———. 1989. "Expenditures, Efficiency, and Equity in Education: The Federal Government's Role." *American Economic Review,* Vol. 79, No. 2 (May): pp. 46–51.

Hargaves-Heap, S. P. 1980. "Choosing the wrong natural rate, accelerating inflation or decelerating unemployment and growth." *Economic Journal,* Vol. 90, No. 359 (September): pp. 611–20

Harris, Howell J. 1982. *The Right to Manage: Industrial Relations Policies of American Business in the 1940s* (Madison: University of Wisconsin Press).

Harris, Seymour E. 1964. *The Economics of the Kennedy Years and a Look Ahead* (New York: Harper and Row).

Harrison, Bennett. 1972. "Education and Unemployment in the Urban Ghetto." *American Economic Review,* Vol. 62, No. 5, pp. 796–812.

Harrison, Harrison and Barry Bluestone. 1988. *The Great U-Turn: Corporate Restructuring and the Polarizing of America* (New York: Basic Books).

———. 1990. "Wage Polarisation in the US and the 'Flexibility' Debate." *Cambridge Journal of Economics,* Vol. 14, No. 3 (September): pp. 351–73.

Hartung, William D. 1999a. "The Shrinking Military Pork Barrel: The Changing Distribution of Pentagon Spending, 1986–1996." In *The Changing Dynamics of U.S. Defense Spending,* ed. Leon V. Sigal (Westport, CT.: Praeger): pp. 29–90.

Hartung, William D. 1999b. "False Expectations: Can Arms Exports Make Up for Cuts in Pentagon Procurement?" In *The Changing Dynamics of U.S. Defense Spending,* ed. Leon V. Sigal (Westport, CT.: Praeger): pp. 177–216.

Hatch, Julie and Angela Clinton. 2000. "Job Growth in the 1990s: A Retrospect." *Monthly Labor Review,* Vol. 123, No. 12 (December): pp. 3–18.

Heede, R. Richard and Amory B. Lovens. 1985. "Hiding the True Costs of Energy Sources." *Wall Street Journal* (17 September): p. 28.

Heller, Walter W. 1966. *New Dimensions of Political Economy* (New York: W.W. Norton).

Hellman, Christopher. 1999. "U.S. Share of World Military Spending Growing." *CDI Defense Monitor* [Center for Defense Information], Volume 3, Issue 44 (11 November 11). <http://www.cdi.org/weekly/1999/issue44.html#3>

Henwood, Douglas. 1990. "A Compendium of Woes." *Left Business Observer,* No. 40 (14 September): pp. 4–5.

———. 1991. "The Uses of Crisis." *Left Business Observer* (3 June): pp. 1–3.

Herz, Diane E. 1990. "Worker Displacement in a Period of Rapid Job Expansion: 1983–87." *Monthly Labor Review,* Vol. 113, No. 5 (May): pp. 21–33.

———. 1991. "Worker Displacement Still Common the Late 1980's." *Monthly Labor Review,* Vol. 114, No. 5 (May): pp. 3–9.

Hickok, Susan. 1991. "The Shifting Composition of U.S. Manufactured Goods Trade." *Federal Reserve Bank of New York Quarterly Review,* Vol. 16, No. 1 (Spring): pp. 27–37.

Hicks, John R. 1932. *Theory of Wages* (New York: St. Martin's Press, 1963).

Hill. T. P. 1977. "On goods and services." *Review of Income and Wealth,* Series 23, No. 4 (December): pp. 315–38.

Hillard, Michael and Richard McIntrye. 1991. "A Kinder Gentler Capitalism? Resurgent Corporate Liberalism in the Age of Bush." *Rethinking Marxism,* Vol. 4, No. 1 (Spring): pp. 104–14.

Hirshleifer, Jack. 1987. *Economic Behavior in Adversity* (Chicago: University of Chicago Press).

Hooks, Gregory. 1991. *Forging the Military-Industrial Complex: World War II's Battle of the Potomac* (Urbana: University of Illinois Press).

Hoover, Herbert. 1952. *The Memoirs of Herbert Hoover,* Vol. 3. *The Great Depression, 1929–1941* (New York: Macmillan).

Hulbert, Mark. 1982. *Interlock: The Untold Story of American Banks, Oil Interests, the Shah's Money, Debts and the Astounding Connection Between Them* (New York: Richardson and Snyder).

———. 1990. "Discussion of Alicia Munnell. 'How Does Public Infrastructure Affect Regional Economic Performance?'" In Alicia H. Munnell, ed. *Is There a Shortfall in Public Capital Investment? Proceedings of a Conference Held in June 1990,* Conference Series No. 34 (Boston: Federal Reserve Bank of Boston): pp. 104–7.

Hulten, Charles R. 1992. "Growth Accounting When Technical Change is Embodied in Capital." *American Economic Review,* Vol. 82, No. 4 (September): pp. 964–80.

Hungerford, Thomas and Gary Solon. 1987. "Sheepskin Effects in the Returns to Education." *Review of Economics and Statistics,* Vol. 49, No. 1 (February): pp. 175–77.

Hunt, Robert M. 1999. "Patent Reform: A Mixed Blessing for the U.S. Economy?" *Business Review of the Federal Reserve Bank of Philadelphia* (November-December): pp. 15–29.

Hunter, Helen Manning. 1982. "The Role of Business Liquidity During the Great Depression and Afterwards: Differences Between Large and Small Firms." *Journal of Economic History,* Vol. 42, No. 4 (December): pp. 883–902.

Institute of Science and Technology, Industrial Development Division, University of Michigan. 1984. "Revitalization of Industrial Buildings: An Investigation of Economic Impact Resulting from Closing of Aged Industrial Plants." U.S. Research and Development Report, NTIS PB 84–162478.

Jackman, Richard and Richard Layard. 1991. "Does Long-term Unemployment Reduce a Person's Chance of a Job? A Time Series Test." *Economica,* Vol. 58, No. 229 (February): pp. 93–106.

Jacoby, Russell. 1994. *Dogmatic Wisdom: How the Culture Wars Divert Education and Distract America* (New York: Anchor Books).

Jenks, Jeremiah. 1890. "The Economic Outlook." *Dial,* 10; cited in Livingston 1986.

Jensen, Michael. 1988. "Takeovers: Their Causes and Consequences." *Journal of Economic Perspectives,* Vol. 2, No. 1 (Winter): pp. 21–48.

Jensen, Richard J. 1989. "The Causes and Cures of Unemployment in the Great Depression." *Journal of Interdisciplinary History,* Vol. 19, No. 4 (Spring): pp. 553–84.

Jerome, Harry. 1934. *Mechanization in Industry* (New York: National Bureau of Economic Research).

Jones, Charles and John Williams. 1998. "Measuring the Social Return to R&D." *Quarterly Journal of Economics,* Vol. 113, No. 4 (November): pp. 1119–36.

Jordan, J. S. 1989. "The Economics of Accounting Information Systems." *American Economic Review,* Vol. 79, No. 2 (May): pp. 140–5.

Joseph, Manu. 2001. "China Threatens India Eminence." *Wired News* (23 February). <http://www.wired.com/news/business/0,1367,41656,00.html>

Juster, F. Thomas, Chairman of the American Economic Association Committee on the Quality of Statistics. 1988. "The State of U.S. Economic Statistics: Current and Prospective Quality, Policy Needs, and Resources." Prepared for the 50th Anniversary Congress on Income and Wealth, Washington, D.C. (12–14 May).

Kadlec, Charles W. and Ralph J. Acampora. 1999. *Dow 100,000: Fact or Fiction* (Englewood Cliffs, NJ: Prentice Hall).

Kanabayashi, Masayoshi. 1990. "Rebuilding Japan: Prompted by the U.S., Tokyo Slates Trillions in Domestic Spending." *Wall Street Journal* (3 January): pp. A1 and A8.

Kaplinsky, Raphael. 1988. "Restructuring the capitalist labour process: some lessons from the car industry." *Cambridge Journal of Economics,* Vol. 12, No. 4 (December): pp. 451–70.

Kapstein, Ethan B. 1990. "From Guns to Butter in the USSR." Vol. *Challenge,* Vol. 32, No. 5 (September/October): pp. 11–15.

Keezer, Dexter M. 1958. *New Forces in American Business* (New York: McGraw-Hill).

Kenney, Martin and Richard Florida. 1988. "Beyond Mass Production: Production and the Labor Process in Japan." *Politics and Society,* Vol. 16, No. 1 (March): pp. 121–58.

Kennickell, Arthur B. 2000. *An Examination of Changes in the Distribution of Wealth From 1989 to 1998: Evidence from the Survey of Consumer Finances.* Jerome Levy Economics Institute, Working Paper No. 307.

Keynes, John Maynard. 1931a. "The Consequences to the Banks of the Collapse of Money Values." *Essays in Persuasion.* vol. ix. *The Collected Writings of John Maynard Keynes,* Elizabeth Johnston, ed. (London: Macmillan, 1972): pp. 150–8.

———. 1931b. "An Economic Analysis of Unemployment." In *Unemployment as a World-Problem: Lectures at the Harris Foundation, 1931,* edited by Philip Quincy Wright (Freeport, NY: Books for Libraries Press), pp. 3–43; reprinted in Elizabeth Johnston (ed.) *The Collected Works of John Maynard Keynes,* vol. XIII, *The General Theory and After,* Part I, *Preparation* (London: Macmillan, 1973): pp. 343–67.

———. 1936. *The General Theory of Employment, Interest and Money* (London: Macmillan).

Kidder, Tracy. 1981. *The Soul of a New Machine* (Boston: Little, Brown.

King, F. H. 1911. *Farmers of Forty Centuries or Permanent Agriculture in China, Korea and Japan* (Emmaus, PA.: Rodale Press, 1972).

Kislev, Yoav and Peterson, Willis. 1982. "Prices, Technology, and Farm Size." *Journal of Political Economy,* Vol. 90, No. 3 (June): pp. 578–95.

Klein, Lawrence R. 1983. *The Economics of Supply and Demand* (Baltimore, Maryland: The John Hopkins University Press).

Kletzer, Lori G. 1998. "Job Displacement." *Journal of Economic Perspectives,* Vol. 12, No. 1 (Winter): pp. 3–26.

Komiya, R. 1975. "Planning in Japan." In M. Bernstein, ed. *Economic Planning: East and West* (New York: Ballinger).

Kopcke, Richard W. 1980. "Potential Growth, Productivity, and Capital Accumulation." *New England Economic Review* (May/June), pp. 22–41.

Kozol, Jonathan. 1991. *Savage Inequalities: Children in America's Schools* (New York: Crown).

Krause, Reinhardt. 2001. "Techbits." *Investor's Business Daily* (25 April): p. A6.

Kravis, Irving B. and Richard E. Lipsey. 1988. "The Effect of Multinational Firms' Foreign Operations on their Domestic Employment." National Bureau of Economic Research Working Paper No. 2760.

———. 1989. "Technological Characteristics of Industries and the Competitiveness of the U.S. and Its Multinational Firms." National Bureau of Economic Research Working Paper No. 2933.

Krugman, Paul. 1990. *The Age of Diminished Expectations* (Cambridge, MA.: MIT Press.

Kulish, Nicholas. 2000. "Economists Group Warns Budget Cuts May Be Hurting Statistics' Reliability." *Wall Street Journal* (23 August): p. A2.

Labaton, Stephen. 1988. "200 Million in Wall St. Fees Seen From Federated Deal." *New York Times* (5 April).

Lamfalussy, A. 1961. *Investment and Growth in Mature Economies: The Case of Belgium* (London: Macmillan).

LaPlante, Alice and Ed Scannell. 1989. "View from the Top." *Infoworld,* Vol. 11, No. 40 (2 October): pp. 53–60.

Lawrence, Robert Z. 1983, "Is Trade Deindustrializing America? A Medium Term Perspective." *Brookings Papers on Economic Activiety,* No. 1, pp. 129–71.

Layard, Richard. 1988. "Comments on Michael Burda. 'Wait Unemployment' in Europe." *Economic Policy,* No. 7 (October): pp. 416–9.

Lazonick, William. 1989. "Controlling the Market for Corporate Control: The Historical Significance of Managerial Capitalism." Barnard Working Paper No. 90–04.

———. 1990. *Competitive Advantage on the Shop Floor* (Cambridge, MA: Harvard University Press).

Lebergott, Stanley. 1990. "'Wage Rigidity' in the Depression: Concept or Phrase?" (March 16). unpub.

Leibenstein, Harvey. 1983. "Property Rights and X-efficiency: Comment." *American Economic Review,* Vol. 73, No. 4 (September): pp. 831–42.

Lekachman, Robert. 1966. *The Age of Keynes* (New York: Random House).

Leontief, W. 1981. "Testimony." In United States House of Representatives. 1981. 97th Congress, 1st Sess. Committee on Energy and Commerce. Subcommittee on Oversight and Investigations. *Capital Formation and Industrial Policy, Part 1. Hearings, 27 and 29 April, 1, 22 and 24 June* (Washington, D.C.: U.S. Government Printing Office).

Levin, Henry M. 1989. "Economics of Investment in Educationally Disadvantaged Students." *American Economic Review,* Vol. 79, No. 2 (May): pp. 52–6.

Levitan, Sar A. and Isaac Shapiro. 1987. "What's Missing in Welfare Reform?" *Challenge,* Vol. 30. No. 3 (July-August): pp. 41–8.

Levy, Frank. 1988. *Dollars and Dreams: The Changing American Income Distribution* (New York: Norton).

Lewis, Michael. 1989. *Liar's Poker: Rising Through the Wreckage on Wall Street* (New York: W.W. Norton).

Light, Jay O. and Andre F. Perold. 1987. "The Institutionalization of Wealth: Changing Patterns of Investment Decision Making." In Samuel P. Hayes, III, ed. *Wall Street and Regulation* (Cambridge, MA: Harvard University Press).

Light, Larry. 1996. "Why Counterfeit Goods May Kill." *Business Week* (2 September): p. 6.

Linbeck, Assar. 1981. "Industrial Policy as an Issue in the Economic Environment." *The World Economy,* Vol. 9, Nos. 11 and 12 (November/December): pp. 391–405.

Lippert, John. 1978. "Shopfloor Politics at Fleetwood." *Radical America,* Vol. 12, No. 4 (July/August): pp. 25–44.

Livingston, James. 1986. *Origins of the Federal Reserve System: Money, Class, and Corporate Capitalism, 1890–1913* (Ithaca, NY: Cornell University Press).

Locay, Luis. 1990. "Economic Development and the Division of Production between Households and Markets." *Journal of Political Economy,* Vol. 98, No. 5 (Part 1) (October): pp. 965–82.

Lucas, Robert E., Jr. 1970. "Capacity, Overtime, and Empirical Production Functions." *American Economic Review,* Vol. 60, No. 2 (May): pp. 23–27; reprinted in his *Studies in Business Cycle Theory* (Cambridge, MA: MIT Press, 1983): pp. 146–55.

Lucia, Joseph L. 1983. "Allan Sproul and the Treasury-Federal Reserve Accord of 1951." *History of Political Economy,* Vol. 15, No. 1 (Spring): pp. 106–21.

Lundberg, Erik. 1985. "The Rise and Fall of the Swedish Model." *Journal of Economic Literature,* Vol. 23, No. 1 (March): pp. 1–36.

Lynd, Staughton. 1989. "Industry goes for the steal." *In These Times,* Vol. 13, No. 11 (1–7 February): p. 20

Macher, Jeffrey T., David C. Mowery, and David A. Hodges. 1999. "Semiconductors." In David C. Mowery, ed. *U.S. Industry in 2000: Studies in Competitive Performance* (Washington, D.C.: National Research Council): pp. 245–86. <http://books.nap.edu/books/0309061792/html>

Maddison, Angus. 1964. *Economic Growth in the West: Comparative Experience in Europe and North America* (New York: Twentieth Century Fund).

Madison, Bernard L. and Therese A. Hart for the Committee on the Mathematical Sciences in the Year 2000. 1990. *A Challenge of Numbers: People in the Mathematical Sciences* (Washington, D.C.: National Academy Press).

Magaziner, Ira and Robert Reich. 1981. *Managing America's Business: The Decline and Rise of the American Economy* (New York: Harcourt, Brace, and Jovanovich).

Magdoff, Harry and Paul Sweezy. 1983. "International Finance and National Power." *Monthly Review,* Vol. 35, No. 5 (October): pp. 1–13.

———. 1985. "The Strange Recovery of 1983–1984." *Monthly Review,* Vol. 37, No. 5 (October): pp. 1–11.

———. 1990. "Investment for What?" *Monthly Review,* Vol. 42, No. 2 (June): pp. 1–10.

Magee, Mike. 2000a. "TSMC Outstrips Intel in Wafer Starts." *The Register* (22 September). <http://www.theregister.co.uk/content/3/13443.html>

———. 2000b. "Taiwanese Axis Beats AMD, Intel to .13 Micron." *The Register* (12 December). <http://www.theregister.co.uk/content/3/15387.html>

Magnusson, Paul, Eric Schine, Barbara Buell and Bruce Hager. 1990. "American Smart Bombs, Foreign Brains." *Business Week* (4 March 1991): p. 18.

Makhijani, Arjun, Stephen I. Schwartz, and William J. Weida. 1998. "Nuclear Waste Management and Environmental Remediation." In Stephen I. Schwartz, ed. *Atomic Audit: The Costs and Consequences of U. S. Nuclear Weapons Since 1940* (Washington, D.C.: Brookings Institution): pp. 353–432.

Malabre, Alfred L., Jr. 1988. "Shaky Statistics Pose Peril for Forecasters." *Wall Street Journal* (9 May): p. 1.

———. 1990a. "Economic Roadblock: Infrastructure Neglect." *Wall Street Journal* (30 July): p. A1.

———. 1990b. "The Economy's Faulty Barometer's." *Wall Street Journal* (26 December): p. 6.

Malcolemson, James M. 1975. "Replacement and the Rental Value of Capital Equipment Subject to Obsolescence," *Journal of Economic Theory,* Vol. 10, No. 1 (February): pp. 24–41.

Malecki, Edward J. 1991. *Technology and Economic Development: The Dynamics of Local, Regional, and National Change* (New York: Longman Scientific and Technical).

Mandel, Michael J. and Aaron Bernstein. 1990. "Dispelling the Myths that are Holding Us Back." *Business Week* (17 December): pp. 66–70.

Manning, Robert. 2000. *Credit Card Nation: The Consequences of America's Addiction To Credit* (New York: Basic Books).

Marglin, Stephen A. 1990. "Lessons of the Golden Age: An Overview." In Stephen A. Marglin and Juliet B. Schor, eds. *The Golden Age of Capitalism: Reinterpreting the Postwar Experience* (Oxford: Clarendon Press): pp. 1–38.

Markides, Constantinos and Norman Berg. 1988. "Manufacturing Offshore Is Bad Business." *Harvard Business Review,* Vol. 66 (September-October): pp. 113–20.

Marshall, Alfred. 1920. *Principles of Economics: An Introductory Volume,* 8th ed. (London: Macmillan & Co.).

Marshall, Andrew. 1987. "Commentary." In United States Congress. Joint Economic Committee. *Gorbachev's Economic Plans,* 2 vols. (Washington, D.C.: U.S. Government Printing Office): pp. 481–4.

May, Ann Mari and Randi R. Grant. 1991. "Class Conflict, Corporate Power, and Macroeconomic Policy: The Impact of Inflation in the Postwar Period." *Journal of Economic Issues,* Vol. 25, No. 2 (June): pp. 373–81.

Mayer, Martin. 1974. *The Bankers* (New York: Ballantine Books).

———. 1990. *The Greatest-Ever Bank Robbery: The Collapse of the Savings and Loan Industry* (New York: Charles Scribner).

McCormack, Gavan. 1996. *The Emptiness of Japanese Affluence* (Armonk, NY: M. E. Sharpe).

McElhattan, Rose. 1985. "Inflation, Supply Shocks and the Stable Rate of Capacity Utilization." *Federal Reserve Bank of San Francisco Review* (Winter): pp. 45–63.

McHugh, Richard and Julia Lane. 1987. "The Role of Embodied Technological Change in the Decline of Labor Productivity." *Southern Economic Journal,* Vol. 53, No. 4 (April): pp. 915–24.

McLemee, Scott. 1995. "Theater of the Absurd." *In These Times* (11 December): pp. 14–16.

Melman, Seymour. 1983. *Profits Without Production* (New York: Alfred A. Knopf).

———. 1988. "Economic Consequences of the Arms Race: The Second-Rate Economy." *American Economic Review,* Vol. 78, No. 2 (May): pp. 55–9.

Melman, Seymour and Lloyd J. Dumas. 1990. "Planning for Economic Conversion." *The Nation,* Vol. 250, No. 15 (16 April): pp. 509 and 522–8.

Meltzer, Allan H. 1988. "Economic policies and actions in the Reagan administration." *Journal of Post Keynesian Economics,* Vol. 10, No. 4 (Summer): pp. 528–40.

Metzenbaum, Senator Howard M. 1991. "Testimony." Hearings of the Senate Committee on Labor and Human Resources, Subcommittee on Labor *Retirees at Risk: The Executive Life Bankruptcy.* (21 June).

Michl, Thomas R. 1988a. "The Two-Stage Decline in U.S. Profitability." *Review of Radical Political Economics,* Vol. 20: No. 4 (Winter): pp. 1–22.

———. 1988b. "The Wage-Profit Frontier and Declining Profitability in U.S. Manufacturing." *Review of Radical Political Economics,* Vol. 20, Nos. 2 & 3 (Summer and Fall): pp. 80–86.

———. 1991. "Wage-Profit Curves in US Manufacturing." *Cambridge Journal of Economics,* Vol. 15, No. 3 (September): pp. 271–86.

Miller, Edward. 1990. "Can a Perpetual Inventory Capital Stock Be Used for Production Function Parameter Estimation." *Review of Income and Wealth,* Vol. 36, No. 4 (March): pp. 67–82.

Miller, James P. 2000. "Berkshire's Buffett Scoffs at Tech Stocks' Valuation." Wall Street Journal (1 May): p. A6.

Miller, John. 1989. "Social Wage or Social Profit? Net Social Wage and the Welfare State." *Review of Radical Political Economy,* Vol. 21, No. 3 (Fall): pp. 82–90.

Mills, David E. and Laurence Schumann. 1985. "Industry Structure with Fluctuating Demand." *American Economic Review,* Vol. 75, No. 4 (September): pp. 758–67.

Minsky, Hyman P. 1982. "Debt Deflation Processes in Today's Institutional Environment." *Banca Nazionale del Lavoro Quarterly Review,* Vol. 143 (December): pp. 375–93.

———. 1986. *Stabilizing an Unstable Economy* (New Haven: Yale University Press).

———. 1990. "Money Manager Capitalism, Fiscal Independence and International Monetary Reconstruction." In *The Future of the Global Economic and Monetary System,* M. Szabo-Pelsoczi, ed. Budapest: Institute for World Economics, Hungarian Academy of Sciences.

Mishel, Lawrence. 1988. *Manufacturing Numbers: How Inaccurate Statistics Conceal U.S. Industrial Decline* (Washington, D.C.: Economic Policy Institute).

Mishel, Lawrence and David M. Frankel. 1991. *The State of Working America, 1990–1991* (Armonk, NY: M. E. Sharpe).

Mishel, Lawrence, Jared Bernstein, and John Schmitt. 2001. *The State of Working America* (Ithaca, NY: Cornell University Press).

Mokyr, Joel. 1990. *The Lever of Riches: Technological Creativity and Economic Progress* (New York: Oxford University Press).

Morgenson, Gretchen. 2001. "How Did They Value Stocks? Count the Absurd Ways." *New York Times* (18 March).

Morse, David. 1985. "The Campaign to Save Dorothy Six." *The Nation* (7 September): pp. 174–5.

Moseley, Fred. 1988. "The Increase of Unproductive Labor in the Postwar U.S. Economy." *Review of Radical Political Economics,* Vol. 20, Nos. 2 & 3 (Summer and Fall): pp. 100–6.

———. 1991. *The Falling Rate of Profit in the Postwar United States Economy* (New York: St. Martin's Press).

Mowery, David C. and Nathan Rosenberg. 1989. *Technology and the Pursuit of Economic Growth* (Cambridge: Cambridge University Press).

Mueller, Hans. 1984. Protection and Competition in the U.S. Steel Market: A Study of Managerial Decision Making in Transition. Monograph Series, No. 30 Middle Tennessee State College, Murfeesboro, TN. (May).

Munnell, Alicia H. 1990. "Why Has Productivity Growth Declined? Productivity and Public Investment." *New England Economic Review of the Federal Reserve Bank of Boston* (January/February): pp. 4–22.

Murnane, Richard J. 1988. "Education and the Productivity of the Workforce: Looking Ahead." In Robert Litan et al. eds. *American Living Standards: Threats and Challenges* (Washington, D.C.: The Brookings Institution): pp. 215–45.

Murnane, Richard J. and Randall J. Olsen. 1990. "The Effects of Salaries and Opportunity Costs on Length of Stay in Teaching: Evidence from North Carolina." *Journal of Human Resources,* Vol. 25, No. 1 (Winter): pp. 106–24.

Murphy, Kevin M., Andrei Shleifer and Robert Vishny. 1991. "The Allocations of Talent: Implications for Growth." *Quarterly Journal of Economics,* Vol. 106, No. 2 (May): pp. 503–30.

Murray, Charles. 1986. *Losing Ground: American Social Policy, 1950–1980* (New York: Basic Books).

Muto, Sheila. 2001a. "About 80% of Bay Area Web Firms Will Fail, San Francisco Study Finds." Wall Street Journal (28 March).

———. 2001b. "Home Prices Begin to Decline In Upscale Parts of San Francisco." *Wall Street Journal* (27 March).

Myrdal, Gunnar. 1962. *An American Dilemma: The Negro Problem and Modern Democracy,* 20th Anniversary Edition (New York: Harper and Row).

Naj, Amal Kumar. 1988. "Chemical Firms Resist Lures to Expand." *Wall Street Journal* (12 January): p. 6.

Nakarmi, Laxmi. 1991. "At Lucky-Goldstar, The Koos Loosen the Reins." *Business Week* (18 February): pp. 72–3.

National Commission on Excellence in Education. 1983. *A Nation at Risk: The Imperative for Educational Reform: A Report to the Nation and the Secretary of Education United States Department of Education.* <http://www.ed.gov/pubs/NatAtRisk/risk.html>.

National Education Association. 1991. *Almanac of Higher Education* (Washington, D.C.: National Education Association).

National Machine Tool Builders Association. 1982–1983. *Economic Handbook of the Machine Tool Industry, 1983* (McLean, Virginia: National Machine Tool Builders Association).

National Science Board. 2000. *Science and Engineering Indicators, 2000* (Washington, D.C.: National Science Federation). <http://www.nsf.gov/sbe/srs/seind00/>

Neal, Alfred C. 1981. *Business Power and Public Policy* (New York: Praeger).

Neild, R. R. 1964. "Replacement Policy." *National Institute Economic Review,* No. 30 (November): pp. 30–43.

Nelson, Richard R. 1989. "What is Private and What is Public About Technology?" *Science, Technology, and Human Values,* Vol. 14, No. 3 (Summer): pp. 229–41.

———. 1990. "U.S. technological leadership: Where did it come from and where did it go?" *Research Policy,* Vol. 19, No. 2 (April): pp. 117–32.

Nelson, Robert A. 1998. "Iridium: From Concept to Reality." *Via Satellite* (September). <http://catalog.com/hitekweb/iridium.htm>

Nieves, Evelyn. 2000a. "Many in Silicon Valley Cannot Afford Housing, Even at $50,000 a Year." *New York Times* (20 February): p. A20.

———. 2000b. "In San Francisco, Renters are Humble Supplicants." *New York Times* (6 June).

Niggle, Christopher J. 1988. "The Increasing Importance of Financial Capital in the U.S. Economy." *Journal of Economic Issues,* Vol. 22, No. 2 (June): pp. 581–8.

Nilsson, Eric A. 1999. "Trends in Compensation for Production Workers: 1948–1995." *Review of Radical Political Economics,* Vol. 31, No. 4 (Fall): pp. 133–163.

Noble, David. 1984. *Forces of Production: A Social History of Industrial Automation* (New York: Alfred A. Knopf).

O'Brien, Anthony Patrick. 1989. "A Behavioral Explanation for Nominal Wage Rigidity During the Great Depression." *Quarterly Journal of Economics,* Vol. 104, No. 4 (November): pp. 719–36.

O'Leary, James J. 1945. "Consumption as a Factor in Postwar Employment." *American Economic Review,* Vol. 35, No. 2 (May): pp. 37–55.

Offer, Avner. 1989. *The First World War: An Agrarian Interpretation* (Oxford: Clarendon Press).

Okun, Arthur M. 1970. *The Political Economy of Prosperity* (New York: W.W. Norton).

Olson, Elizabeth. 1998. "West Hinders Inquiry on Dumping as Rights Issue." *New York Times* (5 April): p. A10.

Orr, Douglas V. 1998. "Strategic Bankruptcy and Private Pension Default." *Journal of Economic Issues,* Vol. 32, No. 3 (September): pp. 669–87.

Oshima, H. T. 1984. "The Growth of U.S. Factor Productivity: The Significance of New Technologies in the Early Decades of the Twentieth Century." *Journal of Economic History,* Vol. 44, No. 1 (March): pp. 161–70.

Pennar, Karen. 1991. "Slash-and-Burn Cost-Cutting Could Singe the Recovery." *Business Week* (6 May): p. 73.

Pentzinger, Thomas, Jr. 1988. "Williams Cos. Transforms 'Lazy Assets' Into No. 4. Telecommunications Service." *Wall Street Journal* (5 May) p. 30.

Perelman, Michael. 1983. *Classical Political Economy, Primitive Accumulation, and the Social Division of Labor* (Totowa, NJ: Rowman and Allanheld).

———. 1987. *Marx's Crises Theory: Scarcity, Labor and Finance* (New York: Praeger).

———. 1989. *Keynes, Investment Theory and the Economic Slowdown: The Role of Replacement Investment and q-Ratios* (London: Macmillan).

———. 1991. *Information, Social Relations, and the Economics of High Technology* (London: Macmillan).

———. 1996. *The End of Economics* (London: Routledge).

———. 1999. *The Natural Instability of Markets: Expectations, Increasing Returns and the Collapse of Markets* (New York: St. Martin's Press).

———. 2000. *Transcending the Economy: On the Potential of Passionate Labor and the Wastes of the Market* (New York: St. Martin's Press).

Peterson, George E. 1990. "Is Public Infrastructure Undersupplied?" In Alicia H. Munnell, ed. *Is There a Shortfall in Public Capital Investment? Proceedings of a Conference Held in June 1990,* Conference Series No. 34 (Boston: Federal Reserve Bank of Boston): pp. 113–30.

Phillips, Albert. 1958. "The Deep Roots of Inflation." *International Socialist Review,* 2 Parts, 19, 3 and 4 (Summer and Spring): pp. 93–98 and pp. 147–52.

Pindyck, Robert S. and Julio Rotemberg. 1983. "Dynamic Factor Demands and the Effects of Energy Price Shocks." *American Economic Review,* Vol. 73, No. 5 (December): pp. 1066–79.

Piven, Frances Fox and Richard A. Cloward. 1971. *Regulating the Poor: The Functions of Public Welfare* (New York: Pantheon).

Pollard, Sidney. 1982. *The Wasting of the British Economy* (New York: St Martin's Press).

President of the United States. 1990. *Economic Report of the President* (Washington, D.C.: U.S. Government Printing Office).

Putka, Gary. 1991. "Making the Grade: Teacher Quality Rises with Improved Pay, Concern for Schools." *Wall Street Journal* (5 December): p. 1A.

Rae, John. 1834. *Statement of Some New Principles of Political Economy* (Boston); Volume II In *John Rae, Political Economist: An Account of his Life and an Compilation of his Main Writings,* edited by R. Warren James (Toronto: Toronto University Press, 1965).

Ramey, Valerie A. and Matthew D. Shapiro. 1998. "Costly Capital Reallocation and the Effects of Government Spending." *Carnegie-Rochester Conference Series on Public Policy,* Vol. 48, No. 1 (June): pp. 145–94.

Rattner, Steven. 1979. "Volcker Asserts U.S. Must Trim Living Standard." *New York Times* (18 October): p. A1.

Raymond, David. 1999. "Show Me the Money." *Forbes ASAP Supplement,* Vol. 163, No. 7 (5 April): p. 20.

Reagan, Ronald. 1984. Speech at Georgetown University's Center for Strategic and International Studies "American Foreign Policy Challenges in the 1980s." *Weekly Compilation of Presidential Documents,* No. 2086, pp. 1–6.

Register, Charles A. and Paul W. Grimes. 1991. "Collective Bargaining, Teachers, and Student Achievement." *Journal of Labor Research,* Vol. 12, No. 2 (Spring): pp. 91–111.

Reich, Robert B. 1990. "Who Is Us?" *Harvard Business Review,* Vol. 90, No. 1 (January-February): pp. 53–64.

Reppy, Judith. 1985. "Military R&D and the Civilian Economy." *Bulletin of the Atomic Scientists,* Vol. 41, No. 9 (October): pp. 10–14.

Richards, E. M. 1933. "To Buy or Not to Buy Equipment." *Factory Management and Maintenance,* Vol. 91 (December): pp. 499–500.

Riddell, Tom. 1987. "Military Build Up, Economic Decline? The Economy's Trillion-Dollar Habit." *Dollars and Sense,* No. 129 (September): pp. 6–9.

———. 1988. "U.S. Military Power, the Terms of Trade, and the Profit Rate." *American Economic Review* Vol. 78, No. 2 (May): pp. 60–5.

Ridgeway, James. 1998. "Dumping on Haiti." *Village Voice* (20 January).

Rivette, Kevin G. and David Kline. 2000. *Rembrandts in the Attic: Unlocking the Hidden Value of Patents* (Boston: Harvard Business School Press).

Robins, Norman. 1979. "Steel Industry Research and Technology." *American Steel Industry Economics Journal* (AISI) (April): pp. 49–58.

Romer, Christina. D. 1989. "The Prewar Business Cycle Reconsidered: New Estimates of Gross National Product, 1869–1908." *Journal of Political Economy,* Vol. 97, No. 1 (February): pp. 1–37.

Romer, Christina D. and David H. Romer. 1989. "Does Monetary Policy Matter? A New Test in the Spirit of Friedman and Schwartz." Olivier Jean Blanchard and Stanley Fischer, eds. *NBER Macroeconomics Annual* (Cambridge, MA: MIT Press): pp. 121–70.

Romer, Paul M. 1987. "Crazy Explanations for the Productivity Slowdown." In Stanley Fischer, ed. *NBER Macroeconomics Annual, 1987* (Cambridge, MA: The MIT Press): pp. 163–202.

Rose, Frederick. 1984. "Occidental's Purchase of Cities Service Does Little to Increase U.S. Oil Reserves." *Wall Street Journal* (5 December): p. 24.

Ross, Edward Alsworth. 1908. *Social Psychology* (New York: Macmillan).

Rothschild, Emma. 1974. *Paradise Lost: The Decline of the Auto-Industrial Age* (New York: Vintage Books).

Rothstein, Richard. 2001a. "Does Money Not Matter? The Data Suggest It Does." *New York Times* (17 January).

———. 2001b. "Lessons: Reducing Poverty Could Increase School Achievement." *New York Times* (7 March).

Rubin, Laura S. 1991. "Productivity and the Public Capital Stock: Another Look." Board of Governors of the Federal Reserve System, Economic Activity Section, Division of Research and Statistics, Working Paper No. 118 (May).

Ruhm, Christopher J. 1991. "Are Workers Permanently Scarred by Job Displacement?" *American Economic Review,* Vol. 81, No. 1 (March): pp. 319–24.

Rüstow, Hanns-Joachim. 1967. "The Development of Shares of Wages and Profits in an Industrial Society." *German Economic Review* No. 5, No. 2, pp. 92–115.

———. 1978. "The Economic Crisis of the Weimar Republic and How it was Overcome—A Comparison with the Present Recession." *Cambridge Journal of Economics,* Vol. 4, No. 2 (December): pp. 409–21.

Ryan, Michael P. 1998. *Knowledge Diplomacy: Global Competition and the Politics of Intellectual Property* (Washington, D.C.: Brookings Institution Press).

Sahling, Leonard and M. A. Akhtar. 1984–85. "What is Behind the Capital Spending Boom?" *Federal Reserve Bank of New York Quarterly Review,* Vol. 9, No. 4 (Winter): pp. 19–30.

Sakellaris, Plutarchos. 1997. "Irreversible Capital and the Stock Market Response to Shocks in Profitability." *International Economic Review,* Vol. 38, No. 2 (May): pp. 351–79.

Salamon, Gerald L. 1985. "Accounting Rates of Return." *American Economic Review,* Vol. 75, No. 3 (June): pp. 495–504.

Salpukas, Agis. 1971. "Workers' Use of Drugs Widespread in Nation." New York Times (21 June): pp. 1 and 16.

Sampson, Anthony. 1975. *The Seven Sisters: The Great Oil Companies and the World They Made* (New York: Viking).

Sansolo, Michael. 1987. "Take this job . . . please." *Progressive Grocer* (January): p. 75.

Santoni, G. J. 1986. "The Employment Act of 1946: Some History Notes." *Economic Review of the Federal Bank of St. Louis,* Vol. 68, No. 9 (November): pp. 5–16.

Sato, Ryuzo and Rama Ramachandran. 1980. "Measuring the Impact of Technical Progress on the Demand for Intermediate Goods: A Survey." *Journal of Economic Literature,* Vol. 18, No. 3 (September): pp. 1003–24.

Scherer, Frederick M. 1980. *Industrial Market Structure and Economic Performance,* 2nd. ed. (Chicago: Rand McNally).

Schlesinger, Arthur M., Jr. 1986. *The Cycles of American History* (Boston: Houghton Mifflin).

Schlesinger, Jacob M. 1990. "Japan Makes Strides in Software Design: 'Factory' Approach Contrasts with U.S. Production." *Wall Street Journal* (8 February): p. B5.

Schmenner, Roger W. 1980. "Choosing New Industrial Capacity: On Site Expansion, Branching, and Relocation." *Quarterly Journal of Economics,* Vol. 44, No. 4 (August): pp. 103–19.

Schmid, Gregory. 1981. "Productivity and Reindustrialization: A Dissenting View." *Challenge,* Vol. 23, No. 6 (January/February): pp. 24–9.

Schoenhof, Jacob. 1893. *The Economy of High Wages: An Inquiry into the Cause of High Wages and their Effects on Methods and Cost of Production* (New York: G. P. Putnam's Sons).

Schor, Juliet B. 1991. *The Overworked American: The Unexpected Decline of Leisure* (New York: Basic Books).

Schorsch, Louis. 1984. "The Abdication of Big Steel." *Challenge,* Vol. 27, No. 1 (March/April): pp. 34–40.

Schultz, Ellen E. 2000. "Companies Quietly Use Mergers, Spinoffs to Cut Worker Benefits." *Wall Street Journal* (27 December): p. A1.

Schultz, Ellen E. 2001. "While Executives See Their Pensions Grow, Regular Workers See Their Benefits Shrink." *Wall Street Journal* (20 June): p. A1.

Schultz, Theodore. 1961. "Investment in Human Capital." *American Economic Review,* Vol. 51, No. 1 (March): pp. 1–17.

Schumpeter, J. A. 1950. *Capitalism, Socialism and Democracy,* 3d. edn. (New York: Harper & Row).

———. 1939. *Business Cycles: A Theoretical, Historical and Statistical Analysis of the Capitalist Process,* 2 vols. (New York: McGraw Hill).

Schwartz, Stephen I. 1998. "Introduction." In Stephen I. Schwartz, ed. *Atomic Audit: The Costs and Consequences of U. S. Nuclear Weapons Since 1940* (Washington, D.C.: Brookings Institution): pp. 1–32.

Scitovsky, Tibor. 1990. "The Benefits of Asymmetric Markets." Journal of Economic Perspectives, Vol. 4, No. 1 (Winter): pp. 135–48.

Scotchmer, Suzanne. 1991. "Standing on the Shoulders of Giants: Cumulative Research and the Patent Law." *Journal of Economic Perspectives,* Vol. 5, No. 1 (Winter): pp. 29–41.

Sell, Susan K. 1999. "Multinational Corporations as Agents of Change: The Globalization of Intellectual Property Rights." In *Private Authority and International Affairs,* eds. A. Claire Cutler, Virginia Haufler, and Tony Porter (Albany: State University of New York Press): pp. 169–98.

Semiconductor Industry Association. 1989. *Meeting the Global Challenge: Advanced Electronics Technology and the American Semiconductor Industry* (Cupertino: Semiconductor Industry Association).

Serrin, William. 1974. *The Company and the Union* (New York: Vintage).

Shaiken, Harley. 1985 *Work Transformed: Automation and Labor in the Computer Age* (New York: Holt, Rinehart & Winston).

Shaikh, Anwar and Ertugrul Ahmet Tonak. 1987. "The Welfare State and the Myth of the Social Wage." In Robert Cherry et al. eds. *The Imperiled Economy.* Book 1. *Macroeconomics from a Left Perspective* (New York: Union for Radical Political Economics): pp. 183–94.

Shelton, Judy. 1989. *The Coming Soviet Crash* (New York: The Free Press).

Sherman, Howard J. 1983. "Cyclical Behavior of Government Fiscal Policy." *Journal of Economic Issues,* Vol. 17, No. 2 (June): pp. 379–88.

———. 1991. *The Business Cycle: Growth and Crisis Under Capitalism* (Princeton: Princeton University Press).

Shiller, Robert J. 2000. *Irrational Exuberance* (Princeton: Princeton University Press).

Shleifer, Andrei and Robert W. Vishny. 1988. "The Efficiency of Investment in the Presence of Aggregate Demand Spillovers." *Journal of Political Economy,* Vol., 96, No. 6 (December): pp. 1221–31.

Shoven, John B., Scott B. Smart, and Joel Waldfogel. 1992. "Real Interest Rates and the Savings and Loan Crisis: The Moral Hazard Premium." *Journal of Economic Perspectives,* Vol. 6, No. 1 (Winter): pp. 155–67.

Shrag, Peter. 1991. "The Myth of Quick School Reform." *The Sacramento Bee* (22 May): p. B6.

Silk, Leonard. 1985. "The Pressures In Geneva." *New York Times* (November 20): p. D2.

Siwek, Stephen E. and Gale Mosteller. 1996. Copyright Industries in the U.S. Economy: The 1996 Report (Economists Incorporated). <http://www.iipa.com/html/pn_executive_summary.html>

Sloan, Allan. 1985. "Why Is No One Safe?" *Forbes* (11 March).

Smith, Adam. 1776. *An Inquiry into the Nature and Causes of the Wealth of Nations* (Oxford: Clarendon Press, 1976).

Smith, Hedrick. 1977. "A Rare Call for Sacrifices." *New York Times* (19 April): pp. 1 and 24.

Smith, James P. and Finis R. Welch. 1989. "Black Economic Progress after Myrdal." *Journal of Economic Literature,* Vol. 27, No. 2 (June): pp. 519–64.

Solow, Robert M. 1963. *Capital Theory and the Rate of Return* (Amsterdam: North Holland).

———. 1987. "We'd Better Watch Out." *New York Times Book Review* (12 July): p. 36.

Spero, John Edelman. 1980. *The Failure of the Franklin National Bank* (New York: Columbia University Press).

Staehle, Hans. 1955. "Technology, Utilization and Production." *Bulletin de l'Institue Internationale de Statistique,* Vol. 34, Part 4, pp. 112–36.

Standage, Tom. 1998. *The Victorian Internet: The Remarkable Story of the Telegraph and the Nineteenth Century's On-Line Pioneers* (New York: Walker and Co.).

Stein, Herbert. 1969. *The Fiscal Revolution in America* (Chicago: University of Chicago Press).

———. 1984. *Presidential Economics: The Making of Economic Policy from Roosevelt to Reagan and Beyond* (New York: Simon and Schuster).

Stewart, James B. 1991. *Den of Thieves* (New York: Simon and Schuster).

Stiglitz, Joseph E. 1987. "The Causes and Consequences of the Dependence of Quality on Price." *Journal of Economic Literature,* Vol. 25, No. 1 (March): pp. 1–48.

Stiglitz, Joseph E. and Andrew Weiss. 1981. "Credit Rationing and Markets with Imperfect Information." *American Economic Review,* Vol. 71, No. 3 (June): pp. 393–411.

Stollman, Rita. 1981. "Economic Diary." *Business Week* (15 June): p. 22.

Stone, Douglas and William T. Ziemba. 1993. "Land and Stock Prices in Japan." *Journal of Economic Perspectives,* Vol. 7, No 3 (Summer): pp. 149–63.

Stout, Hilary. 1989. "Shaky Numbers: U.S. Statistics Mills Grind Out More Data that are then Revised." *Wall Street Journal* (31 August): pp. A1 and A2.

Strachey, Lytton. 1918. *Eminent Victorians* (New York: G. P. Putnam).

Strassman, W.P. 1959. *Risk and Technological Investment* (Ithaca: Cornell University Press).

Streeck, Wolfgang. 1992. *Social Institutions and Economic Performance: Studies of Industrial in Advanced Capitalist Economies* (New York: Sage).

Sullivan, Allanna. 1990. "Stretched Thin: Exxon's Restructuring in the Past is Blamed for Recent Accidents." *Wall Street Journal* (16 March): pp. A1 and A14.

Summers, Lawrence H. 1989. "Some Simple Economics of Mandated Benefits." *American Economic Review,* Vol. 79, No. 2 (May): pp. 177–83.

———. 1990. "What is the Social Return to Capital Investment?" *Growth, productivity, employment: essays to celebrate Bob Solow's birthday,* Peter Diamond, ed. (Cambridge, MA: MIT Press): pp. 113–41.

Summers, Lawrence H. and Victoria P. Summers. 1989. "When Financial Markets Work too Well: A Cautious Case for a Securities Transactions Tax." *Journal of Financial Services Research,* Vol. 3, Nos. 2 and 3 (December): pp. 261–86.

Tanzer, Michael. 1975. *The Energy Crisis: World Struggle for Power and Wealth* (New York: Monthly Review Press).

Tatom, John A. 1991. "Should Government Spending on Capital Goods Be Raised?" *Federal Reserve Bank of St. Louis Review,* Vol. 73, No. 2 (March/April): pp. 3–15.

Terborgh, George. 1949. *Dynamic Equipment Policy* (New York: McGraw-Hill).

Thornton, William Thomas. 1869. *On Labour: Its Wrongful Claims and Rightful Dues* (London: Macmillan).

Thurow, Lester C. 1987. "Economic Paradigms and Slow American Productivity Growth." *Eastern Economic Journal,* Vol. 13, No. 4 (October-December): pp. 333–45.

———. 1989. *Toward a High-Wage, High-Productivity Service Sector* (Washington, D.C.: Economic Policy Institute).

Tilly, Chris. 1991. "Continuing Growth of Part-Time Employment." *Monthly Labor Review,* Vol. 114, No. 3 (March): pp. 10–18.

Tocqueville, Alexis de. 1848. *Democracy in America,* 2 vols. tr. Henry Reeve (New York: D. Appleton, 1899).

Toffler, Alvin. 1990. *Powershift: Knowledge, Wealth, and Violence in the 21st Century* (New York: Bantam Books).

Tonak, E. Ahmet. 1987. "The U.S. Welfare State and the Working Class, 1952–1980." *Review of Radical Political Economy,* Vol. 19, No. 1 (Spring): pp. 47–72.

Turgeon, Lynn. 1996. *Bastard Keynesianism: The Evolution of Economic Thinking and Policymaking since World War II* (Westport, CT: Greenwood Press).

United States Department of Agriculture. 1980. *Agricultural Statistics* (Washington, D.C.: U.S. Government Printing Office).

United States Department of Commerce. Bureau of the Census. 2000a. *Statistical Abstract of the United States* (Washington, D.C.: U.S. Government Printing Office).

United States Department of Commerce. Bureau of the Census. 2000b. Current Population Reports. Consumer Income. Poverty in the United States. P60–230 (Washington, D.C.: U.S. Government Printing Office).

United States Department of Commerce, Bureau of Economic Analysis. 1987. *Fixed Reproducible Tangible Wealth in the United States, 1982–1985* (Washington, D.C.: U.S. Government Printing Office).

Unites States Department of Commerce, Bureau of the Census. 1990. *Statistical Abstract of the United States, 1990* (Washington, D.C.: U.S. Government Printing Office).

United States Department of Education. National Center for Education Statistics. 1991a. *Digest of Education Statistics, 1991* (Washington, D.C.: U.S. Government Printing Office).

United States Department of Education, National Center for Education Statistics. 1991b. *The Condition of Education, 1991.* vol. 1. *Elementary and Secondary Education* (Washington, D.C.: U.S. Government Printing Office).

United States Department of Education. National Center for Education Statistics. 1996. *Schools and Staffing in the U.S.: A Statistical Profile, 1993–94* NCES 96–124 (Washington, D.C.: U.S. Government Printing Office).

United States Department of Education. National Center for Education Statistics. 1999. *The Condition of Education, 1999* (Washington, D.C.: U.S. Government Printing Office). <http://nces.ed.gov/pubs99/condition99/index.html>

United States Department of Education. Office of Educational Research and Improvement. National Center for Education Statistics. 2000. *National Assessment of Educational Performance: 1999 Trends in Academic Progress: Three Decades of Student Performance, NCES 2000–469,* by J. R. Campbell, C. M. Hombo, and J. Mazzeo (Washington, D.C.: U.S. Government Printing Office). <http://nces.ed.gov/nationsreportcard/pubs/main1999/2000469.shtl>

United States Department of Energy, Office of Inspector General, Office of Audit Services. 1996. *Audit of the U.S. Department of Energy's Consolidated Statement of Financial Position (as of September 30, 1995),* Report No. IG-FS-96–01 (29 February). <http://www.ig.doe.gov/text/IGFS9601.txt>

United States Department of Justice. 1990. *Sourcebook of Criminal Justice Statistics* (Washington, D.C.: U.S. Government Printing Office).

United States Department of Justice, Bureau of Justice Statistics. 1999. *Sourcebook of Criminal Justice Statistics* (Washington, D.C.: United States Department of Justice). <http://www.albany.edu/sourcebook/>

United States Department of Labor, Bureau of Labor Statistics. 1977. *Multiple Jobholders in May 1977,* Special Labor Force Report 211.

———. 1989. *Handbook of Labor Statistics,* Bulletin 2340 (Washington, D.C.: U.S. Government Printing Office).

———. 1990. *Employment and Earnings,* Vol. 37, No. 6 (June).

———. Bureau of Labor Statistics. 1989. *The Impact of Research and Development on Productivity Growth,* Bulletin No. 2331 (September) (U.S.G.P.O.: Washington, D.C.).

United States Department of Transportation. 1978. *A Prospectus for Change in the Freight Railroad Industry* (Washington D.C.: U.S. Government Printing Office).

———. 1999. *Transportation Statistics Annual Report, 1999* (Washington, D.C.: Department of Transportation). <http://www.bts.gov/transtu/tsar/tsar1999/>

United States General Accounting Office. 1987. *Dislocated Workers: Local Programs and Outcomes Under the Job Training Partnership Act,* Report to the Congress.

United States General Accounting Office. 1996a. *School Facilities: America's Schools Report Differing Conditions* GAO/HEHS-96–103 (Washington, D.C.: USGPO).

United States General Accounting Office. 1996b. *Resolution Trust Corporation's 1995 and 1994 Financial Statements* GAO/AIMD-96–123 (Washington, D.C. General Accounting Office). <http://frwebgate.access.gpo.gov/cgi-bin/useftp.cgi?IPaddress=162.140.64.21&filename=ai96123.pdf&directory=/diskb/wais/data/gao>.

———. 2000. *Contingent Workers Incomes and Benefits Lag Behind Those of Rest of Workforce.* GAO/HEHS-00-76 (Washington, D.C.: U.S. Government Printing Office). <http://www.gao.gov/new.items/he00076.pdf contingent work>

United States House of Representatives, Committee on Education and Labor, Subcommittee on Elementary, Secondary and Vocational Education. 1989. *Child Nutrition Programs: Issues for the 101st Congress,* One Hundredth Congress, 2d Session (December).

United States House of Representatives. 1981. 97th Congress, 1st Session, Committee on Energy and Commerce, Subcommittee on Oversight and Investigations, *Capital Formation and Industrial Policy, Part I, Hearings, 27 and 29 April, 1, 22 and 24 June* (Washington, D.C.: US Government Printing Office.

United States National Security Council. 1950. "NSC 68: United States Objectives and Programs for National Security." In Thomas H. Etzold and John Lewis Gaddis, eds. *Containment: Documents on American Policy and Strategy, 1945–1950* (New York: Columbia University Press, 1978): pp. 385–442.

United States Pension Benefit Guaranty Corporation. 1999. *Annual Report, 1999* (Washington D.C.: U.S. Government Printing Office). <http://www.pbgc.gov/publications/annual_repts/99annrpt.pdf>

United States President. 2000. *Economic Report of the President* (Washington, D.C.: US Government Printing Office).

United States Senate. 1982. 97th Congress, 2nd Session. Committee on Labor and Human Resources, Subcommittee on Employment and Productivity. *Productivity in the American Economy, 1982., Hearings. 19 and 26 March, 2 and 16 April 1982* (Washington, D.C.: US Government Printing Office).

United States Senate, Committee on the Judiciary, Subcommittee of Separation of Powers. 1970. *The Philadelphia Plan,* 91st Cong., 1st Sess. (27 and 28 October 1969).

United States Department of Transportation. 1990. *Moving America: New Directions, New Opportunities* (Washington, D.C.: U.S. Government Printing Office).

United States President. 1990. *Economic Report of the President* (Washington, D.C.: U.S. Government Printing Office).

Ure, Andrew. 1835. *The Philosophy of Manufactures* (London: Charles Knight).

Valenti, Jack (Chairman and Chief Executive Officer, Motion Picture Association). 1999. "Statement Before the Committee on Ways and Means Subcommittee on Trade, Regarding US-China Trade Relations and the Possible Accession of China to the World Trade Organization (8 June)." <www.mpaa.org/jack/99/99_6_8a.htm>

Varian, Hal R. 1988. "Symposium on Takeovers." *Journal of Economic Perspectives,* Vol. 2, No. 1 (Winter): pp. 3–5.

Vatter, Harold G. 1985. *The U.S. Economy in World War II* (New York: Columbia University Press).

Vedder, Richard K. and Lowell Gallaway. 1991. "The Great Depression of 1946." *Review of Austrian Economics,* Vol. 5, No. 2: pp. 3–32.

Vicker, Ray. 1981. "Hazardous Highways: Deterioration of the Nation's Roads Accelerates, Sparking a Race in States to Increase Fuel Taxes." *Wall Street Journal* (15 October): p. 48.

Vickers, Marcia. 2001. "When Wealth Is Blown Away." *Business Week* (26 March): pp. 39–41.

Vidal, Gore. 1992. "Time for a People's Convention." *The Nation,* Vol. 254, No. 3 (27 January): pp. 73 and 88–94.

Viner, Jacob. 1933. *Balanced Deflation, Inflation or More Depression.* Day and Hour Series, No. 3 (Minneapolis: University of Minnesota Press).

Vives, Xavier. 1990. "Information and Competitive Advantage." *International Journal of Industrial Organization,* Vol. 9, No. 1, pp. 17–35.

Volcker, Paul A., Chairman of the Board of Governors of the Federal Reserve System. 1981. "Testimony before the Committee on Banking, Finance and Urban Affairs of the U.S.

House of Representatives, 21 July 1981." *Federal Reserve Bulletin.* Vol. 67, No. 8 (August): pp. 613–618.

———. 1982. "Testimony before the Joint Economic Committee, 26 January 1982." *Federal Reserve Bulletin.* Vol. 68, No. 2 (February): pp. 88–90.

Wagoner, Harless D. 1968. *The U.S. Machine Tool Industry from 1900 to 1950* (Cambridge, MA: MIT Press).

Waldstein, Louise. 1989. *Toward a High-Wage, High-Productivity Service Sector* (Washington, D.C.: Economic Policy Institute).

———. 1990. *Service Sector Wages, Productivity and Jobs Creation in the U.S. and Other Countries* (Washington, D.C.: Economic Policy Institute).

Walton, Richard E. 1985. "From Control to Commitment in the Workplace." *Harvard Business Review,* Vol. 85, No. 2 (March-April): pp. 76–84.

Warshofsky, Fred. 1994. *The Patent Wars: The Battle to Own the World's Technology* (New York: Wiley).

Water Infrastructure Network. 2000. *Clean Safe Water for the 21st Century: A Renewed National Commitment to Water and Wastewater Infrastructure.* <http://www.usmayors.org/uscm/wash_update/documents/WIN_Report.pdf>.

Waterson, Albert. 1964. "Good Enough for Developing Countries?" *Finance and Development,* Vol. 1 (September): pp. 89–96.

Watson, Bill. 1971. "Counter-Planning on the Shop Floor." *Radical America,* Vol. 5, No. 3 (May-June): pp. 77–85.

Weidenbaum, Murray. 1992. "The Future of the U.S. Defense Industry." *Contemporary Policy Issues,* Vol. 10, No. 2 (April): pp. 27–43.

Weidenbaum, Murray L. and R. DiFina. 1978. *The Cost of Federal Regulation of Economic Activity* (Washington, D.C.: American Enterprise Institute).

Weiner, Tim. 1994. "Inquiry Finds 'Star Wars' Tried Plan to Exaggerate Test Results." *New York Times* (23 July): p. A1.

Weingartner, H. Martin. 1969. "Some New Views on the Payback Period and Capital Budgeting Decisions." *Management Science,* Vol. 15, No. 12 (August): pp. B594–607.

Weisskopf, Tom. 1979. "Marxian Crisis Theory and the Falling Rate of Profit." *Cambridge Journal of Economic,* Vol. 3, No. 4 (December): pp. 341–78.

Weld, Issac. 1799. *Travels thought the States of North America and Provinces of Upper and Lower Canada During the Years 1793, 1796 and 1797* (London: J. Stockdale).

Welles, Chris. 1990. "Exxon's Future: What Has Larry Rawl Wrought." *Business Week* (2 April): pp. 72–6.

Wells, David A. 1885. "The 'Foreign Competitive Pauper Labor' Argument for Protection." In his *Practical Economics: A Collection of Essays Respecting Certain of the Recent Economic Experiences of the United States* (New York: G.C. Putnam; New York: Greenwood Publishers, 1968): pp. 133–52.

White, Merry I. 1991. "Higher Education: A Comparative Examination." *Thought and Action: The NEA Higher Education Journal,* Vol. 7, No. 2 (Fall): pp. 5–18.

Wilgoren, Jodi. 2001. "Education Study Finds U.S. Falling Short." *New York Times* (13 June).

Wilke, John R. 1996. "Showing Its Age: Fed's Huge Empire, Set Up Years Ago, Is Costly and Inefficient." (12 September): pp. A1 and A10.

Williams, Harry B. 1989. "What Temporary Workers Earn: Findings from New BLS Survey." *Monthly Labor Review,* Vol. 112, No. 3 (March): pp. 3–6.

Wion, Douglas W. 1990. "Working Wives and Earnings Inequality Among Married Couples, 1967–1984." *Review of Social Economy,* Vol. 48, No. 1 (Spring): pp. 18–40.

Wolfe, Alan. 1981. *America's Impasse: The Rise and Fall of the Politics of Growth* (New York: Pantheon).

Wolff, Edward N. 1987. *Growth, Accumulation, and Unproductive Activity: An Analysis of the Postwar U.S. Economy* (Cambridge: Cambridge University Press).

Wolfson, Martin H. 1988. *Financial Crises: Understanding the Postwar U.S. Experience* (Armonk, NY: M. E. Sharpe).

Woodham, Douglas M. 1984. "Potential Output Growth and the Long-Term Inflation Outlook." *Federal Reserve Bank of New York Quarterly Review,* Vol. 9, No. 2 (Summer): pp. 16–23.

Wright, Gavin. 1990. "The Origins of American Industrial Success, 1870–1940." *American Economic Review,* Vol. 80, No. 4 (September): pp. 651–68.

Wright, Patrick. 1979. *On a Clear Day You Can See General Motors: John Z. DeLorean's Look Inside the Automotive Giant* (New York: Avon).

Wysocki, Bernard Jr. 2000. "In U.S. Trade Arsenal, Brains Outgun Brawn." *Wall Street Journal* (10 April): p. A1.

Zaslow, Jeffrey. 1985. "Building on the Past: The Challenge of Turning an Aged Plant into a Showpiece Factory of the Future." *Wall Street Journal* (16 September): pp. 6c and 18c.

Zuboff, Shoshana. 1988. *In the Age of the Smart Machines: The Future of Work and Power* (New York: Basic Books).

Index